Liberalism and Catholicism are two of the most important forces shaping the contemporary political culture of the United States. This book explores what is at stake as they encounter each other in new contexts today and what a fresh conversation between them promises for the future of American public life. In light of the conflicts between Catholicism and liberalism in the past, it explores the deeper philosophical, theological, and political issues that must be addressed if such a new conversation is to occur and bear fruit. The book emerges out of the conviction that both traditions continue to have much to learn from each other and that both would contribute more constructively to the resolution of the problems facing the nation if they were to do so. It thus constitutes an invitation to the dialogue that could produce such mutual instruction. It is a collaborative effort that brings together the work of scholars from a wide variety of disciplines. It examines how the relationship between the two traditions came to be what it now is. It projects ways this relationship might develop fruitfully in the years ahead, and addresses practical questions of public life in light of the emerging conversation. Though the book gives particular attention to the United States, it has relevance to debates about the future of both liberalism and Catholicism in many other parts of the world.

CATHOLICISM AND LIBERALISM

CAMBRIDGE STUDIES IN RELIGION AND AMERICAN
PUBLIC LIFE

General editor
Robin W. Lovin

Books in the series

Thomas G. Fuechtmann: *Steeples and Stacks: Religion and Steel Crisis in Youngstown, Ohio*

Merrill D. Peterson and Robert C. Vaughan, eds.: *The Virginia Statute for Religious Freedom*

William R. Hutchison, ed.: *Between the Times: The Travail of the Protestant Establishment in America, 1900–1960*

J. William Frost: *A Perfect Freedom: Religious Liberty in Pennsylvania*

CATHOLICISM AND LIBERALISM

Contributions to American Public Philosophy

EDITED BY

R. BRUCE DOUGLASS

Associate Professor, Department of Government, Georgetown University

AND

DAVID HOLLENBACH

Margaret O'Brien Flatley Professor of Catholic Theology, Boston College

CAMBRIDGE
UNIVERSITY PRESS

Published by the Press Syndicate of the University of Cambridge
The Pitt Building, Trumpington Street, Cambridge CB2 1RP
40 West 20th Street, New York, NY 10011–4211, USA
10 Stamford Road, Oakleigh, Melbourne 3166, Australia

© Cambridge University Press 1994

First published 1994

Printed in Great Britain at the University Press, Cambridge

A catalogue record for this book is available from the British Library

Library of Congress cataloguing in publication data

Catholicism and Liberalism: Contributions to American Public Philosophy / edited by
R. Bruce Douglass and David Hollenbach.
p.   cm.
ISBN 0 521 44528 0 (hardback)
1. Catholic Church – Doctrines. 2. Liberalism – United States.
I. Douglass, R. Bruce.   II. Hollenbach, David.
BX1396.2.C38   1994
261.7′08′822 – dc20   93-1372 CIP

ISBN 0 521 44528 0 hardback

Perhaps the time has come when we should endeavor to dissolve the structure of war that underlies the pluralistic society, and erect the more civilized structure of the dialogue. It would be no less sharply pluralistic, but rather more so, since the real pluralisms would be clarified out of their present confusion. And amid the pluralism a unity would be discernible – the unity of an orderly conversation. The pattern would not be that of ignorant armies clashing by night but of informed men locked together in the full light of a new dialectical day. Thus we might present to a "candid world" the spectacle of a civil society.

John Courtney Murray, SJ, *We Hold These Truths*

Contents

ix

Contributors

R. BRUCE DOUGLASS is Associate Professor in the Department of Government, Georgetown University. A political theorist, he has edited several books, including *Liberalism and the Good* and *The Deeper Meaning of Economic Life*. His work has appeared in *Commonweal*, *The Review of Politics*, and *Political Theory*, among other journals.

LOUIS DUPRÉ is the T. L. Riggs Professor in the philosophy of religion at Yale University. His published work is mainly in the area of social thought (*Marx's Critique of Culture*), philosophy of religion (*The Other Dimension; A Dubious Heritage*), and critique of culture (*Passage to Modernity*, in preparation).

JEAN BETHKE ELSHTAIN is the Centennial Professor of Political Science and Professor of Philosophy at Vanderbilt University. Her books include *Public Man, Private Woman: Women in Social and Political thought; Meditations on Modern Political Thought; Women and War;* and *Power Trips and Other Journeys*. She has been a fellow at the Institute for Advanced Study, Princeton, a scholar-in-residence at the Bellaggio Conference and Study Center, Bellaggio, Italy, and is currently a Guggenheim Fellow at work on an intellectual biography of Jane Addams.

LAURA GELLOTT is Associate Professor of History at the University of Wisconsin-Parkside, in Kenosha, Wisconsin. She holds the PhD in European History from the University of Wisconsin-Madison, and the BA and MA from Marquette University. She has published in the *Austrian History Yearbook*, *Catholic Historical Review*, *Journal of Contemporary History*, and *Commonweal*.

xi

PHILIP GLEASON is Professor of History at the University of Notre Dame. He is the author of *Keeping the Faith: American Catholicism Past and Present* (1987) and *Speaking of Diversity: Language and Ethnicity in Twentieth Century America* (1992).

DAVID HOLLENBACH, SJ, is Margaret O'Brien Flatley Professor of Catholic Theology at Boston College. He is an Associate Fellow at the Woodstock Theological Center, Georgetown University. His publications include *Claims in Conflict: Retrieving and Renewing the Catholic Human Rights Tradition* (1979), and *Justice, Peace, and Human Rights: American Catholic Social Ethics in a Pluralistic World* (1988). He was a consultant to the United States Catholic Bishops for the pastoral letter *Economic Justice for All* (1986).

JOSEPH A. KOMONCHAK is a priest of the Archdiocese of New York and Professor of Theology, Department of Religion and Religious Education, The Catholic University of America. He was ordained in 1963, received the STL degree from the Gregorian University, Rome, in 1964, and the PhD from Union Theological Seminary, New York, in 1976. He is the author of many articles on ecclesiology and Vatican II, and editor of *The New Dictionary of Theology* and *The Reception of Vatican II*.

JAMES H. PROVOST is Associate Professor of Canon Law at The Catholic University of America, where he has chaired the Department of Canon Law since 1987. He was president of the Canon Law Society of America in 1977–78. He is an editor of the international theological journal *Concilium*. He has edited and contributed to several canon law and theological books, including *The Code of Canon Law: A Text and Commentary*, and most recently co-edited *Lex Sequitur Vitam*.

MARY C. SEGERS is Associate Professor of Political Science at Rutgers University, where she teaches political theory, women and politics, and religion and politics. She edited *Church Polity and American Politics: A View from the States* (1990), and co-edited, with Timothy Byrnes, *The Catholic Church and the Politics of Abortion* (1992). She was Visiting Lecturer in Women's Studies at Harvard Divinity School in 1985, and Henry Luce Fellow in Theology at Harvard in 1987–89.

PAUL SIGMUND is Professor of Politics at Princeton University. He has published fifteen books on political theory and Latin American politics, including (with Reinhold Niebuhr) *The Democratic Experience* (1967); *Natural Law in Political Thought* (1981); and *Liberation Theology at the Crossroads: Democracy or Revolution?* (1990).

PETER STEINFELS is Senior Religion Correspondent for *The New York Times*. He formerly served as Editor-in-Chief of *Commonweal*, and was co-editor of the *Hastings Center Report*, published by the Institute of Society, Ethics and the Life Sciences. He is the author of *The Neoconservatives: The Men Who Are Changing America's Politics* (1979) and has contributed to journals such as *The New Republic, Harper's, The Columbia Journalism Review, The Nation*, and *Partisan Review*. He received the Templeton Reporter of the Year Award from the Religion Newswriters Association for his reporting in 1988. He holds a PhD in European History from Columbia University.

DAVID TRACY is the Andrew Thomas Greeley and Grace McNichols Greeley Distinguished Service Professor of Theology at the Divinity School, University of Chicago, where he has taught since 1969. He is also a member of the Committee on the Analysis of Ideas and Methods. Among his recent work are *Plurality and Ambiguity: Hermeneutics, Religion and Hope* (1987) and *Dialogue with the Other* (1990).

Preface

This volume is the product of a study project jointly sponsored by the Woodstock Theological Center and the Department of Government of Georgetown University. The project was designed to facilitate an interdisciplinary and interfaith dialogue on the relevance of the Catholic tradition to the future development of the philosophy that informs the public life of the United States. Because of the special role that liberalism has come to play in the affairs of the nation, the project focused particular attention on the prospects for a fresh Catholic contribution to the shaping of the American mind in the light of what it is that liberal thinking has become. It was predicated on the assumption that *both* the teaching of the church and the premises of liberal thinking about our public life have changed significantly since the days when they stood in principled opposition to one another. The task posed to each of the participants was to take stock, prospectively, of the situation that now prevails in the light of the changes that both Catholicism and liberalism have undergone.

The chapters contained in this volume are revised versions of manuscripts originally presented in a series of meetings extending from the spring of 1989 through the fall of 1990. The meetings were held at the Woodstock Center Library on the campus of Georgetown University.

The directors wish to indicate here their grateful appreciation of J. Leon Hooper, SJ, for his ongoing help in administering the affairs of the project. Special thanks are also in order to James L. Connor, SJ, Director of the Woodstock Center, and John Bailey, who was chairman of the Department of Government at the time of the project, for their active support and encouragement. William Gould, a doctoral candidate in the Department of Government, also provided useful assistance with the minutes of our ongoing discussions. We are also grateful to David Klocek, who prepared the index, and to James Bailey, who helped with the proofreading.

RBD and DH

Introduction

R. Bruce Douglass

> Neither as a doctrine nor as a project is the American Proposition
> a finished thing. Its demonstration is never done once for all;
> and the Proposition itself requires development on penalty of
> decadence. Its historical success is never to be taken for granted,
> nor can it come to some absolute term; and any given measure
> of success demands enlargement on penalty of decline.
>
> John Courtney Murray, SJ

America, scholars are fond of saying, is a nation that owes its
existence to ideas. Perhaps uniquely so. And what they have in mind,
of course, when they speak this way are serious ideas – ideas of the
sort that find expression in solemn declarations and lend themselves
to being characterized as a "philosophy." It is a paradoxical claim,
to be sure, because the way of life that has developed on these shores
is scarcely one that has been conducive to philosophical reflection.
And it cannot be said that philosophical reflection is an activity held
in much respect by Americans, either. But the claim remains true,
nonetheless, and it tells us something important about who we are as
a people.

For even though we may pride ourselves on being "pragmatic" (as
opposed to doctrinaire) and go out of our way to insist that one
person's opinion is as good as the next (almost regardless of who the
person is and what the opinions in question are), there is, at the same
time, no mistaking the fact that there are some things about which we
are *very* principled. We may be disinclined to read philosophical
works very much and impatient with the sort of arguments they
expound. But our attachment to the cluster of ideas associated with
what Abraham Lincoln called the American "proposition" tends to
be so strong, in fact, that it borders on religious devotion. For it is
simply not the case that we are prepared to treat *those* ideas as though
they were just another "point of view." Far from it: they are, each

I

one of us learns from an early age, unlike other political ideas, and deserve to be treated differently. We grow up thinking of them, in fact, as the source of all that our country is as a nation and the secret of its success. And because we are inclined to value that success as highly as we do, we assume they deserve to be treated with a special respect – if not, indeed, reverence.

However, for all the loyalty they command in the hearts of the American people, it cannot really be said the ideas in question have a meaning that is altogether clear and beyond dispute. In broad outline, to be sure, we know – and share – what we are affirming when we pledge allegiance to the flag or sing the national anthem. We know what is meant when we hear our country referred to as "democratic," and we have a pretty good idea, too, of why it is organized the way it is. But at the same time, it does not take much exposure at all to the public life of the United States to see that we vary, too, in myriad ways, in the specific meanings we are inclined to give to key elements of our "public philosophy." So, for example, the Bill of Rights is read in one way by members of the American Civil Liberties Union and quite another by those who take their cues from Robert Bork. And "liberty and justice for all" has one meaning to members of Jesse Jackson's "Rainbow Coalition" and quite another to those who identify with Phyllis Schlafly's "Eagle Forum."

What at first glance has the appearance, therefore, of being a single coherent body of ideas that binds together the richly varied mix of people who go to make up the population of the United States turns out, on closer inspection, itself to be a complex blend of different strains of thought that reflects the diversity of the nation almost as much as it transcends it. Up to a point, there is a common core of belief that can be identified, but it is subject to such diverse interpretations in different parts of the body politic that it is probably better understood as a meeting ground for conversation than a body of shared convictions.

Nor is this really anything new, either. We tend to be, of course, very much aware these days of the pluralistic character of American society. But all along, ever since the moment when people first began to think seriously about joining the original thirteen colonies into a single nation, our country has been a blend of diverse peoples from different sub-cultures engaged in ongoing deliberation about the meaning and purpose of their life together. And not surprisingly, this has found expression in the terms the nation has chosen to capture its self-understanding. So ever since the founders first joined the covenantal theology of New England Calvinism to the Enlightenment rationalism of people like Jefferson to produce the premises on which we subsequently have built, the American "proposition" has in reality always been a synthesis of different beliefs drawn from a variety of sources. And even when it has been woven together as skillfully as it was by the founders, it has been subject to diverse readings as different segments of the American people have sought to make it their own.

The ideas in question have also been subject to change. For over the years, as the country has confronted one new challenge after another and found itself having to accommodate a steady succession of new forces, repeatedly the American people have found it necessary to revisit issues that were confronted at the time of the founding. The conversation about who we are as a people and what we stand for in the world has been, therefore, an ongoing one. And one of the principal reasons why the American "experiment" has turned out as well as it has is surely the fact that its people have been as successful as they have at adapting the ideas and practices inherited from their forebears to new circumstances. So even as they have gone about making one far-reaching change in their way of life after another (ranging from the assimilation of successive waves of immigrants to the emancipation of slaves), somehow they have found it possible to do so without breaking faith with the ideas on which the country was founded. In fact, more often than not, they have done so *in the name of fidelity to those ideas*. And the fact that the ideas involved have lent themselves so well to such adaptation has to be considered one of the main reasons why today they enjoy the respect they do.

REMAKING OURSELVES, AGAIN

Needless to say, this process is something that continues today. And there is more than one reason to think that the era through which we are now living is destined to be another one in which the United States is going to have to rethink rather fundamentally its identity and purpose. From the recurring agitation (in any number of different quarters) for the adoption of new amendments to the Constitution to the declining hold of the two major political parties on the loyalties of the electorate, increasingly it is apparent that the

ideological ground is shifting once again in American life, and people
are feeling the need to rewrite the terms on which our public life is
conducted.

Nor is it hard to understand why. For the nation is in the throes of
a whole series of profound social and cultural changes that are
transforming the conditions under which the American people live
their lives. From the increased ethnic and cultural pluralism that we
are experiencing and the resulting decline of the social and cultural
hegemony previously exercised by WASPs to the revolution that is
now underway in the role women play in society, the country is well
on its way to becoming, once again, something different from what
we have been used to. And as this occurs, it is not in the least
surprising that another round of searching questions – and debates –
have arisen about just who we are and what we mean to make of
ourselves. With the leadership of the nation very much in flux and a
whole series of institutions that have been as basic to our way of life
as the language that we speak, the schools in which we educate our
children, and even marriage and the family undergoing sweeping
change, it would be surprising, in fact, if this were not the case.

Especially so, moreover, since at the same time we are having to
adjust to changes of comparable magnitude in the wider world,
which will almost certainly leave our country in a position quite
different from the one to which we have been accustomed. For now
that Communism has collapsed in all but a handful of places and the
Cold War has come to an end, there is no mistaking the fact that the
United States is no longer going to be called upon to play the same
sort of hegemonic role in world affairs it has played since the end of
World War II. For though it remains a military superpower, it has
ceased to be the leader of a military alliance held together by the
threat posed by an ideological adversary of comparable might. And
even though it continues to be an important economic power, it
enjoys nothing like the economic supremacy it once did. If anything,
in fact, increasingly it is showing signs of finding it hard to keep up
with the competition provided by countries like Germany and Japan.

The more this is so, in turn, and the more the American people find
themselves having to contend with the consequences, the more soul-
searching it can be expected to produce. For a nation that has gotten
used to thinking of itself as preeminent in the world in almost every
respect that matters to it is bound to have certain adjustments to
make in its self-understanding as it goes about learning, anew, how to

conduct itself as one nation among others. And the more it finds that its fate is being determined by forces beyond its control, the greater the adjustments are likely to be. Already we have had some indication of what this can mean in the inclination on the part of a growing number of people (here and abroad) to dwell on the limits of American power, and the more exposure we have to the difference the emerging new global economy makes in the way that Americans live their lives, the more of an effect the changes now taking place in the world can be expected to have on the way that we as a people conceive of our role in it.

THE THREAT OF FRAGMENTATION

Needless to say, the consequence is that a lot is having to be rethought. Especially so, moreover, when it comes to the informal images that we use to flesh out the symbolic meaning and implications of the American "proposition."[1] For it simply is no longer possible to address effectively the challenges we now face on the basis of images that reflect the way the nation *used* to conceive of itself. In part because of the kind of people who are now involved in defining the nation's identity and in part also because of the changed position in which the country now finds itself, they no longer work. So no matter how much nostalgia there may be in some quarters for the day when the United States could still be referred to without fear of contradiction as a "Christian" nation or a "melting pot" or the agency of a "manifest destiny," those days are now gone – for good, presumably. And in their place is emerging what can only be described as a complicated, multi-faceted ongoing process of revision in which little of what such old, familiar images have conveyed is not subject, in one way or another, to change.

Predictably, moreover, this is a process that evokes conflict. Indeed, it is filled with it. For not only are there many people who find it hard to part with the understanding of the American experience reflected in the old images, but those who are prepared to acknowledge the need for change themselves often disagree, too, about the direction it should take. It is one thing to see that the old ways are in need of revision, and quite another to know what deserves to be put in their place. And it is becoming increasingly apparent as the American people come to terms with the deeper issues raised by the changes now taking place in their way of life that there is almost as much room for disagreement once the need for change is acknowledged as when it is not.

For it is not just "traditionalists" and "progressives" who contend against one another these days to define the meaning and significance of the American experience.[2] It is, also, *different kinds* of "traditionalists" and "progressives" contending *against one another* – which each tend to have their own distinctive way of viewing things.[3] That is why our public life is as complex as it is today and why, too, the so-called "culture wars" that have been breaking out as these differences have been joined are not likely to issue in any sort of clear, decisive victory for one "side" or the other.

But precisely for that reason, in turn, the thing that one has to worry about is the absence of any sort of real resolution of the issues that are now being raised as this struggle unfolds. For fragmentation is, in its own way, every bit as much a threat to the health and well-being of a society of the sort the United States is now becoming as polarization. Indeed, we would argue that it is much more the real and present danger that it faces today. This nation is not going to split apart; and neither are the American people likely to square off in anything like a real *Kulturkampf*. But what we could do is splinter in a manner that prevents the attainment of anything like the sort of coherent vision of the nation's purpose that is almost certainly going to be needed if we are to address our present problems effectively.

Indeed, it is what we are already doing, to a considerable extent. So instead of attempting to engage one another in any sort of real dialogue, the partisans of the different visions that now contend for influence in American life are inclined to separate themselves off into distinct social and cultural enclaves and then to attack and stigmatize one another from a distance. And even though they each invoke the American "proposition" in one form or another, they call upon it in such different – and polemical – ways that it ends up being much more a symbol of what divides us than anything we have in common.

Not surprisingly, the result is that people then tend to find it difficult to work together. So no matter what may be said about our need as a society to "pull together," the public life of the nation increasingly has just the opposite quality. It is given over, that is, to a competitive struggle for particular partisan and/or sectional interests, and anything which does not happen to lend itself to being pursued on those terms – including the solution of some of the most pressing and difficult problems we face – ends up being sacrificed.

THE ALTERNATIVE OF ENGAGEMENT

In order for the drift in this direction to be halted, however, we will need to do more than just recognize that this is the case. Such awareness is in fact very much needed and part of our purpose in this book is to promote it. But as a practical matter not much can be expected to change unless the partisans of the various different interests – and creeds – that now contend against one another in the public life of our nation also come to be convinced that it is in fact possible to deal with their differences in some other, more constructive way. And in particular not much is likely to change unless they discover that something constructive can come of *engaging* one another over their differences.

Pursuit of that possibility is, in turn, what this book is about. No one can say with any certainty that it does in fact exist, to be sure. But we think that the reasons people commonly have for *assuming* (and that is what it tends to be – assumption) otherwise are not nearly as compelling as they are often thought to be. Indeed, our sense is that just the opposite is true: they are not compelling at all. And in the pages that follow we seek to show that is so, exploring at some length the prospects for constructive engagement in the case of an ideological difference that has to be considered one of the more difficult and sensitive ones facing us today.

It also happens to be a difference that can be expected to matter a great deal in the conduct of public affairs in our society in the years ahead. Indeed, it could well turn out to matter so much that it ends up being of pivotal importance in determining the course that events take. For it involves two currents of thought that not only are among the more influential forces at work today shaping the cultural life of the United States, but would appear, also, to have a real future ahead of them.

Indeed, the prospects they both have for enlarging their already considerable influence on the thinking of Americans in the years ahead are so promising (albeit for different reasons) that (some) partisans on both sides have been led to entertain the idea that each of them may now be on its way to becoming a dominant cultural influence. Hence the talk we have been hearing of late from some who consider themselves moral and political "liberals" about their way of thinking having finally arrived as *the* public philosophy of the West.[4] And in a comparable vein, hence the talk we have been hearing, too, from proponents of the new role that Catholics are now coming to play in the mainstream of American life about a "Catholic moment," now in the making, that will revitalize the religious roots of American public life.[5]

Even if one believes, moreover (as we do), that claims of this sort exaggerate the significance of the trends on which they are based, there is no mistaking the element of truth in what they suggest. For the trends themselves do exist, of course. And they do lead in the direction that, *broadly*, claims of this sort suggest. Liberalism *is* indeed today enjoying a real renaissance in American life (not to speak of elsewhere in the world), and barring unforeseen developments, it can be expected to enjoy the fruits of that renaissance for years to come. But so, too, is Catholicism. As a result of the process of change set in motion over a quarter of a century ago by Vatican Council II, the church has become a very different institution from the one that it used to be. And the changes that it has undergone (which are by no means yet over), along with the "coming of age" that Catholics have been experiencing in our country in the period since John Kennedy was elected to the presidency, have made Catholicism into much more of a force to contend with than ever it has been before in the affairs of the nation. So much so, in fact, that it is hard to imagine it ever being again anything other than a significant factor in determining the way the nation's affairs are conducted.

AN ENCOUNTER IN THE MAKING

The fact, too, that the church in the United States is becoming as deliberate and outspoken as it is about applying Catholic social teaching to the affairs of the nation,[6] combined with the related consideration that that teaching is itself now a great deal more relevant to the affairs of democratic societies than it has been in the past, only makes it all the more likely that what we now have in store for us is an increasingly explicit encounter of liberalism and Catholicism as distinct intellectual *traditions*. The insistence on the part of liberals that their way of thinking deserves to be recognized as the *de facto* public philosophy of America, combined with the equally firm insistence on the part of Catholics that the way of thinking they favor should now count for something in shaping the nation's identity, makes it almost certain, in fact, that this is the direction in which we are headed.

What is *not* certain, however, we would propose, is the form that this encounter is going to take. And that is fortunate. For what we have seen to date in their interaction has not been (to put it mildly) exactly encouraging. With few exceptions, the occasions when liberals and Catholics have had to deal with one another over matters of principle in the public life of this nation in recent years have been conspicuous for just the sort of antagonism and alienation that make for "culture wars." And if that is all we have to look forward to as Catholics and liberals come increasingly into interaction with one another in the years ahead, it does not bode at all well for the future of our public life.

But things need not turn out this way, we think, and for reasons that have to do with more than just the external pressures that will be brought to bear on liberals and Catholics alike to temper their mutual distrust. For it simply is not the case, we are convinced, that they *have* to be as antagonistic to one another as they have tended to be in recent memory. Especially not at the point where we are *now*. There was a time, to be sure, when such antagonism made good sense. In fact, it was probably unavoidable. For it was a natural result of what both liberalism and Catholicism were. But those days are over. *Both traditions have changed*: they have undergone, in fact, a whole series of changes that have had the effect of redefining rather fundamentally what they stand for. And in the process, of course, a good bit of what is at issue between them has changed as well.

Indeed, so much has changed that, in some respects at least, their relationship is now almost the opposite of what it used to be. For the church is hardly any more the bastion of reaction it once was. Especially not in the United States. Nor is liberalism the unambiguously progressive force it used to be, either (not with its proponents celebrating the *status quo* as they now are inclined to do). Both of them have come a long way, and in the process they have come a lot closer to one another as well. So much so, in fact, that on any number of matters that are of real consequence they now deserve to be thought of much more as allies than as adversaries.[7]

The only reason, moreover, why it is not more recognized that this is the case, we would submit, is myopia born of the heat generated by the "culture wars." The partisans in particular have a hard time appreciating how much has in fact changed because, on both sides, they have allowed themselves to become obsessed with certain particularly divisive issues on which they continue to have deep, abiding differences. And because they *both* have been given to dwelling single-mindedly on those matters – abortion, for example – to the neglect of almost everything else, it has been difficult, if not impossible, to keep in mind that there might be other things that can – and do – matter to them as well. Especially things that matter to them as *much*. So in a classic illustration of the kind of ideologically motivated simplification that has been the curse of American public life in recent years, they have allowed themselves to be defined by their differences, even though this has meant the neglect, if not the denial, of much of what they in fact really are.

THE PRECEDENT OF MUTUAL LEARNING

In suggesting that there is more to the relationship between liberals and Catholics than what now divides them, we do not mean to minimize, of course, the importance of those differences. But what we do intend to do is put them in perspective, and in particular to underscore the need for them to be viewed in *historical* perspective. When they are seen in that light, we would propose, the divisions no longer look the same at all. And this is not just because they cease to be the whole story. For what one also discovers by being at all familiar with the history of the interaction between the two traditions is that *they have had fundamental differences in the past that they have successfully resolved.*

Most of what can now be characterized as the common ground they now occupy is, in fact, a product, in one form or another, of the resolution of just such differences. Everything from the outspoken support that Catholics are now giving to the idea of human rights to the current liberal concern with considerations of distributive (or what Catholics used to call "social") justice is a product of long, difficult struggles in which each of them has, in effect, learned from quarreling with arguments advanced by the other (among others).[8] And it has been only their willingness to engage in such learning – and make the necessary adjustments in previously held positions – that has enabled them to arrive at those positions.

The lesson of their own history, therefore, is that mutual learning is in fact possible even in the face of fundamental differences of opinion. There *can* be successful dialogue among people who find themselves disagreeing in principle even on matters of "ultimate" importance – dialogue that changes the way the people involved end up looking at things. If there is anything that gives the lie to the notion that all that we can do is "agree to disagree," the history that is explored in this book is it. And it is a history, we would submit, that bears close scrutiny by all interested parties for precisely this reason.

The fact, moreover, that so much progress has already been made in this regard makes the frequently drawn conclusion that all that is left for liberals and Catholics to do is do battle against one another all the more anomalous. For it can hardly be said that the differences they have faced – and overcome – in years past have been any less serious than those that divide them today. In fact, if anything, just the reverse is true. And the meeting of minds that they have already achieved should only make it easier for them to be able to appreciate – and respect – one another's arguments.

Even more, it should enable them to appreciate their common need for the kind of conversation that is the source of such agreement. For neither of them would be at all what they are today – or *where* they are, either, for that matter – without it. It is no exaggeration at all, in fact, to say that it is precisely the capacity that both liberals and Catholics have shown over the years to accommodate and even learn from other points of view (whether it be Aristotle or Adam Smith or Karl Marx) that has been the secret of their success. It is the reason why they are still standing and even flourishing when so many of their erstwhile competitors have long since ceased to be viable. And by the same token, it is also the reason why they have a future ahead of them.

THE CONTINUING NEED

But the desirability of learning from one's opponents is something, at the same time, which is very easily lost sight of. No matter how much one may have benefited from the experience, the temptation is great to ignore it, and to act as though there were no need for it. And particularly no need in the future: the last thing that those who have succeeded sometimes want to acknowledge is that they might yet have something more to learn from those with whom they remain in competition. For to do so is to concede not only that one's own thinking might still be wanting, but also that there might actually be some truth in what others have to say.

But difficult as that may be to admit, it is even more difficult to deny. For no matter what success movements like liberalism and Catholicism have experienced in meeting past challenges, it is hardly ever the case that they have learned all they need to learn. Nor is this just because life goes on and is forever posing new challenges; the deeper reason is the partiality of the learning that goes on. And even more fundamentally, it is the partiality of the point of view that is reflected in even the best of what they have to offer.

For as the history of modern ideologies shows, every one of them is the reflection of a particular sort of experience (and a particular sort of person, typically, as well). And no matter how much they may attempt to adapt and revise what they stand for in order to take into account a larger range of human experience, they always end up seeing things *from a particular point of view*.[9] They cannot do otherwise. For they are what they are by virtue of seeing things in that way. And that means, in turn, that they cannot help but learn selectively, so that there are some features of human experience whose significance they are in a better position to grasp than others.

So even though the Catholic church, for example, has made enormous strides in coming to terms with the challenge presented by the democratic aspirations that find expression in contemporary thinking about human rights, it has hardly learned all that it needs to learn in that respect. Especially with regard to the status of women it still has, needless to say, a long way to go. And one can clearly see in the Catholic hierarchy's struggle with the challenge posed by contemporary feminism continuing evidence of the same habits of mind that in the past prevented the church from appreciating the human promise of democratic aspirations. So what it has learned in that regard it has obviously learned in an incomplete way, and it still has a lot to overcome. And as it struggles to do that, it can hardly dispense with the stimulus provided by the kind of pointed and insistent affirmation of the rights of the human person that finds expression these days in liberalism.

But in like manner, liberals continue to need exposure to the kind of principled affirmation of the import of attending to the *common good* that finds expression in the witness and teaching of the church. For even though liberals have come a long way in appreciating the need for the assumption of collective responsibility for social outcomes, they still have an unmistakable ambivalence about doing so. So even though economic individualism in the old "rugged" form that they used to champion is gone, it still persists in a new, modified form that ends up yielding no little human misery. And even though many liberals are now committed in principle to overcoming that misery, in practice they have a hard time taking the steps that would be necessary to make it happen – which is why, after years of talk, poverty is still so much a reality in the United States today.[10]

Even more do they tend to have a hard time, moreover, doing what it would take to enhance the quality of the way of life we share in more fundamental ways. For apart from the value they are inclined to place on material well-being and personal liberty, they are not much prepared to enter into a serious discussion of what it is that constitutes the human good. And even less are they prepared to pursue it actively. So even as it becomes (painfully) evident that it is going to take more than just a combination of prosperity and freedom to bring about a truly *good* society, they shy away from saying – or doing – much of anything about it.[11] In particular, they tend to shy away from anything approaching the sort of critical reflection on how we should use the opportunities now available to us that will be the *sine qua non* of any successful attempt to resolve the issues of meaning and purpose that are increasingly surfacing in our public life.[12]

FROM CIVILITY, VISION

So there is still plenty of room for further learning, on both sides. And a good part of what lies ahead, in turn, in this book is given over to mapping out just where that is. In chapters that take up subjects as diverse as the prospects for the family as an institution, the role of women in society (and the church), the fate of human rights in the church, and the effect of relying on market economies on both our politics and our cultural life, those of us who have been a part of the project that produced this book seek to show where liberals and Catholics might beneficially continue to learn from one another in the years that lie ahead.

The thing above all, moreover, that we hope emerges from the analysis presented in these chapters is a clear sense of what there is to be gained from doing so. And not merely for liberalism and Catholicism themselves, either. Part of the argument made in the pages that follow is, of course, that both traditions themselves have something to gain from continuing their mutual learning: not only will each of them have more of a capacity to influence the course of events, but there will also be, we believe, a further enrichment of what they themselves intrinsically are. Mutual learning presents them both with an opportunity to *grow*, and in ways that could make it possible for them to realize their potential much more fully. But what is also at stake, we are convinced, is growth of another sort. For the quality of our public life would almost certainly be enhanced, too, were such mutual learning to begin to take place between liberals and Catholics. Nor would it just be the resultant civility that would be the benefit, either. In view of the problem that we now face in that regard, that would be, to be sure, no small gain. But it could also improve the chances of a coherent vision of the nation's mission and purpose emerging out of the process of rethinking that we are now undergoing.

But not only that, it could also do a great deal to enhance the *quality* of that vision: not only would the resources brought by liberals and Catholics to the realization of such a vision be enhanced, but there would be a greater likelihood of that vision doing justice to what they both have to offer. And that above all is what we think is the real promise that all of this holds. For a vision of the nation's purpose appropriate to our time that even began to do justice to the richness of the aspirations expressed by liberalism and Catholicism would be a good deal more than just the solution to the practical problem we now face. It would be an enlargement – and refinement – of what we stand for, too. And as such, it would be just the sort of creative *development* the American "proposition" now needs if it is not to turn into a recipe for our decline.

NOTES

1 One of the most important points that needs to be grasped in order to make sense of the "civil conversation" that goes on in a society like the United States is that it is about many different kinds of things, ranging from very specific policy matters to the most general images and metaphors that are used in our public life to define the nation's identity. Needless to say, moreover, some of the most important debates of all have to do with the latter – which is why the struggle over symbolism is so hard to avoid in any of our debates that touch on matters of principle in any way. What also needs to be appreciated is that much of the debate that goes on in moral and political theory is in fact a debate about symbols. See in this connection Michael Walzer, "On the Role of Symbolism in Political Thought," *Political Science Quarterly* 72 (June 1967): 191–204.
2 This is what is problematic about the otherwise instructive analysis provided by James Davison Hunter in his recent book, *Culture Wars* (New York: Harper/Collins, 1991). For while the realignment of the

political culture of the USA along the "orthodox" – "progressivist" divide that he identifies captures well *some* of what is now taking place, it does not really do justice to its full complexity. In particular, it does not adequately take into account how diversely the American people now respond to the issues that are being contested in the controversies he examines.

3 The difference between a "progressive" Catholic and a more "traditional" one, for example, can loom large when one focuses on their relationship to the exclusion of all else. But it does not take much exposure to the differences that can surface when such "progressive" Catholics enter into conversation with "progressives" of other sorts (Rawlsian liberals, for instance) to see that there remain plenty of other grounds for "difference" in the public life of the United States. (The same goes for conservatives, too.) And one can rest assured that they will manifest themselves, given the right setting. The challenge of holding together the diverse forces that compose the primary base of support of both of the major political parties in the United States would not be what it is, were it not for the fact that such varied differences have to be dealt with.

4 See Francis Fukuyama, *The End of History and the Last Man* (New York: Free Press, 1992).

5 See Richard John Neuhaus, *The Catholic Moment: The Paradox of the Church in the Postmodern World* (San Francisco: Harper & Row, 1987).

6 The best evidence of this is, of course, the two pastoral letters that have been issued in the course of the 1980s by the National Conference of Catholic Bishops on national security policy and the functioning of the economy. For both documents seek explicitly – and elaborately – to bring the historic teaching of the church to bear on major policy issues confronting the United States government. See National Conference of Catholic Bishops (NCCB), *The Challenge of Peace: God's Promise and Our Response – A Pastoral Letter on War and Peace* (Washington: NCCB, United States Catholic Conference, 1983); and *Economic Justice for All: A Pastoral Letter on Catholic Social Teaching and the U.S. Economy* (Washington: NCCB, United States Catholic Conference, 1986).

7 Nothing illustrates this better, moreover, than the two major pastoral letters that have been issued on matters of public policy by the US Catholic bishops in the course of the 1980s. For as conservative critics correctly have observed, both of those documents have had a lot to say that was in keeping with the tenor of liberal thinking in recent years.

8 We do not mean to suggest, of course, that the evolution through which liberalism and Catholicism have gone is attributable solely to the interaction they have had with one another. Both of them have had to respond, over the years, to a complex mix of different forces and ideas, only one element of which has been the liberal or Catholic (as the case may be) influence. But what we *do* mean to suggest is that, in each case,

that element has formed an important part of what they have had to take into account. And that means, in turn, that we are skeptical of accounts suggesting that the development undergone by either one of them can be adequately understood without taking into account the interaction they have had. The increasingly firm insistence on the need for distributive justice on the part of *a certain kind* of liberal, at least, is in part a response to socialist critiques, to be sure. But that is not the whole story. Especially in the United States, every bit as important has been the kind of religiously inspired insistence on the need for social justice that has been the stock-in-trade of Catholic social teaching ever since the time of the encyclical *Rerum Novarum* (1891).

9 To this day, no one has explained this better than Karl Mannheim in his classic *Ideology and Utopia* (New York: Harcourt, Brace & World, 1936).

10 The thing that always needs to be kept in mind in considering the state of liberalism today is that there is not one liberalism but several. And on issues of political economy in particular there is a deep fissure that continues to run right through the center of the liberal family. For the kind of project engaged in by a figure like John Rawls is being fought, of course, every step of the way by those who have a more "traditional" view of what liberalism stands for. Hayekian liberals are inclined, after all, to dismiss the quest for distributive justice in and through the welfare state as an "illusion" – and a dangerous one at that.

11 For an extended treatment of the issues at stake here, see R. Bruce Douglass, Gerald R. Mara, and Henry S. Richardson, eds., *Liberalism and the Good* (New York and London: Routledge, 1990).

12 "Quality of life" issues are almost certainly going to loom increasingly large in the public life of societies like the United States in the years ahead. And those issues are not at all easily addressed by liberals. For they require – almost by definition – a "thicker" conception of the human good than liberals tend to want to affirm. Catholics, in contrast, have no such compunctions. In fact, it is their forte. And our expectation is that the more attention is paid to such issues, the more obvious the contrast between them in this regard will become. For a particularly vivid illustration of the relevance of the Catholic facility to think in these terms to contemporary problems, see the distinction drawn by Pope John Paul II between development which is "only economic" (and therefore counterproductive) and that which is "truly human" in the encyclical of December 30, 1987, *Sollicitudo Rei Socialis* (Of Social Concern).

PART I

Historical conflicts and developments

The failed encounter: the Catholic church and liberalism in the nineteenth century

Peter Steinfels

I

The outline of the nineteenth-century encounter between Roman Catholicism and liberalism is familiar to readers of almost any modern history text.

The drama begins when the French Revolution tries first to retailor the church to a revolutionary pattern and then, having fallen short in the effort, attempts to replace Christianity altogether. The church casts its lot with counter-revolution. During the restoration the papacy renews and reinforces the bonds between the throne and altar with a series of concordats and with support for Metternich's Holy Alliance.

For the rest of the century this post-revolutionary settlement is repeatedly challenged and gradually dismantled – by revolutionary forces in 1830 and 1848; by the loss of the papal states to a unified Italy in 1870; by Bismarck's 1873–78 *Kulturkampf* against the church in a unified Germany; by the French Third Republic's turn to Gambetta's anti-clericalism in 1877 and, after the debacle of the Dreyfus Affair, by the harsh separation of church and state in 1905; by the seemingly inexorable rise of an anti-religious socialism among the working class and an anti-religious science among the educated. At the century's end, the pope has sentenced himself to becoming a "prisoner in the Vatican" and the church is forced to the margins of cultural and political life.

Meanwhile, there has been a parallel series of challenges from within the church itself. First there is the meteoric rise and fall of Félicité de Lamennais and his dramatic appeal to replace the alliance of throne and altar with an alliance between people and altar based on universal suffrage and freedom of religion and opinion. In an early issue of *L'Avenir*, Lamennais and his followers willingly take on the title of "liberal Catholics." He and his doctrine are swiftly repudiated by his bishops and, in the encyclicals *Mirari Vos* (1832) and *Singulari Nos* (1834), summarily condemned by Gregory XVI.

The pattern appears to be set. Support for liberal freedoms of religion, press, association, constitutional and parliamentary rule, and for free scientific inquiry gradually builds up – only to be repeatedly rejected by the papacy. After the uprising of 1848, Pope Pius IX disabuses those who imagined him a liberal sympathizer; he spurns the dreams of Italian nationalists and reinstalls rigorous papal rule in his territories with the power of French arms. The pragmatic Catholic liberalism that gained influence for the church in the 1840s is now stymied by the all-absorbing question of the pope's temporal powers and the interrelated question of support for the "empire" of Louis Napoleon. The papacy and zealous ultramontanes in every country react sharply to anything that may risk the retention of the papal states.

In England, Newman falls under suspicion and the liberal Catholic publications, *The Rambler* and the *The Home and Foreign Review*, teeter on the edge of condemnation. Neoscholasticism becomes the official form of theology as all its rivals to the Enlightenment left or the Romantic right fall under the ban.

In 1863, the Vatican censures the Comte de Montalembert's appeal for a reconciliation of Catholicism and liberalism at a liberal Catholic gathering at Malines. Similarly condemned is the appeal for freedom of scholarly investigation sounded that same year at the Congress of Munich by Ignaz Döllinger. In 1864, Pope Pius IX issues *Quanta Cura* and the Syllabus of Errors. Only the dialectical skills of interpreters like Bishop Dupanloup of Orléans allow the liberal Catholics to survive. The First Vatican Council and the definition of papal infallibility seem to remove their legitimacy even further.

Liberalism revives among Catholics after the election of Pope Leo XIII. He repeats many of his predecessors' animadversions on the papal states, liberal freedoms, and links between church and state, but his more flexible diplomacy and new concern for industrial social problems indicate a greater sensitivity to contemporary conditions. In 1890 the pope urges French Catholics to support the Third Republic rather than cling to hopes of restoring a monarchy. But his last years and the succeeding reign of Pius X bring condemnations of Americanism, Christian Democracy, and Modernism. At all levels of the church, an interlocking system of surveillance, oaths, accusations, and rebukes purges theological deviance.

The cycles of revival and rejection continue. The common suffering of World War I brings Catholics and non-Catholics together; in France, the war binds Catholics to the Republic in a way that Leo XIII's directive failed to achieve. The right-wing Action Française is condemned in 1927. But to stem threats of chaos and revolution in Italy, Germany, France, Portugal, Spain, and Austria, both pope and hierarchies prefer authoritarian forces rather than alliances with liberals and socialists.

With the World War II victory of the liberal democracies in Western Europe and the opening of the Cold War against Communism, the church aligns itself with Christian Democracy. The anti-Modernist barriers against free inquiry last longer. But Vatican II ultimately endorses most of the planks in the platform of nineteenth-century liberal Catholicism.

II

This basic story line is subject to different interpretations. First there is melodrama. As E. E. Y. Hales noted in the preface to his biography of Pius IX, this view long dominated British historiography. "On the one side were the 'obscurantists' and 'fanatics' – the intransigent Ultramontanes. On the other side were the liberals, fighting for freedom and truth." It was "still shocking to suggest that aught but obstinacy and ill-will toward his fellow human beings dictated" the papacy's desire to remain sovereign in Rome, the Syllabus, and ultramontanism.[1]

The roles, of course, can be reversed. Brave conservatives defend the fortress of truth against the ever-encroaching armies of liberalism until the defenders go down in tragic (but, God willing, only temporary) defeat. This was not only the official view of the papacy, it long dominated Catholic opinion and remains strong in conservative circles as well as among Lefebvrists.

Mr. Hales and others have offered more nuanced interpretations explaining why the clash between Catholicism and liberalism, although unfortunate, was nonetheless unavoidable. Liberalism, it is said, was a political threat to the church. Betraying its own anti-statist principles, it remained determined to use state power to achieve dogmatically secularist or anticlerical ends. Not until it had lost that ideological edge could the church come to terms with it. The papal condemnations, especially the Syllabus, should not be read in the universal terms in which they were couched but as applying only to the concrete circumstances which quite justifiably gave rise to them.

More nuanced yet: even if liberalism was not actually a danger to religion, given the traumatic experience of the church with the Enlightenment and the French Revolution, it was inevitable that the church leadership should perceive it as such.

Or again: the anti-liberalism of the papacy was an unfortunate but necessary prerequisite for building a tight Catholic counter-culture, a fortress Catholicism that, however much it sometimes ironically mirrored its opponents, enabled the church to survive a hostile and self-destructive century and offer its healing message to the chastened age that has followed.

Yet another interpretation draws strength from Marxism although frequently advanced by non-Marxists, even by integralist critics of modernity. Liberalism is simply a legitimating ideology for bourgeois hegemony or capitalism. Behind the sometimes unattractive details of the church's clash with liberalism, therefore, was a sound refusal to bless the narrow interests of a particular class or a passing phase in economic history.

To choose among these interpretations requires a thorough historical survey of evidence beyond the scope of this essay. What follows is meant to suggest that in the first two-thirds of the nineteenth century there was more of a window of opportunity for a mutually instructive encounter between liberalism and Catholicism than is frequently assumed. Grounds for this encounter were available, it is suggested in passing, in the mood of much early nineteenth-century liberalism and – here the argument is more extensive – in the potentially mediating movement of liberal Catholicism. Whatever serious challenges liberal Catholicism posed to the church, the movement was quite distinct from the skeptical individualism of the Enlightenment or the statist Jacobinism of the Revolution.

The opportunity for a positive exchange passed with the 1864 Syllabus and was made impossible by united Italy's seizure of papal Rome. Not only was the reinvigorated Voltairean and positivist liberalism of the latter third of the century beyond the church's reach, but the church had no part in the reformulations of liberalism that eventually emerged in response to democratic and socialist pressure.

Instead an anti-liberal tradition implanted itself in Catholicism, the depth and vehemence of which contributed mightily to the church's inability to resist authoritarian regimes in the twentieth century.

This essay can only be suggestive, providing illustration more than demonstration (insofar as demonstration is possible in history in any case). It is deliberately meant as a counter to an apologetic tone, perhaps inherited from pre-Vatican II writers like Hales, that lingers in many Catholic discussions of the church's confrontation with liberalism, a tone that has the effect of minimizing the tragedy involved. But the emphasis in this essay is finally proposed as only one more entry into the lists of contending interpretations.

III

What was the liberalism that Catholicism encountered in the nineteenth century? Of defining liberalism, of course, there is no end. "Confused, vague, contradictory," writes Owen Chadwick, "the idea of liberalism dominated the nineteenth century, more a motto than a word, more a programme of what might be than a description of what was; a protean word, which some claimed to rest upon coherent philosophies and economic theory and others saw as the destruction of the stable structure of a reasonable society."[2]

Another historian, Irene Collins, is more encouraging: "To embrace all the variations of liberalism throughout the century a complicated definition would be required," she writes, "yet liberals themselves, certainly up to 1860 or 1870, saw nothing complicated in their creed. Whatever twists and turns were demanded of them by circumstances, they held at heart a simple faith: a belief that progress, leading to final perfection, could be achieved by means of free institutions,"[3] such as freely elected parliaments, accountable ministers, independent judiciaries, freedom of speech, press, religion, assembly, careers open to talent, the protection of property, and due process before the law.

There are "tight" definitions of liberalism and "loose" definitions. Tight definitions insist that liberalism constitutes a finely linked whole in which its political program cannot be separated from an economic outlook, a view of human nature, a social theory, an ethics, an epistemology, even a metaphysics. Such analyses usually construct an ideal type – "classic liberalism" – or choose certain liberal thinkers as paradigmatic, a canon within the canon. Other positions claiming liberal affiliation are considered unstable hybrids or half-hearted compromises. Under pressure, they will gravitate to the pure liberal model or cease to be liberal. Why is this the case? Does logic compel it? Has history demonstrated it? These analyses do not reply.

"Loose" definitions avoid this problem. Liberalism is a current, a school, a "family" in which all the cousins are equally welcome. Liberalism is defined by a set of leading principles, doctrines, or goals, a general perspective on history or even a certain temperament. The set need not display a tight inner coherence. Liberal principles or attitudes could coexist more or less peacefully with non-liberal or even anti-liberal ones. It is sufficient that the liberal genes predominate, a matter for acrimonious dispute in particular cases.

"Loose" definitions appeal to historians. "Tight" definitions appeal to theorists and critics of liberalism, allowing them to connect aspects of liberalism enjoying a prima facie appeal with what they allege are its fatal, underlying flaws. Critics find "loose" definitions an annoyingly moving target.

There are also philosophical definitions of liberalism and institutional ones. Philosophical definitions treat liberalism's advocacy of such institutional arrangements as parliamentary government, regular elections, a free press, an independent judiciary, separation of church and state as a highly likely but not necessarily crucial function of their underlying philosophy. Thus there is no real problem about holding Hobbes to be liberal – if not even the liberal – despite his justification for absolutism, since in important respects his philosophy is continuous with that of Locke and other empiricists and contractarians. Institutional definitions, on the other hand, begin with advocacy of "free" or "liberal" institutions, and include in the circle of liberalism whatever philosophical positions provide reasonable grounds for that advocacy.

IV

These distinctions are pertinent for this reason: by some accounts, neither the secular nor the Catholic liberalism of the nineteenth century qualifies as true liberalism! True liberalism is either an ideal type or an historic standard taken from the seventeenth or eighteenth centuries. The reality was there before the label was invented. What later passed under the label was only a shadow or even a counterfeit of the reality.[4]

Of liberalism in the nineteenth century, it must be said that its stance toward the French Revolution and toward religion was highly mixed. Much of the century's liberalism was consciously anti-revolutionary. When liberals did favor revolution they did so largely in the context of struggles for national liberation – Polish, Greek, German, Italian – from the absolutist thrones of the East – Prussia, Russia, Austria, and the Ottomans. Social unrest was typically met by liberal regimes with "prudential" restraints on those liberties – of speech, press, and assembly – that the church, too, found threatening.

Likewise, in the wake of the French Revolution and Romanticism, liberalism's attitude toward religion and the church, at least at the level of fresh thought rather than the level of, say, the entrenched secondary school teachers of the July Monarchy, was far from Voltaire's "Ecrasez l'infame!" It included a polite skepticism as well as a wistful sympathy, a self-doubting faith, a scholarly questioning, a highly developed private conscience, a romantic pantheism. The anti-dogmatic principle for which Newman used the term liberalism should not be confused with aggressive attacks on the position of the church, unless one considers, as Newman did in his Tractarian days, any weakening of the church's privileged and established status as an aggressive attack. Although Gambetta's cry "Le cléricalisme, voilà l'ennemi!" had its predecessors in the first half of the century, particularly in places like Italy where the church exercised state power, it should be remembered that many of the fiercest conflicts between Catholicism and liberals arose in the latter half of the century after Rome had unmistakably thrown down the gauntlet in the struggle over constitutional and limited government.

In the early part of the century, liberalism in Britain and Germany had national reasons to recall the French Revolution in negative terms, but in France, too, as Guido de Ruggiero and other historians of liberalism agree, liberalism "was definitely conservative in tendency."[5] French liberals urged that liberalism was a new creed. Its desired liberty should not be confused with that of ancient Greece or, sometimes sotto voce, the French Revolution. "This anxiety to show that a break had been made with the past arose from an anxiety to deny all connection with the excesses of the French Revolution. Most people in France and indeed in Europe dreaded a recurrence of the turmoil and bloodshed of the revolution, and most liberals felt obliged to fight these memories of the revolution as their worst enemies."[6] Perhaps the most supple, but not unrepresentative, French liberal thinkers of this era were Benjamin Constant and Alexis de Tocqueville, the one steadfastly opposed to democracy, the other warily welcoming it, but both fiercely anti-revolutionary and anti-Jacobin.

v

Was there any possibility that Catholic authorities, especially the papacy, could have seen anything but a single, undifferentiated bloc of forces in the Enlightenment, the Revolution, and the liberalism of the nineteenth century? Certainly one can conclude that a different outcome was unlikely by simply recalling the years 1790–1814. That quarter century saw the church of France torn apart during the Revolution. Venerable church properties and privileges were suppressed throughout Napoleonic Europe. Finally, two popes were ignominiously kidnapped and imprisoned.

The appearance of inevitability is strengthened, however, by a tendency to read back into the Enlightenment, the Revolution, and the Napoleonic era's encroachments on the church's power the categorical division that eventually emerged. Papal and anti-clerical defenders have converged in picturing the conflict in terms of two monolithic and irreconcilable forces. It is good to keep in mind, as Sheridan Gilley points out, that the relationship between Catholicism and the Enlightenment was by no means simply the picture of conflict that has been popularized.[7]

Furthermore, long before encroachments on church positions were perpetrated by revolutionaries, they were policies of eighteenth-century monarchies. Whether or not these policies reflected Enlightenment ideals, they almost always reflected traditional state power over church matters: nominating bishops, suppressing religious orders, secularizing monastic holdings, prescribing theological textbooks, repressing or requiring religious devotions. The Civil Constitutions of the Clergy stood in a line stretching from Josephism to Bonaparte's Organic Articles and his depredations of the papal states.

Thus no small amount of the restrictions placed on church activities that church authorities attributed to liberalism in fact came from the assumptions of state control over religious matters that ran from Enlightened absolutism through the Revolution to Bonapartism and the Restoration. Even the loss of the papal states was the handiwork in good measure of the second Bonaparte, who proved less faithful to the papacy than did French public opinion. Were there not grounds here for welcoming some aspects of liberalism as well as criticizing others – thus opening up a fruitful interaction?

The question is precisely the one that liberal Catholics posed. Perhaps the most important thing to be kept in mind about their movement, one so obvious that it can only be obscured by taking for granted later patterns, is that it began with a concern for freedom, not of the individual, not of the dissenting conscience, not of an aspiring class, but of the Catholic church.

Liberal Catholics began as restorationists not revolutionaries. They began as ultramontanes and in 1863, on the eve of the Syllabus, Lord Acton was still trying to salvage this title for liberal Catholics. They dreamed of restoring Catholic cultural hegemony. To begin with, they did not rebel against the alliance of throne and altar because the altar was aggrandizing itself or violating consciences by wielding the power of the throne. They first rebelled because the throne was using its power to intervene in the affairs of the altar. Then they rebelled because they saw the possibility of reconquering society for Catholic Christianity doomed as long as the church remained chained to hopelessly bankrupt regimes. Only at the end of this process of reasoning did they reach the conclusion that the freedom necessary for the church to conquer implied the general freedom of all.

The dramatic case, as always, was that of Lamennais. In line with de Maistre and de Bonald, he rejected the Enlightenment's reliance on individual reason. In his *Essai sur l'indifférence en matière de religion*, a book that had an enormous impact when the first volume appeared in 1817, he demonstrated that from Descartes to Hume the reason of the philosophers had inevitably ended in the cul-de-sac of a practically unworkable skepticism. Truth could only be found in what was universally held by humankind. This *sensus communis* ultimately stemmed from God's primitive revelation, was handed on through tradition, and could only be verified through the authority of the church – in the last resort, of the pope.

Academic ingenuity could probably link Lamennais's views to "the linguistic turn" (de Bonald: thought is impossible without the vehicle of a preexisting language) or to anti-foundationalism, but in many ways his argument seems hopelessly naive. It was not, however, relativist or individualist. The word "indifference" in the title did

not refer primarily to the apathy of individuals but to the attitude
that adherence to one belief rather than another made no difference.[8]
As for individualism, "Man must be viewed, not as an isolated being,
but as a link in a vast hierarchy of beings, as a member of an eternal
society of intellects."[9] The trinitarian God, in the depths of the divine
life, is an eternal society of relations – and has created human nature
as intrinsically relational.

Lamennais's passage to liberalism was hardly direct. In his longing
for a triumphant Catholic restoration, he confronted with dismay the
large degree of toleration and practical religious neutrality that
existed even in the Bourbon regime with its established Catholic
church. If the French state condemned sacrilege – one of the more
inflammatory issues of the Restoration – it condemned sacrilege
against all faiths alike. From this Lamennais concluded rather
hyperbolically that the Restoration monarchy was "atheistic." That
fact made all the more intolerable a whole catalogue of restrictions,
of the traditional Gallican variety, that the state placed on the church
in matters of education, discipline, and relations with Rome,
restrictions that Lamennais imagined to be hobbling the Catholic
renewal he so passionately desired.

In all this there was a certain parallel to what led the heralds of the
Oxford Movement to raise the alarm of "national apostasy." Repeal
of the Test Act, Catholic emancipation, and the suppression of
Church of Ireland sees were all expressions of a religious and political
liberalism that in the eyes of the Oxford activists raised the threat of
a religiously indifferent government deciding the course of the
church. The first response – whether of Lamennais or Gladstone or
Newman – was to imagine a church which had the best of two
worlds, enjoying both a privileged relationship with the state and an
untrammeled predominance over it, an independence and authority
to be guaranteed for Lamennais by vesting spiritual power in the
pope rather than the national church. The second response, however,
was to recognize as unrealistic in modern conditions any solution that
did not entail a much greater severing of church and state. By way of
hostile reaction to liberal measures within a framework of church–
state union, these religious reformers came to accept a liberal
framework of church–state separation.

In Lamennais's case, this development was spurred when he
suffered prosecution for anti-Gallican writings and finally when
restrictions on Catholic schooling were ordered in 1828 by a ministry

hoping to appease anti-clerical opposition to the regime. On the eve of the 1830 revolution that would replace the Bourbons with the Orleanist July Monarchy, Lamennais took the startling step of urging the church to shift its hopes from princes to people and to trust in the new opportunities opened by freedom of conscience, press, and education.

The goal of increasing the church's direct influence on society can be seen in the argument for religious liberty presented in *L'Avenir*, the daily paper Lamennais and his followers founded after the July revolution. Freedom of individual conscience played its part in the argument, but more prominent was the conviction that under modern conditions, when states are populated by people of diverse beliefs, the union of church and state leads to a condition of "permanent political and civil warfare" in which one belief after another dominates while suppressing the rest. The result is that force replaces discussion, conflict and passion make understanding impossible, anarchy becomes interminable. "The only remedy to such a great evil is to let this spiritual warfare be waged and resolved with purely spiritual weapons. Truth is all powerful." Freedom of religion was not just a safeguard for the individual conscience, it was a condition for the successful pursuit of dialogue, debate, and ultimately, the editors of *L'Avenir* believed, the reconversion of Europe and the world. "Nous croyons fermement que le développement des lumières modernes ramènera un jour, non seulement la France, mais l'Europe entière à l'unité catholique, qui, plus tard et par un progrès successif, attirant à elle le rest du genre humain, le constituera par une même foi dans une même société spirituelle."[10] The traditionalist, Burkean strand in their thought could be seen in the large place they gave over to defending local liberties and attacking the rational centralization inherited from the Bourbons, the Enlightenment, and Bonaparte.[11] Finally, their Catholic militancy passed from words to action when they ended up convicted in court for publicly opening an independent Catholic school – deliberately challenging the new regime's refusal to put into practice its theoretical commitment to freedom of education.[12]

Other examples could be given of the distinctively Catholic sources, preoccupations, and character of Catholic liberalism. Even as he adopted liberal positions, Lamennais continued to excoriate liberalism per se as ultimately a form of anarchy. The moderate Catholics who accepted in the late 1820s the label of Catholic liberals

(or liberal Catholics, an ordering of words giving rise to refined
discussions that will be ignored here) were still objecting in the 1850s
to the terms Catholic liberalism or liberal Catholicism, with their
suggestion of a special doctrine. Lord Acton was a rare case, a liberal
Catholic who was actually a member of a liberal political party,[13]
although he too entered public life interested in winning the world for
Catholicism rather than liberalism in any party or doctrinal sense.
In the 1840s Montalembert, recovered from the condemnation of
L'Avenir and once more in pursuit of educational freedom, kept his
distance from secular liberals, sometimes to the detriment of his
cause.[14] In the traumatic events of the 1850s and 1860s that led to the
loss of the papal states, Catholic liberals were, with a few exceptions,
outspoken champions of the papal cause. Montalembert's attacks on
Louis Napoleon's double-dealing diplomacy were polemic master-
pieces. He was far more prescient about the French leader's
untrustworthiness than the ultramontane Louis Veuillot. At the
Congress at Malines, in the very speeches that would earn a papal
condemnation and seal the fate of liberal Catholicism for decades,
Montalembert denounced the appropriation by Cavour of the
formula "a free church in a free state" to mean "a despoiled church
in a despoiling state." Acton and Döllinger were equally fierce in
condemning the Piedmontese court at Turin for its encroachments on
Rome. Finally, there is the personal religious devotion of many of the
Catholic liberals, a traditional piety, a strict moral discipline. "En
aucune manière le libéralisme catholique n'est un laxisme moral ou
doctrinal, une religion diluée, 'coupée d'eau,' comme Manning le
disait à propos de Newman."[15]

VII

But granted distinctively Catholic, even conservative, roots and traits
in liberal Catholicism, did any basic premises, underlying its overt
commitment to liberal institutions, define it and link it to liberalism
proper? As with liberalism itself, any attempt at definition immediately becomes an occasion for caveats and exceptions. Catholic
liberal ranks included constitutional monarchists and republicans,
democrats and aristocratic critics of democracy, nationalists and
internationalists, defenders and opponents of laissez-faire economics.
Despite its strong, initial ultramontanism, there were always some
liberal Catholics of a different opinion, and eventually the movement

as a whole was anti-ultramontane. There were Catholic liberals whose liberalism became a matter of universal, unalterable principles; there were those whose liberalism always contained a large element of the tactical and circumstantial. Catholic liberalism found expressions across Europe, from the Ireland of Daniel O'Connell, which provided an early inspiration to continental movements, to Belgium, England, Germany, Poland, Italy, Austria, Hungary. There was a high degree of communication between leading figures and journals, but each outcropping was shaped by its special national circumstances.

Beyond the catalytic thirteen months of *L'Avenir*, it is hard to point to a single place or a single person for a well-developed and representative statement of Catholic liberal doctrine. The leaders of liberal Catholicism were not theoreticians, not systematic thinkers. Many were brilliant men who appreciated scholarship but were not scholars. Instead they were journalists and ecclesiastics and parliamentarians. They were orators and wordsmiths like Lacordaire and Montalembert. They were historians like Acton and Döllinger. History, not philosophy, was in fact their native element. History, after all, was the flower of Romanticism; it was the nineteenth-century discipline par excellence; and throughout their speeches, articles, and correspondence, they are always reaching for historical examples and comparisons with which to fix and analyze the modern flux that they were calling the church to address.[16]

Is the absence of a clear and comprehensive liberal Catholic doctrine to be deplored? Or is it a question of accepting the movement on its own terms, realizing in addition that repeated thunderbolts from Rome and conservative adversaries did not encourage these thinkers to present larger targets than necessary? Montalembert, for instance, repeatedly disclaimed any ambition of setting forth universal principles. Look, after all, what happened to his mentor, Lamennais, for whom everything was a matter of universal principle. His aim, Montalembert said, was only to propose solutions appropriate to the immediate circumstances.

Lacking a doctrine or a classical statement with which to define this movement, we can still discern some important traits:

1. Catholic liberals rejected a blanket condemnation of the French Revolution and its consequences.

Sharp differences existed between them on the topic of the Revolution. Lacordaire and Montalembert jousted over the topic in their correspondence. Their contrasting views reflected the split among the one-time disciples of Lamennais in 1848 as well as their different attitudes toward democracy. Lacordaire had greeted the fall of the July Monarchy with enthusiasm in 1848, started a paper, *L'Ere nouvelle*, with Ozanam and others, gained a seat in the Assembly where he placed himself on the far left, then promptly resigned after the riots of May 15. Montalembert had lamented the Revolution grievously, briefly rallied to Louis Napoleon's authoritarian regime, then reasserted his liberal principles in opposition. In their letters, Lacordaire chides Montalembert for his censorious tone toward even the word "revolution," warning him that "there are two men in you," a defender of liberty and a reactionary, and one or the other will establish his reputation for posterity. Montalembert replies that liberty has been endangered by revolution, not achieved by it, that Lacordaire's attitude is indulgent and enthusiastic, that in the Revolution as in the Reformation God might draw good from evil, but that we should not therefore approve the evil, since the good might have been accomplished in less destructive fashion.[17] Neither, however, could accept the French Revolution totally, nor could they reject the world that had sprung from it. This insistence on distinctions separated Catholic liberals from many fellow believers, laity and hierarchy.

2. Catholic liberals felt that change had become not the exceptional moment but the very medium of human existence, the chief reality of modern life. They believed that the church could embrace this condition as an opportunity rather than denounce it as an affliction.

René Rémond has said that liberal Catholics were marked by "a certain historicism."[18] But their outlook fell short of an articulated philosophy of history like Auguste Comte's or Herbert Spencer's stages of society. It was closer to the nineteenth-century consciousness that one finds in Thomas Carlyle's 1829 "Signs of the Times": "The thinking minds of all nations call for change. There is a deep-lying struggle in the whole fabric of society: a boundless grinding collision of the New with the Old."[19] Or two years later, in the young John Stuart Mill's "Spirit of the Age": "It is an age of transition. Mankind have outgrown old institutions and old doctrines, and have not yet acquired new ones."[20] Like Alexis de Tocqueville and Matthew Arnold, Catholic liberals advised their listeners to accept and prepare for a democratic society that was inevitable but not irredeemable. Catholics, declared Montalembert in his speech at the Congress of Malines,

experience an overwhelming mixture of embarrassment and timidity in the face of modern society. It frightens them; they have not yet learned either to understand it, or to love it, or to act in it. In mind and heart, many of them still unconsciously dwell in the Ancien Regime, that is to say, in a society that granted neither civil equality nor political liberty nor freedom of conscience.

This Ancien Regime had its great and beautiful aspects: I do not pretend to judge it here, still less to condemn it. It is enough to recognize that it suffers from a single fault but a capital one: it is dead.

The new society, democracy, to call it by its name, exists. One can almost say that it alone exists; everything else has little force and life...

As for me, I am not a democrat; but I am still less an absolutist. I try above all not to be blind...

On this immense ocean of democracy, with its depths, its maelstroms, its reefs, its dead calms, and its tempests, the church alone can venture without misgiving or fear...

If we directly and boldly engage this new world in order... to combat the dangers inherent to democracy with the immortal resources of liberty... we will not be invulnerable but we will be invincible.[21]

Arguments like this have been assailed, and justly, for substituting inevitability – the "wave of the future" – for justification, a shortcut admitting of intellectual and moral abuse. Yet to deny such arguments altogether is to pretend that history is entirely open to all possibilities at all moments. Certainly such arguments are more convincing when made by a Tocqueville or a Montalembert on behalf of a historical shift about which they are not entirely happy.

3. Catholic liberals had an almost unbounded confidence in the power of truth.

This faith in "the march of mind" was one of their links with the Enlightenment and secular liberalism, although the Catholic liberals conceived of it in terms of philosophical and religious verities rather than the encyclopédistes' practical science of material well-being or the technological progress of the utilitarians' "steam-engine intellect." Truth, simply because it was the truth, would conquer error if it were allowed free play on the terrain of open discussion. Like John Stuart Mill, they believed that free speech and every form of liberty was the best guarantee of truth's victory.[22]

Their adversaries, like Mill's critic James Fitzjames Stephen, did not share this confidence.[23] When Gregory XVI condemned "that absurd and erroneous maxim, or rather that madness, that it is necessary to assure and guarantee liberty of conscience to everyone," he did so speaking of human nature as "inclined to evil." Throughout *Mirari Vos*, his assumption is that in any competition between truly religious writings and malicious or "suspect and harmful" ones, the latter will prevail.[24]

This special concern with things of the mind set Catholic liberals off from their coreligionists whose intellectual state the liberals were always bemoaning. In France, Lamennais drew young enthusiasts to his Congrégation de Saint Pierre at La Chesnaie in an effort to set afoot a vast enterprise of learning and publication that would overshadow the work of the encyclopédistes. Abbé Gerbet undertook a parallel effort in the publication *L'Université catholique*. The need for educating English and Irish Catholics was a constant concern of Newman, Acton, Simpson, and the other stalwarts of *The Rambler* and *The Home and Foreign Review*. Newman threw himself into the abortive founding of a Catholic University of Ireland, the project of retranslating Scripture and efforts to educate young Catholics at Oxford and elsewhere. "Now from first to last, education, in this large sense of the word, has been my line," he wrote, with a keen sense that it had mainly earned him enemies in Rome and at home.[25]

Again in France, it was not just a Catholic share in primary education (effectively handed over to the church in 1833 by Guizot) that mobilized the Catholic liberals but breaking the state's monopoly in secondary and higher education. Yet Catholic liberals, led by Bishop Dupanloup, also came to the defense of secular learning after Abbé Guame attacked the study of classical writers in 1851.

In an 1833 lecture, Abbé Gerbet decried those Catholics "who have a secret fear of every movement of thought. In their mind, they have linked the unchangeable truths of religions with the particular knowledge of an age." They have imagined that "this human edifice held up the heavens, and so it is that each time a stone comes loose, they cry that the stars are falling." He contrasted this attitude with what he said was confidence of the Church Fathers in "the progress of reason."[26]

The church must take part in the century's impressive development of secular knowledge, both to learn and to contribute. The failure of Catholics to do this was the source of Acton's slashing attacks in his 1859 essay on the Catholic press: "Religion is not served by denying facts, or by denouncing those who proclaim them. A fire is not put out by a policeman's whistle, nor a thief taken by the cry of 'Stop thief!' Authority can only condemn error; its vitality is not destroyed until it is refuted..." At a time "when science has made such progress," Acton wrote, "it is necessary for the church to accept science as her necessary and trusty ally."[27]

4. Catholic liberals insisted on the autonomy of distinct spheres of human activity – whether politics or religion or science.

Although ultimately the formed conscience must make a final judgment, each field has its independent criteria that must be scrupulously respected. In this conception, liberal Catholicism reflected the modern differentiation of life and segmentation of activities, and here surely was one of the prime sources of its conflict with the church.

This characteristic emerges most strongly in Acton's attitude toward historical scholarship, although one could trace it in a dozen other major figures. Acton's 1863 essay, "Ultramontanism," tracing the degeneration of what he considered a fundamentally sound impulse, brings together the Catholic liberals' attitude toward truth, free inquiry, and the autonomy of different spheres. It begins with the premise that an unwavering progress in truth, "secured against loss or deterioration," is of the essence of the Catholic church. The penultimate pages of the essay wove together many ideas and frustrations of liberal Catholicism. The central Christian beliefs – God's existence, the immortality of the soul, the punishment of sin, and so on, had developed "by the organic action of the church" into full-blown doctrines, none of which could be "destroyed by the progress of knowledge":

But there is an outward shell of variable opinions constantly forming round this inward core of irreversible dogma, by its contact with human science or philosophy, as a coating of oxide forms round a mass of metal where it comes in contact with the shifting atmosphere. The Church must always put herself in harmony with existing ideas, and speak to each age and nation in its own language. A kind of amalgam between the eternal faith and temporal opinion is thus in constant process of generation, and by it Christians explain to themselves the bearings of their religion, so far as knowledge allows...

But as opinion changes, as principles become developed, and as habits alter, one element of the amalgam is constantly losing its vitality, and the true dogma is left in an unnatural union with exploded opinion. From time to time a very extensive revision is required, hateful to conservative habits and feelings; a crisis occurs, and a new alliance has to be formed between religion and knowledge, between the Church and society. Every victory thus gained is in reality a victory of truth over error, of science over opinion. It is a change not to be deplored but to be accepted with joy... The danger is only for those who fail to distinguish the essential from the accidental, and who cling to their religion, not for its substance, but for its appendages...

The fear of giving scandal, and the unwillingness to question too closely the limits of authority, are therefore the two motives which make the best informed Catholics very circumspect in destroying opinions which have become amalgamated with faith. But these motives are misplaced in an age when Catholics can no longer shut themselves out from contact with the world, nor shelter themselves in ignorance... Catholics cannot help attempting to solve the problems which all the world is discussing. The point is, that while they solve them religiously, they should likewise solve them scientifically on grounds quite external to religion.

When a man has really performed this double task – when he has worked out the problem of science or politics, on purely scientific and political principles, and then controlled this process by the doctrine of the Church, and found its results to coincide with that doctrine, then he is an Ultramontane in the real meaning of the term – a Catholic in the highest sense of Catholicism. The Ultramontane is therefore one who makes no parade of his religion; who appeals to no extrinsic considerations – benevolence, or force, or interest, or artifice – in order to establish his point; who discusses each topic on its intrinsic merits – answering the critic by a severer criticism, the metaphysician by a closer reasoning, the historian by deeper learning, the politician by sounder politics and indifference itself by a pure impartiality... Not that this labour is an easy one, or one capable of being brought to a close... There will always be some progress to be made, some new discoveries to adopt and assimilate, some discord to harmonize, some half-truth which has become an error to lop away. It is a process never to be terminated, till God has finished the work of educating the human race to know Him and to love Him.[28]

5. Catholic liberals generally tried to minimize the implications of their attitudes for the interior life of the church, but these could not be avoided.

Although many Catholic liberals began as defenders of the papacy, repeated condemnations by Rome and their general belief in preserving the vigor of local power against a domineering central government could not help but make them unenthusiastic about papal centralization. Their belief in law as a protection against arbitrary power ran against the increasing Roman rule by fiat. Their commitment to deliberation, representation, and public participation put their views at odds with the church's closed, monarchical institutions. Their moderation clashed with the devotional enthusiasms of the era. Their faith in freedom of inquiry could not be halted at theological borders.[29] When *The Rambler* in England discussed Catholic education or legal freedom of religion or respect for scholarly criteria of truth, it incurred the wrath of church authorities.

VIII

Historians have argued that the papacy's unyielding attitude toward liberalism, even Catholic liberalism, was rooted as much in immediate politics as in deeper divisions of outlook. Metternich's agents intercepted Lamennais's correspondence, and the Austrian leader pressed the Holy See to condemn the French priest. E. E. Y. Hales maintained that the church's welfare "appeared much more likely to be served by maintaining the alliance with political conservatism."[30] He pointed to successful efforts at winning favors from Austria and the obstacle that Pius IX's early liberal reputation posed to negotiations with the Russian and Prussian monarchies. The commitment of the church to a system of concordats aligned it with governments against their critics and adversaries. Liberal ideas, according to other historians, were incompatible with "theocratic government" as it existed in the papal states.

These political factors should not be underestimated, especially when seen in conjunction with Catholic liberalism's support of basic political freedoms, its refusal to issue a blanket condemnation of the French Revolution, its optimism about free discussion, its recognition of relatively autonomous spheres of human endeavor reflecting the differentiation of modern society, and its largely implicit critique of the internal life of the church. There were indeed real philosophical differences between Catholic liberalism and church authorities of the papal persuasion. In addition, however, there were contingent factors in the church's rejection of Catholic liberalism. One was certainly the character of its first exponent to capture widespread attention, Hugues-Félicité Robert de La Mennais. Lamennais was a loose cannon temperamentally, philosophically, theologically, politically. It is not surprising that the French church and the papacy could not endorse him. It is even understandable why in cases like Lamennais's the church went further and issued a condemnation. It does not follow, however, that the papacy had to erect and maintain, with but occasional relaxations, the most extreme counter-position. It could have left open middle ground for the evolution of the pragmatic, moderate liberal Catholicism that was much more typical than the apocalyptic visions of a Lamennais.

Why did Rome and its supporters equate liberal Catholicism with the Revolution and the Enlightenment, with relativism, with philosophical individualism, with qualified or watered-down Catholicism, with revolutionary or anti-clerical enemies of the church, when liberal Catholics manifestly opposed all of these?

It is proposed in defense of the papacy's anti-liberal stance that the church was only objecting to liberalism's absolute claims. The evidence in regard to liberal Catholicism cuts in the other direction. What the church objected to was that movement's failure to support the church's own absolute claims. Catholic anti-liberalism was based on the principle that if you are not for me one hundred percent, you are against me. Anything less than an institutionally enforced monopoly on spiritual power was equivalent to persecution and amounted to the great but largely undefined heresy of the century – "indifferentism."

The "perverse opinion," "poisonous spring," "widespread pestilence," and "hideous error" of indifferentism, as mentioned in *Mirari Vos*, the Syllabus, and dozens of other documents, referred primarily to the belief that salvation could well be available to those outside the Catholic church. But evoked in reference to concordats, legislation, education, mixed marriages, and other contexts, it became a protean label for whatever might offer legitimacy, acceptance, or parity to anything but Catholic belief. It showed its face in guarantees of free speech, press, religious practice, "removal of restraints," and "desire for novelty."

If Catholic liberals' major offense was their principled objection to using state power to enforce the church's spiritual monopoly (they rather naively envisaged the church someday enjoying a similar monopoly but one achieved through cultural energy and not buttressed with legal coercion), their lay encroachment on the clergy's, hierarchy's, and Holy See's monopoly of spiritual authority within the church was a nearly equal transgression.

The full scope of Catholic anti-liberalism can be seen by looking more closely at two documents among many. In 1866, Louis Veuillot published *L'Illusion libérale*. Before Pius IX and his advisors decided on the format of the Syllabus, the pope had considered using an earlier draft of the pamphlet as the condemnation of prevalent "errors of the times."[31]

Essential to Veuillot's argument is the denial of all middle ground. On the one side was the removal of religion and morality from public life and their relegation to "the privacy of the conscience" by "godless, soulless, anti-Christian liberalism." On the other side was the unembarrassed use of civil power to affirm and enforce true religion. If Christian society is to be maintained, the state should be at the bidding of the pope. The Christian duty is to transform force and use it charitably but never to renounce it. God himself is might. "Force in the hands of the church is the force of right, and we have no desire that right should remain without force." The church may have to forgo such exercise of divine prerogatives in the face of unbelieving or heretical states, but the church must never abandon its claims.

Veuillot backed this defense of "the theocentric principle" with two arguments. The first was the argument from authority: a barrage of biblical and magisterial teachings that Catholic liberals, he said, try to evade or rebut. The second was stated after an extensive review of the Catholic liberal case. Despite the surface reasonableness of this case, Veuillot said that he was not reassured. He imagined not the refined audience that he thought Catholic liberals catered to, but "the general public," and "instantly there came upon me the sad realization of the utter helplessness of reason."

"The multitude obeys its passions, it loves destruction"; it is "naturally inclined to error" and therefore to "death." "Human souls are sick, and sick with a terrible disease," the desire of error. The duty of Christ's kingly people is "to protect the multitude of our weak and ignorant brothers both as regards their souls and as regards their bodies." The main way to do this is "to enact such laws as will make it easier for them to know God and to be in communion with God." Any other response will leave us excusing ourselves with Cain's plea, "Am I my brother's keeper?"

Veuillot portrays Catholic liberals as attempting "to reconcile the irreconcilable." He acknowledges their uprightness, piety, learning, enthusiasm – but deftly incorporates these virtues into a picture of illusion and priggishness, "cant" and "verbiage." Catholic liberals are on the verge of heresy, yearning for the "fleshpots of unorthodoxy," trafficking with the Tempter, ingratiating themselves with the enemy, and receiving nothing but scorn in return.

Needless to say, Veuillot's response to this compromising liberal Catholicism was a clarion call to battle for the Rock of Peter and the reign of Christ the King, regardless of whether the prospect be triumph or martyrdom.[32]

In the appreciations of Veuillot by his admirers printed in a special issue of L'Univers following his death, liberal Catholics are denounced more often than anyone else. Liberal Catholics are even more dangerous than liberalism itself because they threaten to divide and confuse the troops. To make distinctions about liberalism implied reliance on categories and evidence other than the simple upholding of "faith."[33]

Another example of the depth of Catholic anti-liberalism can be found in El Liberalismo es Pecado (Liberalism Is a Sin), a small book by Don Felix Sarda y Salvany. Published in Spanish in 1886, it was quickly translated into other European languages and widely circulated; it remains in print a century later.[34] A campaign to rebut it and have it condemned ended with a Holy Office commendation of Sarda y Salvany's book and a rebuke to its detractors.

Liberalism, the book declares, is "a greater sin than blasphemy, theft, adultery, homicide, or any other violation of the law of God." It is pervasive, protean, insidiously seductive, "the evil of all evils," the "offspring of Satan and the enemy of mankind." The more reasonable or practical that liberalism shows itself, the more dangerous it is – and therefore "the odious and repulsive attempt to unite Liberalism with Catholicism" results in a monstrosity. The Catholic liberal is "both a traitor and a fool," a pagan at heart, a pawn of the Devil, corrupted by pride and worldliness, and "less excusable than those Liberals who have never been within the pale of the Church."

The world of the book is Hobbesian and stark. One must choose between dogmatically affirming the absolute independence of the individual and subordination of the social order to the revealed Law of God. It takes the greatest care even to live among Liberals without being infected, barring all friendship or affection, keeping relations to a minimum, maintaining a lively "horror of heresy," never "attempt-ing to be impartial" in evaluating liberal ideas. "Guided by these rules one could live without injury to his faith amidst a population of Jews," the book declares.

El Liberalismo es Pecado repudiates accusations that Catholic anti-liberalism is uncharitable. To repel an aggressor with every means possible is an obligation of charity. "A disease is inseparable from the persons of the diseased." "Is it sufficient to dodge their blows? Not at all; the first thing necessary is to demolish the combatant himself." It is "thus lawful, in certain cases, to drag his name in the mire," to use "every means and method" as long as one does not lie. "Let the sword of the Catholic polemicist wound, and when it wounds, wound mortally."

x

The loss of the papal states and the intellectual isolation of Catholicism in the last third of the century created in the church the sense of being a lonely voice resisting the tide of the times. As far as liberalism was concerned, the reality was different. Behind the apparent triumph of parliamentary regimes throughout Europe after the downfall of Louis Napoleon and the unification of Italy and Germany, liberalism was in decline. Its ambiguous stance toward democracy, reflecting its class basis and philosophical ambiguities, limited its capacity to respond to demands for political equality and social welfare, which were taken up by competing forces of socialism. Its anti-militarist, free-trade principles faced new forces of political and economic nationalism and imperialism. Its rationalist and humanitarian premises were increasingly dismissed by generations imbued with a harsher Darwinian perspective on the world and human nature or haunted by glimpses of reality that seemed beyond the reach of liberal reason. Ultimately an attenuated liberalism, no longer able to command the energies of either masses or elites, would stagger beneath the brutal attack of racist and neo-pagan auth-oritarian mass movements.

From this perspective, Catholic anti-liberalism was not a lonely critic but one more assailant among a growing number. Catholicism had no truck with socialism – indeed its inability to distinguish different strands of liberalism and engage in a dialogue with those most accessible set the pattern for its response to socialism as well. Catholicism was theoretically opposed to nationalism and had been its victim in Germany and Italy. Its teachings ran directly counter to militarism, Darwinianism, irrationalism, anti-Semitism, and, above all, racist neo-paganism. Eventually, a Catholic–liberal hybrid emerged in the form of Christian democracy – reinvented, it seemed, not from the liberal Catholicism of 1825–65, but from intransigent forces pledged to the Syllabus and Catholic anti-liberalism. Christian democracy's always halting growth came too late. Meanwhile, in nation after nation, Catholicism aligned itself with anti-liberal forces or risked their triumph rather than join hands with liberals or parliamentary socialists.

It is not fanciful to imagine that liberalism could have been strengthened and deepened by Catholicism's rejection of relativism, continuing contact with the masses, internationalism, and insistence on a spiritual and heroic dimension to life. This, of course, would have been a Catholicism that, in turn, learned from liberalism the value of freedom of conscience and discussion, learned that respect for truth and human dignity did not demand the imposition of absolute claims but could be found in tolerant and tentative social arrangements, respectful of unresolved differences without denying the possibility of ultimate resolution.

Chains of cause and effect can never be traced with certainty in history, but at least one cause for the widespread Catholic complicity or abdication in the face of twentieth-century right-wing authoritarian movements and regimes was the failed encounter with liberalism in the first half of the preceding century and the open field left to a vehement Catholic anti-liberalism in the era that followed.

NOTES

1 E. E. Y. Hales, *Pio Nono* (Garden City, NY: Doubleday, 1962), 12–13.
2 Owen Chadwick, *The Secularization of the European Mind in the Nineteenth Century* (Cambridge University Press, 1975), 21.
3 Irene Collins, "Liberalism in Nineteenth Century Europe," in Eugene C. Black, ed., *European Political History, 1815–1870* (New York: Harper & Row, 1967), 106.
4 This seems to be the view of Anthony Arblaster in *The Rise and Decline of Western Liberalism* (New York: B. Blackwell, 1984). For Arblaster the French Revolution is the "climax" of liberalism, after which comes its decline into laissez-faire.
5 Guido de Ruggiero, *The History of European Liberalism*, trans. R. G. Collingwood (Boston: Beacon Press, 1959), 171.

6 Collins, "Liberalism," 109–110.
7 Sheridan Gilley, "Christianity and Enlightenment: An Historical Survey," *History of European Ideas* 1 (1981): 103–121.
8 Alec R. Vidler, *Prophecy and Papacy* (New York: Scribner, 1954), 73.
9 Ibid., 88.
10 Quoted in Marcel Prêlot and Françoise Gallouédec Genuys, eds., *Le Libéralisme catholique* (Paris: Colin, 1969), 85–86.
11 Ibid., 91–98.
12 Ibid., 148–57.
13 Victor Conzemius, "Les Foyers internationaux du Catholicisme libéral hors de France au XIXe siècle: esquisse d'une géographie historique," in *Les Catholiques libéraux au XIXe siècle*, Actes du Colloque international d'histoire religieuse de Grenoble des 30 september – 3 octobre 1971, Centre d'Histoire de Catholicisme de l'Université de Lyon (Presses universitaires de Grenoble, 1974), 42.
14 André Latreile, "La Croisade pour la liberté d'enseignement: Montalembert et les libéraux," in *Les Catholiques libéraux*, 302.
15 Prêlot and Genuys, *Libéralisme*, 15–16.
16 See Philip Herbert Spencer, *The Politics of Belief in Nineteenth Century France: Lacordaire, Michon, Veuillot* (London: Faber and Faber, 1954).
17 Charles de Montalembert, *Catholicisme et liberté, Correspondence inédite avec le P. Lacordaire, Mgr de Mérode et A. de Falloux (1852–1870)* (Paris: Editions du Cerf, 1970), 24, 40–47, 63–79.
18 René Rémond, "Rapport de Conclusion," in *Les Catholiques libéraux*, 554.
19 Thomas Carlyle, *Selected Writings*, ed. Alan Shelston (Baltimore: Penguin Books, 1971), 84.
20 John Stuart Mill, *Essays on Politics and Culture*, ed. Gertrude Himmelfarb (Garden City, NY: Doubleday, 1963), 1–2.
21 Prêlot and Genuys, *Libéralisme*, 229–230.
22 Rémond, "Rapport," 555, and Maurice Larkin in the "Discussion," *Les Catholiques libéraux*, 570.
23 Chadwick, *Secularization*, 43.
24 Published as Appendix C in Peter N. Stearns, *Priest and Revolutionary: Lamennais and the Dilemma of French Catholicism* (New York: Harper & Row, 1967), 190, 192.
25 John Henry Newman, *Autobiographical Writings*, ed. Henry Tristram (London: 1956), 259, quoted in J. M. Cameron, "Newman the Liberal," in *Nuclear Catholics* (Grand Rapids, MI: Eerdmans, 1989), 221.
26 Quoted in Joseph Lecler, "La Spiritualité de Catholiques libéraux," in *Les Catholiques libéraux*, 381–382.
27 John Emerich Edward Dalberg-Acton, *Selected Writings of Lord Acton*, vol. III: *Essays in Religion, Politics, and Morality*, ed. J. Rufus Fears (Indianapolis, IN: Liberty Classics, 1988), 48–49.
28 Ibid., 191–194.

29 Jacques Gadille and Jean-Marie Mayeur, "Les Milieux catholiques libéraux en France: Continuité et diversité d'une tradition," *Les Libéraux catholiques*, 203–204.

30 Hales, *Pio Nono*, 56.

31 Ibid., 268.

32 If anyone would dismiss Veuillot's pamphlet as unrepresentative, despite Pope Pius IX's approval of both the man and the work, it should be noted that the pamphlet was translated and published in the United States by the National Catholic Welfare Conference in 1939.

33 Émile Poulat, *L'Église c'est un monde* (Paris: Editions du Cerf, 1986), chap. 6: "Louis Veuillot, l'instituteur du clergé français," 131–158.

34 The English translation is titled less belligerently *What Is Liberalism?* – the question, evidently, for which the Spanish title is the answer – and contains emendations and adaptations "to our American conditions" by the translator, Condé B. Pallen. Originally issued in 1899 by B. Herder Book Co., St. Louis, the translation is now published by TAN Books, Rockford, IL, n.d.

CHAPTER 2

American Catholics and liberalism, 1789–1960

Philip Gleason

"Liberalism" has meant different things to different people at different times and places. Before saying anything about the historic relationship between Catholicism and liberalism in the United States we must therefore take a moment to indicate briefly how it will be understood in what follows. We begin by recalling a distinction made by the once-famous Catholic historian Carlton J. H. Hayes between "ecumenical liberalism" and "sectarian liberalism."

Hayes introduced the distinction in his *Generation of Materialism* (1941), a work covering Europe as a whole in the late nineteenth century.[1] By "ecumenical," or "general," liberalism, he meant the spirit animating developments from the Reformation through the French Revolution and its aftermath that sought to limit despotism and promote representative government, eliminate restrictions on commerce and industry, protect freedom of conscience in matters of religion, and in general champion the rights of the individual against the claims of traditional authority in church or state. This broad and diffuse liberalism included many subspecies – political, economic, intellectual; conservative, moderate, radical, atheistic, even Christian.

Of "ecumenical liberalism" thus understood, Hayes clearly approved. The sudden emergence of "sectarian liberalism" in the 1870s, however, struck him as "something like a calamity," for the excesses of its adherents, who appropriated the name to themselves alone, went far toward discrediting the whole tradition.[2] The new version was not, of course, unrelated to ecumenical liberalism; the Liberals with a capital "L" did indeed take over genuine elements of the tradition, such as concern for personal liberty, devotion to science and secular schooling, and a commitment to parliamentary government and laissez-faire economics as the master keys to material progress. But they transformed these and other themes of liberalism

45

into a doctrinaire ideology. Most relevantly for us, many sectarian liberals were agnostics or scientific materialists who regarded ecclesiastical authority, particularly that of the Roman Catholic church, with abhorrence. On the continent, where the church still wielded considerable institutional power, sectarian liberals were "not merely anti-clerical but rampantly anti-Christian."[3] Their willingness to use repressive measures against religion, and an accompanying weakness for other forms of *Realpolitik*, accounted in large part for Hayes's reservations about sectarian, as contrasted to ecumenical, liberalism.

Hayes was of course writing about Europe where the situation of both liberalism and Catholicism was quite different from what it was in the United States. Even so, the distinction he made is a useful one, and can be applied in a general way to the topic at hand. The American Revolution was surely a major landmark in the development of liberalism in the ecumenical sense, and it does not distort things unduly to interpret the whole of our national history along similar lines.[4] And while Hayes's late nineteenth-century "sectarian liberalism" never developed a clear identity in this country, an American liberalism that can legitimately be called sectarian did emerge as a self-conscious ideological position after the turn of the century. This kind of sectarian liberalism differed sharply from the earlier version in that it rejected laissez-faire economics and endorsed an activist state. But at its apogee in the second quarter of the twentieth century, its leading intellectual spokesmen shared fully in the scientism and hostility to supernatural religion, especially Catholicism, that marked their ideological predecessors.

The United States likewise differed from Europe in the degree to which a Protestant ethos and outlook permeated public life through the nineteenth century and even into the twentieth.[5] This deeply religious strain in American public life complicated the interaction of Catholicism and liberalism because most Protestants regarded their religious heritage as a key element in the development of (ecumenical) liberalism as such. More than that, they believed Protestantism furnished the bedrock on which the distinctly American variant of (ecumenical) liberalism rested; and they had no doubt whatever that the Catholic church was an integral part of the old regime against which liberalism struggled.[6] Catholics, for their part, conventionally portrayed the Reformation as the first episode in the modern world's revolt against God; and even when willing to credit the religious sincerity of their Protestant fellow-countrymen, they regarded the various forms of Protestantism as little more than way-stations on the road to complete unbelief – an unbelief that had always been associated with certain forms of liberalism.

These connections and interconnections between religion and liberalism are difficult to sort out even in retrospect; they were, to say the least, no less confusing for earlier generations of American Catholics. As the historical sketch that follows will attempt to show, Catholics in the early republic welcomed the ecumenically liberal regime established by the Constitution, which they interpreted as recognizing a duality of realms that meshed nicely with the natural–supernatural dualism so strong in Catholicity. As the state moved into areas where the church claimed competence (such as education), and as the clash between Catholicism and liberalism in Europe grew more intense, the situation became more complex and conflicts multiplied. But not until the second quarter of the twentieth century did Catholics find themselves in open conflict with the American form of sectarian liberalism.

REPUBLICAN BEGINNINGS: THE ERA OF CARROLL AND ENGLAND

When John Carroll was named the first bishop in the United States in 1789, Catholics were a tiny minority in the American population – about 30,000 out of four million. Since Catholics in colonial Maryland had, as Carroll put it, "smarted... under the lash of an established [Anglican] church," practical considerations alone might explain why they welcomed religious freedom and the separation of church and state.[7] But beyond that, Carroll had been a strong supporter of the patriot cause and was deeply committed to the new polity that emerged from the War for Independence. "Republicanism" has become a talisman for scholars of the late eighteenth century, and many would extend its influence far into the nineteenth.[8] It would lead us too far afield to inquire what this kind of republicanism means as interpreted by Gordon S. Wood, J. G. A. Pocock, and other scholars who employ the concept; the relevant point here is that recent Catholic historical work likewise emphasizes the broadly "republican" orientation of early American Catholic development. This Catholic republicanism – which can be called liberal in the ecumenical sense – made itself felt both at the level of episcopal leadership (especially in the cases of Carroll and John England, who became bishop of Charleston, SC, in 1820) and, as manifested in the phenomenon of lay trusteeism, among the ordinary faithful.[9]

Some formulations of this interpretation seem to me over-ideologized (if that barbarism can be permitted). For example, I do not think John Carroll ever worked out anything that could properly be called a "republican blueprint" for Catholic development in the new republic.[10] In my view, Carroll's approach was shaped less by abstract devotion to a self-consciously adopted theoretical position than by a pragmatic, but principled, willingness to adjust to the realities of the post-revolutionary situation.

Of course, these are matters of emphasis: the prevailing ideas of the time were certainly part of the situation to be adjusted to, and Carroll was undoubtedly affected by the ideas of his time, including moderate Enlightenment ideas, just as he was affected by the practical needs of ecclesiastical governance.[11] John England, who was more of an intellectual (and whose background in Ireland disposed him even more to republicanism), worked out a systematic "republican" position on church government which had obvious implications for the broader issue of the relation of the Catholic church to the social and political institutions of the new nation.[12] And broadly speaking, it is surely correct to say that Carroll, England, and early American Catholics as a group welcomed religious freedom, separation of church and state, and (for as long as it prevailed) a kind of live-and-let-live ecumenism with their non-Catholic neighbors.

This generally positive attitude towards the political and social system of the United States extended to the French priests put to flight by the French Revolution who played so important a role in the early development of the American church.[13] One should add, however, that the French émigrés differed among themselves in personality and outlook. In some, admiration for the American system was by no means unmixed with more hostile feelings toward the "heretics" among whom they lived, with an ideological horror of republicanism in its revolutionary form, and with suspicion of their Irish coreligionists for trouble-making proclivities that were in some cases believed to be tinctured by radical republicanism – with the latter anxiety being particularly marked in the attitude of Ambrose Maréchal toward John England (an attitude communicated by

Maréchal to James Whitfield, his English-born successor as Archbishop of Baltimore.)[14]

But in spite of the atheism associated with the French Revolution, and in spite of what Catholic observers saw as growing religious indifferentism on the part of Americans generally, thoroughgoing "infidelity" – i.e., rejection of supernatural religion – was not an issue Catholic apologetics had to take seriously in the era of republicanism. John England's address to Congress in 1826 clearly illustrates his assumption, characteristic of Catholic thinking at the time, that Americans in general – non-Catholics as well as Catholics – shared the traditional Christian belief in a transcendent God Who had revealed Himself to humankind, and to Whom obedience and worship was owed.[15] The great difference between Catholics and Protestants, which England proceeded to elaborate, centered on the role of the church as the interpreter of God's revealed truth.

The distinction of realms as set forth in England's discourse was sharply disjunctive. Matters relating to God and the supernatural fell within the purview of the church; matters having to do with "our civil rights, our civil concerns" fell within that of the state. And just as the separation of church and state meant that political authorities could not meddle in religious matters, neither was the church to interfere in matters properly belonging to the state. This strongly dualistic formulation was, of course, shaped by the apologetical exigencies of the case as interpreted by England – that is, by his determination to correct the view that the Catholic church claimed the right to depose rulers, persecute those who dissented from its religious teachings, or otherwise encroach on the civic realm. His exposition left untouched all sorts of problems having to do with areas of common concern to church and state; indeed, it would be unreasonable to expect him to have dealt with them, given the apologetical context in which his talk to Congress must be situated. England's acceptance of "republican" institutions and practices in his famous constitution for the diocese of Charleston shows clearly that his theoretical dualism did not exclude positive *practical* interaction between the political and ecclesiastical spheres.

Despite its obvious incompleteness, England's formulation rested on two assumptions that remained fundamental in American Catholic thought into the mid twentieth century: The first of these was the conviction that a dualistic distinction of realms constituted the *premise* of American-style separation of church and state, from which flowed the incompetence of the state in religious matters. This, John Courtney Murray and his followers argued in the 1950s, was what distinguished the religiously neutral American state from the aggressively anti-religious state of continental liberalism. The former, while liberal in the ecumenical sense, recognized the existence of a spiritual realm into which political authority did not extend. The latter, animated by sectarian liberalism, denied the existence of any spiritual realm beyond the reach of political authority and, after ostensibly "separating" church and state, actually made the state itself a religious object.[16]

The second, and closely related, assumption – tacit in England's discourse, but implied by what he took for granted about the beliefs of non-Catholics – was that American society is fundamentally religious, indeed Christian, and that separation of church and state does not, therefore, entail the separation of religion from society or from culture. Orestes A. Brownson and Isaac T. Hecker, the leading spokesmen for American Catholicism in the mid nineteenth century, both held this view, which was stated most succinctly by Hecker in 1887: "the basis of our [American] civilization is not atheism or rationalism, but Christianity."[17] And Catholics of the 1950s heartily endorsed the Supreme Court's avowal in the *Zorach* case that "We are a religious people whose institutions presupposed a Supreme Being." Murray cited this dictum as clinching evidence that "it is not permissible to read into the concept of separation of church and state a philosophy of hostility to religion" – which meant, of course, that Catholics could wholeheartedly endorse the American system.[18]

AMERICANISM AND LIBERALISM

Mention of Brownson and Hecker moves us into a new epoch. Ascending to even greater heights of generalization, let us consider as one era the span from shortly before 1844, the year in which both men came into the church as converts, to the late 1890s, when controversy over what was called "Americanism" swirled posthumously around the figure of Isaac Hecker (who died in 1888). Institutionally speaking the church was firmly established by the opening of this era, which was fortunate for it proved to be a much stormier period in terms of controversies, both external and internal, than was the earlier epoch of republican beginnings.

The principal causes of controversy were three: (1) the great evangelical revivals that swept through American Protestantism animating, among other things, religiously grounded anti-Catholicism; (2) the alarming growth of what evangelicals took to be the "Catholic threat," not only in numbers (resulting from massive immigration), but also in terms of the church's intellectual and spiritual resurgence (manifested, for example, in Romanticism and the Oxford Movement); and (3) the fall-out in the United States from clashes in Europe between an increasingly sectarian liberalism and an increasingly ultramontane Catholicism – especially the revolutions of 1848, which prompted Pius IX to pursue an aggressively anti-liberal policy that caused American Catholics serious discomfiture and gave great offense to their non-Catholic countrymen.[19] Know-Nothingism in the 1850s and the American Protective Association in the 1880s and 90s represented the high-points of tension between Catholics and external foes; and it is no accident that controversies *among* American Catholics pretty well coincided with those climaxes of anti-Catholic nativism.

The perennial nativist charge that Catholicism is incompatible with Americanism was not exactly new to this era – many earlier Protestant and deist Americans would have agreed in substance – but this was when it emerged as a full-blown issue because the Catholic church was no longer so negligible a factor that it could be safely overlooked. The questions this charge raises about Catholic Americanism, or the impossibility thereof, lead us straight into a conceptual minefield. We cannot avoid it, however, because of the intimate relationship that exists between liberalism and Americanism. For Americans have always regarded their system as liberal in the ecumenical sense, and the Catholic "Americanists," or "Americanizers," of the late nineteenth century were also known as "liberals." To deal with the topic of Catholics and liberalism in this era, we must therefore grasp the nettle of "Americanism."[20]

First of all we must note that the issue did not, in this era, center on church-and-state as an explicit constitutional question. The major controversies over Catholic Americanism (or un-Americanism) dealt rather with the more diffuse area of the relationship of religion to society and culture. The church and state issue was, to be sure, implicitly involved, because opposing ideological relationships between religion and the sociopolitical realm were assumed by most Americans to be built into Protestantism and Catholicism, the former being held compatible with the American system and the latter not.[21]

This excessively abstract formulation can perhaps be made clearer by a brief examination of the "school question."

Education became a "question" because it is an activity in which both religious and secular authorities have an interest. In other words, it takes place in an area where the distinction of realms is very fuzzy. Insofar as it had been formalized beyond the circle of the family (which included apprentices), education had historically been a responsibility of the church. Only in the nineteenth century did the state begin to assume it, often shouldering the church roughly aside in the process.[22] Indeed, it is revealing that the word "secularization" found early employment in respect of the shift from religious to state schools. In this country, the so-called common schools (i.e., state-supported public schools) had very close ties to the Protestant churches; they were in fact permeated by cultural Protestantism throughout the nineteenth century, a heritage that lingered well into the twentieth in many parts of the country.[23] The intimate association between public education and Protestantism thus provides clear evidence for the second of the perennial assumptions listed above, namely, that American society was to be understood as *religious*, despite church–state separation. But what happened in respect of the school question likewise illustrates the difficulties this assumption encountered as the religious pluralism of American society grew more pronounced.

When the school question first erupted as a Catholic issue in the 1840s, Catholics were protesting the channeling of public money into what they perceived as Protestant institutions.[24] They appealed to the state for a share of public funds to support their own schools. Although not successful in this respect, Catholic pressure did contribute to the gradual elimination of institutionalized Protestant influence over the public schools. In this manner, Catholics involved themselves in the often-noted irony of contributing to the secularization of public education – which indicates that secularization occurred in this country much more as a result of the circumstances of pluralism than from conscious intention. At least that was true in its first phases; in the later nineteenth century, and more so in the twentieth, secularization did become a conscious policy pursued by those who no longer held traditional religious beliefs.

We will return to the matter of secularization, but for the moment the main point to be noted is that when the school question first arose, all parties accepted the view that religion had a role to play in education. What Catholics objected to was the tendency of Protestants to identify the national sociopolitical culture exclusively with their own position, to make Protestantism and Americanism practically synonymous. The Protestants, who still shaped public policy on the matter, for their part refused to countenance the funding of Catholic schools because they regarded them as being, not just religiously depraved, but also socially divisive, culturally substandard, and ideologically subversive – in short, un-American.[25]

So much for the point that the school question illustrates the way in which "Americanism" centered primarily on the relation of religion to society and culture rather than on the church–state issue as such. But what about ecumenical Catholic liberalism of the Americanist variety? Once again, education serves well as an illustration because the school question figured prominently in the earliest articulation of an explicitly Americanist version of liberal Catholicism – that of Orestes A. Brownson.

Brownson, a Vermont-born Yankee, was a thoroughgoing American in his cultural outlook. As both Catholic immigration and nativist Know-Nothingism moved toward a climax in 1854, Brownson denounced the failure of his Irish coreligionists to distinguish with sufficient clarity between nationality and religion. Catholicity was one thing; "Irishism," as Brownson called it, something else. Tightly interwoven though the two had been in Ireland, this was America; here Irishism was out of place. Even more out of place was the use of Catholic schools to inculcate and preserve, not the Catholic religion as such, but the cultural accoutrements associated with Catholicism in Ireland. Here the church should adjust itself to American circumstances in every way not directly opposed to faith or morals. Where possible, Catholic youngsters should attend the common schools, and grow up as birthright participants in the national community. Where actual religious prejudice operated in the common schools, Brownson granted that Catholic schools were needed. But he vehemently opposed using religion as a pretext to keep young people attached to an ethnic tradition that would make them aliens in the land of their birth.[26]

At the same time as these domestic issues were bringing Brownson around to the view that one had to distinguish between the "Catholic tradition" and the "traditions of Catholics," events in Europe reinforced the same conclusion and gave it a more distinctively ideological coloration.[27] Although he had strongly criticized the "red republicanism" of the revolutions of 1848, Brownson was equally critical of the repressive regimes that succeeded the revolutions, especially that of Napoleon III in France. Reflection on these developments, his contacts with the French Catholic liberal Count de Montalembert, and the ethnicity-and-education issue at home led Brownson to adopt a position in the late 1850s and early 1860s that can legitimately be called both liberal and Americanist.[28]

Brownson repented of his liberalism after the Civil War, but the same outlook inspired a new generation of liberal Catholic leaders in the 1880s and 1890s. This brings us to the controversy over "Americanism" as such.[29] Its history is tangled, but may be summarized as follows: difficulties arising in the 1880s between German-speaking and English-speaking Catholics persisted through the 1890s, becoming interwoven in the process with liberal–conservative splits on a wide range of other issues, such as the establishment of the Catholic University of America, parochial schools, membership of Catholics in secret societies, and Catholic participation in interfaith gatherings. These controversies involved intense politicking in Rome and eventually drew the attention of European Catholics, both progressive and conservative, to what was happening in the United States. The conflict reached its climax in 1897–98 when French Catholic liberals hailed Father Hecker (whose biography had just appeared in French) as the prophet of a new reconciliation between Catholicism and the modern world, while French conservatives portrayed the founder of the Paulists as a heretic and "Americanism" as a betrayal of the faith.

Leo XIII brought the crisis to a conclusion in January, 1899, with the apostolic letter *Testem Benevolentiae*. Here the pope condemned certain doctrinal views "which some comprise under the head of Americanism," but excluded from his condemnation Americanism understood in a purely social, cultural, or political sense.[30] The liberals, whose best known leader was Archbishop John Ireland of St. Paul, claimed that their Americanism was strictly of the latter type, but their conservative opponents insisted that the errors condemned by the pope did indeed exist in this country. Historians have also differed in their assessments, with scholars in the post-Vatican II era tending to see more theological content in Americanism, and hence a closer kinship with Modernism (which had a very limited impact in the United States) and other forms of continental theological liberalism.[31]

Without attempting to settle the issue, we can observe that the liberalism of the Americanists took its origin from, and consisted primarily in, a desire to bring Catholicism into a positive relationship with American ecumenical liberalism, particularly freedom, democracy, and individualistic self-reliance. Although charges of doctrinal deviation were raised early in the controversial era and became the central issue (at least ostensibly) in its final phase, the disputes arose mainly from differences of prudential judgment in respect of the Americanization of immigrants, the importance of parochial schools, and other matters of concrete socioreligious policy. Whatever the logical implications of their stance, the Americanists seem to have been firmly traditional in their belief in a transcendent God, and in their acceptance of the natural–supernatural dualism. The only possible exception among the leading liberals was Bishop John Lancaster Spalding of Peoria, some of whose writings tend toward an immanentism that would invest "culture" with religious value in the manner of Matthew Arnold.[32]

Enlightened non-Catholic commentary heavily favored the progressivism of the Americanists over the conservatism of their opponents. But the nativists were more impartial: they attacked the liberals too, especially Archbishop Ireland's so-called Faribault Plan, whereby parochial schools might be turned over to public authorities for a nominal fee, with the state paying the salaries of the (Catholic) teachers, and with religious instruction being restricted to after-school hours. Militant anti-Catholics viewed this arrangement as a devious scheme to insinuate Romanism into American public education. As to the higher-level intellectual questions of the day (religion and science, Darwinism, etc.), Catholic Americanism was not really in the picture. It was too much an intra-Catholic squabble over matters ecclesiastical to attract the attention of the thinkers taken up with the warfare of science and theology, or committed to the work that the intellectual historian Merle Curti called "delimiting the supernatural."[33] Catholicism would not become a real problem for liberal intellectuals until the second quarter of the twentieth century.

THE NEW FRAMEWORK OF THE CATHOLIC–LIBERAL ISSUE

Developments that took shape in the opening decades of the twentieth century gave the Catholic–liberal question so distinctive a new framework that we must describe them in general terms before proceeding to sketch the course of interaction between Catholics and liberals.

In the first place, what we can call the organizational question became a far more important matter than it had been before, both for liberals and for Catholics. This transpired because social developments like massive population increase, the growth of cities and urban problems, technological advances, business consolidations, economic dislocations, and industrial conflict required all elements in society to regroup in order to deal more effectively with the new level of complexity that characterized modern life. The organizational issue was a prominent theme in the so-called "Progressive Movement," which one historian links with "the response to industrialism," and another associates with "the search for order."[34]

What contemporaries called "the social question" (which referred primarily to capital–labor issues) was particularly difficult for liberals, since their tradition was closely linked to individualism. An attractive alternative was socialism, which seemed in the progressive era to be establishing itself as a major social and political force in American life, and to which a good many liberal intellectuals were attracted. And even those who rejected socialism turned toward far greater reliance on state action than had nineteenth-century liberals. Herbert Croly, the founder of the *New Republic*, explained that changing circumstances required this shift in his book *The Promise of American Life* (1909), and an even greater oracle of liberalism, John Dewey, repeated it a generation later in his *Liberalism and Social Action* (1935).[35]

Catholics too responded to the organizational imperative. The American Federation of Catholic Societies (1901–19), although weak and already outdated in terms of its organizing principle, was significant as a sign of the times. Of much greater significance, both in itself and symptomatically, was the Catholic Educational Association (est. 1904), the first of the Catholic professional associations that burgeoned in later years. But the most important organizational step was the creation in 1917 of the National Catholic War Council, which evolved after the war into a permanent secretariat for the American hierarchy, the National Catholic Welfare Conference (NCWC).[36]

Catholic concern over the social question, although it sprang from conservative roots, nonetheless furnished a point of positive contact with American liberalism. That was particularly true in the case of Monsignor John A. Ryan, who was by far the best known *and* the most liberal of Catholic social theorists, particularly in his willingness to expand the powers of the state to deal with social problems.[37] Generally speaking, however, Catholics strongly opposed "statism," not only because enhanced state power threatened immediate Catholic interests (especially in education), but also because they feared that the state's appetite for expansion had no natural limit and would not be satisfied until the church was reduced to a social nullity.[38] In other words, Catholics feared the "secularizing" tendency of the social changes of the era, a great many of which did, in fact, have the effect of diminishing the religious dimension of activities (e.g., charity work and higher education) which the churches had earlier dominated, or at least influenced to a marked degree.

The secularizing tendency was even more obvious in the intellectual realm. Agnosticism established itself among the intellectual elite in the late nineteenth century; by the 1920s, such persons were, by and large, no longer believers in any traditional sense, and what Walter Lippmann called "the acids of modernity" had eaten deeply into the faith of ordinary people. Among American Protestants, the "Fundamentalist Controversy" of the 1920s sprang, as George Marsden has shown, from the realization by evangelical Christians that what the culture had formerly accepted as religious truth was now regarded as outmoded superstition – and the outcome of that controversy discredited traditional faith even more.[39]

Catholics spoke of the resulting condition as "secularism." What they meant by that term, as applied to the culture at large, was not so much active unbelief as the *absence of belief*. But "liberals," as that term had come to be understood by the 1930s, were associated with secularism as its agents – that is, as self-conscious promoters of the ideas that produced secularism as a diffuse assumption about the nature of things more or less unreflectively adopted by the society as a whole. Viewing liberals in this manner, it is understandable that Catholics regarded them as religious adversaries whose erroneous views had to be overcome because they exerted a pernicious influence on the religious and moral fabric of the whole society.

As they contemplated this challenge in the interwar years, American Catholics were heartened by the conviction that they were witnessing – and taking part in – a tremendous "Catholic Revival," a resurgence of the Church's spiritual and intellectual energies that was capable of "restoring all things in Christ." The best known study of this phenomenon – William M. Halsey's *Survival of American Innocence* (1980) – does not, in my opinion, do justice to it. But it is, nonetheless, a very valuable book, and nowhere more so than in emphasizing that the beginnings of this shift in the spirit and outlook of American Catholics were closely linked to the First World War.[40]

Negatively, if I may overstate to convey the sense Catholics had of the situation, the war confirmed Pius X's condemnation of "Modernism" – that is, it shattered prevailing illusions about human perfectibility, mocked the optimism of evolutionary immanentism, and revealed the demonic potentialities of science, technology, and the modern state. The disillusionment, despair, and sense of cultural crisis thus engendered created an atmosphere more receptive to persuasive restatement of the traditional Christian message than had obtained for almost a century. In these circumstances, European Catholicism experienced a restoration of morale, a burst of new energy that constituted in the words of the German writer Peter Wust a "return from exile."[41]

American Catholics experienced this aspect of the revival at second hand, but the war affected them in an even more positive way.[42] The mobilization of Catholic energies for the war effort, the creation of a national organization (the NCWC), and the heightened sense of patriotic identification that accompanied these developments acted as a tonic to the American Catholic spirit. As a result, American Catholics entered the 1920s with new confidence, a feeling of having come of age, a sense of mission – with what might even be called a new Americanism. It deserved that name because it assumed a kind of built-in harmony between American and Catholic principles. This conviction, which is strikingly revealed in the thinking of the liberal Catholics associated with *The Commonweal* (est. 1924), particularly Michael Williams and George Shuster, was based on what can be called the Catholic-roots-of-democracy theory.

Now remembered (if at all) as a silly and embarrassing effort to derive Thomas Jefferson's ideas from the writings of Robert

Bellarmine, SJ, this theory was in fact not at all ridiculous.[43] Though sometimes overstated, it rested on the best recent scholarship about the medieval origins of constitutionalism and limited government, the general drift of which is suggested by Lord Acton's remark that St. Thomas was the first Whig. Hence there was no conflict between Catholicism and Americanism; properly understood, the latter rested on religious and natural-law foundations.[44] By explaining this to their countrymen, Catholics would not only vindicate their own Americanism, they would also offer a saving message to a nation that was losing contact with its religious roots.

But that was not all there was to the saving message Catholics brought to a society overtaken by confusion, doubt, and despair. Its essence was, of course, the traditional Christian message of repentance and salvation; but now it was presented in the new articulation provided by a revived and invigorated Scholasticism. For Neoscholasticism was the intellectual basis and bedrock of the whole Catholic Revival. Although it had been developing in Europe for two generations, Neoscholasticism did not attain the level of a general movement among educated American Catholics until the late twenties – at the very moment when their pride was stung by the defeat of Al Smith, their energies galvanized by Pius XI's call for "Catholic Action," their conviction of crisis reinforced by the economic collapse, and their confidence bolstered by the expression of sentiments similar to their own by the "New Humanists," most notably Irving Babbitt and Paul Elmer More, and, to an even greater extent, by the new Aristotelians, Robert M. Hutchins and Mortimer J. Adler. From the late twenties through the middle fifties, Neoscholasticism reigned supreme, not only in departments of philosophy and theology of Catholic colleges and universities, but as the cognitive armature of the worldview held by educated American Catholics as a group.[45]

Neoscholastic Catholicism was, it need hardly be said, thoroughly supernaturalistic and strongly dualistic – although the two realms were to be understood, not as opposed to each other, but in the grace-builds-upon-nature relation of superordination–subordination. It was looked upon as the basis on which a comprehensive and unified Catholic culture could be erected – one that extended outward from its properly "religious" center into every phase of life, from the marriage bed to international relations. It included among its proponents persons as diverse as the liturgist Virgil Michel, OSB; the social actionist John A. Ryan; the poet-educator Sister Madeleva Wolff, CSC; the media personality Fulton J. Sheen; and the theologian John Courtney Murray, SJ.

This Neoscholastic worldview, which differed *toto caelo* from that of secular intellectuals and which seemed to them perversely "medieval," provided the basis from which American Catholics mounted their critique of secularism, "the practical exclusion of God from human thinking and living." The clashes between Catholics and liberals, which reached their historical climax in the Neoscholastic era, stemmed basically from this diametrical opposition of fundamental viewpoints, although they were occasioned by more contingent historical developments, both foreign and domestic.

THE COURSE OF CATHOLIC–LIBERAL INTERACTION, 1920–60

Catholic and liberal relations in the 1920s were relatively good by comparison with what they were to become in the next two decades.[46] Indeed, liberals were pleasurably surprised by the socially progressive stand taken by the so-called "Bishops' Program of Social Reconstruction" in 1919, and by the continuation of that stance in the work of John A. Ryan and the Social Action Department of the NCWC. Nor could liberals condone the excesses of anti-Catholicism represented by the Ku Klux Klan and the nativism of the immigration restriction movement. From their viewpoint, the religious bugbear of the era was not the Papist, but "the Puritan" (i.e., the stiff-necked, hypocritical, prohibitionist "Dry"), and Fundamentalism dominated the landscape of religious obscurantism.

Liberals, however, were far from comfortable with the Catholic position on church and state, which emerged as an explicit political issue in the twenties. If they supported Al Smith in 1928, it was because they liked his politics, and believed that his "Americanism... was far more deeply rooted in his nature than any Roman Catholic doctrines ever had been." Liberals were also uneasy about the Lateran treaty of 1929, which they interpreted as a rapprochement between the Catholic church and fascism, and it is worth noting that the passage quoted above occurs in a *Nation* editorial prompted by the first book to appear from the Vatican's newly independent printing house, a new edition of the Index of Forbidden Books.

Granting that "liberal Catholics" might not pay much attention to the Index, the editorialist went on to assert that the conflict between Catholicism and liberalism was such that "The liberal who follows where abstract logic would lead him cannot be other than anti-Catholic, and Catholicism insists upon the supremacy of abstract logic." This drew from John A. Ryan an article on "Catholicism and Liberalism" which distinguished informal (i.e., ecumenical) liberalism from the anti-clerical (sectarian) variety typical of continental Europe. Ryan insisted that Catholics could be liberal in attitude toward economic and political questions while rejecting absolutely "the anti-church variety."[47] Unfortunately, events in the thirties and forties were to drive Catholics and liberals further apart, and something closer to the continental attitude toward the church gained ground among American liberals.

Matters first took a serious turn for the worse in the mid thirties. On the domestic scene, Father Charles E. Coughlin's shift to an anti-New Deal position in 1935–36 alerted liberals to the fascist potentialities of his influence. Over the next few years, their fears were reinforced by his growing extremism on the menace of Communism, his increasingly open anti-Semitism, and the sometimes violent behavior of his "Christian Front" followers, especially in New York City.[48]

Internationally, the Spanish Civil War, which broke out in 1936, was the decisive issue. To American liberals, the war was a clear-cut contest between fascism and democracy and the church had shown its true colors by rallying to the fascists. But American Catholics, deeply shocked by the widespread desecration of churches and slaughter of priests that marked the early months of the war, saw the struggle as a conflict between Christian civilization and atheistic Communism. They bitterly resented the indifference displayed by American liberals to the persecution of the church in Spain (and in Mexico too). Catholics' support for Franco, and the campaign they waged to prevent lifting the embargo on arms sales to the Spanish Republicans, infuriated liberals who interpreted it as Catholic dictation of American foreign policy.[49]

By the eve of World War II, liberals took the fascist–Catholic linkage for granted. George Seldes summed up their case in his book, *The Catholic Crisis* (1939). Besides the Spanish Civil War, which was his centerpiece, Seldes contrasted the Vatican's softness toward Italian and German fascism with its exaggerated hostility toward

Communism and liberalism. On the domestic front, he scored the anti-Semitism of the Coughlinites, Catholic ties with corrupt political bosses, and objectionable pressure-group tactics brought to bear on Congress, state legislatures, the press, the film industry, and private groups or individuals who espoused causes of which Catholics disapproved, such as birth control. He did not stress "Catholic Action" as the generic form of these objectionable activities, but other critics sometimes did.[50]

Late the same year Seldes's book appeared, President Roosevelt announced the appointment of Myron C. Taylor as his personal representative to the Vatican. This action created new allies for the liberal critics of the Catholic church by arousing more conservative Protestants, who were traditionally hostile to Catholicism and especially sensitive about the issue of church–state separation.[51] The publication a few months later of *Catholic Principles of Politics*, by John A. Ryan and Francis J. Boland, CSC, made matters worse by reaffirming the traditional teaching that ideally Catholicism should be the religion of the state. Ryan's renown as a champion of progressive social legislation made the book especially shocking, and seemed to confirm the worst fears of Protestants and liberals.[52]

During the wartime years, tensions were masked by the drive to promote national unity through mutual tolerance among all groups in American society. But they did not entirely disappear. Protestants were deeply concerned about the growing strength and self-confidence of the Catholic community, every manifestation of whose organized energies they interpreted as a part of a hierarchical plot to "take over" the country.[53] Liberals were, for their part, incensed by Catholic criticism of secularism, particularly by the charge that the relativism of naturalistic thinkers like John Dewey opened the way for totalitarianism. According to the liberal diagnosis, acceptance of absolutes in philosophy led to absolutism in politics; hence, it was the views of Catholics and their obscurantist allies, Hutchins and Adler, that constituted the true fountainhead of totalitarianism.[54] Indeed, the reaction of liberals at times betrayed a note of outrage – as though Catholics, in addition to their substantive offenses, had committed a kind of intellectual *lèse majesté*.

The stage was thus set for a major eruption when the war ended, and it was not long in coming. US representation at the Vatican continued to be a sore point, but the issue of public funds for Catholic schools, which arose in the context of postwar plans for federal aid to education, raised the church–state conflict to a new level of intensity. The Supreme Court's decision in the *Everson* case (1947), which set forth a stringent definition of the "wall of separation" between church and state, but at the same time permitted bussing parochial schoolchildren at public expense, left both sides dissatisfied and galvanized into action a new organization, Protestants and Other Americans United for the Separation of Church and State, which thereafter pursued a militantly anti-Catholic line. Subsequent Court decisions in the *McCollum* (1948) and *Zorach* (1952) cases steered a somewhat zigzag path in respect to religion and education and kept the school question in the forefront of controversy.[55]

Secular liberals might differ from Protestants on many matters, but not on the "Catholic question." Seldes brought out a second edition of his *Catholic Crisis* in 1945, but it attracted little attention, perhaps because the foreign-policy issues of the late thirties were by that time outdated. The person who took over Seldes's role as liberal scourge of Catholicism, and performed it with far greater effect, was Paul Blanshard. First in a series of articles in *The Nation*, then in his *American Freedom and Catholic Power* (1949), Blanshard continued the critique of Catholic pressure-group tactics, which he portrayed as not only improper in themselves, but also as infringements of church–state separation.

Blanshard disclaimed opposition to Catholicism as a private religious faith, or to Catholics as an element in American society. But the church's public role was a different matter. The "authoritarianism" built into its hierarchical structure could not be squared with democracy. Hence the Catholic church was intrinsically un-American, a condition which manifested itself in the reactionary moral and political teachings the hierarchy imposed upon lay Catholics – and attempted to impose on all Americans by boycott, censorship, and raw political clout. In a second book on the subject, Blanshard elaborated the totalitarian implications of Catholic ecclesiology by pointing out parallels between the church and the Soviet Union under Stalin.[56]

Catholic authoritarianism and disregard for civil liberties had long been associated in the minds of liberals with the church's fervent anti-Communism. That association was reinforced when "McCarthyism" erupted as an issue at the height of the controversies over school aid, Blanshard's book, and other incidents such as Cardinal Spellman's public criticism of Eleanor Roosevelt. But while McCarthyism added a new and explosive element to the situation, it – and the outbreak of the Korean War – served to distract attention from the Catholic question as such. McCarthy was, to be sure, a Catholic and he had much Catholic support. But influential Catholics also opposed him, and Catholicism itself was not the central issue in the controversy over McCarthyism.[57] Although suspicions lingered after the Wisconsin senator's downfall, the religious issue had receded from prominence by that time.

When Will Herberg published his *Protestant–Catholic–Jew* (1955), he barely mentioned the controversies, and no one seemed disposed to quarrel with his characterizing Catholicism as one of the "three great faiths of democracy."[58] John F. Kennedy's religion, of course, played a significant role in the 1960 election. But the fact that JFK was elected showed how much things had changed since the Al Smith campaign. And from the viewpoint of this essay, it is even more important that, insofar as there was a "liberal candidate" in 1960, it was Kennedy. The Catholic–liberal relationship had in fact improved markedly in the few years since Blanshardism reached its crest.

Perhaps the most important reason for this rapprochement, if that is not too strong a term for it, was that a new and more ideologically self-conscious species of Catholic liberalism emerged in the midst of the post-World War II controversies and gained ground during the 1950s. It was not the dominant strain in American Catholic life as a whole, but, at least among the Catholic intellectual elite, it contested for dominance. As in the late nineteenth century, the mediating ground of its emergence was Americanism – in this case, the highly positive evaluation of "what America stands for" that took shape in the wartime struggle against totalitarianism and carried over into what has been called the "American celebration" of the postwar decade.

In looking back at this phenomenon in American culture generally, historians have tended to deplore its nationalistic excesses and pervasive self-satisfaction, to say nothing of the hypocrisy of the American people's failure to live up to their high ideals in the area of race. But on the latter point, there was plenty of self-criticism at the time; and more broadly considered, there were solid reasons for celebrating what the nation stood for: freedom, equality, tolerance for diversity, and "pluralism."[59] The last named of these values commended itself particularly to Catholic intellectuals made more keenly sensitive by their wartime experience to the admirable features of the American system, and to the goodwill of their non-Catholic neighbors. Although deeply loyal to the church, and fierce in their denunciation of "Blanshardism," these intellectuals were discomfited by criticism from people whom they respected of rigidities in the church's stance and gratuitous abrasiveness on the part of her spokesmen. Hence "pluralism" emerged as the key word for Catholic liberals who undertook to rethink the relation of their religion to American life.[60]

The historiographic recovery of the Americanist episode of the 1880s and 1890s, which began in the war years and gathered momentum through the fifties, testifies to the new spirit.[61] The Americanists, who were the heroes in virtually all of these works of scholarship, were, after all, the liberals – optimistic, forward-looking, irenic in attitude, positive about American civilization, and sanguine in their expectations for the church's future. As a group, the historians of Americanism were far from being activists or ideologues, but their work accorded with, and no doubt furthered, the new liberal outlook that was gaining ground as they wrote.

"*Commonweal* liberalism" was much more self-conscious and topical. The magazine's orientation had, of course, been liberal since its founding. But in the late forties and early fifties, *Commonweal* liberalism came to be more clearly associated with a critique of "Catholic separatism." Catholics, the editors insisted, must break out of their self-imposed "ghetto" and involve themselves more actively in the "pluralistic" society of which they were a part, and toward which they had responsibilities that went beyond purely Catholic concerns. "*Commonweal* Catholics" were New Deal liberals in political outlook; although strongly opposed to McCarthyism, they were also anti-Communist internationalists; they espoused an enlightened liberality on matters relating to artistic expression, and were regularly chagrined by the moralistic excesses of Catholic "crusades" against indecency in books and movies. The degree to which this pluralistic liberalism was linked to Americanism as it was understood at the time is illustrated in the series of articles entitled "Catholicism in America," which was published as a book in 1954.[62]

John Courtney Murray's "project," as it has been called, was incomparably the most important instance of liberal Catholic Americanism in the post-World War II era. Although nothing like a systematic review of Murray's work can be undertaken here, some comment about its relationship to the overall theme of this discussion is required.[63]

Murray's project was, first of all, thoroughly American in that the basic task he set for himself was to provide a new rationale for his fellow religionists' historic claim that their faith was fully compatible with American principles. In this respect, and in the general line of argument he followed, Murray was solidly in the ecumenically liberal tradition of Brownson, Hecker, and the Catholic-roots-of-democracy writers of the 1920s.

Murray's work was also thoroughly Catholic, for though he applied the resources of Neoscholasticism in new and creative ways, his thinking was steeped in the Thomism that had been the official Catholic philosophy since Leo XIII's *Aeterni Patris* of 1879. He was impatient with Niebuhrian "ambiguists" who dealt in ironies, dilemmas, and paradoxes; and there was no mistaking the pride with which he affirmed his belonging to the "tradition of reason" that reached back through the medieval scholastics to the origins of Western philosophy in classical Greece. He made the concept of natural law the starting point for much of his analysis, even though he realized full well that American Protestants found it "alien... [and] unassimilable."[64] His use of the concept, along with the social and political writings of Jacques Maritain, helps explain why the natural law loomed so large in the thinking of a liberal Catholic journalist like John Cogley.[65]

Rooted as it was in the Catholic tradition, Murray's work was at the same time obviously affected by the distinctive historical situation of American Catholicism in the postwar era, particularly by the centrality of the church–state issue in the "Catholic question" of the day. Equally topical was the prominence Murray accorded "pluralism" – a concept which referred, in his usage, not simply to a pleasing degree of cultural diversity, but to a social condition in which people who differed from each other in deeply held beliefs were nevertheless constrained to live together and aspired to do so in peace and reasonable harmony.

Murray's approach was irenic, but he stoutly defended what he regarded as legitimate Catholic claims, as in the matter of aid to parochial schools. He also entered actively into the polemical wars set off by Paul Blanshard, whose position he characterized as "the new nativism." And he was uncompromising in his rejection of monistic secularism as a theoretical position and as the (unacknowledged) foundation of Blanshard's (and other liberals') criticism, not just of the abuses of "Catholic authoritarianism," but of the church's claim to exist as a source of authority independent of the state. On at least one occasion, Murray explicitly identified this secularist position as "(in Carlton Hayes's term) sectarian Liberalism, or (in the more definitive term used today) totalitarian democracy."[66]

As the foregoing point suggests, Murray's project was fundamentally an exercise in the distinction of realms; as such, it assumed the traditional dualities of nature and grace, secular and sacred, temporal and spiritual. These distinctions, though far more subtly worked out, were the same as those that underlay Bishop England's 1826 discourse before Congress. They ruled out liberalism of the totalitarian-democracy type precisely because of its monistic tendency, its disallowance of any realm beyond the reach of the state or of any source of authority independent of the state. At the same time, they left room for the kind of ecumenical liberalism so well represented by Murray's "reflections on the American proposition."

It is notorious that Murray's project aroused opposition within the church, and that he was forbidden to write on church-and-state in the mid fifties. Even so, his work, along with the increasing respectability of *Commonweal* liberalism among Catholic intellectuals, did a great deal to defuse the "Catholic question" in that decade.[67] It seems likely that tensions eased in part because liberals suspected that the logic of "pluralism" would carry the process of Catholic liberalization beyond the delicate equipoise in which Murray's fine distinguishing of realms left it. To those who did not think the realm of the sacred really existed – or who believed with Horace Kallen that "secularism is the will of God" – this sequel must have seemed inevitable.[68]

Whatever Murray's consultative role might have been, John F. Kennedy's handling of the religious issue in the campaign, and his performance as president, did nothing to dispel such expectations on the part of liberals. For the practical implication of JFK's campaign statements and conduct in office was that his Catholic faith was a purely private matter that had no bearing whatsoever on matters of public policy. And when the liberal Jewish academic, Lawrence Fuchs, undertook to explain *John F. Kennedy and American Catholicism* (1967), it was clear that he (Fuchs) accepted a version of American civil religion as the appropriate standard by which to judge the politically relevant beliefs and actions of Catholics.[69]

But Fuchs's book belongs to a later period. The preconciliar Catholic–liberal relationship reached its classic moment in the postwar decade. It was classic in the sense that a monistic-secularist version of sectarian liberalism clearly furnished the basis for the critique of "political Catholicism" mounted by Paul Blanshard, while, on the other hand, the Catholic distinction-of-realms that could accommodate ecumenical liberalism was stated by Murray with a lucidity and nuance never before achieved. The conflict between these two versions of liberalism was not settled, to be sure, but at least the issues could be clearly discerned. And raising a discussion to the level where clear-cut disagreement becomes possible is, as Murray himself pointed out, no easy thing. We will do well, indeed, if we can attain the same level in our reflections on Catholicism and liberalism today.

NOTES

1 Carlton J. H. Hayes, *A Generation of Materialism, 1871–1900* (New York: Harper & Brothers, 1941), esp. 46–50, 74–87. Hayes once (p. 357) called the broader version of liberalism "general" instead of "ecumenical."

2 Hayes, *Generation*, 48–49.

3 Ibid., 134 for quotation; 123–151 for general treatment of religious developments.

4 Louis Hartz, *The Liberal Tradition in America* (New York: Harcourt, Brace, 1955) particularizes this argument somewhat, since it is Lockeian liberalism he has in mind. Despite criticism by more recent scholars, Hartz's interpretation has genuine merit. For pertinent comments, see Daniel T. Rodgers, *Contested Truths: Keywords in American Politics since Independence* (New York: Basic Books, 1987), 8–9.

5 An anecdote reported by the American intellectual historian Henry F. May is revealing. When he remarked at a conference in Poland "that evangelical Protestantism was the usual religion of the people, whereas religious liberalism was usually associated with the upper middle class," some of his listeners "found this statement not so much wrong as incomprehensible. Religion was associated with authority; the people were revolting against authority and therefore against religion." However applicable such a view may be to Europe, May concludes, "it certainly will not work for the United States." Henry F. May, "Religion and American Intellectual History, 1945–1985: Reflections on an Uneasy Relationship," in Michael J. Lacey, ed., *Religion and Twentieth-Century American Intellectual Life* (New York: Cambridge University Press, 1989), 19.

6 Generalizations of this magnitude cannot really be documented, but the whole literature dealing with American civil religion is relevant. For bibliography see James A. Mathisen, "Twenty Years After Bellah: Whatever Happened to American Civil Religion?" *Sociological Analysis* 50 (1989): 129–146. Also highly relevant is Robert T. Handy, *A Christian America: Protestant Hopes and Historical Realities*, 2nd edn. (New York: Oxford University Press, 1989). For a mid-twentieth-century example of a Protestant church historian's proprietary attitude toward Americanism, see William Warren Sweet, *American Culture and Religion* (Dallas: Southern Methodist University Press, 1951), esp. 39.

7 Carroll used the expression quoted here in writing to his English friend Charles Plowden, February 2, 1785. See Thomas O'Brien Hanley, ed., *The John Carroll Papers*, 3 vols. (Notre Dame, IN: University of Notre Dame Press, 1976), 1: 168.

8 For orientation to this literature, see Robert E. Shalhope, "Toward a Republican Synthesis: The Emergence of an Understanding of Republicanism in American History," *William & Mary Quarterly*, 3rd ser., 29 (January 1972): 49–80, and Shalhope, "Republicanism and Early American Historiography," ibid., 3rd ser., 39 (April 1982): 334–356.

9 Jay P. Dolan, *The American Catholic Experience: A History from Colonial Times to the Present* (Garden City, NY: Doubleday, 1985), chap. 4; David O'Brien, *Public Catholicism* (New York: Macmillan, 1989), chap. 2; Thomas W. Spalding, *The Premier See: A History of the Archdiocese of Baltimore, 1789–1989* (Baltimore: Johns Hopkins University Press, 1989), esp. 17–20; Margaret Mary Reher, *Catholic Intellectual Life in America: A Historical Study of Persons and Movements* (New York: Macmillan, 1989), chap. 1; Patrick W. Carey, *People, Priests, and Prelates: Ecclesiastical Democracy and the Tensions of Trusteeism* (Notre Dame, IN: University of Notre Dame Press, 1987); Patrick W. Carey, *An Immigrant Bishop: John England's Adaptation of Irish Catholicism to American Republicanism* (Yonkers, NY: U.S. Catholic Historical Society, 1982).

10 This expression, introduced by Dolan (*American Catholic Experience*, chap. 4), is employed in highly ideological fashion in Dennis P. McCann, *New Experiment in Democracy: The Challenge for American Catholicism* (Kansas City, MO: Sheed & Ward, 1987), 162ff.

11 For Enlightenment influence, see Patrick W. Carey, *American Catholic Religious Thought: The Shaping of a Theological and Social Tradition* (New York: Paulist Press, 1987), 5–15; and Joseph Chinnici, *Living Stones: The History and Structure of Catholic Spiritual Life in the United States* (New York: Macmillan, 1989), Part 1, "An Enlightenment Synthesis, 1776–1815"; for general background, Henry F. May, *The Enlightenment in America* (New York: Oxford University Press, 1976).

12 Besides Carey, *Immigrant Bishop*, see Peter Clark's essay on England in Gerald P. Fogarty, ed., *Patterns of Episcopal Leadership* (New York: Macmillan, 1989), 68–84.

13 The Americanist orientation of the French émigrés was first argued by Thomas T. McAvoy, "The Formation of the Catholic Minority in the United States, 1820–1860," *Review of Politics* 10 (January 1948): 13–34. For recent studies, see Richard Shaw, *John Dubois: Founding Father* (New York: U.S. Catholic Historical Society, 1983); Annabelle M. Melville, *Louis William DuBourg*, 2 vols. (Chicago: Loyola University Press, 1986); Clyde F. Crews's essay on Benedict J. Flaget in Fogarty, *Patterns of Episcopal Leadership*, 52–67; and Christopher J. Kauffman, *Tradition and Transformation in Catholic Culture: The Priests of Saint Sulpice in the United States from 1791 to the Present* (New York: Macmillan, 1987).

14 Spalding, *Premier See*, 93–94, 102–103.

15 For the address, see Sebastian G. Messmer, ed., *The Works of the Right Reverend John England, First Bishop of Charleston*, 7 vols. (Cleveland, OH: Arthur H. Clarke, 1908), VII: 9–43; for background and summary, Peter Guilday, *The Life and Times of John England, First Bishop of Charleston (1786–1842)*, 2 vols. (New York: America Press, 1927), II: 48–67; for elaboration of the interpretation offered here, Philip Gleason, *Keeping the Faith: American Catholicism Past and Present* (Notre Dame, IN: University of Notre Dame Press, 1987), 98–100.

16 John Courtney Murray, *We Hold These Truths: Catholic Reflections on the American Proposition* (New York: Sheed & Ward, 1960), esp. 67–69, and chap. 9, "Are There Two or One?"; for a representative statement by a Murray follower, see Edward Duff, "The Church in American Public Life," in Philip Gleason, ed., *Contemporary Catholicism in the United States* (Notre Dame, IN: University of Notre Dame Press, 1969), 99–103.

17 Quotation from Isaac T. Hecker, "Leo XIII," *Catholic World* 46 (December 1887): 291–298; see also Hecker, *The Church and the Age* (New York: Office of the Catholic World, 1887), esp. chaps. 2 (on church and state in America) and 3 (on Cardinal Gibbons and American institutions); Orestes A. Brownson, "The Mission of America," *Brownson's Quarterly Review* 13 (October 1856): 409–444. For fuller discussion of Hecker, see my article "Father Hecker's Last Book: A Look Back at *The Church and the Age*," *Catholic World* 232 (March–April 1989): 70–73.

18 Murray, *We Hold These Truths*, 151; see also 28–30.

19 When Pius IX's Syllabus of Errors appeared in 1864, Archbishop John McCloskey of New York (later to be the first American cardinal) wrote to Archbishop Martin J. Spalding of Baltimore: "It is consoling to think that our Holy Father has in all his official acts a light of guidance from on High – for according to all the rules of mere human prudence and wisdom... [the Syllabus] would be considered ill timed. It can hardly be doubted that it places us in a state of apparent antagonism, at least as far as our principles are concerned, to the institutions under which we live..." Quoted in Thomas W. Spalding, *Martin John Spalding: American Churchman* (Washington: Catholic University of America Press, 1973), 241.

20 My *Speaking of Diversity: Language and Ethnicity in Twentieth-Century America* (Baltimore: Johns Hopkins University Press, 1992), chap. 11, surveys the literature on Americanism.

21 Both Brownson and Hecker maintained that Catholicism was more compatible with American principles than Protestantism because the former stressed free will and the ability of human reason to attain truth in the natural order, while the founders of Protestantism taught that human nature was totally depraved, that reason could not reach truth, and that free will was an illusion. Catholic teaching was thus in line with the assumptions on which republicanism rested, and the founding principles of Protestantism were not. See Brownson, "Mission of America," 426–430; Hecker, *Church and Age*, chap. 8. The prevailing American view, of course, held that Protestantism represented freedom and progress, while Catholicism stood for authority and reaction.

22 See Hayes, *Generation of Materialism*, 82ff.; and for the particularly embattled French situation, Joseph N. Moody, *French Education Since Napoleon* (Syracuse, NY: Syracuse University Press, 1978).

23 Classical on this point is Timothy L. Smith, "Protestant Schooling and American Nationality, 1800–1850," *Journal of American History* 53 (March 1967): 679–695; see also Robert Michaelsen, *Piety in the Public School* (New York: Macmillan, 1970); and Lloyd P. Jorgenson, *The State and the Non-Public School, 1825–1925* (Columbia, MO: University of Missouri Press, 1987), esp. chaps. 3–4.

24 See Vincent P. Lannie, *Public Money and Parochial Education: Bishop Hughes, Governor Seward and the New York School Controversy* (Cleveland, OH: Press of Case Western Reserve University, 1968); for background, Jorgenson, *Non-Public School*, and Charles Leslie Glenn, Jr., *The Myth of the Common School* (Amherst, MA: University of Massachusetts Press, 1988).

25 For further discussion, see Gleason, *Keeping the Faith*, 122–124.

26 For Brownson on the ethnic issue, see "Native Americanism" and "The Know Nothings," *Brownson's Quarterly Review* 11 (July, October 1854): 328–354, 447–487; for education, "Public and Parochial Schools," *Brownson's Quarterly Review* 16 (July 1859): 324–342; "Catholic Schools and Education," *Brownson's Quarterly Review* 19 (January 1862): 66–84. For a general treatment, see James M. McDonnell, *Orestes A. Brownson and Nineteenth-Century Catholic Education* (New York: Garland Press, 1989).

27 Brownson made this distinction in a highly controversial article entitled "The Rights of the Temporal," *Brownson's Quarterly Review* 17 (October 1860): 464, and repeated it in an editorial note, *Brownson's Quarterly Review* 19 (January 1862): 133–134. For discussion, see Thomas T. McAvoy, "Orestes A. Brownson and Archbishop John Hughes in 1860," *Review of Politics* 24 (January 1962): 19–47.

28 Thomas R. Ryan, *Orestes A. Brownson: A Definitive Biography* (Hun-

tington, IN: Our Sunday Visitor, 1976), chaps. 27–40, covers this period in detail; for Brownson's liberalism as such, see pp. 597–612.

29 James Hennesey, *American Catholics: A History of the Roman Catholic Community in the United States* (New York: Oxford University Press, 1981), chap. 15, is excellent; for a more extended treatment, see Gerald P. Fogarty, *The Vatican and the American Hierarchy from 1870 to 1965*, paperback edn. (Wilmington, DL: Michael Glazier, 1985), chaps. 2–7; and for a superb biography of the chief figure among the Americanists, Marvin R. O'Connell, *John Ireland and the American Catholic Church* (St. Paul, MN: Minnesota Historical Society Press, 1988).

30 For the text, see the appendix to Thomas T. McAvoy's standard work, *The Great Crisis in American Catholic History, 1895–1900* (Chicago: Regnery, 1957).

31 For Modernism see R. Scott Appleby, *"Church and Age Unite! The Modernist Impulse in American Catholicism* (Notre Dame, IN: University of Notre Dame Press, 1991); Carey, *American Catholic Religious Thought*, 30–39; Reher, *Catholic Intellectual Life*, chaps. 4–5; Chinnici, *Living Stones*, Part III, esp. chap. 11. See also Margaret M. Reher, "Americanism and Modernism – Continuity or Discontinuity?" *U.S. Catholic Historian* 1 (Summer 1981): 87–103.

32 See John Lancaster Spalding, *Education and the Higher Life* (Chicago: A. C. McClurg, 1890), 199–204; and, more generally, David P. Killen, "Americanism Revisited: John Spalding and *Testem Benevolentiae*," *Harvard Theological Review* 66 (October 1973): 413–454.

33 Merle Curti, *Growth of American Thought*, 3rd edn. (New York: Harper & Row, 1964), chap. 21. A minor Americanist, John A. Zahm, CSC, was censured for his writings on evolution, but that issue did not loom large in the controversy. Appleby, however (*"Church and Age Unite,"* chap. 1), places Zahm among the American Modernists.

34 The literature on Progressivism is enormous. The works mentioned are Samuel P. Hays, *The Response to Industrialism 1885–1914* (University of Chicago Press, 1957), and Robert Wiebe, *The Search for Order, 1877–1920* (New York: Hill and Wang, 1967).

35 For Croly's reinterpretation of liberalism, see Charles Forcey, *The Crossroads of Liberalism: Croly, Weyl, Lippmann, and the Progressive Era* (New York: Oxford University Press, 1961); for Dewey, see Jerome Nathanson, *John Dewey: The Reconstruction of the Democratic Life* (New York: Scribner, 1951).

36 See esp. Elizabeth McKeown, "War and Welfare: A Study of American Catholic Leadership" (Ph.D. diss., University of Chicago, 1972); John B. Sheerin, *Never Look Back: The Career and Concerns of John J. Burke* (New York: Paulist Press, 1975); and Douglas J. Slawson, *The Foundation and First Decade of the National Catholic Welfare Council* (Washington: Catholic University of America Press, 1992).

37 For a distinctively conservative dimension in Catholic social reform, see

Philip Gleason, *The Conservative Reformers: German–American Catholics and the Social Order* (Notre Dame, IN: University of Notre Dame Press, 1968); for Ryan, see Joseph McShane, *"Sufficiently Radical": Catholicism, Progressivism, and the Bishops' Program of 1919* (Washington: Catholic University of America Press, 1986).

38 See Lynn Dumenil, "'The Insatiable Maw of Bureaucracy': Antistatism and Education Reform in the 1920s," *Journal of American History* 77 (September 1990): 499–524; and Dumenil, "The Tribal Twenties: 'Assimilated' Catholics' Response to Anti-Catholicism in the 1920s," *Journal of American Ethnic History* 11 (Fall 1991): 21–49.

39 George M. Marsden, *Fundamentalism and American Culture: The Shaping of Twentieth-Century Evangelicalism, 1870–1925* (New York: Oxford University Press, 1980); for "acids of modernity," Walter Lippmann, *A Preface to Morals* (New York: Macmillan, 1929); for general background, Owen Chadwick, *The Secularization of the European Mind in the Nineteenth Century* (Cambridge University Press, 1975), and James Turner, *Without God, Without Creed: The Origins of Unbelief in America* (Baltimore: Johns Hopkins University Press, 1985).

40 William M. Halsey, *The Survival of American Innocence: Catholicism in an Era of Disillusionment, 1920–1940* (Notre Dame, IN: University of Notre Dame Press, 1980). My review of this book in *Catholic Historical Review* 67 (October 1981): 640–643, spells out my reservations. For important supplements to Halsey, see Chinnici, *Living Stones*, chaps. 13–14, and Arnold Sparr, *To Promote, Defend, and Redeem: The Catholic Literary Revival and the Cultural Transformation of American Catholicism, 1920–1960* (Westport, CT: Greenwood Press, 1990).

41 Halsey, *Survival of American Innocence*, chap. 1.

42 My interpretation here and in what follows is derived from ongoing research on the history of Catholic higher education in this period. Indications of the general direction it takes may be found in my *Keeping the Faith*, chaps. 1, 5, 7, and 8.

43 Halsey, *Survival of American Innocence*, 71ff.

44 Brownson, "Mission of America," 422, 427–429, and Hecker, *Church and Age*, 83–87, make the same argument.

45 Halsey, *Survival of American Innocence*, chaps. 8–9; Philip Gleason, "Neoscholasticism as Preconciliar Ideology," *U.S. Catholic Historian* 7 (Fall 1988): 401–411.

46 Fuller documentation for what follows may be found in Gleason, *Speaking of Diversity*, chap. 8.

47 "A Moral Pestilence," *Nation* 129 (December 25, 1929): 767–768; John A. Ryan, "Catholicism and Liberalism," *Nation* 131 (August 6, 1930): 150–152. Ryan's biographer calls this article "the most important statement on liberalism during his whole career." See Francis L. Broderick, *Right Reverend New Dealer: John A. Ryan* (New York: Macmillan, 1963), 150, and, more generally, 140–164.

74 PHILIP GLEASON

48 Charles J. Tull, *Father Coughlin and the New Deal* (Syracuse, NY: Syracuse University Press, 1965), 78, 80, 82–88, and chap. 6; Alan Brinkley, *Voices of Protest: Huey Long, Father Coughlin and the Great Depression* (New York: Knopf, 1982), esp. Appendix 1, "The Question of Anti-Semitism and the Problem of Fascism"; and Ronald H. Bayor, *Neighbors in Conflict: The Irish, Germans, Jews, and Italians of New York City, 1929–1941* (Baltimore: Johns Hopkins University Press, 1978), chap. 5.

49 J. David Valaik, "American Catholics and the Spanish Civil War, 1931–1939" (Ph.D. diss., University of Rochester, 1964); Allen Guttman, *The Wound in the Heart: America and the Spanish Civil War* (New York: Free Press of Glencoe, 1962); George Q. Flynn, *Roosevelt and Romanism: Catholics and American Diplomacy, 1937–1945* (Westport, CT: Greenwood Press, 1976), esp. 43–53.

50 George Seldes, *The Catholic Crisis* (New York: J. Messner. Inc., 1939; 2nd edn., 1945). For a Catholic response to the pro-fascist charge, see Theodore Maynard, "Catholics and the Nazis," *American Mercury* 53 (October 1941): 391–400.

51 See Lerond Curry, *Protestant–Catholic Relations in America: World War I through Vatican II* (Lexington, KY: University Press of Kentucky, 1972), 36ff.

52 John A. Ryan and Francis J. Boland, *Catholic Principles of Politics* (New York: Macmillan, 1940), chaps. 22–23, esp. pp. 316–321. This was the revised version of a book originally published in 1922 which had been a focal point of controversy in the Al Smith campaign. See Broderick, *Right Reverend New Dealer*, 118–120, 170–179, 247–248.

53 This is best illustrated in Harold E. Fey's eight-part series, entitled "Can Catholicism Win America," which ran in *Christian Century* from November 29, 1944, through January 17, 1945, and circulated thereafter as a pamphlet.

54 For liberal irritation with Catholics, see Sidney Hook, John Dewey, and Ernest Nagel, "The New Failure of Nerve," *Partisan Review* 10 (January–February, 1943): 11, 17–20, 28ff., 50–53; for background, see Edward A. Purcell, Jr., *The Crisis of Democratic Theory: Scientific Naturalism & the Problem of Value* (Lexington, KY: University Press of Kentucky, 1973), esp. 164ff., 179–180, 203–204, 224–225, 241.

55 See Curry, *Protestant–Catholic Relations*, chap. 2; John J. Kane, *Catholic–Protestant Conflicts in America* (Chicago: Regnery, 1955); G. H. Williams et al., "Issues Between Catholics and Protestants at Mid-century," *Religion in Life* 23 (Spring 1954): 163–205; Diane Ravitch, *Troubled Crusade: American Education, 1945–1980* (New York: Basic Books, 1983), 29–41; Anson Phelps Stokes and Leo Pfeffer, *Church and State in the United States*, rev. edn. (New York: Harper & Row, 1964), 278–279, 436–440.

56 Paul Blanshard, *American Freedom and Catholic Power* (Boston: Beacon

Press, 1949); Blanshard, *Communism, Democracy, and Catholic Power* (Boston: Beacon Press, 1951).

57 Donald F. Crosby, *God, Church, and Flag: Senator Joseph R. McCarthy and the Catholic Church, 1950–1957* (Chapel Hill, NC: University of North Carolina Press, 1978).

58 Will Herberg, *Protestant–Catholic–Jew: An Essay in American Religious Sociology* (Garden City, NY: Doubleday, 1955), esp. chap. 10.

59 For a recent and balanced survey, see John P. Diggins, *The Proud Decades: America in War and Peace, 1941–1960* (New York: Norton, 1988).

60 For Catholics and pluralism, see Gleason, *Speaking of Diversity*, 63–69, and chap. 8.

61 Gleason, *Speaking of Diversity*, 286–289.

62 *Catholicism in America: A Series of Articles from The Commonweal* (New York: Harcourt, Brace, 1954). For a general study, see Rodger Van Allen, *The Commonweal and American Catholicism: The Magazine, the Movement, the Meaning* (Philadelphia: Fortress Press, 1974).

63 Donald E. Pelotte, *John Courtney Murray: Theologian in Conflict* (New York: Paulist Press, 1976), situates Murray's work in the context of mid-twentieth-century American Catholicism. Murray's genre was the essay or learned article, rather than the book. His *We Hold These Truths*, which is a collection of essays on closely related themes, furnishes the main basis for the generalizations that follow.

64 Murray, *We Hold These Truths*, 282–286, for ambiguists and the tradition of reason; p. 17, for Protestants and natural law.

65 Jacques Maritain, *Man and the State* (University of Chicago Press, 1951); John Cogley, et al., *Natural Law and Modern Society* (Cleveland, OH: World Pub. Co., 1963).

66 Murray, *We Hold These Truths*, 67; see also Murray, "Paul Blanshard and the New Nativism," *The Month* 191 (1951): 214–225.

67 For an early appreciation of the value of Murray's work in easing tensions, see George H. Williams's contribution to "Issues Between Catholics and Protestants," *Religion in Life* 23 (Spring 1954): 176–186.

68 For discussion of Kallen's position, see Gleason, *Speaking of Diversity*, 213–222.

69 Lawrence H. Fuchs, *John F. Kennedy and American Catholicism* (New York: Meredith Press, 1967), see index heading "Americanism, culture-religion of."

CHAPTER 3

Vatican II and the encounter between Catholicism and liberalism

Joseph A. Komonchak

The Second Vatican Council can be read as the event in which the Catholic church significantly reassessed modern society and culture and the attitudes and strategies it had adopted towards them in the previous century and a half. Those earlier attitudes and strategies had been founded in a consistent repudiation of an ideology and praxis summed up in the word "liberalism."

"Liberalism" is, of course, notoriously difficult to define, and the history we are studying in this volume is in good part also a history of interpretations and evaluations of the word. But in the minds of most Catholic popes, bishops, and apologists over the last two centuries, it had a clear reference which may first be illuminated by the literally diabolical lineage they imagined for it. Liberalism had its origins in Satan's "Non serviam" but only took on systematic form in the Lutheran revolt against the church's authority and on behalf of free examination, in the naturalism of the Renaissance, in the Enlightenment's repudiation of tradition, authority and community, in the secularization of the political sphere, in the possessive individualism of capitalist economics, and in the cultural anarchy produced by an unrestrained freedom of opinion, speech, and the press. Common to all these developments were an exaltation of the individual and a definition of freedom as exemption from external constraint.

If on this view the original sin that gave rise to liberalism was Satan's and Adam's rejection of God's will, its modern triumph was accomplished by the emancipation of large areas of human life from the Lordship of Christ exercised through the teaching and laws of the church. The separation of church and state implied that political society can be organized and directed without being undergirded and legitimated by religious unity. Economic life ceased to be regulated by religious and moral norms and was now to be governed by its own laws, which could be expected to function automatically.

76

Philosophy became autonomous, defining itself by the absence of authority. Religion no longer had anything to do, then, with the spheres of politics, economics, and culture and now would find its sole place at the margins of society where it became a personal ornament of those so disposed. "Liberalism," in the mind of this typical Catholicism, was the theoretical and practical system which denies religion significance for the public sphere. This liberalism was, therefore, rejected as "sin," as "the rendez-vous of all heresies," and, because it denied the need for Christ the Redeemer and the role of the church, "apostasy."[1]

It was this privatizing of religion that the church consistently opposed since the time when, so it was thought, it first displayed its true colors in the French Revolution. This is the common thread that runs, despite some important changes, through the actions of the popes from Pius VI's repudiation of the Declaration of the Rights of Man, to Gregory XVI's condemnation of an emergent "liberal" Catholicism, Pius IX's Syllabus of Errors, Leo XIII's repudiation of the liberal notion of church–state relations, Pius X's battle-cry: "To restore all things in Christ," Pius XI's exaltation of the Kingship of Christ, down to Pius XII's consecration of a sick world to the Queenship of Mary. God and Christ had been denied their rights in favor of "the rights of man," and the task of the church in the modern world was to bring it back to the Redeemer and to his church.

Throughout the nineteenth century and the first half of the twentieth, the church constructed itself as a counter-society legitimated by the counter-culture of its basic faith. Central dogmas and devotions were articulated in such a way as to stress their anti-modern, anti-liberal meanings and implications. This counter-ideology was embodied in the structures of an alternate society. Catholic organizations and movements multiplied to insure that Catholics would primarily associate with one another, and, thus immunized from the contagion of liberalism, would be equipped to undertake the battle to restore Christ's rights. These popular forms of association were designed to supply for the absence of the political support the church had once been able to count on. But while the church had grave reservations about the centralized, bureaucratized nation-state, it did not hesitate to borrow from it new ways of organizing its own political structure, as when a *Code* of canon law replaced the body of traditional case-law, and new ways of legitimating an increasingly centralized regime, as when the First

Vatican Council defined a universal primacy of the pope in terms of modern models of sovereignty.[2]

Most of the internal controversies in the Catholic church during the nineteenth and twentieth centuries have revolved around the accuracy and adequacy of this often undifferentiated, religiously motivated rejection of the modern liberal experiment. In most instances from Lamennais to Murray, those who suggested differentiations or accommodations were made to suffer for their efforts by those who had made their own Pius IX's blanket condemnation of the proposition that "the Roman Pontiff can and should reconcile and accommodate himself to progress, liberalism, and recent civilization."[3] It would be the Second Vatican Council that would permit the most dramatic and important challenge to the apocalyptic reading of the modern world that occasioned and legitimated the modern Roman Catholic counter-culture. I propose in this essay to discuss how the Council's engagement with liberalism challenged the attitudes and strategies of this sub-culture, to explore the historical and methodological issues that were at stake in the conciliar debate, and to reflect on their continued relevance today.

VATICAN II

The first major challenge came in a famous passage in the opening address of Pope John XXIII.[4] The Pope complained that he often encountered people around him who could see nothing but calamity and ruin in the modern era, who believed things were always becoming worse, as if the end of the world were near. They spoke as if in the past everything had been advantageous to the church, ignoring the degree to which the protection and favor of the state were often purchased at the loss of the church's freedom. In a dramatic statement, Pope John flatly declared his disagreement with "these prophets of doom."

The pope's sharp words were a repudiation of the idealized picture of medieval Christendom which some were still using as the criterion by which to assess and repudiate the developments that mark the modern era. It is likely that the pope was referring to the authors of the doctrinal texts that had been prepared over the previous two years for discussion and, it was expected, rapid approval by the bishops at the Council. With the exception of the draft on the Liturgy, these documents were a concise reaffirmation of the positions and strategies adopted by the church, under Roman direction, for the previous century and a half. They had been composed under the direction of officials of the Roman Curia who also occupied key roles in the preparatory commissions.

Behind the theological texts, there lay a view of modern social, political, and cultural developments that was expressed most clearly and succinctly by the Holy Office, two years earlier, when it indicated what challenges and threats the Council should address.[5] In the introduction to its proposal, it described the errors which, although condemned by Vatican I, were reviving and threatening to subvert Christianity. Philosophical rationalism, theological emanationism, and political liberalism were now taking on new forms: naturalism, atheistic humanism, evolutionism, relativism, indifferentism, materialism, Marxism, laicism, immanentism. The doctrinal texts produced during the following two years by and large reflected this negative assessment of modern society and culture.

It was this "almost neurotic denial of all that was new"[6] that Pope John was criticizing in his opening remarks. Where the preparatory texts saw calamity and ruin, the pope insisted could be found opportunity for the Gospel, "a new order of human relations," the challenge of fulfilling "God's higher and inscrutable designs." He therefore proposed that the Council undertake a different task from the simple repetition of what had been taught before, for which a Council was not necessary. The Council instead should undertake a twofold task: a renewed exploration of the church's biblical and traditional patrimony and a simultaneous review of the "new conditions and forms of life introduced into the modern world." Two slogans at the time encapsulated the two projects: *ressourcement* and *aggiornamento*.

In a speech delivered only a month before the Council opened,[7] Pope John had proposed a distinction which was taken up by others and became an easy and perhaps over-simplified way of describing the Council's work: the distinction between the church *ad intra* and the church *ad extra*. Some people have even used the distinction to sort out the conciliar documents, with such texts as the documents on the Liturgy, the church, and Divine Revelation falling under the first rubric, while the texts on Religious Freedom, Non-Christian Religions, and the church in the Modern World are placed under the second. Tensions both at the Council and since have led some to harden the obvious differences in the two kinds of texts, and a choice of one or the other has even been presented as a way of typifying receptions of the Council.[8]

In Pope John's mind, the two tasks of *ressourcement* and *aggiornamento* were not to be divorced from one another, nor did they represent distinct moments in the Council's work. It was a sense of inappropriateness to modern conditions which led the Council to discard the language and many of the assumptions of anti-modern Catholicism and to adopt instead a much more biblical, traditional, and discursive language. Furthermore, one of the great instruments of the recovery of the primary tradition was precisely that example of modern rationality, historical criticism. Above all, Pope John's own insistence that the Council be primarily a *pastoral* exercise of the teaching office was itself not simply a matter of simple adaptations or applications of perennial principles, but a new reading of the Gospel undertaken under the impulse of the "signs of the times."[9] The primarily doctrinal and "internal" texts of the Council themselves, then, also reflect a new and far more positive encounter with modernity.

Nonetheless, in the context of this study most interest will probably fall on the texts in which the Council more explicitly addressed the problematic of modern society and culture. Of these the most important are the Pastoral Constitution on the church in the Modern World (*Gaudium et Spes*) and the Declaration on Religious Freedom (*Dignitatis Humanae*).

Gaudium et Spes

The novelty of this document consists first in its not being a discussion of the general theme, "Church and World," but of the church in the *modern* world, the world of *today*. This explains its methodology of "reading the signs of the times and of interpreting them in the light of the Gospel" (*GS* 4). Among the principles and developments identified in the course of the document as characterizing "today" we find: the rapidity and depth of social and cultural transformations; the impact of the natural and social sciences and technology; modernization, industrialization, urbanization, mass media; a dynamic sense of nature; calls for greater freedom of self-realization and human rights; the spread of democracy; the changed relationship between church and state.[10]

The Council's method thus included a moment of simple observation and description, an attempt to state what sets the modern experience apart from earlier ages. The Council did not refrain from judgments and evaluations about the problems created by modern developments, but the attitude of "solidarity," "respectful affection," and "dialogue" which the Council chose to adopt towards the modern world (*GS* 3) required a prior effort to understand and evaluate its distinctive character.

A similar effort is visible in the Council's description of the modern understanding of freedom as autonomy and self-responsibility, giving birth to "a new humanism, for which man is primarily defined by his responsibility for his brothers and for history" (*GS* 55). It also led the Council, in responding to the widespread belief that religion endangers rightful human autonomy, not only to reject the idea that autonomy must mean disregarding our relation to the Creator but also to insist on the legitimate meaning of the word:

If by the autonomy of earthly affairs we mean that created things and societies themselves have their own laws and values which are gradually to be discovered, exploited and ordered by man, then it is entirely legitimate to demand it, and this is something which not only is claimed by men of our day but agrees also with the Creator's will. For by the very nature of creation, all things are endowed with their own solidity, truth, and goodness, their own laws and order. For that reason methodical research in all branches of knowledge, if it is carried out in a truly scientific way and in accord with moral norms, will never really conflict with faith, since profane realities and the things of faith have their origin from the same God... That is why we must deplore certain attitudes, which sometimes have been present among Christians because of a failure to perceive the rightful autonomy of science, attitudes which have occasioned conflicts and controversies that have led many to think that faith and science are opposed to one another.[11]

Only after this fundamental distinction did the Council then address the concrete history of human activity, interpreting it theologically in terms of the age-old dialectic of sin and grace and offering the central Christian message of redemption by which "all human activities, which are daily endangered by pride and inordinate self-love, are to be purified by the cross and resurrection of Christ and brought to their perfection" (*GS* 37). Human activity is not obliterated by the grace of the Gospel, but purified and fulfilled in Christ. As *Gaudium et Spes* says later, "The fact that the same God is both Savior and Creator, Lord of human history and of the history of salvation, does not mean that in this divine order the autonomy of the creature and particularly of man is taken away; on the contrary, this autonomy is restored to its dignity and confirmed in it" (*GS* 41).

The pertinence of this fundamental methodology to the discussion of liberalism should be apparent. The modern church's repudiation of liberalism opposed an ideal of freedom and autonomy which rested on a belief that one must choose between freedom and order, autonomy and creaturehood. This led, on the one hand, to Feuerbach's famous cry, "To enrich man, one must impoverish God," and, on the other, to the not uncommon Catholic habit of counterposing "the rights of God" to "the rights of man." The result was the cul-de-sac in which "Enlightenment" was considered by some to require emancipation from religion and modernity was thought by others to be nothing but "apostasy." The only way out of that dead-end was to start making distinctions which both sides had often been unwilling to make.

On the Council's part, this resulted in a much more positive appreciation of the driving principles of modernity than had been common before. The church not only had something to teach and to give the modern world; it had something to learn and to receive as well (GS 40–45). The distinctive forces and principles of the modern achievement could be acknowledged, not simply as an unfortunate present condition, but as ways in which the human race has begun more effectively to assume its God-given self-responsibility: "Far from considering the conquests of man's genius and courage to be opposed to God's power as if he set himself up as a rival to the Creator God, Christians ought to be convinced that the achievements of the human race are a sign of God's greatness and the fulfillment of his mysterious design" (GS 34).

This does not mean that the Council found nothing to criticize. In fact, *Gaudium et Spes* pointed out in many places the imbalances, injustices, and anxieties that modern developments had produced. As its distinctive response, the church offered its central teachings about God, Christ, and human persons – a Christologically centered humanism. This humanism can fully respect today's impetus towards human self-responsibility and self-realization, while identifying and responding to the evils that attend this impetus by proclaiming the message about Christ, sin, and redemption. In this broad and deep Christian humanism, the adjective does not cancel out the noun, as too often happened in "Catholic catastrophism." Nor does the noun exile the adjective, as too often occurred in doctrinaire liberalism.

On the foundations articulated in the first four chapters of *Gaudium et Spes*, the Council went on to speak about particular spheres of the modern world: marriage and the family, the world of culture, economic and social life, the political community, and the international community. In each sphere it attempted to articulate the encounter between fundamental Catholic beliefs and values and the specific conditions of modern life.

Perhaps most pertinent to our interests are the sections on economics and politics. The Council's statements on both spheres were governed by the general principle articulated in *GS* 43: "One of the gravest errors of our time is the dichotomy between the faith which many profess and the practice of their daily lives." These chapters were aimed at the individualistic morality that often underlies this split, the danger that modern differentiations of human life will consign religion to the sphere of the private and the intimate. If this is part of what is considered to constitute liberalism, then the Council clearly repudiates it, as, for example, when it insists on the pertinence to the field of economics of basic Christian truths and values (*GS* 63–72).

If political liberalism is taken to mean the assumption that the ordered life of society can do without those truths and values, the Council clearly opposed that also. The Council believed it possible to provide a religious legitimation for modern developments toward constitutional democracy (*GS* 73–75). But, given the modern Catholic attitude towards the question of church–state relations, it is quite striking that the Council did not deal with this issue in terms of institutional relationships. There is only the very quiet repetition of the traditional thesis: "The political community and the Church are autonomous and independent of each other in their own fields" (*GS* 76). Traditionally, this sentence prefaced a long and detailed analysis of the juridical relations that ought to exist between the two "perfect societies."[12] The Council, however, was content to speak simply of the need for the two communities to cooperate, with the church's contribution deriving from her preaching of her distinctive message: "By preaching the truth of the Gospel and by clarifying all the spheres of human activity through its teaching and the witness of the faithful, the Church respects and promotes the political freedom and responsibility of citizens." But if, in turn, the church makes use of temporal realities to accomplish its purpose, there is one that it would no longer count on: "It never places its hopes in any privileges accorded to it by civil authority; indeed, it will give up the exercise of certain legitimately acquired rights whenever it becomes clear that their use will compromise the sincerity of its witness or whenever new circumstances require another arrangement" (*GS* 76). If not a formal or complete rejection of the policy of concordats, this statement notably relativized an important practice of the Catholic church over the last two centuries. The church's effort to influence modern society would no longer be tied to or considered to coincide with its relationship with the state. This new stance was spelled out in more detail and consequence in the Council's Declaration on Religious Freedom.

Dignitatis Humanae

It was over the text of *Dignitatis Humanae* that the contest between liberalism and Catholicism was most dramatically fought at the Council. The Declaration on Religious Freedom remains the trump card played by those who accuse the Council of departing from Catholic truth and of capitulating to liberalism,[13] by which, of course, they mean the evil archetype condemned by Council authorities and apologists in the previous century. The evaluation of the Council's stance very much depends on whether this ideal-type represents all that can be meant by the word "liberalism."

The Declaration formally committed the Catholic church to the principle of religious freedom in modern society. It first defined this freedom negatively as "freedom from coercion in civil society" (*DH* 1). The civil right was then said to rest on the dignity of human persons who, if they are obliged to pursue truth and especially religious truth, cannot do so if they do not enjoy both "psychological freedom and immunity from external coercion" (*DH* 2). The truth can only be discovered by free inquiry and only acknowledged by free acts of faith. And this search and discovery transcend the sphere of the state's proper authority: "Civil authority, whose proper purpose is to care for the common temporal good, should acknowledge and favor the religious life of citizens, but it must be said to exceed its limits if it presumes to direct or to impede religious acts" (*DH* 3). The right to public exercise belongs to all religious groups and must be acknowledged and defended by civil authority. And, "if, because of the circumstances of a particular people, special civil recognition is given to one religious community in the constitutional organization of a society, the right of all citizens and religious communities to religious freedom must be recognized and respected as well" (*DH* 6).

Even this brief summary indicates how in this text, as Archbishop

Lefebvre was later bitterly to complain, the Council abandoned the ideal of the confessional state. Lefebvre sees in this act something close to an apostate capitulation to liberalism because he, first, identifies the latter with secularism, indifferentism, and relativism and, second, maintains that the only appropriate response to these threats is the confessional state. For Lefebvre, freedom does not rest on human dignity; freedom and human dignity itself rest ultimately on the possession of the truth: "The truth shall make you free." That is why it is intolerable to him that the one true religious community should be placed on a par with false religious communities. For him liberalism can only mean indifference to rival truth-claims in religion, while respect for the truth of Christianity implies the possibility and desirability of a Catholic state. For Lefebvre, therefore, *Dignitatis Humanae* was a major departure from the consistent and definitive anti-liberalism of modern Roman Catholicism.[14]

But in fact *Dignitatis Humanae* does not surrender the Catholic church's claim to be the true religion, and neither it nor any other conciliar document maintains that religion is a matter of indifference to the life of civil society. In that respect, the Council makes no concessions to doctrinaire liberalism. But the Council does adopt the modern political tradition of constitutional separation of church and state and its attendant guarantee of religious freedom to all persons and all religious groups. In that respect, the Council does accept the solution to the question of church and state often identified as political liberalism.

Historical and methodological presuppositions

Two sets of developments, one historical and one methodological, permitted the Council to adopt its more nuanced attitude toward liberal modernity. The historical development was largely the work of John Courtney Murray, who in the two decades before the Council attempted to introduce some distinctions into the massive repudiation of liberalism characteristic of modern Catholicism.[15] Murray argued that the liberalism so defined and so rejected was a distinctively continental (i.e., European) ideology. From it he distinguished an Anglo-Saxon liberal tradition whose roots he found in the medieval tradition and whose distinction between the *duo genera* of societies, the church and the civil order, was quite compatible with the Catholic insistence on the public significance and necessity of religion.

Continental liberalism, on the other hand, was the heir of the absolutism of the *ancien régime* and understood the separation of church and state to imply the irrelevance of religion to the public order and the sole right of the state to control all aspects of public life. For Murray, the church was correct in repudiating this ideology and practice, but it failed to take note of the quite different philosophy underlying the liberal tradition that inspired the American political experiment.[16]

The methodological development that enabled the Council to adopt its attitude toward the modern world was obscured during its debates, particularly in the early sessions. The bishops and theologians who constituted the "progressive" majority at the Council came together initially because of a common opposition to the faction that had dominated the preparation of the Council and that wished to see it do nothing more than ratify the attitudes and strategies of the previous century and a half. For a time, and particularly when dealing with questions about the church's internal life, this group formed a united body that was generally successful in breaking open the tight system into which Catholic Christianity had been stuffed before. But when the Council began to consider other questions and to undertake a consideration of what attitudes and strategies might take the place of the counter-modern sub-society, it began to become apparent that there were serious differences among the "progressives" themselves, not least of all over questions of theological method.[17]

At the risk of considerable over-simplification, one of these tensions might be described in terms of the traditional opposition thought to exist between "Augustinians" and "Thomists." (I prescind here from the question of how fair this contrast is to either Augustine or Thomas.) Two questions characterize the presence of this tension at the Council. The first might be put in this way: Granted that we can no longer be content with the anti-modern neurosis of recent Roman Catholicism, what attitude should the church adopt before the modern world? And, if we are to look to our past for examples of the church's engagement with contemporary culture, which is most pertinent to our day: the great Patristic enterprise which led to the creation of the Christian intellectual and cultural world, or the great Thomist effort to meet, confidently and discriminatingly, the challenge to that world represented in the medieval period by the introduction of Aristotelian philosophy and Arab science? Is the modern challenge more like one than the other? Or, perhaps, does it have features so distinctive that neither past cultural engagement provides useful lessons?

The second question concerns the method of critical engagement with the modern world, the theological epistemology one brings to bear. The typically Augustinian approach works with a sharp and unmediated distinction between sin and grace, natural reason and faith. The natural world appears to have no solidity or substance except as a sign pointing beyond itself to the spiritual and supernatural. The dramatic contest between sin and grace monopolizes attention, distracting it away from the natural, or rather subsuming the natural under the religious categories so that, on the one hand, we are *natura filii irae* and, on the other, our "true" nature is only recognized in the supernatural.

The typically Thomist approach, in contrast, effects a theoretical differentiation of the natural, not in order to deny that the drama of sin and grace is the only real drama of human history but in order to promote a more accurate understanding of it. "Nature," if you will, theoretically mediates the practical drama. It has its own solidity or substance, its own laws, its created autonomy. Sin is what falls short of or contradicts nature, and grace is what heals and transcendently fulfills nature. This permits one at once to differentiate the genuine limitations of nature without having to label them as sinful and to affirm the power of grace as the fulfillment and not the destruction of nature. This is why St. Thomas could embrace the new world opened to Christian culture by Aristotle's philosophy and by Arab science without believing, as many Augustinians did at the time, that this was a profanation of the sacred because it implied that an understanding of nature was possible in other than religious terms.

Two examples illustrate this: the ideas of freedom and of human intelligence. Typically an Augustinian will ask only about the uses to which freedom is being put and deal exclusively with the alternatives of freedom for the Lord or freedom for the self.[18] The typical Thomist will not deny that in fact these are the only two practical alternatives, but will seek also to understand freedom in its own structure and dynamics as these are displayed both in the sinner and in the one in love with God, and will use this understanding to show why the latter is the fulfillment of the inner dynamics of freedom while the former is its contradiction.

Similarly, Augustine's explanation of how a person comes to know spiritual truth, that is, truth beyond the sensibly given, appeals to divine illumination. Only God's direct enlightenment can bring the human mind beyond the sensible and transitory to the intelligible and eternal. St. Thomas, in contrast, domesticated the Augustinian illumination by speaking of the light of agent intellect as the created generative principle of understanding and judgment in each knower. For St. Thomas this light was also a participation in the uncreated Light of God's mind, but it was a created power, resident in each individual and making the human knower the active coagent in understanding and judging rather than the simply passive recipient that the knower appeared to be in the Augustinian view.

From this digression we can perhaps better appreciate what was at stake in the debates that took place late in the Council, particularly in connection with *Gaudium et Spes*.[19] The principal influence on the text came from French and Belgian bishops and theologians who might be called typically Thomist in orientation. Their text showed the Thomist effort to make distinctions, to try to identify the generative principles of the modern world, to understand them in and for themselves, only then to apply the categories of sin and grace to their development, and in doing this to be careful not to confuse nature and sin.

At a certain point in the discussion, a group of German bishops and theologians accused the text of indulging in a naturalism and "naive optimism." In typically Augustinian fashion, some of them read the Thomist distinctions as separations or at best juxtapositions of philosophy and theology, making Christianity a second world simply attached to the natural or reduced to the role of sacralizing contemporary progress. They felt that the reality of sin was being underemphasized both in the general anthropology and in the concrete analysis of the modern world. They asked for a stronger emphasis on the theology of the cross as symbolizing the necessity of conversion before the distinctive features of modernity could be welcomed. This was the same sort of criticism which St. Thomas received from the Augustinians in the thirteenth century; it was also a prominent element in the critique of the baroque Scholasticism that had hardened Thomas's distinction into a separation.[20] For some critics, the changes made in the final text of *Gaudium et Spes* were not enough to prevent its being accused of a naturalistic semi-Pelagianism or of naive optimism, which a larger dose of Augustinianism might have prevented.[21]

THE RECEPTION OF THE COUNCIL

The twenty-five years since the Council closed have seen such dramatic developments in both church and modern society as to make the discussion of Catholicism and liberalism during this period so complex as to prohibit analysis or evaluation in a single essay.[22] I wish to focus the question by exploring the continued relevance of the distinction Murray made between the broad liberal tradition he believed not only to be compatible with fundamental Catholic beliefs and values but in part to be inspired by them and the doctrinaire liberalism whose exclusion of religion from public consequence he believed to be radically incompatible with Catholicism, both philosophically and theologically.

There is a certain validity in seeing this as a distinction between liberal political *structures*, which the church can accept, and a liberal *ideology*, which it must repudiate. The establishment of constitutional democracy and the guaranteeing of civil rights, after all, are not minor achievements. In general, Catholics since the Council have been unreserved in their adherence to them. Popes since the Council have powerfully endorsed democratic constitutional government, generalized religious freedom, and human rights as criteria of political justice. Several concordats have been revised and brought into accord with *Dignitatis Humanae*. Some years ago, it is true, concern over outrageous economic inequalities led a few theologians to dismiss questions of political rights as either irrelevant to or trivial in comparison with questions of economic rights; but this flirtation with Marxist ideas was largely confined to countries with little experience of liberal democracy and has lately been almost universally abandoned. Only in marginal figures like Archbishop Lefebvre has the Council's surrender of the ideal of the confessional state been severely criticized. In that sense one could say that the Council's acceptance of the political structures of the broad liberal tradition has been echoed in the larger Catholic body. In principle church–state relationships are no longer a theoretical problem, and we appear to be at the end of the long era of constitutional controversy over the question of the confessional state.

The question that remains cannot be left at the level of formal constitutional structures. After the question of church–state relationships – the question of the confessional state – is settled, there remains the question of the relation between church and society. If freedom is the operative word in both questions, settling the question of freedom as immunity from coercion must raise the question of the uses to which freedom is put. Here too the point is to follow the Council in insisting that the church must have a role in the definition and constitution of what Murray called "the spiritual substance of society."[23]

The question of truth and genuine value thus returns even more acutely. The issue is whether the construction of society is possible simply on the basis of a formal notion of freedom, as "freedom from," which leaves in suspense or perhaps even considers unresolvable the question of "freedom for." This is the question not only of the purposes for which freedom of conscience is being used, but also of the cultural, ethical, and even religious presuppositions which underlie the very choice of a liberal political order. Put most simply, does the *constitutional* indifference of the state imply *substantive* cultural indifference to questions of truth and value?

It is perhaps at this point that the real problem of the church with liberalism lies: the question of genuine values cannot be avoided, nor that of the foundation of these rights. Even in the midst of Vatican II's acceptance of the liberal political solution, there persists a view of the foundations of rights which differs from that of classical political liberalism. Rights do not belong to isolated individuals, pre-political monads, for whom society is a later, man-made artifact. Rights adhere in persons living in communities. Strictly speaking, a monad has no rights, for there is no one to respect them. Embodiment in society is precisely the origin of rights, and this embodiment is prior to and explains the construction of a political order to secure them. On this point the Council did not make any concession to liberal philosophy.

At least on Murray's reading of the history and the theories, then, the confrontation with liberalism raised issues deeper than those of formal structure. Behind the broader liberal tradition which he defended there also lay a set of ideas about the relationship between these political structures and the truths and values contained in what he called "the public consensus." This consensus was so basic to the political arrangement that without it the structures could not achieve their desired ends. It included the central conviction that religious and moral principles were constitutive elements of the spiritual substance of human society. The Council's endorsement of the broad liberal tradition, then, was legitimate not simply because it included a repudiation of the liberal ideology, but also because and to the degree that it also continued to insist on the public relevance of religion enshrined in the broad tradition.

Thus the more acute question concerns the *substance* of the societies now organized on the liberal premise, what Bruce Douglass in his essay for this volume calls "the cultural foundations of our public life." In the early 1950s, in the midst of the controversy caused by his views, Murray complained about the inability of even his Catholic opponents to distinguish between the continental ideology and the American "proposition" and about their consequent reduction of the question of church and society to the question of church and state. Not so oddly, doctrinaire liberals suffered from the same inability and made the same mistake. And, if, as it sometimes seems, the same faults return today when questions about the spiritual substance of our society are again confused with the question of church and state, it may be because something close to doctrinaire liberalism has largely replaced the consensus which underlay the original American experiment.

Murray was always addressing two audiences, Catholic intransigents and doctrinaire liberals. If in the end he succeeded in confuting the Catholic opposition, he was far less successful with his secularist opponents. In one of his early essays Murray noted that some people were beginning to abandon "the original principles of American constitutionalism" and to justify the separation of church and state with a theory similar to nineteenth-century doctrinaire liberalism.[24] By the time, seven years later, when he put together his book, *We Hold These Truths*, this trend had reached the point that it became a chief target of his argument. The substance of society had been evacuated as the broad religious and moral principles which had once directed and legitimated it were replaced by a consensus which had now only one tenet: "an agreement to disagree."

When Murray argued that "no society in history has ever achieved and maintained an identity and a vigor in action unless it has had some substance, unless it has been sustained and directed by some body of substantive beliefs," he was met by an appeal to the "free society," for which a purely procedural consensus could suffice:

It involves no agreement on the premises and purposes of political life and legal institutions; it is solely an agreement with regard to the method of making decisions and getting things done, whatever the things may be. The substance of American society is our "democratic institutions," conceived as purely formal categories. These institutions have no content; they are simply channels through which any kind of content may flow. In the end, the only life-or-death question for American society is that it should live or die under punctilious regard for correct democratic procedures.[25]

Murray regarded these views as the return in democratic form of the same monism that the church had earlier resisted when it appeared in absolutist and Jacobin forms. Its rejection of the public pertinence of substantive beliefs was being assisted by a spreading sense that basic philosophical and moral differences were not publicly adjudicable, because faith in reason was collapsing and people were coming to regard them as merely matters of personal decision. The result was "the contemporary idolatry of the democratic process":

What is urged is a monism, not so much of the political order itself, as of a political technique. The proposition is that all the issues of human life – intellectual, religious, and moral issues as well as formally political issues – are to be regarded as, or resolved into, political issues and are to be settled by the single omnicompetent political technique of majority vote.[26]

In Murray's view, this procedural monism surrendered belief in transcendent norms, attainable by reason, for passing judgment on civil polities. These transcendent norms defined the distinction of realms which Christianity had contributed to Western political thought.

If there is any truth to these observations on American society and if, as I would be tempted to argue, the tendencies Murray identified have grown and spread even more in the subsequent thirty years, then the question arises whether the debate has not returned to the central issue which in the last century set Catholicism and liberalism over against one another. Only the basic issue is now much more clearly seen to be, not the indifferentism and laicism of *the state*, but the indifferentism and laicism of *society*. Murray did not regret that the state was now considered incompetent to judge among rival religious claims. He did regret that, increasingly, the society was coming to believe that religion and morality were realms in which truth-questions either do not arise or are not capable of being publicly debated and resolved. His endorsement of "the lay state" was never an acceptance of a lay, that is, secularized, society.

This perspective sheds considerable light on recent discussions of the relationship of church and society. One senses, for example, that the sudden intervention of some Protestant fundamentalists in the social and political arenas was prompted by a rather belated recognition that the United States had ceased to be a society in which Christian beliefs and values are respected and honored. A year or so ago, many people were astonished to read that the Supreme Court had once taken it for granted that the United States is a "religious people," even a Christian one. Richard John Neuhaus's "naked public square" in many ways describes the substantive vacuum which Murray had predicted.

Murray's distinction also illumines recent statements of the church's social teaching. Recent popes have addressed the problem of the Western social consensus in their severe critiques of consumerism and materialism. Long before Gorbachev began to speak of "a common European home," John Paul II was trying to evoke the substantive beliefs and values that marked "the common Christian roots of Europe." Cardinal Ratzinger's analysis of the condition of the post-conciliar church includes an indictment of Catholics' surrender to the culture of "the tertiary bourgeoisie," an invocation of a post-modern "return to the sacred" aroused by the spiritual vacuity of modern society, and an argument that the proper point of insertion of the church is not a "political theology" but a "political ethic," that is, the mediation of the moral principles on which a genuine democracy must be built.[27] Finally, there are the difficulties encountered by the US bishops in their efforts to claim a voice in the public debates on war and economics and in their efforts to define the public responsibilities of Catholics on the issue of abortion.

The latter incidents are perhaps particularly illustrative of the contemporary debate. The descriptive language often heard in the debates is here especially revealing, as, for example, when the bishops are said to have been "liberal" in their pastoral letters on nuclear weapons and on economic justice, whereas on the abortion issue several of them are considered by many to be quite anti-liberal, an accusation which arises not solely out of legitimate concerns about methods but also out of substantive ideas about a "liberal" society.

But it can be argued that in both cases the bishops were making the same fundamental effort. They were trying, that is, to address, to shape, to evoke a societal consensus on the moral issues involved. This is an effort which is quite compatible with Murray's broad liberal tradition, which acknowledged the need for a basic public consensus that the state could neither guarantee nor do without. It is not compatible with classic continental liberalism, whose individualism and indifferentism either saw no need for a public consensus or denied religion a role in shaping it. Nor is it compatible with a procedural monism which resolves all issues into political issues for which the sole determining rule is majority-vote.

But behind this procedural monism and partly explaining the differing assessments of the legitimacy of the bishops' interventions often lie sets of substantive assumptions which deny them a right to a "prophetical" voice in one or the other of the two cases. One group will deny them a right to address issues of military or economic policy but concede it on matters of family morality; the other group will welcome them into the first arena but, accepting the reduction of the issue of abortion to a matter of "choice," "privacy," and "reproductive freedom," will see in their actions here an illegitimate intrusion into public morality and invoke the spectre of an attack upon the separation of church and state.

The US bishops' task has been rendered more difficult because of the loss of a common belief that a public consensus on anything more substantial than democratic procedures is either possible or desirable. The bishops argue, of course, that their intervention into the public debates is not based solely on confessional religious principles but can be justified by appeals to moral principles presumably held generally throughout the society. But in neither case do they seem to have convinced anyone not already in agreement with their particular conclusions. It may be that the chief problem which they face and which they have not been notably successful in addressing is a widespread belief that *no* ethical, much less religious, beliefs or values are more than the products of personal choice.

That this may be the case is indicated by the similarity between contemporary controversies over American culture, which pit individualists over and against communitarians or relativists over and against defenders of a public reason, and the confrontation between doctrinaire liberals and Catholics in the last two centuries. Atomistic and possessive individualism is precisely what Catholic apologists considered to be the original sin of the liberal ideology. That societies could be constructed around a consensus that is no longer substantive but merely procedural was what they meant when they accused liberals of relativism and indifferentism. When they condemned the liberal project as a modern form of Pelagianism, they were giving a theological interpretation of what they took to be the liberal claim that the procedures and structures of democracy could by themselves guarantee the construction of a just and genuinely free society.

What is the relevance of all this for an assessment of Vatican II's confrontation with liberal modernity? It seems to me to make it far more difficult to be content with simplifying interpretations, for these are defined by a refusal or reluctance to make distinctions. Those who see the Council's achievement as a naive capitulation to modernity often fail to distinguish not only between the particular social form Catholicism adopted in the last century and a half and the permanent essence of the church but also between the liberal political structures of modern democracies and the liberal ideology which often legitimates them. Those who celebrate the Council as a long-overdue accommodation to modernity often focus on its acceptance of many of the liberal structures of the day but ignore or play down the Council's insistence on the substantive relevance of religion to society. If the one group tends to demonize modernity, the other tends to deify it; and it is not hard to see why they encourage one another's simplicities. I would myself continue to insist that the key is still St. Thomas's general methodological injunction: "Distinguendum est!" and its more particular embodiment in the attempt to elaborate a basic social anthropology for which human nature and the dynamics of its individual and social self-constitution are respected for what they are, a dynamic structure which is neither utterly corrupted by sin nor rendered superfluous by grace.

This is not to say that the Council represents a completely adequate solution to our questions today. The Council defined a major shift (some have not hesitated to call it "epochal"[28]), and it is not to be expected that it saw everything clearly or got everything right or anticipated all eventualities. But one thing it did get right: that it was possible to address the church's rights and responsibilities in the modern world without relying on the easy certainties of either liberalism or anti-modern Catholicism.

NOTES

1 See *What is Liberalism?* Englished and Adapted from the Spanish of Dr. Don Felix Sarda y Salvany by Condé B. Pallen (St. Louis: Herder, 1899) (the original Spanish title of this book was: "Liberalism is Sin"); A. Roussel, *Liberalisme et catholicisme. Rapports présentés à la "Semaine*

Catholique" en *Février 1926 sous les auspices de la Ligue Apostolique pour le retour des Nations à l'ordre social chrétien* (Paris: Aux Bureaux de la "Ligue Apostolique," 1926) (a work on which Archbishop Lefebvre continues to draw). For an illustration of this assessment of liberal modernity, see the early work of Jacques Maritain, *Antimoderne*, 2nd edn. (Paris: Desclée, 1922), particularly chapter 5: "Réflexions sur le temps présent," 195–223.

2 See Joseph A. Komonchak, "The Enlightenment and the Construction of Roman Catholicism," *Annual of the Catholic Commission on Intellectual and Cultural Affairs* (1985): 31–59.

3 Syllabus of Errors, prop. 80 (Henricus Denzinger and Adolphus Schömetzer, eds., *Enchiridion Symbolorum*, editio xxxii [Rome: Herder, 1963], no. 1780).

4 An introduction to and a critical text of the Pope's speech can be found in Giuseppe Alberigo and Alberto Melloni, "L'allocuzione *Gaudet Mater Ecclesia* di Giovanni XXIII (11 ottobre 1962)," in *Fede Tradizione Profezia: Studi su Giovanni XXIII e sul Vaticano II* (Brescia: Paideia, 1984), 187–283.

5 The Holy Office's "Schema pro Concilio Oecumenico" can be found in *Acta et Documenta Concilio Oecumenico Vaticano II Apparando*, Series I (Antepraeparatoria), vol. III (Typis Polyglottis Vaticanis, 1960), 3–17.

6 Joseph Ratzinger, *Theological Highlights of Vatican II* (New York: Paulist Press, 1966), 23.

7 See *AAS* 54 (1962): 678–685.

8 See Joseph Ratzinger, "Church and World: An Inquiry into the Reception of Vatican Council II," in *Principles of Catholic Theology: Building Stones for a Fundamental Theology* (San Francisco: Ignatius Press, 1987), 378–379.

9 See the important essay by Giuseppe Ruggieri, "Appunti per una teologia in Papa Roncalli," in *Papa Giovanni*, ed. Giuseppe Alberigo (Bari: Laterza, 1987), 245–271, particularly his comment on p. 256 that Pope John did not counterpose the "doctrinal" to the "pastoral," as if the latter were simply a matter of "applications," but saw the pastoral dimension as an "historical imperative" intrinsic to doctrine: "the historical hermeneutics of Christian truth."

10 There is a good description of them all in *GS* 54.

11 *GS* 36. The translations of the documents of Vatican II are from Austin Flannery, ed., *Vatican Council II: The Conciliar and Post-Conciliar Documents*, revised edn. (Northport, NY: Costello, 1988). This discussion of autonomy is the closest the Council comes to a treatment of effect of the differentiations usually referred to as "secularization," a term the Council never uses.

12 A chapter on church–state relations prepared for a document on the church had repeated the "classical" teaching on the ideal "thesis" and the tolerated "hypothesis;" see *Acta Synodalia Sacrosancti Concilii Oecu-*

menici Vaticani II, 1/iv (Typis Polyglottis Vaticanis, 1971), 65–74, and, for a brief summary, Richard J. Regan, *Conflict and Consensus: Religious Freedom and the Second Vatican Council* (New York: Macmillan, 1967), 24–26.

13 See Archbishop Marcel Lefebvre's two books, *Lettre ouverte aux catholiques perplexes* (Paris: Albin Michel, 1985) and *Ils l'ont découronné: Du liberalisme à l'apostasie, La tragédie conciliaire* (Excurolles: Ed. "Fideliter", 1987), in which he stops just short of regarding this document as heretical. Francesco Spadafora, *La tradizione contro il Concilio* (Rome: Volpe, 1989), 239–247, has recently asked whether the Congregation for the Interpretation of the Decrees of Vatican II should not respond to the accusation that the Council, by surrendering in this text to liberalism, has called into question the infallibility of the magisterium.

14 Joseph Ratzinger's description of *Gaudium et Spes* as "a revision of the *Syllabus* of Pius IX, a kind of countersyllabus" (*Principles of Catholic Theology*, 381–382), is cited by Archbishop Lefebvre as evidence for his view that Vatican II departed from orthodox tradition; see *Ils l'ont découronné*, 184n.

15 See Donald E. Pelotte, *John Courtney Murray: Theologian in Conflict* (New York: Paulist Press, 1976); J. Leon Hooper, *The Ethics of Discourse: The Social Philosophy of John Courtney Murray* (Washington: Georgetown University Press, 1986).

16 In general it may be said that Vatican II chose Murray's historical analysis over the one which underlies Lefebvre's position.

17 "What was at stake was not this or that theory, this or that special scholarly question, but the form in which the Word of God was to be presented and spiritually interpreted. Here the preparatory text [on the sources of revelation] was unsatisfactory, and the Council rejected the extant texts. But the question at this point was: What now?" (Ratzinger, *Theological Highlights of Vatican II*, 148). Later he describes the split that occurred when the draft of *Gaudium et Spes* began to be debated in 1965: "it became clear that the old conflict of 'integrists' and progressives promised to break down. No longer was there the old majority and the old minority; new lines had formed to face new tasks and new problems... a certain conflict between German and French theology began to be visible" (*Ibid.*, 151).

18 For an example, see Joseph Ratzinger, "Freedom and Liberation: The Anthropological Vision of 1986 Instruction *Libertatis Conscientia*," in *Church, Ecumenism and Politics: New Essays in Ecclesiology* (New York: Crossroad, 1988), 255–275, where the "two contrasting conceptions of history and freedom between which we have to choose" are described as "anarchy" and "constraint."

19 For this discussion, see Charles Moeller, "History of the Constitution," in *Commentary on the Documents of Vatican II*, 5 vols. (New York: Herder and Herder, 1969), v: 58–61; Philippe Delhaye, "Histoire des textes de

la Constitution pastorale," in *L'Eglise dans le monde de ce temps*, vol. I (Unam Sanctam, 65a; Paris: Editions du Cerf, 1967), 267–273; Ratzinger, *Theological Highlights*, 147–171.

20 See J. A. Komonchak, "Theology and Culture at Mid-Century: The Example of Henri de Lubac," *Theological Studies* 51 (1990): 579–602. Although de Lubac's *Surnaturel* was in good part an effort to rescue Thomas from the Thomists, it is also clear that de Lubac believed that many traces of original sin remained after Aquinas's effort to "baptize" Aristotle.

21 See, for example, the interplay between Thomism and Augustinianism in Ratzinger's discussion of the anthropology found in *GS* 12–17, in *Commentary on the Documents of Vatican II*, vol. V, 119–140.

22 A full treatment would have to include at least such topics as: the rapid collapse of the Roman Catholic sub-culture and of its theological legitimation in Neoscholasticism; the peripaties of theological developments from "secularization-theology" to political theology to liberation theology to a theology of democratic capitalism; the development of Catholic social teaching from *Populorum Progressio* to the Medellín documents to *Octagesima Adveniens* to the Synod of 1971 to *Laborem Exercens* to the Vatican critique of liberation theology to *Sollicitudo Rei Socialis*; the critique of liberalism in the 1960s; the transformation of Western culture; the affirmations of "post-modernity" and the "return of the sacred"; the return of "fundamentalism"; the efforts of the church to make its voice heard in the public arena (US bishops' pastoral letters); the responsibilities of Catholic public officials, etc.

23 This phrase and variants on it occur often in Murray's writings: "the traditional substance of Western society," "the social relevance of the Christian patrimony," "the Christian substance of society," "the spiritual substance of social life," etc. In *We Hold These Truths* (New York: Sheed & Ward, 1960) it seems to be what is described as the "social consensus": "It is not the residual minimum left after rigid application of the Cartesian axiom, '*de omnibus dubitandum*.' It is not simply a set of working hypotheses whose value is pragmatic. It is an ensemble of substantive truths, a structure of basic knowledge, an order of elementary affirmations that reflect realities inherent in the order of existence. It occupies an established position in society and excludes opinions alien or contrary to itself. This consensus is the intuitional a priori of all the rationalities and technicalities of constitutional and statutory law. It furnishes the premises of the people's action in history and defines the larger aims which that action seeks in internal affairs and in external relations" (pp. 9–10).

24 John Courtney Murray, "Leo XIII: Separation of Church and State," *Theological Studies* 14 (1953): 151n.

25 *We Hold These Truths*, 84.

26 *Ibid.*, 208.

27 See *Church, Ecumenism and Politics,* 204–275.
28 This view, which was popularly expressed even during the Council in such phrases as "the end of the Constantinian, or the Counter-Reformation, or the Tridentine age," has been argued more carefully in many of the writings of Giuseppe Alberigo. It also appears in Hermann Joseph Pottmeyer's hermeneutics of the Council as a "transitional event"; see "A New Phase in the Reception of Vatican II: Twenty Years of Interpretation of the Council," *The Reception of Vatican II,* ed. G. Alberigo, J.-P. Jossua, and J. A. Komonchak (Washington: The Catholic University of America Press, 1988), 27–43. It is severely criticized in the revisionist interpretation of the Council given in *The Ratzinger Report.*

CHAPTER 4

Liberalism after the good times: the "end of history" in historical perspective

R. Bruce Douglass

What we may in fact be witnessing is not just the passing of a particular period of postwar history, but the endpoint of mankind's ideological evolution and the emergence of Western liberal democracy as the final form of government.

Francis Fukuyama

In culture, as well as politics, liberalism is now up against the wall.

Daniel Bell

This is an essay about the future of liberalism in the light of its past. It is designed to recall some of what liberals have been through in the recent past in order to make sense of where they are now headed. And in particular it is intended to bring to light the complexity – and uncertainty – of the fate that awaits them.

This is not something, needless to say, which can be taken for granted. For now that events are turning out well for them, there is a predictable tendency on the part of liberals (as well as many others) to assume that their present success has a simple, straightforward meaning. Hence the talk we are hearing of their having "won" the great ideological competition of our time and even of "history" having come to an end in the process – all of which gives the impression that it is obvious what has taken place and where it leads.[1] But it is not. And the more one knows of the actual history of the events in question, I would submit, the more evident it is that this is the case.

In particular, moreover, I mean to challenge the suggestion of finality that is implicit in talk of this sort. For no matter what conclusion may be drawn about the fate that has befallen its competitors, it is just not the case that anything permanent has been settled about the fate of liberalism itself. Not even concerning its role in the public life of rich, technologically advanced societies like the

United States. This is true despite the fact that there is, I think, no denying that it is well on its way to establishing itself as just the sort of hegemonic force in such societies that liberals tend to assume it is. For even though, as the reader will discover, I am prepared to concede that this is so, I do not think that it makes sense to draw from this success the conclusions that liberals are now inclined to draw. Not at all. Indeed, it will be my argument that it makes better sense to conclude just the *opposite*.

Specifically, my thesis is this: far from having now secured for itself a position as the "end point of mankind's ideological evolution,"[2] liberalism has, by virtue of the victory that it has won, actually entered a period in its development in which it is likely to be tested as severely as it has ever been before. And it cannot be taken for granted it will successfully rise to the challenge. For even though in the past it has shown extraordinary adaptability (which is the reason, in my view, why it is still viable when most of its erstwhile competitors are not), it is not at all clear that it is going to have what it will take to meet *this* particular test.

The test I have in mind is a result of the success enjoyed by liberalism in recent years. And it will be my argument that it is unavoidable. I see it arising as a natural by-product of the decline in influence of alternative ways of thinking that an ascendant liberalism can be expected to supplant. For the other side, of course, of allowing ourselves to fall increasingly under the sway of the kind of mentality that is characteristic of liberals is that we shall be less influenced by other ways of looking at things. People can be expected, therefore, to conduct their lives in a manner that is (ever) more consistently liberal. And as we contemplate this prospect, one has to wonder what it will mean for the benefits that, historically, have come from thinking in other ways. Some of them, at least (virtues of the sort that have come from religious belief or strong family ties, for example), will be hard to do without. In fact, *liberals themselves* will need to be able to rely on them if they are to be successful in pursuing the projects (distributive justice, for example) that matter to them. And it will be up to them to see to it, in turn, that substitutes are found.

What makes this so urgent, moreover, is that one can well imagine things working out in just the opposite way. One can imagine, that is, the emergence of what can only be described as a liberal nightmare. In fact, as we know all too well, this is not just something to be imagined: in some respects, at least, it is materializing right before our eyes. For in several different ways, ranging from what is happening to the family to the state of popular culture in our time, it is clear that we are well on our way to creating a way of life that in important respects is subversive of the habits of mind and heart that are needed if the humane ends that liberals profess to serve are to stand a chance of being realized.

Indeed, if the tendency that these developments represent is carried very far, it can easily end up being subversive of almost everything we value – which is why, increasingly, it is becoming a matter of public concern. And it is also, of course, why liberals themselves are beginning to be concerned about it.[3] But it is one thing to recognize a problem and quite another to solve it. And there is more than one reason, I believe, for doubting that they will in fact be able to take the necessary steps to come to terms effectively with the challenge that it poses. For to do so would be not just to recast fundamentally what the liberal project is about (which has been done before, of course, more than once), but also to redefine the relationship liberals have to the entire trajectory that modern societies are on (which has *not* been done). It would thus be to redirect liberalism, turning it into a serious critic of the very way of life that has been the source of the success that it now enjoys.

That is a tall order. And it is why it does not make sense for liberals to pay a lot of attention to their recent press clippings. For if the change of direction I am proposing turns out to be something that they cannot accomplish, in a few years liberalism itself could end up looking just as flawed (and dated) as its old competitors do now. But if that were in fact to happen, we would all be the worse for it. Given the hegemonic role that liberalism has come to play in our way of life, a good deal more is at stake than just the fate of an ideology. And that above all, I shall argue, is why it is not a foregone conclusion how things will turn out. There are – and will continue to be – formidable practical pressures drawing liberals to rethink what they stand for along the lines I am suggesting.

All of this, however, needs to be explained more fully. I need to say more about what sort of rethinking I have in mind. And I need to say more about what I understand liberalism now to be, as well as how – and why – it came to be that way. For it is clearly liberalism of a certain sort, one which is the product of a particular phase in the development of liberal thinking, that is at issue. So in what follows I shall be focusing attention on the past just as much as on the present, starting with an account of the last major crisis liberals had to face. For the fact that that crisis was resolved as it was is, in a very real sense, the reason why liberalism is what – and where – it is today.

The idea that liberalism occupies a privileged place in the experience of nations that have succeeded in making democratic institutions work is not, to be sure, exactly a new one. One need only have a passing familiarity with the writing of liberals from decades past to know this is an idea they have long harbored. But until recently this idea could not possibly be held in the form that we are now familiar with. In fact, as late as half a century ago, there would have been no sense in making the sort of claims that are presently being made on its behalf. For liberal thinking and the institutions with which it was associated all too obviously were in crisis, and even its staunchest adherents had to wonder whether the crisis was one that could successfully be weathered.

We all too easily forget how widespread was the disaffection with liberal thinking in the inter-war period. In particular, by the 1930s a large part of the population of Europe was prepared to go along with what amounted to a principled repudiation of most of what liberals stood for. From both the Right and the Left came attacks that went to the very core of liberalism, and events showed all too clearly how prepared those who held such views were to act on them. It was a time, even in countries that did not succumb to the lure of illiberal thinking, of ideological polarization, when it simply would not have occurred to informed observers to speak of anything like a liberal hegemony.

It was readily apparent, too, why this "counter-revolution" (as Walter Lippmann was to characterize it) had the force that it did.[4] Especially as the consequences of the Depression made themselves felt, the economic arrangements in particular with which liberals were identified could not help but come under fire. Nor did it take long before the vulnerabilities of the political practices they favored were exposed as well. With mass unemployment and epidemic bankruptcies, the sheen soon went off representative government in all but a few countries, and it all too readily took on the appearance of a luxury that could not be afforded. Even in the better established democracies, in fact, there was no little uncertainty about whether the institutions that liberals favored would successfully weather the storm, and the democratic prospect was anything but taken for granted.[5]

For their part, liberals, too, were hard put to avoid taking responsibility for the crisis into which Western institutions had fallen. There continued, to be sure, to be purists who conceded nothing and insisted that all would have been well if only the societies in question had not allowed themselves to be beguiled by the nostrums offered by their opponents. But for every Hayek there were several Keyneses and Deweys who were quite prepared to admit that it was liberal ideas themselves that in no small part lay behind the troubles the industrialized countries were having, and they took it as axiomatic that major revisions of liberal thinking were in order. Many of the very things that the purists were inclined to celebrate about liberalism were singled out, in fact, by the reformers as being in need of revision, and it was not at all uncommon to find liberals acknowledging the obsolescence of much of their theoretical inheritance.[6]

Nor was it just the more obvious sources of political and economic discontent that were called into question as this self-criticism unfolded, either. The presumption against an active role for government in economic life that was dictated by the historic liberal commitment to *laissez-faire*, for example, could scarcely help but come in for criticism, and with results that were predictable. But a good deal more came under fire as well. The unsettling experience of running directly up against the wave of anti-democratic sentiment that made itself felt in the inter-war years threw the apologetic resources available to liberals into sharp relief, and not surprisingly, it prompted doubts about their adequacy. Especially as many liberals themselves went out of their way to deny the possibility of reasoned discrimination among ends (political and otherwise) was there bound to be uncertainty – and uneasiness – in this regard. It could only grow, moreover, as critics proposed that it was *liberal* skepticism, born of positivist influences, that had contributed significantly to the breakdown of democratic government in some countries.[7]

THE UNCERTAIN AFTERMATH

Nor did this mood pass away quickly. The decisive victory of the Allies in their military showdown with the Axis powers went a long way, admittedly, toward relieving liberal anxieties, and the re-establishment of constitutional democracy in one country after another gave reason for renewed optimism about the prospect of a successful recovery from the crisis of the Depression era. But these events did not lead at all to an immediate recovery of liberal confidence. For a number of years after the cessation of hostilities, in fact, the mood was anything but confident, and with good reason.

In the countries that had been ravaged by the war there was particular uncertainty about the course that events would take as the reconstruction unfolded. The anti-democratic Right might have been discredited as a political force, but its counterpart on the Left was not. Because of the role which they had played in the Resistance, Communists emerged out of the experience of the war in a number of countries with more popular appeal than ever, and they made no bones about what their intentions were.

For all the desire to establish the regimes in question on a more secure foundation, moreover, there was no guarantee the old sources of instability would not reappear. The Fourth Republic in France, for example, was all too reminiscent of its predecessor, and as late as de Gaulle's seizure of power at the end of the 1950s, it was still an open question among informed observers whether democratic government could in fact be constituted in that country in a form that would not yield paralyzing divisions. And even with the effort that was devoted to purging Germany and its allies of fascist influences, it was scarcely to be taken for granted that the democratic reconstruction of their politics was going to succeed.[8] Nor was there any reason to assume that the economic troubles were over, either. Especially in view of the toll that the war had taken on the productive capacities of much of the European heartland, optimism was anything but justified. The likely prospect, it appeared, was for a protracted period of rebuilding, fraught with uncertainties. The memory of the events that had followed the previous war was all too vivid, and few informed observers were confident they would not be repeated.

As the Cold War took shape, too, it was evident that liberal thinking was still laboring under the spell of the traumatic events of the previous quarter century. It was a time when even American liberals spoke darkly of the threat to civilization posed by the anomic tendencies in modern life,[9] and a recovery of Augustinian pessimism was greeted as intellectual progress. Among intellectuals in particular optimism was out of fashion, and it was not just radical ideas that met with skepticism.

RECOVERY (OF NERVE)

Even as this mood was coming into its own as a climate of opinion, however, the way was being prepared for something very different to take its place. With the realization that a sustained economic recovery of unprecedented proportions was in the making, it became evident that the days of liberal self-doubt were numbered. One fear after another dissolved as the effects of the resulting affluence began to be felt, and it was not long at all before there was an optimistic, if not triumphant, assurance in the pronouncements of liberal spokesmen of a sort that had not been heard in decades.

It was not just, of course, the mere fact of affluence that brought this about. The sheer magnitude of the economic progress Western Europe experienced was impressive by any standard, to be sure, and it could not help but catch the imagination of people who were expecting so much less. But what really altered the tenor of liberal thinking was the fact that the growth was as sustained as it was, and that there was reason to believe that this was no accident. There was scarcely any historical precedent for the continuous expansion of output, consumption, and investment that took place, and it could not escape attention that the governments of the countries in question had devoted themselves to the active management of economic life in ways that had shown themselves to be conducive to this result. A "new" sort of capitalism was clearly in the making, learned from hard lessons about the pursuit of stable prosperity. And the longer the growth went on, the more people were inclined to assume the economic problems of the past had been effectively solved.[10]

Every bit as impressive, too, was the fact the prosperity being achieved was not purchased at the price of deprivation for the majority of the population. Quite the contrary. The benefits were spread widely, and in fact high levels of employment and steadily expanding consumer demand were treated as essential to economic progress. As John K. Galbraith in particular emphasized, affluence for the many was coming to be an economic as well as a political necessity.[11] If production was going to be maintained at the desired level, consumption had to be cultivated as a way of life.

Social policy underwent a comparable development as the welfare state came into its own as a source of entitlements. As a result of common hardships imposed by both the Depression and the war, the prejudice against collective provision faded, and in its place emerged a commitment to insuring each citizen freedom from want as a matter of right. Nor was it merely the avoidance of poverty that was intended, either. From "cradle to grave" (in the words of a famous liberal apologist for the English version of this development[12]) the state was to see to it that no one lacked access to basic goods and services. Especially as tax revenues multiplied and the idea of equality of opportunity caught on, there was even a tendency to think in terms of guaranteeing a certain quality of life as well.

Once these arrangements began to fall into place, there was no mistaking their political effectiveness, either. For it soon became evident how effective they were in dissolving opposition. The dissolution was never complete, to be sure, but it did not take long before opponents found themselves marginalized. Not least because of the enormous popular appeal that this blend of policies elicited, a consensus was building among the forces in serious contention for power. And the longer the recovery lasted, the stronger it tended to be. Instead of falling into conflict, therefore, the democracies suddenly began to look like models of stability. Even the newly constituted ones, such as the Federal Republic of Germany, took on an appearance of strength that would have been unthinkable only a few years before. And the fears of instability that had figured so prominently in political analyses then were promptly dispatched to memories of a time gone by.

THE (MOMENTARY) END OF IDEOLOGY

It was compromise that made all of this possible, of course. Especially between liberals and socialists, whose ideas tended to dominate public debate after the war. Liberal individualism was being significantly qualified to make room for the assumption of public responsibility for the fate of individuals. And for their part socialists abandoned a doctrinaire belief in "collectivism." Social Democrats, at least, made it clear in practice as well as pronouncements that they were no longer wedded to thinking in the old categorical terms and were prepared to pursue their objectives on the terrain provided by the emerging blend of public and private power. The more experience each had with collaboration on what was clearly turning out to be common ground, moreover, the stronger the appeal of accommodation tended to become.

This, in turn, is what made it thinkable that the end of ideology might be at hand. And, as part of the same argument, it was what made it possible, too, to hazard the thought that at long last a set of political and economic practices was emerging that actually would fulfill the promise of modern life.[13] With ideological passions cooling and partisans in a mood to look beyond past mistakes, it was not at all unreasonable to infer, in fact, that what was in the making was a creative blend of the old opposites. So planning would be joined with reliance on the market, and the old choices – liberty *or* equality, efficiency *or* justice, etc. – would fade away. And in their place would emerge (*was* emerging, in fact) a set of arrangements that would allow for most of what was worthy in *both* traditions to be pursued while overcoming their previous excesses.

As long as one was willing to make certain assumptions this argument made perfectly good sense. In particular, it made sense if one was part of the emerging "consensus," and shared the accompanying assumptions about the ends to be pursued and the manner in which this was to be done. It was no accident, as critics were quick to observe, that virtually all those who favored this way of interpreting what was happening were also proponents of the process it purported to explain. Indeed, most of them, in fact, were *liberals*, who made no bones about their dislike of the sort of politics that were supposedly being overcome.

But if one did not share in the alleged consensus or accept the assumptions on which it was based, a different interpretation was called for. And it was not long in coming. The ink was barely dry, in fact, on the pages of the first announcements of the end of ideology before events revealed dramatically that there could be another way of looking at the matter. The new generation of radicals who surfaced in the 1960s were not at all inclined to accept the verdict that was being passed on ideology, of course. For as dissidents, they saw clearly that something more was going on than just a clearing of the ideological mists.[14]

Nor did it take much time at all for the progress of ideas to confirm this intuition. The proposition that ideology was on its way out was a product of a period in which liberals had momentarily lost their philosophical nerve as a result of the influence of positivism.[15] But once John Rawls in particular showed it was possible to break out of this paralysis and give coherent philosophical expression once again to the ideas that in practice were guiding the course of events, it quickly became evident that liberals themselves were prepared to put a different construction on what was happening. Especially as the renaissance of liberal theory inaugurated by Rawls's path-breaking *A Theory of Justice*[16] unfolded, talk of the obsolescence of ideology faded, and in its place emerged a confident reassertion of the hegemonic intent of liberalism.

THE IDEOLOGY OF "CHOICE"

Rawls in particular has devoted much effort to establishing the capacity of liberalism to be neutral among "sectarian" creeds.[17] But it takes little scrutiny even of his version to see that the project that he and by now many others are currently engaged in involves something other than just the securing of a neutral ground from which to pursue any and all purposes. The principled embrace of pluralism in recent liberal theory notwithstanding, it remains today what it has always been: an apology for a particular way of life that is conducive to the realization of certain ends and distinctly unconducive to others.[18] Its content may have changed considerably since the period when it would be characterized as unambiguously bourgeois, but it remains every bit as partisan.

The impression of partiality only deepens the more one is acquainted with the actual logic of the theories in question. As a simple presumption in favor of civil liberties, the rule of law, and the like, contemporary liberalism looks neutral enough, to be sure. But as a body of argument in support and explanation of such a presumption – which is, after all, what gives liberalism its distinctive character – it is something else again.[19] For not only does it involve a particular way of construing the character of nearly every human relationship that is anything but neutral, but it also entails a preference for one particular way of acting on the liberties in question as well. Again and again, in fact, contemporary liberal theory shows itself to be partisan in this regard, and typically it ends up, when all is said and done, with little pretense of compromise. With a thoroughness that is unprecedented, it carries the case for self-*creation* through to its logical conclusion.[20]

Nor is there any mistaking the fact, either, that people who think this way tend to respond to events in predictably partisan ways. Social and cultural conservatives, for example, can scarcely avoid noting the challenge which liberal thinking poses for much of what they value. From divorce to abortion to pornography, liberalism these days more and more presents the spectacle of an expansive campaign for "liberation" on many different fronts, and it takes no particular scrutiny to discover that this is not in the least accidental. Or that it is likely to continue, and even intensify, in the years ahead.

However, even as liberalism is today at the cutting edge of change in this regard, it will not escape the notice of radicals in the more conventional sense that the liberal outlook tends not to be at all conducive to change of the sort they have in mind. For the essentially private way of construing the human good that it breeds is hardly designed to get people to entertain aspirations beyond life as we now know it. It is hardly a recipe, that is, for visionary thinking. Indeed, it probably discourages such thoughts.[21] For the preoccupation with "self-realization" which it fosters (doing one's own "thing") all too easily lends itself to a suspicion of the sort of collective measures typically involved in radical projects, and now that "collectivism" has been tarred with the brush of totalitarianism, such a reaction is well nigh automatic.

Especially is this the case, moreover, with liberals going out of their way to characterize the freedoms they associate with the existence of stable constitutional democracies as "humanity's most precious achievements,"[22] and strongly implying that there is not much more that we have a right to hope for. There is an unmistakable sense of satisfaction with things as they are in the "rich democracies," on the one hand, and a skepticism about the likelihood of a feasible alternative, on the other, that is reflected in even the most balanced versions of liberal teaching available today; and any suggestion to the contrary is greeted with disbelief.

HEGEMONIC LIBERALISM

Little wonder it is, therefore, that talk of the end of ideology has gone out of style, and in its place has emerged what can only be described as a new phase of ideological partisanship. Especially among liberals, who now tend to go out of their way to declare themselves as such. Ever since the radical resurgence in the 1960s, in fact, it has been clear that the post-ideological consensus supposedly arriving with the achievement of stable affluence was not going to materialize. Even as that radicalism has waned, moreover, peace has not exactly broken out. Particularly as the liberal agenda for change has come clearly into focus, a conservative reaction has set in, which has posed in its own way every bit as principled a challenge as anything that came from the Left in the moment of its reactivation.[23]

But still, for all the evidence of continuing cleavages, this is ideological politics with a difference. It is manifestly not the same sort of thing as Shils, Bell, Lipset, et al. had in the back of their minds when they came to the conclusion that the era of ideological politics was coming to an end. And it is the product of a very different set of circumstances. Not even in principle are the challenges posed to liberal thinking of late of anywhere near the same magnitude as those that it had to face a generation ago, and as a practical matter they amount to even less.

In particular it is striking how little evidence there is of the old inclination to challenge root and branch the liberal understanding of how public life ought to be ordered. For no matter how pointed they may be in their criticism of liberal thinking on other grounds, few (if any) of those who today present themselves as opponents of liberalism are prepared to call into question in principle its basic orientation toward public affairs. Quite the contrary. The "fact" of pluralism, as Rawls has spoken of it, in its particular liberal interpretation, is not only taken for granted by critics but even incorporated into their own self-understanding. So whatever they themselves may think – and say – about the relative merits of the particular partisan views they hold, they are quite prepared to have those views treated as though they were but one more "point of view" among others. And so they abstain from making any stronger claim.

It takes little examination of the thinking behind behavior of this sort to see, too, that it reflects more than just a respect for pluralism. It is not simply that people who think in this way acknowledge the legitimacy of the existence of other points of view, each of which deserves to be heard. It goes deeper than that. They are also under the influence of a certain conception of human existence – one which over the years has figured prominently in the development of liberalism and is distinguished by the premium it places on choice. And the appeal that it exercises tends to be so strong that it is proving to be nearly impossible to resist. So even those currents of thought dedicated in principle to giving primacy to other goods end up paying their respects to the "elective" self, thereby conceding, in effect, much of what has been at issue all along in past debates over the adequacy of liberalism as a public philosophy.[24]

Predictably, too, the alternatives held out by critics have much more the character of amendments (and even refinements) than new departures. They are thus more post- than anti-liberal, and the claim made for them is, almost without exception, that they offer a way of doing better – in one way or another – what is now already being done. Or, alternatively, they provide a way of securing other goods as well while preserving the existing gains. Gone are the days when liberals had to face opponents who stood for alien values, and in their place has emerged what have to be considered, by comparison, a series of variations on what are essentially the same themes. Regardless of whether they are socialists or Catholics, Aristotelians or Nietzscheans, the vast majority of those who today define themselves ideologically in other than liberal terms hold views comfortably within the parameters of what Rawls characterizes as the "overlapping consensus." So they pose no fundamental threat to its hegemony whatsoever.[25]

AFTER THE GOOD TIMES

It is precisely for this reason, of course, that the claim Rawls makes is so plausible. We may not all literally now be liberals, but few of us hold ideas that are seriously at odds with the liberal viewpoint. Nor, more importantly, is it easy to imagine ourselves being at odds with it. With respect to considerations of culture every bit as much as political economy, liberal ideas have now come to acquire an authority so pervasive that it is possible for them to be stipulated as common ground with little fear of contradiction.

They are not, however, the last word. And for all the confidence and even self-satisfaction that liberal thinking tends now to exude, it is not at all to be taken for granted that what the future holds is only more of the same. For there is no guarantee that the conditions that have made possible the liberal resurgence will last. In fact, for some time now there has been evidence that a somewhat different set of conditions was in the making. And the more time has gone by, the more unlikely it has come to be that future generations will experience anything like the environment that existed in the post-war era. The resurgence was barely underway, in fact (Rawls's book was published in 1971), when the first of several "rude shocks" ushered in the end of the economic miracle produced by the postwar reconstruction, and ever since a very different mood has come to prevail.

This does not mean, to be sure, that the affluence to which we have become accustomed has evaporated. Or that there has been a retreat from the dedicated pursuit of it that accompanied the accelerated growth of the 1960s. Indeed, if anything, in some respects it is pursued more intensely than ever. But at the same time there is no mistaking the fact that increasingly it is pursued on different terms – and with a different outlook as well. For ever since OPEC quadrupled the price of oil and the industrialized nations were thrown into the worst recession since the 1930s, economic growth has been harder to come by. And often it has been accompanied by disturbingly high levels of inflation. The disease that we have come to know as "stagflation" has made its appearance, confounding the conventional economic wisdom and exposing government policy-makers to unexpected new uncertainties.

As real wages have fallen, in turn, and unemployment has risen, a sense of limits has returned, and with it, a waning of confidence in economic macromanagement. What in particular has waned, moreover, is confidence in the possibility of reconciling growth with social welfare in the seemingly unambiguous manner that characterized the postwar era. The optimism generated by the success of the policies pursued in the years of growth has slipped away almost as quickly as it came, and even among policy-makers the tendency of late has been to revert to conceding the inescapability of "trade-offs." Especially as the tax burden has grown as a result of the steady expansion of the welfare state has it become routine, once more, to pit efficiency against equity, and insist that the one must be sacrificed for the other. Zero-sum thinking has reasserted itself, and in the process redefined the political landscape in one country after another.

There is more than one reason, moreover, to wonder whether the choices that need to be made can (or will) in fact be made. Precisely because they are hard choices, requiring *self*-discipline every bit as much as a willingness to tighten others' belts, it is not at all to be taken for granted that anything like prudent policies will be embraced. Especially in the absence of governments with both a mandate *and* an effective capacity to impose coherent order on the myriad demands generated by modern industrial societies, there is little incentive to make the necessary choices. For the willingness of one group to refrain from aggressively asserting its interests can easily become just another's opportunity, and in a time when group identifications tend increasingly to be the defining identifications in political life, such a policy hardly can seem practical.[26]

THE WANING OF CONFIDENCE

As a result, talk of social "contradictions" and even crisis tendencies has surfaced once again across a surprisingly broad range of opinion in recent social analysis and commentary. Not just radicals and conservatives but even a surprising number of observers who are sympathetic to the existing order have been given once again to speaking darkly about its prospects, and the sentiment they reflect is by no means confined just to elites. In the general public, too, there is abundant evidence of a waning of confidence in the capacities of established institutions that is fast making the confident optimism of the post-war era a faint memory. In place of a "can do" mentality, there is an increasing inclination to assume that the best we can do is "muddle through," and even our ability to accomplish that successfully is something that is no longer taken for granted.

Gone – as fast as it came – is the comfortable optimism about the future that only decades ago was thought to be a natural by-product of affluence, and in its place has emerged, especially among those with any economic awareness at all, what has begun to look like just the opposite frame of mind. There is little confidence that the standard of living that we now enjoy can be maintained, much less improved, for the generations to come. With good reason, middle-class families in particular sense that it is probably going to be difficult for the succeeding generation just to preserve the standard of living they have achieved.

Nor is it just economic considerations that inspire such pessimism, either. Above all what must give informed observers pause when they see the course that events now appear to be taking is the steadily increasing political complexity of the task of keeping the economic forces at work under any sort of rational control.[27] And it is surely the public's intuition that such control is proving to be elusive more than any other single factor that lies behind its unease. But it is not just that. On a number of other fronts as well events appear to be anything but under control, and those who are supposed to be in charge seem to be powerless to do much about it.

In spite of the fact, for example, that the harmful effects of years of abuse of the natural environment are now unmistakably upon us, we insist on clinging to patterns of behavior that can only compound the damage that has already been done. For all the attention that has been focused on the subject and the alarms that are now routinely sounded by acknowledged experts, precious little changes. Hydrocarbons continue to be poured into the air, the rivers and oceans keep on being used as dumping grounds for waste, and virtually every attempt to alter our behavior that is of any consequence meets with concerted, effective resistance.

The social environment hardly fares much better, moreover. For not only do we confront social pathologies (drug addiction, violent crime, etc.) which threaten to become epidemic, but the most basic social institutions are being subjected to sweeping change, seemingly by accident, which places them under severe strain, as well. And the results are then treated as though they were facts of nature. In scarcely a generation, for example, divorce has gone from being a comparative rarity to a commonplace occurrence, and in the process family life has been turned upside down. And so, too, has child-raising, of course. Especially with the return of women to the (employed) labor force in growing numbers, the trend toward reliance on care-providers outside the home has increased dramatically. And even in families where it continues to be possible for parents themselves to function as the primary providers of child care, the drift away from family-centered socialization is unmistakable. From day care to television to adolescent culture, the young today are routinely being exposed to a wide variety of different influences emanating from outside the family, many of which are in direct competition with the authority of parents.

Nor can there be much doubt, either, about the direction in which much of this beckons. For the ethos of modern life today is oriented heavily toward self-absorption, on the one hand, and the gratification of desire, on the other. And it is not conducive to the emergence of many of the virtues that in past years (not least in the development of modern economies) have been taken for granted as socially necessary. Indeed, as late as a generation ago, such "bourgeois" virtues as sobriety, frugality, and self-restraint (not to speak of piety) were commonly looked upon as the price that most people, at least, paid for the benefits of civilization. But at a time when people are being invited almost as a matter of duty to be faithful to their own desires and to fulfill them as expansively as possible, these qualities can scarcely help but seem antique. Especially to a generation which has known mass consumption, easy credit, and the cultural liberalization which has accompanied the affluence of the last half-century this must be the case. And the more typical their experience becomes, the more evident it is how much of a revolution of manners and mores is in the making.

LIBERAL CONTRADICTIONS

None of this, admittedly, is the whole story. The contradictions are by no means so aggravated, for example, that growth is precluded altogether. The 1980s demonstrated that. Up to a point, they also showed, too, that learning can take place. Especially with regard to the fiscal problems of the state, there is clear evidence of a willingness on the part of some voters, at least, to undertake the rethinking that will be needed to avoid catastrophe.

But the question is whether this can occur on anything like the scale necessary to make possible the changes that are called for. It is one thing to admit in principle the need for fiscal discipline and quite another to apply it in particular cases. So, too, even more, is it one thing to recognize the jeopardy into which institutions like the family have been put by the social and cultural environment they now face and quite another to be prepared to take the measures required to change things. Hardly anyone, presumably, can be completely indifferent any more to the danger that we are running in this regard, but doing something about it is quite another thing. In particular, it is uncertain that we are capable of taking the sort of *concerted* action that would be required to make a real difference in addressing almost any of the more important long-term challenges the "liberal" democracies now face, and in the absence of crises it is difficult to imagine the uncertainty being relieved.

When one reflects on why this is so, moreover, it is difficult to avoid the suspicion that the reason has to do in no small part with the liberal character of the thinking that tends to prevail in their public life. For the very same tendencies that find expression in liberalism today happen to be among the most important sources of the resistance to remedial action. And for all the effort that has been devoted of late to showing that another result is possible, liberal ideas more often than not end up functioning as a legitimation for such resistance.

Superficially, to be sure, there is plenty of evidence to the contrary. The appeal in most of the influential liberal writing today is consistently to *enlightened* self-interest, and its proponents generally pride themselves on identifying with the most up-to-date understandings of what in practice this might mean. Their heads are anything but in the sand, and they are full of proposals for addressing the dangers we face. From stagflation to crime to education, they are as attuned to the need for reform as anyone, and much of what they say is designed specifically to make the case for it. Intent is one thing, however, and delivery quite something else again. And more often than not what is said in this vein ends up being, in practice, highly artificial. In theory it makes sense, but because it is embedded in a larger view of things that supports weakly, at best, the sentiments it needs in order to be effective, it has little to do with anything that is real.

It is all well and good, for example, to develop elaborate theories of distributive justice of the kind that liberals have produced at such great length in recent years. And it is all well and good to say, in turn, that the scramble for competitive advantage among groups needs to be replaced by "explicit equity decisions" made in the interests of all.[28] But in the absence of a strong sense of shared purpose which *transcends interest*, it is hard to see how such a prescription can be anything more than idle talk. Especially is this so if every effort at creating a culture that sustains the capacity to make such decisions meets with resistance at every turn on the grounds of respect for the autonomy of persons.

"Fairness" may well in principle provide a way of balancing interests that could effectively relieve the pressures now threatening the well-being of future generations. But the commitment to it – the sense that it is in any way *binding* – is, to say the least, not to be taken for granted, and it has to be wondered how well it is served by a politics that is so much concerned to avoid taking any stand on how life ought to be lived. Especially when the wider setting is so decidedly *un*neutral. The constant, almost relentless invitation to self-absorption which is the climate of the time can scarcely help affecting the moral sentiments people are capable of, and without strong, active countervailing forces, it is not at all surprising that distributive justice turns out to be so difficult to achieve in practice.[29]

Even less surprising is the ongoing abuse of nature. The more enlightened liberals may acknowledge that things can no longer go on in this regard as they have in the past. But there is little basis in the larger teaching they hold (especially their moral theory) for creating an effective sense of limits, and much to discourage it. Especially does the absence of anything like a strong sense of continuity between the generations make itself felt in this regard. And when it is combined with the erosion of restraint that characterizes contemporary liberalism, it is all too easy to see why actual practice tends to be so much at variance with what is presumed in principle to be needed.

So, too, with marriage and the family. It is all well and good for the occasional liberal theorist to acknowledge the need for strong, stable families and affirm the attendant virtues. But without a different way of conceiving the relationship between institutions and individuals than the one that is characteristic of liberals these days, it is difficult to see how such a gesture can amount to much. Especially not when the trend of events runs so much in the other direction.

It goes without saying, moreover, that liberals are not well equipped to confront the challenge posed by a culture dedicated to the cultivation of desire. Indeed, if anything, the emphasis that they tend to place on toleration is one of the most potent arguments for doing nothing to resist the pull in this direction. So whatever it is that they may say – and believe – about the virtues needed to preserve the way of life that they cherish, they are hardly in a position to take the steps necessary to promote them effectively. And the more liberal thinking prevails, the harder it is for anyone else to undertake such measures, either.

THE LIBERAL PROSPECT

There continues to be, of course, more to our practice than what now finds expression in liberal theory. Even as a hegemonic force, it does not literally define how we in fact live. At best, it is nothing more than a stylized abstraction which points up certain distinctive features of our way of life. Other influences are at work in our lives, too, and numerous other practices, some of which conform to an altogether different logic. So traditions continue to be upheld, restraints observed, and moral obligations fulfilled in a way that would be inexplicable if the experience reflected in liberal ideas were all we knew. And the danger that is posed by the opposing tendencies in modern life is, in turn, correspondingly relieved. Though they may not find much place in liberal theory, there are resources available to us, we sense, for resisting those pressures, and because they are as effective as they are, dire conclusions need not be drawn about where we are headed. Not yet, at least.

Indeed, in the eyes of many liberal theorists, such reliance on forces beyond itself is just what distinguishes liberalism as a political philosophy. It offers a framework within which other influences can develop, and it is precisely the invitation that it provides for such spontaneous self-definition by individuals and groups that is its genius. Instead of taking upon itself the burden of prescribing how life should be lived and attempting to generate all the resources needed for civilized existence, it leaves much of what is required to the initiative of others. Experience has shown, moreover, that such initiative is in fact forthcoming, and can be relied upon.

But the question now, increasingly, as liberalism comes into its own as a hegemonic force is whether this will continue to be the case in the years ahead. For the more pervasive liberalism's influence becomes, the less likely it is that it will be able to function as just such a neutral framework. Already it is evident that thinking in liberal terms can affect the way people conceive of virtually everything else in their lives. And the more effects of this sort come to be felt, the harder it can be expected to be for other practices to take root, much less flourish. It will be *liberal* understandings of the family, education, culture, etc. to which people will find themselves drawn, and anything else will be made anomalous.[30]

As I indicated at the outset of this discussion, the other side, therefore, of living in a time when principled opposition to the liberal project is fading is having to face up to the consequence of doing without the benefits of alternative ways of thinking (and living). From the sense of social solidarity fostered by working-class movements to the respect for family and nation cultivated by conservatives, liberal practice has long lived parasitically off the fruits of ideas to which liberal theory itself has not been particularly congenial. And the more complete the hegemony of the liberal way of looking at things becomes, the less possible that dependence is going to be. Unless liberal substitutes can be found, it is difficult, moreover, to imagine the result being anything else but the gradual attenuation of inherited beliefs and practices of which the critics of liberalism have always warned.

The attainment of such substitutes cannot, of course, be ruled out. Their pursuit is obviously what a good bit of the more suggestive recent work in liberal theory has been about, and it has yielded arguments with definite promise. From the searching criticism of the atomistic tendencies in contemporary liberalism that one finds in the writing of such figures as Michael Sandel and Charles Taylor to the insistence on the part of people like William Galston and Thomas Spragens, Jr. that liberals pay attention to considerations of character, a response to the dilemma posed by the costs of the liberal triumph is clearly in the making.[31] And if a serious attempt is in fact made to turn such arguments into a full-blown alternative conception of the liberal project it is reasonable to expect that the liberal capacity to respond will be significantly enhanced. A liberalism that was really attentive to the "dependence of sound politics on sound culture" would be in a far different position to respond than any version currently available.[32]

Those who pursue such a project are correct, moreover, when they say that there is ample warrant for it in the prior history of liberalism.[33] For better than a century, in fact, liberal theorists have been periodically engaged in a dialogue with one or another version of what is now coming to be thought of as "communitarian" thinking, and there can be little doubt that liberals have benefited greatly from the exchange. The "social" liberalism pioneered by figures like Leonard Hobhouse in England and John Dewey in the USA helped prepare the way for the policy innovations that resolved the last liberal crisis, and it surely makes sense for liberals harboring comparable concerns today to seek the contemporary equivalent.

At the same time, however, one cannot help being aware of how different their situation is from the one faced by those in whose path they hope now to follow. For unlike those who had the task of weaning liberal thinking away from a doctrinaire attachment to laissez-faire economic policies toward the kind of mixed economy with which we are now familiar, they do not have the prevailing trend of events going for them. Not in the eyes of other liberals, at least. In fact, if anything, as the criticism that they are receiving from other liberals routinely shows, what they represent tends to be viewed as just the opposite. It is perceived to be *the wave of the past*. And it is easy to see why. For to anyone who identifies progress with the expansion of opportunities for the exercise of personal autonomy in the unqualified way that liberals tend to do these days, talk of returning to anything like the deliberate pursuit of community – much less virtue or the "common good" – can only mean one thing; and it is something they assume we need to be *liberated from*, not to preserve.

Needless to say, such defenders of the current liberal orthodoxy are not alone. The idea that setting people free from anything that might limit or constrain personal autonomy is by definition "progressive" and even "democratic" is so widely shared these days that it tends to be treated as self-evident. And for that reason anything that seriously calls it into question invites being misunderstood – which is why I think it has to be said that the odds are distinctly against liberals in particular changing their minds on this matter.

But at the same time, the fact is that the idea in question is not one that is self-evident. Not at all. And if the analysis of our present predicament that has been explored in this paper is at all valid, there will be a high price to pay for holding on to it. For people will find that the longer they try to do so, the more they will have to put up with the consequences of refusing to take responsibility for the quality of the common life. They will learn from experience, in other words, just how *unprogressive* and even *undemocratic* a single-minded pre-occupation with the autonomy of individuals can be. And experiences of that kind can make a difference in the way people think. Indeed, they can even cause them to rethink things fundamentally. That is the lesson of liberalism's own past, and it is the best hope for its future as well.

NOTES

1 See Francis Fukuyama, "The End of History," *The National Interest* 16 (Summer 1989): 19–35. The more extended statement of this argument appears in the same author's *The End of History and the Last Man* (New York: Free Press, 1992).

2 Fukuyama, "End of History," 24.

3 The most important example of the growing awareness of this problem among a *certain kind* of liberal thinker is William A. Galston's recent book

Liberal Purposes (Cambridge University Press, 1991), which is addressed to what Galston pointedly characterizes as the "relentless tribalization and barbarization of American life." Another volume which reflects a similar concern is James S. Fishkin's *Beyond Subjective Morality* (New Haven and London: Yale University Press, 1984).

4 See Walter Lippmann, *The Public Philosophy* (New York: Mentor, 1955). This well-known diagnosis of the "malady of democratic states," which was begun in the eventful summer of 1938, provides a vivid illustration of the sense of crisis that gripped liberals in this period.

5 Karl Mannheim was hardly atypical when he warned: "Realism prevents us from prophesying a Utopian future. It must be said in all seriousness that there is only a chance that the Western states with their deep-rooted democratic traditions will grasp the position in time, and will be enthusiastic enough to revitalize their ancient heritage to meet the new situation." *Man and Society in an Age of Reconstruction* (New York: Harcourt, 1940), 7. This volume was originally published in German in 1935 in Holland.

6 See John Dewey, *Liberalism and Social Action* (New York: Capricorn, 1935).

7 See John H. Hallowell, *The Decline of Liberalism as an Ideology* (Berkeley: University of California Press, 1943).

8 See Hans J. Morgenthau, ed., *Germany and the Future of Europe* (University of Chicago Press, 1951).

9 See Arthur Schlesinger, Jr., *The Vital Center* (Boston: Houghton Mifflin, 1949).

10 Andrew Shonfield's *Modern Capitalism* (Oxford University Press, 1965), published at the height of the optimism generated by this development, is a perfect illustration of the frame of mind it generated.

11 See John Kenneth Galbraith, *The Affluent Society* (Boston: Houghton Mifflin, 1958).

12 William H. Beveridge, *Social Insurance and Allied Services* (the Beveridge Report) (New York: Macmillan, 1942).

13 The two assertions, of course, almost always went hand in hand. The end of ideology was routinely presented by those who found it an apt characterization of what was taking place as a by-product of a successful resolution of the problems of the past. Indeed, more. It was, as one of the more influential proponents of this way of thinking put the matter, the realization of "the good society itself in operation" that made ideology obsolete. See Seymour Martin Lipset, *Political Man* (Garden City, NY: Anchor, 1960), 439.

14 Prophetic in this regard was the critique provided by C. Wright Mills in his "Letter to the New Left," *New Left Review* 5 (September–October 1960).

15 The end of ideology was proclaimed, it needs to be remembered, at a time when it was also fashionable to wonder whether political *theory* had

a future. See Alfred Cobban, "The Decline of Political Theory," *Political Science Quarterly* 67/3 (1953).

16 See John Rawls, *A Theory of Justice* (Cambridge, MA: Harvard University Press, 1971).

17 This aspect of Rawls's argument is developed most fully in his more recent work. See especially "Justice as Fairness: Political not Metaphysical," *Philosophy and Public Affairs* 14 (1985): 223–251; and "The Idea of an Overlapping Consensus," *Oxford Journal of Legal Studies* 7 (1987): 1–25.

18 Brian Barry is refreshingly frank (if somewhat overly simple) when he characterizes the way of life that liberals favor as the pursuit of "self-expression, self-mastery, control over the environment, natural and social; the acceptance of personal responsibility for the decisions that shape one's life..." *The Liberal Theory of Justice* (Oxford: Clarendon Press, 1973), 127.

19 This above all is what is obscured by the way in which the concept of "liberal democracy" tends currently to be used. For it is one thing to affirm the political institutions and practices liberals typically advocate, and quite something else to place on them the particular interpretation that they favor.

20 I take this to be Michael Sandel's point when he characterizes the self that is presupposed in Rawls's work as "unencumbered." Literally, of course, it is impossible for the self to be distanced from the particular circumstances of its existence to the degree that such a notion suggests. To some extent, our identities are bound to be given, and cannot be the object of choice. But by presupposing the sort of image of the self that he does, Rawls places a premium on choice and thereby renders the acceptance of contingencies problematic. "As long as it is assumed," says Sandel, "that man is by nature a being who chooses his ends rather than being, as the ancients conceived him, one who discovers his ends, then his fundamental preference must necessarily be for the conditions of choice rather than, say, self-knowledge." *Liberalism and the Limits of Justice* (Cambridge University Press, 1982). Though liberals have objected to this charge on the grounds that it imputes undue metaphysical weight to Rawls's *methodological* assumptions, it strikes this reader, at least, as perfectly justified – and applicable much more widely as well.

21 I take this to be the deeper issue that is at stake in Martha Nussbaum's critique of contemporary liberalism in "Aristotelian Social Democracy," which appears in R. Bruce Douglass, Gerald R. Mara and Henry S. Richardson, eds., *Liberalism and the Good* (New York and London: Routledge, 1991), 203–252.

22 See Richard Rorty, "Thugs and Theorists: A Reply to Bernstein," *Political Theory* 15 (November 1987): 567.

23 See James Davison Hunter, *Culture Wars* (New York: Basic Books, 1991).

24 A perfect illustration of this phenomenon is provided, of course, by the evolution that Catholic teaching has undergone in the period since Vatican II. More and more, the church has found itself affirming parts of the liberal credo that in years past it opposed root and branch. It does not take much exposure to the steps that it has taken in this regard to see that the change goes very deep. It pertains, that is, not just to institutions and policies that in the past the church would have opposed, but to its more basic philosophical and even *theological* teaching as well.

25 It is interesting to note in this relation how even the more severe critics of liberal teaching hardly ever end up espousing a politics which entails anything like a systemic departure from the sort with which we are currently familiar. A figure like Alasdair MacIntyre, for example, has scarcely a good word to say about liberalism, yet he can hardly be counted as a principled opponent in the old sense.

26 See Robert Skidelsky, "The Decline of Keynesian Politics," in Colin Crouch, ed., *State and Economy in Contemporary Capitalism* (New York: St. Martin's, 1979), 55–87; and Robert O. Keohane, "Economics, Inflation and the Role of the State," *World Politics* 31 (1978): 108–128.

27 See Suzanne Berger, "Introduction," *Organizing Interests in Western Europe: Pluralism, Corporatism and the Transformation of Politics* (Cambridge University Press, 1981); John H. Goldthorpe, "The Current Inflation: A Sociological Account," in Fred Hirsch and John H. Goldthorpe, eds., *The Political Economy of Inflation* (Cambridge, MA: Harvard University Press, 1978), 186–216; and Charles S. Maier, "Preconditions for Corporatism," in John H. Goldthorpe, ed., *Order and Conflict in Contemporary Capitalism* (Oxford University Press, 1984), 39–59.

28 See Lester Thurow, *The Zero-Sum Society* (New York: Penguin, 1980).

29 This is why Alasdair MacIntyre's critique of contemporary liberal theories of justice is so telling. See *After Virtue*, 2nd edn. (Notre Dame, IN: University of Notre Dame Press, 1984), esp. chap. 17, which ends with the observation that "modern politics is simply civil war carried on by other means."

30 It is evident, too, from the substance of recent liberal writing that liberals themselves are beginning to sense that this is the case. A work like Amy Gutmann's *Democratic Education* (Princeton University Press, 1987), for example, which gives expression to a liberal understanding of education that is geared to the issues facing the makers of educational policy in this country, reflects the clear sense that it is now the responsibility of liberals to define how education is to be conducted and what it is for.

31 Much of this literature is reviewed critically in Amy Gutmann's "Communitarian Critics of Liberalism," *Philosophy and Public Affairs* 14/3 (1985): 308–322.

32 Galston, *Liberal Purposes*, 6.

33 See William N. Sullivan, "Bringing the Good Back In," in *Liberalism and the Good*, 148–166.

PART II

New encounters and theoretical reconstructions

A communitarian reconstruction of human rights: contributions from Catholic tradition

David Hollenbach, SJ

There is considerable irony in the relationship between Roman Catholic thought and recent discussions of human rights. During the last century and a half, the Roman Catholic church has moved from strong opposition to the rights championed by liberal thinkers of the eighteenth and nineteenth centuries to the position of one of the leading institutional advocates for human rights on the world stage today. In 1832, for example, Pope Gregory XVI had declared that the right to freedom of conscience is an "insanity" (*deliramentum*).[1] The dramatic change is evident if one juxtaposes this condemnation with the Second Vatican Council's declaration that "the right to religious freedom has its foundation in the very dignity of the human person, as this dignity is known through the revealed word of God and by reason itself."[2] Indeed Vatican II linked its support for human rights with the very core of Christian faith when it declared that "by virtue of the gospel committed to it, the Church proclaims the rights of the human person."[3]

Thus in a relatively short period, the Catholic church moved from being a staunch opponent of liberal rights and freedoms to activist engagement in the struggle for human rights from Poland to the Philippines, from Central America to South Africa. This shift is one of the most dramatic reversals in the long history of the Catholic tradition. Despite this clear volte-face, however, this essay will argue that the changed stance of the church toward the modern idea of rights was not the result of an across-the-board acceptance of classical liberal thinking. More specifically, it will argue that there are notable elements of continuity between official Catholic support for human rights today and its rejection of certain aspects of the theoretical structure of earlier liberalisms. Though the shift in the official Catholic attitude toward modern rights and freedoms has been profound, there is a continuing tension between the substance of

Catholic thinking and the arguments offered by many contemporary liberals for these rights.

The thesis proposed here is that Catholic teaching on human rights today presupposes a reconstruction of the classical liberal understanding of what these rights are. The pivot on which this reconstruction turns is the traditional natural-law conviction that the human person is an essentially social being. Catholic thought and action in the human rights sphere, in other words, are rooted in a communitarian alternative to liberal human rights theory. Because of this stress on the communal rather than the individualist grounding of rights, contemporary Catholic discussions of constitutional democracy and free-market capitalism diverge in notable ways from the liberal theories of rights that are regnant today.

One disclaimer is in order before moving to the substance of the argument. This essay is not a historical survey of the development of either Catholic or liberal thinking about human rights.[4] Rather, an *interpretation* of Catholic thought and action will be proposed, not simply a report on what popes, bishops, or other Catholic thinkers have said. This essay seeks to make more explicit the idea of human rights that is implicit in recent Catholic thinking and to give it more adequate theoretical expression.

The argument will be set forward in five steps. First, it will examine recent claims that the use of human rights categories in recent Catholic thought stands in problematic or even contradictory relation to the traditional natural law emphasis on the social reality of human personhood. Second, it will sketch the reasons these criticisms would be quite valid if the use of rights language were to commit Catholic thinkers to adopting some of the central presuppositions of some contemporary liberals. Third, a communitarian reconstruction of the idea of human rights that is implicit in recent Catholic thought will be proposed. Fourth, a brief detour will be made to explore the problem of historicism and relativism as it affects debates about political rights such as freedom of speech and religion. Finally, some implications of the proposed reconstruction for issues such as torture, hunger, and unemployment will be noted.

CATHOLIC USE OF RIGHTS LANGUAGE: PLAUSIBLE
OBJECTIONS

Several recent commentators who are sympathetic to the Thomistic and Aristotelian roots of Catholic social thought have raised objections to the recent adoption of the language of human rights by this tradition. They suggest that the natural law tradition of Aquinas and Aristotle is not self-evidently compatible with the liberal emphasis on individual freedoms that undergirds modern human rights theories. For example, Ernest Fortin argues that the Aristotelian-Thomistic natural law ethic granted primacy of place to the duties all persons have to the common good of the community and to the virtues that must be nurtured if these duties are to be carried out in action. Human rights theory, in contrast, stresses what each person can claim as his or her own, and the individual freedom that grounds such claims. Fortin's examination of the writings of recent popes, bishops, and Catholic scholars leads him to conclude that

What once presented itself as first and foremost a doctrine of duties and hence of virtue or dedication to the common good of one's society now takes its bearings, not from what human beings owe to their fellow human beings, but from what they can claim for themselves.[5]

In Fortin's view, recent church teachings have not altogether abandoned natural law concern with duty, virtue, and the common good. These traditional concerns are still present. But liberal human rights theory, in its origins, was fundamentally antithetical to the tradition of the common good. Thus Fortin thinks recent Catholic social thought is trying to blend two different moral visions of social existence in a way that is almost certain to produce confusion. "It suffers from a latent bifocalism that puts it at odds with itself."[6]

The most pointed objection to human rights theory on Aristotelian-Thomistic grounds is that of Alasdair MacIntyre.[7] MacIntyre maintains that the language of rights is not really a moral language at all. It is simply an ideological club wielded to defend self-interest and secure political concessions from other individuals and from society at large. For him, the idea of human rights is an illusion. "There are no such rights, and belief in them is one with belief in witches and unicorns."[8]

MacIntyre asserts this because, in his view, the claim that human rights are *universal* is illusory. It conflicts with the nature of morality itself. Morality is a historical institution sustained by traditions of shared vision of the good and by communal social roles that educate us in virtue. To be a person is necessarily to live in particular historical circumstances, with a particular social identity and set of relationships. In MacIntyre's view, the way I should treat others and the way they ought to treat me cannot be determined apart from these traditions, social relations, and roles.[9] Morality is a "practice" that one must learn much as an apprentice learns a skill under the tutelage of a master craftsman. The idea of rights assumes an entirely different view of morality. It maintains that all persons are entitled to certain forms of treatment independent of their communal bonds, social roles, historical period, and cultural traditions. The notion of human rights abstracts from these historical and communal dimensions of human existence. It rests on a concept of the person as an "unencumbered self" – a self whose personal identity is established prior to and independent of its ends, history, and communal relationships.[10] Moral norms are simply given in uncultivated, unpracticed human nature. We need not "learn" how to be moral from a communal tradition. We can simply read the demands of morality in the conditions that are necessary for human action to occur at all. For the liberal tradition, in other words, morality specifies and protects human freedom. And liberals, MacIntyre claims, identify freedom with autonomy, the ability to set one's own goals and ends, to determine what is good for oneself and for society as a whole. The notion of universal human rights, therefore, leads to an individualistic understanding of morality. But if MacIntyre and the common good tradition are right when they argue that morality is essentially a matter of community and virtuous pursuit of the good of community, talk of human rights will undermine morality itself. So MacIntyre wants to abolish such talk. For the Catholic tradition to embrace a liberal human rights ethic would be subversive of its own insights into the importance of community and the common good.

What is one to make of these criticisms of the ethic of human rights and its alleged incompatibility with an ethic of virtue and the common good? To respond fully would require a survey of the arguments in favor of the idea of rights in liberal thought from Hobbes through Locke, Jefferson, Madison, Smith, and Kant down to the present. This is clearly impossible here. There are major differences among the thinkers who have shaped the liberal tradition. Hobbes comes closest to the individualist anthropology rejected by the critics of Catholic use of rights language. His moral philosophy and theory of government are grounded on the individual good of those who make up the commonwealth: "foresight of their own preservation, and a more contented life thereby."[11] The case of Locke is more complex. For Locke, rights are grounded in the condition of human beings in the state of nature: "a state of perfect freedom to order their actions and dispose of their possessions and persons as they see fit... without asking leave, or depending on the will of any other man." But Locke placed constraints on freedom of self-disposition even prior to the establishment of the social contract. It must be exercised "within the bounds of the law of nature."[12] For example, the right to private property is limited by the imperatives that there be "enough, and as good left in common for others" and that no one appropriate more perishable goods than can be used before they spoil.[13] Kant based all morality in the self-legislating autonomous will. But his understanding of practical reason led directly to the strongly communal notion of human beings as members of a "kingdom of ends," an idea with at least some echoes of the Christian notion of the kingdom of God.[14] Thus a sweeping generalization that the historical antecedents of the modern ethic of human rights have been utterly individualistic and uninterested in commitment to the common good is hazardous.

Nevertheless, there is little doubt that these understandings of human rights led modern Western culture to value autonomous freedom more highly than virtuous commitment to the common good. Philosophical presuppositions about autonomous freedom entered into mutual symbiosis with commitments to the institutions of democratic politics and free market economics. Freedom to be a self-legislating source of one's own morality, freedom to be a self-governing citizen in political society, and freedom of exchange and initiative in the economic sphere have been clustered together in an identifiable cultural tradition. Philosophically, the rights to freedom of conscience, religion, thought, and expression must be guaranteed because they are preconditions for a self-legislated or freely chosen vision of the good life. In turn, rights to suffrage, free exchange, and private property are prerequisites for the protection of autonomy in the political and economic domains. It is this cultural gestalt that critics of Catholic use of rights language object to. If human rights are understood this way, objections to grafting them onto the trunk of the Catholic tradition have plausibility.

LIBERALISM AND HUMAN RIGHTS: A NECESSARY
CONNECTION?

The question is whether there is a necessary link between human rights and this individualistic cultural framework. The Catholic thinkers whose work led up to the endorsement of the human rights ethic by the church in recent decades sought to draw a sharp distinction between the individualist presuppositions of someone like Hobbes and the idea of human rights as criteria for constitutional government.[15] John Courtney Murray, for example, argued in the 1950s and 1960s that earlier condemnations of freedom of thought and belief by Pope Leo XIII were the result of the pope's failure to distinguish between the political institutions that would protect the freedom of the church precisely by protecting the religious freedom of all, and a liberal ideology that saw conscience as the arbiter or even the creator of religious and moral truth.[16] In Murray's view, Gregory XVI and Leo XIII viewed human rights in an "archaistic" way by linking them with an ideology of individual autonomy no longer plausible in the mid twentieth century.[17] He stressed that Catholic endorsement of the right to religious freedom could in no way be based on a claim that religion or morality are "self-legislated." Rather, Vatican II's assertion that religious freedom "is to become a civil right" was a *juridical and political* statement about a freedom that is rightfully exercised in the civil and political spheres. It says nothing about autonomy as the metaphysical ground of the truth of religion or morality, nor does it imply that religion is a purely private matter.[18]

By calling the right to religious freedom "simply juridical," Murray was making a claim about the competence of government to determine the truth in matters religious (certainly not embracing legal positivism). Government simply lacks the capacity to make such judgments. Therefore it has no business either imposing or restricting the exercise of those beliefs, so long as the fundamental concern of government for justice and public peace is not threatened. This juridical-political understanding of religious freedom makes an assertion about the function of government, not about the truth of religious beliefs or their salience for the well-being of society. On this level, the Second Vatican Council is in continuity with Pius IX's and Leo XIII's condemnations of an idea of religious liberty based on the notion that all religions should be equally free because they are all equally true (or equally false). As Murray pointed out, the achievement of the Council was its recognition that it was both possible and necessary to separate the juridical and political institutions that support freedom of religion from the liberal ideology that was initially identified with these institutions in continental Europe.[19]

Murray further argued that the charter of human rights laid out by Pope John XXIII in *Pacem in Terris* in 1963[20] was based on a growing awareness of both the personal and social nature of human beings – the "self-in-society." John XXIII's understanding of human rights was structured by "natural law thinking at its best," not by the presuppositions of "liberalist individualism." It saw freedom as a key to "the dynamism of social progress toward fuller humanity in social living." In this view of the self-in-society, Murray maintained, "the historical problematic " of earlier liberal ideologies that was the source of church opposition to human rights "is completely dissolved."[21]

This analysis enables us to formulate the question we face today sharply. Is the link between the idea of human rights and a liberal ideology of individual autonomy as "archaistic" as Murray thought it was? It will be argued below that achieving a synthesis of the idea of human rights with concern for the common good is a crucial condition for any viable moral-political theory in our time. But there are grounds for being less sanguine than was Murray about how this might be achieved. Several examples will serve to illustrate the continuing ambiguity of the issue today.

The first is that of John Rawls. Rawls's 1971 *Theory of Justice* is the magna charta of that form of late twentieth-century liberal democracy that includes a commitment to the principles of the modern welfare state. In many ways, Rawls's work has strong affinities with the emphases of Catholic social thought as it developed at and since the Second Vatican Council. Rawls stresses the importance of freedom as an essential expression of human dignity. His "difference principle" – which maintains that inequalities in the distribution of primary human goods can be justified only when they are to the advantage of the least advantaged – bears a notable resemblance to what recent Catholic thinkers, including the present pope, have called "the preferential option for the poor." Therefore there is a substantial convergence of the practical implications of Rawls's elegant theory of justice with the ethical and political recommendations of both official and unofficial Catholic discussions of the same issues.

The theoretical underpinnings of Rawls's theory, however, raise serious questions. When *A Theory of Justice* was published Rawls had not yet fully taken the "pragmatist turn" that has characterized his more recent work. The 1971 *Theory* appeared to hold firm to Kantian presuppositions about the ability of practical reason to reach universally binding conclusions about freedoms to which all persons were entitled and about norms of economic distribution. *Theory* was careful not to say that it was making universalist claims that transcend cultures or history. But the structure of the work implied otherwise. The so-called "original position" that was the fulcrum of its argument appeared to be a description of practical reason as such.

Since 1971, Rawls has been gradually modifying this position (or trying to show that he had not intended to advocate it in the first place). In his recent writings, the "original position" of disinterested rationality has been largely replaced by the historical presuppositions of Western constitutional democracy. An adequate political theory of justice looks to "our public political culture itself, including its main institutions and the historical traditions of their interpretation" as a fund of ideas and principles that the theory then organizes and systematizes.[22] What counts as reasonable in generating a theory of justice (or human rights) is what the Western tradition has already taught us. The theory of justice, now, is not expected to be able to produce an argumentative *coup de grace* to those who do not already share its presuppositions. And among these presuppositions is the conviction that disagreement about the ultimate good in human life must finally be a private affair. Virtue becomes a matter of cooperation among people with conflicting views of what ultimately matters. Human rights become the conditions necessary for them to cooperate in public, while pursuing their visions of the full human good in private.

There are some important resemblances between Rawls's claim that his revised version of the theory of justice is "political not metaphysical," having no presuppositions about the ultimate good, and Murray's assertion that the Catholic defense of the right to religious freedom is "juridical." If Rawls meant that his newly pragmatic approach to the justice of political institutions would ensure public space for debate about larger and more encompassing visions of the good, then the Catholic tradition would have no difficulty entering the fray. But Rawls denies that debates about our common life in the *polis* should grapple with "comprehensive" visions of the social good. He accurately points to the deep disputes that exist about what the common good really is in our society. But for Rawls there is no way to resolve these disputes.

Therefore Rawls argues that the fact of pluralism demands that in politics we deal with disagreements about the comprehensive good of human life by what he calls "the method of avoidance." This method demands that "we try, so far as we can, neither to assert nor to deny any religious, philosophical or moral views, or their associated philosophical accounts of truth and the status of values."[23] Avoidance of such basic questions is necessary in politics, Rawls thinks, if we are to have any chance of achieving consensus. "We apply the principle of toleration to philosophy itself" when debating the basic political and economic institutions that will structure social life.[24] Argument about the common good is also to be avoided in debates about more specific public policies. Each man or woman must be free to hold his or her view of what the full good really is. But these comprehensive views of the good life must remain private convictions. This privatization of "thick" visions of the good is not only a sociologically given fact; it is a moral constraint of how human beings must relate to each other in our kind of society.

Thus has Rawls the defender of the rights of liberty and the demands of equality on grounds of neo-Kantian practical reason been transformed into Rawls the apologist for welfare-state liberalism on the grounds that it is the reigning tradition in Western democracies. The convergence with MacIntyre's stress on tradition is notable, and ironic. For as MacIntyre has insisted, Rawls's argument has a serious flaw. The regnant Western moral-political tradition is formed at least as much by utilitarian ideas and the institutions of the marketplace as it is by ideas of fundamental human rights and the institutions of constitutional democracy. Thus Rawls's recent, tradition-dependent defense of liberal democracy must be highly selective in choosing which elements of received tradition it will systematize in a theory of justice. And if there is no possibility of adjudicating among competing elements of this tradition in *public*, Rawls's theory must remain one more proposal among many for how to organize social existence. Once a philosopher or a culture makes the decision to privatize or "avoid" basic questions of the full human good, it will be very difficult to prevent this "method of avoidance" from undermining even that "thin" conception of the good enshrined in the notion of human rights.[25]

The irony of Rawls's convergence with MacIntyre on the role of tradition in generating a morality and political philosophy is heightened when the views of a thinker like Richard Rorty are introduced into the argument. In Rorty's vision, tradition and the language that mediates it "goes all the way down" in human existence. There is no aspect of human personality or of human thought that has not been historically shaped by language. For example, the language and tradition of Western liberalism has created the idea of a "self" who is the bearer of the rights that claim to be transcultural moral touchstones. For Rorty, however, this claim is illusory. The historicity of all things human means that there can be no such transcultural norms at all.

He calls his conclusion "post-modernist bourgeois liberalism" – a form of liberalism that denies there are any natural or human rights. This denial does not take the form of philosophical refutation of the existence of these rights. Philosophical refutation of the idea of human rights would call for the same transcendence of the particularities of tradition and language as proving their existence would demand. For Rorty the appropriate response to anyone who would be gauche enough to use the antiquated absolutist or realist language of human rights is simply to "change the subject." As he puts it, directly but poignantly:

I want to contrast bourgeois liberalism, the attempt to fulfill the hopes of the North Atlantic bourgeoisie, with philosophical liberalism, a collection of Kantian principles thought to justify us in having such hopes.[26]

These "bourgeois" hopes are that no one ever be treated with cruelty. Cruelty is the ultimately evil thing. But no transcultural notion of human dignity can be invoked to argue why this is so. Immoral action is simply something "we don't do." Our tradition has constituted "us" as a "we" who abhor cruelty. No further argument is needed or possible. In one of the characteristic passages that have led Hilary Putnam to call Rorty's writing "ever so slightly decadent,"[27] the matter is put this way:

[In an objection to] my view a child found wandering in the woods, the remnant of a slaughtered nation whose temples have been razed and whose books have been burned, has no share in human dignity. This is indeed a consequence, but it does not follow that she may be treated like an animal. For it is part of the tradition of *our* community that the human stranger from whom all dignity has been stripped is to be taken in, to be reclothed with dignity. This Jewish and Christian element in our tradition is gratefully invoked by free-loading atheists like myself... The existence of human rights, in the sense in which it is at issue in this meta-ethical debate, has as much or as little relevance to our treatment of such a child as the existence of God. I think both have equally little relevance.[28]

Note the linkage of three ideas here: the denial that any communal tradition (e.g. Western bourgeois liberalism) can or should transcend its presuppositions and encounter alternative truth-claims, the denial of the reality of anything called human rights, and the trivializing of the question of God. These denials mean that Rorty's ideal liberal culture would be one that

was enlightened through and through. It would be one in which no trace of divinity remained, either in the form of a divinized world or a divinized self... It would drop, or drastically reinterpret, not only the idea of holiness but those of "devotion to truth" and of "fulfillment of the deepest needs of the spirit"... Doubts about whether the aims of liberal society were "objective moral values" would seem merely quaint.[29]

This vision of liberalism goes beyond Rawl's "method of avoidance" as a tactic for seeking whatever consensus can be obtained in a pluralistic society. It makes the avoidance of the question of the truth of any claim about moral or political norms an epistemological necessity, for it denies the validity of the notion of truth itself. Thus Rorty's version of liberalism *denies* the existence of human rights on the same ground that Popes Gregory XVI and Pius IX thought early liberals were *affirming* these rights: indifference to the truth of all moral and religious claims.

I do not mean to imply that all liberals today are epistemological agnostics or that most contemporary liberals reject the idea of human rights. Rather the purpose is to point out a new irony in the relationship between Catholicism and liberalism regarding the question of human rights. Contemporary liberals like Rawls and Rorty have increasingly come to accept the idea that has been central to the Aristotelian and Thomistic traditions: that human beings are fundamentally social beings whose "selves" are constituted by historical traditions and communities. But Rorty has radicalized this thesis in a way that turns liberalism into a tribal morality. If his vision of an ideal liberal culture were to prevail it would become a major threat to the dignity of others, especially those who are not members of the "North Atlantic bourgeoisie." It would become a bulwark of the political and economic status quo against transformative forces that invoke an idea of human rights transcending any tribal "we."

This irony points to a way of construing the Catholic tradition's recent adoption of rights language that is in deep continuity with its ancient stress on virtuous commitment to the good of community. The vision of community that generates the idea of human rights is the community of all human beings as such.

"THE MINIMUM CONDITIONS FOR LIFE IN COMMUNITY"

The effort to uncover the communitarian understanding of human rights implicit in recent Catholic discussions might usefully begin with a look at some of the relevant texts. The Second Vatican Council's Pastoral Constitution on the Church in the Modern World (*Gaudium et Spes*) sought to adapt Catholic tradition to make it more intelligible and communicable to modern consciousness. To the extent that "modernity" is identified with the emergence of the autonomous person or "self," however, the Council is at least as critical as it is adaptive.

On the one hand, the Council strongly affirmed the dignity of the human person as the basis for human rights, as do most modern rights theories. The Declaration on Religious Freedom noted that "a sense of the dignity of the human person has been impressing itself more and more deeply on the consciousness of contemporary humanity." This new consciousness is "greatly in accord with truth and justice."[30] *Gaudium et Spes* provided theological warrants for this affirmation: the creation of the human person in the image of God, and the death of Christ for the redemption of all people.[31] It also affirmed non-theological warrants for this dignity: the capacity of human beings to understand and know the truth, their ability to discern the good through conscience, and the freedom that is the precondition for the pursuit of goodness.[32]

But the next chapter of *Gaudium et Spes* immediately challenges all individualistic interpretations of human dignity for both empirical and normative reasons. Empirically, "one of the salient features of the modern world is the growing interdependence of human persons one on the other, a development very largely promoted by modern technical advances."[33] Normatively, the Council echoed Aristotle and Aquinas by asserting that social relationships are constitutive of personality.

The social nature of human beings makes it evident that the progress of the human person and the advance of society itself hinge on each other. For the beginning, the subject and the goal of all social institutions is and must be the human person, which for its part and by its very nature stands completely in need of social life. This social life is not something added on to human beings. Hence, through dealings with others, through reciprocal duties, and through fraternal dialogue they develop all their gifts and rise to their destiny.[34]

As one of the subtitles of *Gaudium et Spes* puts it: more than an individualistic ethic is required.[35] We could rephrase this: an individualistic conception of human rights is inadequate.

Is such a communitarian view of human rights coherent? Or is it marred by a confusion of incompatible ideas, as Fortin maintains? The 1986 Pastoral Letter of the United States Catholic bishops on economic justice deals with this issue more explicitly than other recent church documents. The US bishops do not present a developed theory of rights. But their discussion can be elaborated in a way that responds to the fear that all talk of rights threatens the common good. This is not to make a revisionist historical claim that Locke or Jefferson held the view of human rights proposed. Rather it is a normative proposal for what human rights *ought* to mean in our time. Contrary to MacIntyre, human rights are not ahistorical moral concepts. The meaning of human rights is subject to ongoing argument and development; it is not simply a historical *given*.[36]

The definition of human rights contained in the pastoral letter is the key to this argument. Human rights are called "the minimum conditions for life in community."[37] Here human rights have a social or relational meaning from the very start. It flows directly from the understanding of justice that I have elsewhere called "justice-as-participation."[38] The bishops spell out what this means this way:

Basic justice demands the establishment of minimum levels of participation in the life of the human community for all persons. The ultimate injustice is for a person or group to be treated actively or abandoned passively as if they were nonmembers of the human race.[39]

The bottom line in the debate about the meaning of justice, therefore, is that it calls for all persons to be enabled to function as participating members of the commonwealth. The antithesis of such participation is called marginalization – exclusion from active membership in the human community.

Such injustice has many faces. Murder is the most obvious, for it eliminates the possibility of any participation in historical community. Political oppression through denial of the vote or restriction of free speech and assembly also attacks forms of social participation that are crucial to a just society. Injustice can also be economic in nature. Where persons remain unemployed even after extensive job-searches, they are effectively marginalized. They are implicitly told by the community: "we don't need your talent, we don't need your initiative, we don't need *you*."[40] If society fails to take steps to alleviate such unemployment, injustice is being done.

It is on the basis of such an understanding of justice that the pastoral letter builds its understanding of human rights. This approach agrees with Michael Perry and John Finnis that "rights-talk is also a way of talking about duties and obligations from the side of the beneficiary of the duty."[41] But the notion of rights is retained rather than entirely subsumed into the language of the duties of justice because it emphasizes that public morality is not simply a matter of the virtues of those who are the subjects of these duties. Public morality is also concerned with the fact that persons have a moral claim to be the "beneficiaries" of these duties simply because they are members of the human community. Human rights specify the *minimum standards* for what it means to treat people as members of this community. Rights language has the advantage of specifying these minima in greater detail than does the more general notion of justice.[42] Rights claims also add an element of urgency to the demands of community membership. These claims insist that justice and virtue *demand at least this much* from the community toward all its members: not to be tortured or summarily killed, not to be silenced in political debate, not to be prevented from proposing a vision of the good life (including a religious vision) as salient for the public weal, not to be excluded from a decent share in material well-being or from the participation in economic life necessary to achieve it. Understood this way, rights language does not presuppose an individualistic view of the person. It is a language that expresses the demands of the common good when these demands are being ignored or spurned.[43]

This way of defining human rights only makes sense by noting its relation to the overall structure of the moral theory presented in the pastoral letter. This theory does not take rights as its starting point. It begins rather with a discussion of "the responsibilities of social living." These responsibilities are first outlined in a sketch of biblical ethics. Love for one's neighbor as oneself, of course, is a summary of the biblical vision of the moral life. Consequently, the Bible does not regard freedom as autonomous independence; rather liberation is *from* bondage *into* community. Further, the decalogue specifies the demands of the covenantal solidarity of the Israelites with God and with each other. The Ten Commandments, therefore, specify the conditions that must be present if a genuine community is to exist at all.[44] The Commandments function in a way somewhat analogous to contemporary declarations of human rights. Such biblical perspectives are at the basis of the pastoral letter's insistence that "respect for human rights and a strong sense of both personal and community responsibility are linked, not opposed."[45] They also support the bishops' argument that the violation of human rights not only threatens individual persons but is also a threat to the commonweal. "Any denial of these rights harms persons and wounds the human community. Their serious and sustained denial violates individuals and destroys solidarity among persons."[46]

For such an interpretation of human rights to have plausibility in a pluralistic culture, however, it must be provided with secular warrants, not simply biblical or religious ones. These secular warrants have not been developed in any full way in recent church statements. Nevertheless they can be extrapolated from what the statements do say.

Basic to this interpretation is the primacy granted to the idea of rights as positive empowerments over rights as negative immunities. In classical liberalism rights are identified with certain freedoms that are protected against coercion or interference by others. They are defenses against the intrusions that other persons or the government might try to make into the individual's zone of freedom. Freedom of religion, speech, association, and assembly are all viewed as analogous to the right to private property. These rights are like the fenceposts that define the turf no one may enter without the owner's consent. The argument for a communitarian understanding of rights questions whether this view of the political rights stressed by classical liberalism does justice to their true importance and meaning.

Consider freedom of speech as an example. The central importance of the right to free speech in a constitutional democracy is not simply that it protects a zone of privacy where isolated individuals can utter whatever they please. Rather its deeper significance is that it enables citizens to try to convince others of ideas that they think make a difference to the way they live together in society. Repressive governments do not shut down newspapers simply because they do not like the ideas that are being printed. They shut them down because they are afraid these ideas might lead people to try to take power away from the generals or the party apparatchiks who have been running these governments. Similarly, freedom of religion is important so that believers may worship in private as their consciences dictate. But as the Second Vatican Council observed, religious freedom also means that persons or groups should be free to seek "to show the special value of their doctrine in what concerns the organization of society and the inspiration of the whole of human activity."[47] This way of interpreting freedom of speech and religion views immunity from interference in these domains as in service of active participation in the public life of society. People should be free to express their political and religious beliefs in public in order that the true nature of the common good of the community might be more adequately understood and pursued.

INQUIRY AND RELATIVISM

This can be clarified by a brief excursus on Alasdair MacIntyre's more recent book, *Whose Justice? Which Rationality?* Here MacIntyre continues to maintain, as he did in *After Virtue*, that all moral visions are tradition-dependent. All moral reflection "begins in and from some condition of pure historical contingency, from the beliefs, institutions, and practices of some particular community which constitute a given."[48] The entire argument of *Whose Justice?*, however, is directed at showing that the fact that moral virtue and reflection are rooted in historically contingent texts and communities need not lead to the denial of the possibility of assessing the rational adequacy of competing traditions. The historicity of moral practice and theory do not entail relativism, as some critics of *After Virtue* thought that book implied.

This argument rests on a recovery of a concept of tradition as a tradition of *inquiry*. In a mature tradition which is in good working order, the process of "traditioning" is not simply a matter of retelling stories, citing classic texts and authorities, and socializing young people into preexisting roles. "Conservative action on the past" was indeed one of the criteria that distinguishes authentic developments from corruptions of a tradition, according to John Henry Newman, to whom MacIntyre acknowledges "a massive debt." But a living tradition is also marked by its power to assimilate ideas originally discovered or generated elsewhere. In Newman's words, ideas about human existence "are not placed in a void, but in the crowded world, and make way for themselves by interpenetration, and develop by absorption."[49]

Relying on such insights from Newman, MacIntyre proposes an understanding of tradition that is dynamic, self-critical, and open to new knowledge gained from elsewhere. He also seeks to counter the challenge of relativism that must be faced by any theory as committed to the historicity of all knowledge as his is. It is his understanding of a mature tradition as a tradition of inquiry that enables him to argue for such a proposal. He acknowledges that such a process of inquiry can never lead one to a conclusion that is in principle not revisable. Is this relativism? His answer is a strong no. Stated with utter brevity, this conclusion rests on the fact that a serious encounter between persons shaped by two different traditions can sometimes compel a change of conviction by some of them. The adherents of a particular historical tradition can and sometimes do recognize that their received beliefs *must* be revised or abandoned because of what they have learned from outside that tradition. Such a recognition depends on acknowledging that there is a truth that can cause such a revision to be necessary.[50] Relativists don't bother to argue at all; they just coexist or "cooperate." MacIntyre will have none of such minimal cooperation. He wants real intellectual engagement.

In other words, MacIntyre rejects Rawls's proposal that we deal with disagreements about the comprehensive good and final purpose of human life by "the method of avoidance." MacIntyre is proposing something altogether different, though he is at least as aware of pluralism and of the historicity of knowledge as is Rawls. I would call it the "method of dialogue and mutual inquiry," or, if you will, the method of ecumenism.[51] In principle, therefore, MacIntyre's stress on tradition is not simply backward-looking. His theory of practical rationality demands creativity, encounter with other traditions, and the search for truth wherever it leads in the light of dialectical investigation. But he has failed so far to reflect sufficiently on the institutional implications of his commitment to inquiry as constitutive of any tradition that is in working order. This has led some of his critics to suspect that he harbors reactionary intentions.[52]

I do not wish to speculate on MacIntyre's intentions. But if he is to follow through on his commitment to philosophical inquiry as the route to greater truth and as the only way to sustain a working tradition, I think he *must* endorse rights such as freedom of speech and religion. Without these rights, participation in inquiry must come to an end. And the importance of these rights is not only necessary if the theoretical work of philosophers like MacIntyre is to go forward. They are crucial to popular participation in public debate about the full good of social existence. Therefore, MacIntyre's animus against the idea of human rights is self-contradictory. His theory of practical reason necessarily leads to affirmation of these rights as well as the institutions of constitutional government. It is on grounds very much like those that shape MacIntyre's recent book that recent Catholic teachings have joined a strong sensitivity to the role of tradition, community, and practical rationality with an unambiguous affirmation of the human rights to freedom of speech, religion, association, and assembly. The value of MacIntyre's work is that it points the way to a communitarian reconstruction of the political rights asserted by classical liberalism, even though MacIntyre himself seems not to recognize this. Martin Luther King in the United States, Nelson Mandela and Desmond Tutu in South Africa, Andrei Sakharov in the Soviet Union, Lech Walesa in Poland, and Václav Havel in Czechoslovakia all would agree, I think, on the urgent importance of these rights for the creation of the virtuous community MacIntyre so cherishes.

CONCLUSION: TORTURE, HUNGER, AND WORK

This reconstruction of political rights as positive empowerments for life in community has direct consequences for thinking about other rights proclaimed by recent declarations.

The right to bodily integrity and the right not to be tortured initially appear to be grounded in utterly individualistic considerations. What could be of greater concern to a person as an individual than immunity from the violence of torture? Elaine Scarry's recent study of the documentation produced by Amnesty International on this grotesque attack on persons, however, reveals that it too has fundamentally communitarian dimensions. The most radical purpose of torture is to "unmake" the world of the victim. Torture is not the infliction of pain as an end in itself. The pain is a means by which the torturer uses brute power to destroy the relationships that enable the victim to share in a common world of language and communication. It reduces the victim to a state where "in the most literal way possible, the created world of thought and feeling, all the psychological and mental content that constitutes both one's self and one's world, and that gives rise to and in turn is made possible by language, ceases to exist."[53] By degrading the victim to a state where only "cries and whispers" – or groans and screams – are possible, the torturer seeks to destroy the commonality among persons that is born with the birth of language. This barbarity eliminates the victim's "ability to project himself out of his private, isolating needs into a concrete, objectified, and therefore sharable world."[54] Its purpose is the replacement of a mutually shared world with a world in which the power of the torturer becomes utter domination.

The right not to be tortured, therefore, is not adequately described as a negative right to be left alone. It is a positive claim to be treated as a self-in-society, a person-in-relation-to-other-persons. A Hobbesian view that what human beings seek is simply "their own preservation and a more contented life thereby" does not come close to describing what they lose when they are subjected to this heinous abuse. Scarry's phenomenology shows that the loss of self, the loss of community, and the domination of one human being by another are *simultaneous* in this extreme case. By unmaking the human world of mutual relationship, the barbarism of torture reveals what participation in a community achieves when it makes a world with others. The right of persons not to be tortured, therefore, is one of the "minimum conditions for life in community." If any solidarity among persons is to exist, it demands at least this much: "No one shall be subjected to torture" (Universal Declaration of Human Rights, article 7).

Finally, recent Catholic efforts to reconstruct the idea of human rights in a more communitarian way have direct implications for the question of economic rights to minimum nutrition, housing, and employment. It shows why economic rights are indispensable conditions for any sort of life in common with other human beings.

Like the political rights of classical liberalism, economic rights involve immunities from interference by others. They rule out stealing the last loaf of bread from a person facing starvation. They mean not preventing relief organizations from getting food to a region of an African nation suffering from famine because the inhabitants of that region are political adversaries. They mean not discriminating against blacks or women in ways that prevent them from obtaining the jobs and education they need and are capable of.

These economic rights also have a positive dimension that expresses the fact that all rights are rights to participation in community. First, respect for these rights means that individuals and society as a whole have obligations to take the positive steps necessary to assure that all persons obtain the nutrition, housing, and employment necessary if they are to live minimally decent and active lives. Some of these steps will take the form of direct acts of assistance by one person to another. Others will be indirect, such as the creation of the social and economic institutions needed to secure these rights in a stable way for all over time.

Second, these economic rights call for enabling persons to express their agency through positive participation in the life of society.[55] For example, the protection of rights to economic well-being is not simply a matter of assuring that all persons are minimally fed and housed. When individuals and societies have the resources to do this it is surely required. But respect for human agency demands more than this. It requires that people not only be maintained alive, but alive as active agents of their own well-being through participation in social life, for example through being able to get a job with adequate pay and decent working conditions. Recent Catholic teachings continue to support the right to private ownership of property. But, as Pope Paul VI insisted, echoing Thomas Aquinas rather than Locke, the negative immunities connected with the institution of private property are limited by the positive claim of all persons to a share in the resources that only participation in social life can provide.[56]

There is more to be said if this proposal is to be made persuasive in a society where such issues are far too often dealt with using the "method of avoidance" rather than the "method of dialogue and mutual inquiry" advocated here. In particular, virtually nothing has been said about the institutional and political issues that must be dealt with if the idea of economic rights is to be interpreted in a way compatible with equally important political rights. Other essays in this volume address some of these institutional questions.[57]

But one can hope that the conclusion is evident. The blending of rights language and common good language in recent Catholic thought is not a result of conceptual confusion. It is the consequence of a clear-eyed vision of the human person whose dignity is social through and through.

NOTES

1 Gregory XVI, *Mirari Vos Arbitramur*, trans. in J. Neuner and J. Dupuis, *The Christian Faith in the Doctrinal Documents of the Catholic Church*, rev. edn. (Staten Island, NY: Alba House, 1982), no. 1007. The antagonism between the papacy and the emergent liberalism in modern Europe, especially France, is treated in Peter Steinfels's essay in this volume.

2 Vatican Council II, *Dignitatis Humanae* (Declaration on Religious Freedom), in Walter M. Abbott and Joseph Gallagher, eds., *The Documents of Vatican II* (New York: America Press, 1966), no. 2. All citations from the Vatican II documents are from this edition, with the translation sometimes emended to include both genders.

3 Vatican Council II, *Gaudium et Spes*, no. 41.

4 I have attempted such a historical overview of Catholic understandings of human rights since 1878 in *Claims in Conflict: Retrieving and Renewing the Catholic Human Rights Tradition* (New York: Paulist Press, 1979), esp. chap. 2. Ian Shapiro has provided a interpretation of the twists and turns of liberal thinking about rights from Hobbes to the present in *The Evolution of Rights in Liberal Theory* (Cambridge University Press, 1986).

5 Ernest L. Fortin, "The Trouble with Catholic Social Thought," *Boston College Magazine* (Summer 1988): 37–38.

6 Ibid., 37. See Fortin, "The New Rights Theory and Natural Law," *Review of Politics* 44 (1982): 590–612. A similar critique is that of R. Bruce Douglass and William Gould, "After the Pastoral: The Beginning of a Discussion?" *Commonweal* 113 (December 5, 1986): 652–653. For a contrary argument that the pastoral letter moves "far beyond the bounds of philosophical liberalism" see Gerald M. Mara, "Poverty and Justice: The Bishops and Contemporary Liberalism," in R. Bruce Douglass, ed., *The Deeper Meaning of Economic Life: Critical Essays on the U.S. Bishops' Pastoral Letter on the Economy* (Washington: Georgetown University Press, 1986), 157–178.

7 Alasdair MacIntyre, *After Virtue: A Study in Moral Theory* (Notre Dame, IN: University of Notre Dame Press, 1981). It will become clear below that I think MacIntyre's more recent book *Whose Justice? Which Rationality?* points toward a reconciliation of the tradition of the virtues and the common good with the tradition that has generated the idea of human rights in a way that MacIntyre himself fails to recognize.

8 Ibid., 67.

9 Ibid., 205.

10 See Michael Sandel, *Liberalism and the Limits of Justice* (New York: Cambridge University Press, 1982), 59–65; Sandel, "The Procedural

Republic and the Unencumbered Self," *Political Theory* 12 (1984): 81–96.

11 Thomas Hobbes, *Leviathan*, Part II, chap. 17, in *Leviathan, Parts I and II*, with an introduction by Herbert Schneider (Indianapolis, IN: Bobbs-Merrill, 1958), 159.

12 John Locke, *Second Treatise on Civil Government*, in *Social Contract*, with an introduction by Sir Ernest Barker (New York: Oxford University Press, 1967), 4.

13 Ibid., 18–19. Shapiro observes that, in theory, these provisos could lead to a Lockean argument for the welfare state or even socialism. But he also observes that such an argument can and will be countered by claims that Locke believed that unlimited accumulation of land and durable capital generates productivity for the benefit of all, thus rendering Locke's provisos moot. *The Evolution of Rights in Liberal Theory*, 294–295.

14 Immanuel Kant, *Foundations of the Metaphysics of Morals*, trans. Louis White Beck (Indianapolis, IN: Bobbs-Merrill, 1959), 55–59. Philip Rossi discusses the similarities between Kant's kingdom of ends and the kingdom of God in *Together toward Hope: A Journey in Moral Theology* (Notre Dame, IN: University of Notre Dame Press, 1983), chap. 3.

15 The essays in this volume by Philip Gleason and Paul Sigmund trace this current in Catholic responses to liberalism in the United States and Latin American contexts.

16 John Courtney Murray, *The Problem of Religious Freedom*, Woodstock Papers, no. 7 (Westminster, MD: Newman Press, 1965), 54.

17 Ibid., 77.

18 In Murray's words, "Here, of course, it is possible to see the vast difference between religious freedom in its contemporary juridical meaning and 'freedom of conscience' and 'freedom of cult' in the sense of nineteenth century continental laicism. These latter formulas were not simply juridical; they were ideological. Inherent in them was the moral judgment that the individual conscience is absolutely autonomous, and the further theological-social judgment that religion is a purely private affair, irrelevant to any of the public concerns of the political community." "The Declaration on Religious Freedom," in John H. Miller, ed., *Vatican II: An Interfaith Appraisal* (Notre Dame, IN: University of Notre Dame Press, 1966), 568–569.

19 Murray, *The Problem of Religious Freedom*, 83.

20 John XXIII, *Pacem in Terris*, nos. 8–33, in Joseph Gremillion, ed., *The Gospel of Peace and Justice: Catholic Social Teaching since Pope John* (Maryknoll, NY: Orbis, 1976).

21 Murray, *The Problem of Religious Freedom*, 80–83.

22 John Rawls, "Justice as Fairness: Political not Metaphysical," *Philosophy and Public Affairs* 14 (1985): 228.

23 Rawls, "The Idea of an Overlapping Consensus," *Oxford Journal of Legal Studies* 7/1 (1987): 13.

24 Rawls, "Justice as Fairness: Political not Metaphysical," 223.
25 Rawls's concern in his recent writings with the stability of his political ethic shows that he is aware of this problem.
26 Richard Rorty, "Postmodernist Bourgeois Liberalism," in Robert Hollinger, ed., *Hermeneutics and Praxis* (Notre Dame, IN: University of Notre Dame Press, 1985), 216.
27 Hilary Putnam, "Liberation Philosophy," *London Review of Books* 8/5 (March 1986): 5, cited in Jeffrey Stout, *Ethics after Babel: The Languages of Morals and Their Discontents* (Boston: Beacon Press, 1988), 230.
28 Rorty, "Postmodernist Bourgeois Liberalism," 219–220.
29 Rorty, *Contingency, Irony, and Solidarity* (New York: Cambridge University Press, 1989), 45.
30 *Dignitatis Humanae*, no. 1.
31 *Gaudium et Spes*, nos. 12 and 22.
32 Ibid., nos. 15, 16, 17.
33 Ibid., no. 23.
34 Ibid., no. 25.
35 Ibid., no. 30, section subtitle.
36 MacIntyre himself asserts that "a living tradition" is "an historically extended, socially embodied argument, and an argument precisely in part about the goods which constitute that tradition." *After Virtue*, 207. However, MacIntyre rejects out of hand the idea that the Western human rights tradition could develop in a way that would appropriate his Aristotelian concerns or that the tradition of the virtues could appropriate insights from the liberal human rights tradition. This essay proposes a development in both traditions that MacIntyre thinks is impossible.
37 National Conference of Catholic Bishops [NCCB], *Economic Justice for All: Pastoral Letter on Catholic Social Teaching and the U.S. Economy* (Washington: NCCB, 1986) no. 79, section title.
38 David Hollenbach, *Justice, Peace, and Human Rights: American Catholic Social Ethics in a Pluralistic World* (New York: Crossroad, 1988), chap. 5, "Justice as Participation: Public Moral Discourse and the U.S. Economy," 71–83.
39 NCCB, *Economic Justice for All*, no. 77.
40 Ibid., no. 141.
41 Michael J. Perry, *Morality, Politics, and Law* (New York: Oxford University Press, 1988), "Appendix A: Not Taking Rights Too Seriously," 185–188; see John Finnis, *Natural Law and Natural Rights* (Oxford: Clarendon Press, 1980), 205–210.
42 NCCB, *Economic Justice for All*, no. 79.
43 This is thoughtfully developed by Jon Gunnemann, who relies on Jürgen Habermas, in "Human Rights and Modernity: The Truth of the Fiction of Individual Rights," *Journal of Religious Ethics* 16/1 (1988): 160–189.

44 This interpretation of the decalogue has been developed in Walter Harrelson, *The Ten Commandments and Human Rights* (Philadelphia: Fortress, 1980).

45 NCCB, *Economic Justice for All*, no. 79.

46 Ibid., no. 80.

47 *Dignitatis Humanae*, nos. 2 and 4.

48 MacIntyre, *Whose Justice? Which Rationality?* (Notre Dame, IN: University of Notre Dame Press, 1988), 354.

49 John Henry Newman, *An Essay on the Development of Christian Doctrine* (Garden City, NY: Doubleday Image, 1960), 189.

50 MacIntyre, *Whose Justice? Which Rationality?*, chaps. 18 and 19, esp. 364–365, 387–388.

51 Michael Perry's argument for "a politics that is, not neutral, but ecumenical" develops this notion. See his "Neutral Politics?" *Review of Politics* (Fall 1989): 479–509, and *Morality, Politics and Law*, esp. chaps. 1–3.

52 See, for example, the reviews of *Whose Justice? Which Rationality?* by Thomas Nagel in *The Times Literary Supplement* (July 8–14, 1988): 747–748, and by Martha Nussbaum in *The New York Review of Books* 36/19 (December 7, 1989): 36–41.

53 Elaine Scarry, *The Body in Pain: The Making and Unmaking of the World* (New York: Oxford University Press, 1985), 30.

54 Ibid., 41.

55 As Alan Gewirth puts it, "Even where the rights require positive assistance from other persons, their point is not to reinforce or increase dependence but rather to give support that enables persons to be agents, that is, to control their own lives and effectively pursue and sustain their own purposes without being subjected to domination and harms from others. *Human Rights: Essays on Justification and Applications* (University of Chicago Press, 1982), 5.

56 Paul VI, *Populorum Progressio*, nos. 23–24, in Gremillion, ed., *The Gospel of Peace and Justice*.

57 See especially the essays in this volume by Jean Bethke Elshtain and Paul Sigmund.

CHAPTER 6

Catholic social thought, the city, and liberal America

Jean Bethke Elshtain

The horizon for this essay is framed by the notion of subsidiarity, drawn from Catholic social thought, by the history of "the city" as a site of public, rather than exclusively individual freedom, and by the current state of a particular liberal society – our own. I begin with the third of these concerns, which translates into a focus on the fate of *civil society* in the US. By this I mean "the many forms of community and association that are not political in form: families, neighborhoods, voluntary associations of innumerable kinds, labor unions, small businesses, giant corporations, and religious communities."[1] When we think of civil society we think of networks of voluntary associations and the obligations they involve. Some may cavil at the notion that such associations are not "political," but theorists of civil society would insist, in response, that this network and the many ways we are nested within it lie outside the formal structure of state power.

THE FATE OF CIVIL SOCIETY

It is by now a familiar lament that all is not well with us, that something has gone terribly awry with the North American version of market-modernity. The man, and woman, in the street speaks of a loss of neighborliness, of growing fear and suspicions, of the enhanced sexual, commercial, and contractual pressures upon the young. Things used to be better, and easier, they say. Now there is not enough time to be a parent and a citizen and a worker. All the evidence is consistent on this score. Explanations for our discontents vary, as do prescriptions for a cure. But analysts from left and right alike speak of an erosion in a sense of civic responsibility and the entrenchment of a brittle conviction that self-interest is all.

Recent surveys, for example, offer a profile of apathy and alienation among the young, to which one must add the rising tide of violence that threatens to engulf whole sections of American youth. Since 1975, murders committed by juveniles have increased threefold, rape twofold, robberies fivefold. In 1989, the House Committee on Children, Youth and Families reported a "national emergency" of growing violence by and against youth, with homicide now the leading killer of black males between the ages of fifteen and twenty-four and the leading crime among black youths in the same age bracket. On what might be called the female side of the ledger, matters are similarly critical. Nearly one in four American infants is born to an unmarried mother, six times as many as four decades ago. This litany could go on for pages, but perhaps a few additional pieces of evidence will suffice: the continuing decline of voter turnout, the drop in charitable contributions, the de-socialization of life as measured by declining contacts with parents, siblings, and neighbors, and the plummeting rate of professed social trust.[2]

Most often indicated as the source of such troubles is a breakdown of our basic institutions – families, churches, neighborhoods, schools. Others see such breakdown as a symptom of our contemporary malaise. One group of strong communitarians wants to restore these institutions to the robustness and definitiveness they once had. Others seek solutions by turning to the state, to more and better welfare programs. Some statist politicians and philosophies go so far as to design programs and policies aimed at destroying particular, local loyalties and identities in favor of a prescriptive universalism. There the matter is joined – and checkmated: localists versus universalists, on one reading of the situation; individualists versus communitarians on a second. My approach offers a third option, one which focuses on the mediating institutions of civil society in a way that, ideally, nurtures both rights *and* responsibilities, that sees persons as irreducibly social, and that locates such persons in the overlapping relations – public and private – of civil society. I shall argue that this approach is profoundly at odds with the dominant rights-based, individualist thrust of contemporary American culture in order to frame my own speculative musings about an alternative.

Consider Tocqueville's classic, *Democracy in America*, as our entry point into American liberalism.[3] Tocqueville praised the practices of American democracy but feared what might be America's fate. In his view, even as the reality of American democracy freed individuals

from the constraints of older, undemocratic structures and obligations, atomism, individualism and privatization were also unleashed. Tocqueville's fear was not that this invites anarchy; rather,
he believed that the individualism of an acquisitive bourgeois society
would engender new forms of social and political domination.
Individual disentanglement from the web of overlapping social
bodies invites the tyranny of mass opinion and centralized political
authority. The lure of private acquisitiveness spawns political apathy
and invites democratic despotism. All social webs that once held
persons intact having disintegrated, the individual finds himself
isolated and impotent, exposed and unprotected. Into this power
vacuum moves "the organized force of the government," the
centralized state.

This is a pretty bleak picture, to be sure, but Tocqueville also
insisted that American democracy had the means to avoid this fate,
to respond to atomization and disassociation. The cure could be
found in *political* liberty, in remnants of a civic republican tradition
that stresses civic participation, and in a religious identity that invites
social responsibility. Tocqueville noted the plethora of voluntary
political and beneficent associations in which Americans participated
as well as structured guarantees of genuine power at municipal and
state levels.

Nineteenth-century America, then, was a society whose ideals bred
simultaneous strengths and weaknesses. As a new world, freed from
the orthodox and corporate constraints of the old, American
democracy would either fulfill its bracing promise of liberty with
equality or sink into a privatized, individualistic apathy accompanied
by an unchecked momentum toward centralization and ultimate
despotism. Tocqueville's political hope rested in a society honey-
combed by multiple, voluntary political associations – civil society –
checkmating tendencies toward coercive homogeneity.

If this is where we were, on one of the great "readings" of America
as a civic culture, where are we today? In the danger zone presaged
by Tocqueville, it seems. Our public discourse is increasingly
dominated by a doctrine I tag "ultra-liberalism."[4] I distinguish
"ultra-liberalism" from the liberal tradition as such, for liberalism is
not of a piece. Although I believe sources for political renewal are
present within contemporary American liberalism, I also find these
options under pressure to succumb to the combined force of those
beliefs, practices and commitments I am about to criticize. This is a

worry. If I am even partially correct, it means that the version of liberalism that dominates our public life and our media's constructions of that life has become more and more self-defeating. For the priorities and doctrines it deploys serve as vehicles and rationalizations for newer modes of social control: deeper dependency of the self on anti-democratic bureaucracies and modes of social engineering; continued stripping away of the last vestiges of personal authority (negatively construed as domination), the undermining of traditional identities (construed as irrational and backward), and so on.

What makes ultra-liberalism run? The motor that moves the system is a particular notion of the self. There is no single, shared understanding of the self that grounds all forms of liberal theorizing. The transcendental subject of Kant's deontological liberalism, for example, is a being at odds with the prudential calculator of Bentham's utilitarianism. Ultra-liberalism's vision of self flows from seventeenth-century contractarian discourse, a doctrine linked to the names of Hobbes and Locke (very different thinkers, to be sure). Contractarianism of an atomistic sort posits the self as given prior to any social order – ahistorical, unsituated, a bearer of abstract rights, an untrammeled chooser in whose choices lie his freedom and autonomy (and initially this character was a "he").

One uneliminable feature of atomism, then, is "an affirmation of what we would call the primacy of rights."[5] Although atomism ascribes primacy to rights, it denies the same status to any principle of belonging or obligation. Primacy of rights has been one of the important formative influences on the political consciousness of the West. We remain so deeply immersed in this universe of discourse that most of us most of the time unthinkingly grant individual rights automatic force. In our political debates rights are trumps. Atomism makes this doctrine of primacy plausible by insisting on the "self-sufficiency of man alone or, if you prefer, of the individual."[6] Closely linked to the primacy of rights is the central importance atomists attach to a version of freedom – not freedom as that free-domain within which citizens debate and struggle to achieve goods in common that are not reducible to self-interest alone – but freedom to constitute and choose values for oneself. In making this notion of freedom of choice an absolute, atomism "exalts choice as a human capacity. It carries with it the demand that we become beings capable of choice, that we rise to the level of self-consciousness and autonomy where we can exercise choice, that we not remain mired through fear, sloth, ignorance, or superstition in some code imposed by tradition, society, or fate which tells us how we should dispose of what belongs to us."[7]

Solidified by market images of the sovereign consumer, this atomistic self was pitted against the self of older, "unchosen" constraints. The atomist picture of freedom, this overarching *Bildung* that valorizes a market model of choice, is so deeply entrenched that we modern (or post-modern, as the case may be) Americans tend to see the *natural* condition or end of human beings as one of self-sufficiency. At least this is what we are told; this is the vision that saturates the cultural air we breathe. Atomism's absolutizing of choice and its celebration of radical autonomy all cast suspicion on ties of reciprocal obligation or mutual interdependence and help to erode the traditional bases of personal identity and authority in families and civil society alike. Once choice is made absolute, important and troubling questions that arise as one evaluates the writ over which individual right and social obligation, respectively, should run are blanked out of existence. One simply gives everything, or nearly so, over to the individualist pole in advance.

Clearly, the cluster of assumptions I have characterized signify much more than currents of thought: they point to habits and dispositions, to actions and ways of being. In his recent book, *The True and Only Heaven*, Christopher Lasch tells the tale in this way. In the eighteenth century, the founders of modern liberalism embraced an argument that posited human wants and needs as infinitely expandable. It followed that an indefinite expansion of the productive forces of economic life was needed in order to satisfy and fuel this restless and relentless cycle of needs-creation. This ideology of progress was distinctive, Lasch claims, in exempting its world from the judgment of time, leading to an unqualified and altogether unwarranted optimism that a way of life could persist untarnished and undamaged, moving always toward a glowing future.

This ideology of progress has been the joint property of various liberalisms and conservatisms (both "ultra-liberal," on my construal) since its historic birth. But the chief twentieth-century purveyors of progressivism as ideology have been those on the left who valorized a political philosophy of growth, which means in practice "more and better" consumerism. Moving from a glorification of producer to consumer was key because of the conclusion that underconsumption leads to declining investment. No real alternative to laissez-faire celebrations of the untrammeled operations of the market, then, can be found in most left-wing ideologies generated within the culture of liberal individualism, fueled by the teleology of history as a story of progress. Promoting a brittle present-mindedness, the idea of progress weakens our capacity to think intelligently about the future and undermines our ability to make intelligent use of the past. Thus says Lasch.[8]

I take this critique to be similar to John Paul II's criticism of "liberal capitalism" in his encyclical on social concerns, *Sollicitudo Rei Socialis*. Rejecting the smugness of the teleology of Progress, John Paul criticizes a phenomenon he calls "superdevelopment, which consists in an excessive availability of every kind of material goods for the benefit of certain social groups." Superdevelopment, in turn, "makes people slaves of 'possession' and of immediate gratification, with no other horizon than the multiplication or continual replacement of the things already owned with others still better. This is the so-called civilization of 'consumption' or 'consumerism,' which involves so much 'throwing away' and 'waste.'"[9]

The "sad effects of this blind submission to pure consumerism," John Paul continues, are a combination of materialism and relentless dissatisfaction, as the "more one possesses the more one wants." Aspirations that cut deeper, that speak to human dignity within a world of others, are stifled. John Paul's name for this alternative aspiration is "solidarity," not "a feeling of vague compassion or shallow distress at the misfortunes of so many people" but, instead, a determination to "commit oneself to the common good; that is to say, to the good of all and of each individual because we are really responsible for all." Through solidarity we *see* "the 'other'... not just as some kind of instrument... but as our 'neighbor,' a 'helper' (cf. Gen. 2 : 18–20), to be made a sharer on a par with ourselves in the banquet of life to which all are equally invited by God."[10] The structures that make possible this ideal of solidarity are the many associations of civil society "below" the level of the state (it is difficult not to spatialize this imagery).

To the extent that John Paul's words strike us as forbiddingly utopian or hopelessly naive, to that extent we have lost civil society. Or so, at least, Alan Wolfe concludes in *Whose Keeper? Social Science and Moral Obligation*. Wolfe updates Tocqueville, apprising us of how far we have come, or how rapidly we have traveled, down that dangerous road to more and more individualism requiring more and more centralization of political and economic power. Wolfe speaks directly to our discontents. For all our success in modern societies, especially in the United States, there is a sense, desperate in some cases, that all is not well. We citizens of liberal democratic societies understand and cherish our freedom but we are "confused when it comes to recognizing the social obligations that make...freedom possible in the first place."[11] This confusion permeates all levels, from the marketplace, to the home, to the academy.

The political fallout of our current moral crisis is reflected in the irony of a morally exhausted left embracing rather than challenging the logic of the market by endorsing the relentless translation of *wants* into *rights*. Although the left continues to argue for taming the market in a strictly economic sense, it follows the market model where social relations are concerned, seeing in any restriction of individual "freedom" to live any sort of lifestyle an unacceptable diminution of choice. On the other hand, many conservatives love the untrammeled (or the less trammeled the better) operations of the market in economic life but call for a restoration of traditional morality in social life, including strict sexual role definitions for men and women. Both rely either on the market or the state "to organize their codes of moral obligation" when what they really need is "civil society – families, communities, friendship networks, solidaristic workplace ties, voluntarism, spontaneous groups and movements – not to reject, but to complete the project of modernity."[12]

Wolfe reminds us that early theoreticians of liberal civil society were concerned to limit the sphere of capitalist economics by either assuming or reiterating the very different logic of the moral ties that bind in the realms of family, religion, voluntary association, community. The market model, Adam Smith insisted, should not be extended as a metaphor for a process of all-encompassing exchange. Were we to organize "all our social relations by the same logic we use in seeking a good bargain," – and this *is* the direction we are pushed in by the atomist, contractarian project – we could not "even have friends, for everyone else interferes with our ability to calculate conditions that will maximize self-interest."[13]

Nor is the welfare state as we know it a solution to the problems thrown up by the operations of the market. The welfare state emerged out of a set of ethical concerns and passions that ushered in the conviction that the state was the "only agent capable of serving as a surrogate for the moral ties of civil society" as these began to succumb to market pressure. But over forty years of evidence is in and it is clear that welfare statism as a totalizing logic erodes "the very social ties that make government possible in the first place." Government can strengthen moral obligations but cannot substitute for them. As our sense of moral responsibilities to future generations falters and the state moves in to treat the dislocations, it may temporarily "solve" delimited problems. But these solutions, over time, may serve to thin out the skein of obligation further. Eventually support for the welfare state begins to plummet and a politics of resentment grows apace. This is evident in tax evasion, black markets, proliferation of asocial behavior, all adding up to socially generated selfishness as a form of revolt against an intrusive and abstract "caregiver." Wolfe's primary case in point is Sweden, where what Jürgen Habermas calls a "therapeutocracy" is everywhere in evidence, a world in which "professional expertise comes increasingly to substitute for family autonomy." Just as the family has corroded in Sweden, so have all other intermediary social bodies.[14]

Wolfe today, like Tocqueville in the nineteenth century, appreciates that a social crisis is also an ethical crisis. Although he presents no menu of policy options, Wolfe calls for a "third perspective on moral agency different from those of the market and the state," one that "allows us to view moral obligation as a socially constructed practice negotiated between learning agents capable of growth on the one hand and change on the other."[15] This is strikingly similar to Hollenbach's "pluralist-analogical understanding of the common good and human rights." Hollenbach, with Wolfe, recognizes that social and institutional change is not only inevitable but needed "if all persons are to become active participants in the common good, politically, economically and culturally."[16] Wolfe does not deploy the language of common good but he does call upon "obligation" to others as a form of "genuine freedom." We cannot rely on either markets or states alone to make us decent, or to create a decent society. Wolfe is alarmed, rightly so, for he fears we are in peril of "losing the gift of society."

SUBSIDIARITY AND THE GIFT OF SOCIETY

At this point, Catholic social thought makes contact with the non-atomistic theory of liberal civil society – and with such thinkers as Tocqueville and others who follow in his vein.[17] Latter-day Tocquevillians and Catholic social thinkers share a hope that the social practices of everyday life in modern liberal democracies can be richer and reflect greater sociality than current atomistic liberal doctrine allows. Perhaps, they muse, most of us most of the time do *not* govern our lives by principles of exchange, despite the totalizing logic of contractarians and hard-line individualists (including, alas, one powerful school of feminism.) Liberalism historically has been a notoriously unshapely thing, open to many assessments, interpretations, definitions, permutations, possibilities.

Perhaps, just perhaps, there is a distinction to be made between how we are compelled to talk, given the dominant rhetoric of individualism, and how, in fact, we act as members of families, communities, churches, neighborhoods. Perhaps. But surely it is the case that our social practices are under extraordinary pressure. What might be called the unbearable lightness of liberalism in fact disguises a heavy hand that swats back more robust notions of an explicitly social construction of the self. I have in mind here not an antinomy that poses individualism against a strong, collective notion of *the* good, but a less stark, less dichotomous set of possibilities. Tocquevillians and Catholic social thinkers indebted to the principle of subsidiarity offer conceptual possibilities not locked into binary oppositions. They allow us to pose such questions as: Is there any longer the possibility for the existence of multiple *civitates* not wholly dependent upon, or brought into being by, the state? What are the possibilities for reanimating these civic entities, including the city as a home for citizenship and solidarity, in order to stem the individualist-market tide? Is there available to us an understanding of rights tied to a social rather than atomistic theory of the self? Does this understanding really have any purchase on our current self-understandings and social practices? These are but a few of the concerns I will put into play as I turn to a discussion of Catholic social thought and subsidiarity.

The easiest question to tackle is the alternative understanding of rights imbedded within Catholic social thought. More difficult by far is determining if this alternative is among the repertoire of civic possibilities we contemporary Americans can call up or call upon as an alternative to what C. B. Macpherson called "possessive individualism." Lisa Sowle Cahill insists that in the Christian view generally, persons are creatures for whom rights are the counterparts of duties. Contra "natural rights" liberalism, there is no claim to personal goods "which are prior to social relationships and obligations."[18] Rights are grounded in an ontology of human dignity, but this dignity of the self cannot be dehistoricized and disembodied from the experience of human beings as creatures essentially, not contingently, related to others.

The modern social encyclicals of Leo XIII, Pius XI, John XXIII, Paul VI, and John Paul II "affirm much more strongly the importance of the individual and, as Thomas never did, of his or her rights."[19] But these rights are not "spoken of primarily as individual claims against other individuals or society. They are woven into a concept of community that envisions the person as a part, a sacred part, of the whole. Rights exist within and are relative to a historical and social context and are intelligible only in terms of the obligations of individuals to other persons."[20] This understanding of persons steers clear of the strong antinomies of individualism versus collectivism. Catholic social thought does *not* offer a "third way," as if it were simply a matter of hacking off bits and pieces of the individualist–collectivist options and melding them into a palatable compromise. Rather, it begins from a fundamentally different ontology from that assumed and required by individualism, on the one hand, and statist collectivism, on the other. The assumptions of Catholic social thought provide for individuality and rights as the goods of persons in community, together with the claims of social obligation.

Thus Pope John XXIII argues that society must be ordered to the good of the individual and that good is achievable only in solidarity with others, in cooperative enterprises tailored to an appropriate human scale. This version of individuality makes possible human unity as a cherished achievement and acts as a brake against coerced uniformity.[21] Or take these words from the US bishops' pastoral letter on the economy: "The dignity of the human person, realized in community with others, is the criterion against which all aspects of economic life must be measured." All economic decisions must be judged "in light of what they do *for* the poor, what they do *to* the poor and what they enable the poor to do *for themselves*."[22] The bishops draw upon the principle of subsidiarity to guide action based on such judgments. They speak of the need "for vital contributions from different human associations" and for institutional pluralism as guarantees of "space for freedom, initiative and creativity on the part of many social agents."[23] In Pius XI's words, the principle of subsidiarity affirms that

> it is an injustice and at the same time a grave evil and disturbance of right order to assign to a greater and higher association what lesser and subordinate organizations can do. For every social activity ought of its very nature to furnish help (*subsidium*) to the members of the body social, and never destroy and absorb them.[24]

Hollenbach calls this "justice-as-participation," noting that the bishops' contribution to the current, dead-locked "liberal/communitarian debate" lies in the way justice is conceptualized "in terms of this link between personhood and the basic prerequisites of social participation."[25]

Summing up subsidiarity, Joseph A. Komonchak lists nine basic elements: (1) the priority of the person as origin and purpose of society; (2) the essential sociality of the human person, whose self-realization is through social relations – the principle of solidarity; (3) social relationships and communities exist to provide help to individuals and this "subsidiary" function of society does not supplant self-responsibility, but augments it; (4) "higher" communities exist to perform the same subsidiary roles toward "lower" communities; (5) communities must enable and encourage individuals to exercise their self-responsibility and larger communities do the same for smaller ones; (6) communities are not to deprive individuals and smaller communities of their rights to exercise self-responsibility; (7) subsidiarity serves as a principle to regulate interrelations between individuals and communities, and between smaller and larger communities; (8) subsidiarity is a formal principle that can be embodied only in particular communities and circumstances; (9) subsidiarity is a universal principle, grounded in a particular ontology of the person.[26] Subsidiarity thus favors Tocqueville's associative version of democracy at its best and works to exclude "unnecessary centralization and suppression of self-government" by favoring the "construction of society 'from below' up."[27] Subsidiarity is a theory of, and for, civil society. It refuses stark alternatives between individualism and collectivism.

My hunch is that most Americans affirm the "principle of subsidiarity" without calling it that or positing it in any formal sense. Surely most Americans believe that the state should, for the most part, allow families, neighborhoods, associations, even cities and states to try to work things out as much as possible for themselves. Opinion polls repeatedly show that Americans favor some rough and ready association of rights with responsibilities. So what has happened? Why are we faced with the prospect of the loss of civil society, the drying up of the wellsprings of sociality? A partial answer to that question yields a set of proposals for social and political transformation that build upon subsidiarity and the conviction that civil society is a precious gift. In pursuit of such an answer I will make what may appear, at first, to be a rather strange move. I turn, briefly, to Aristotle and to the concept of "the city," going on to track the fate of the city in American political thought and history. I do this in the recognition that if we fail to create civic homes for citizens, we will become more and more homeless, more and more civically bereft. None of us can be a "universal" citizen. We must begin in our own backyards.

THE CITY AS CIVIC HOME

To the *polis*, then. Book III of Aristotle's *Politics* opens with the question, "Whatever is the city?" – in some translations, "What is the nature of the *polis*?" Aristotle offers throughout the *Politics* a strongly teleological appreciation of the city as the supremely authoritative association that encompasses all others. He also cautions against speaking of "the city" in the abstract, for there are many cities, many ways to create this public entity. The roots for the words "city" and "citizen" derive from the Latin *civitas*, but the ideas of the city and citizen go back to the *polis* and *polites* of ancient Greece. The city was public, the property of a country or locality, that which was in common. It was contrasted to the private, that which belonged to a particular individual (or was even construed as a condition of privation).

Classical Western political thought arose out of this form of city-thinking, structuring our theorizing about the civic. The city was a particular setting. It had to transcend the household. Hence Aristotle opens his *Politics* by distinguishing between household and city. Self-sufficiency was a requirement for city life. The citizen shared honors and burdens, rights and responsibilities. He deliberated and ruled, but he could also be called upon to forfeit his life for that of the civic body. (The citizen was a "he" and a minority of "he's" at that.[28])

The ancient city ended in Empire, first Macedonian, later Roman, and Cicero's lament over the grave of the Roman republic echoes still through the years, "We have lost the *res publica.*" To hear these echoes more clearly we need to consider another chapter in the story of city-thinking, one that brings us closer to our contemporary target. I refer to the medieval city, an entity quite different from its classical counterpart, constituted in and through an amalgam of ideas derived from Roman law, Germanic tribal codes, and, of course, Christianity. This latter combines suspicion of any political formation with insistence, ever more exigent following the twelfth century revival of Aristotle in the West, that communal entities are necessary to sustain some common good and to achieve certain earthly possibilities, including justice.

In his classic work, *Die Stadt*, Max Weber extols the medieval city as a site of free-dom, a free domain.[29] "Stadtluft macht frei." This free domain was available to anyone within its boundaries. Although the city nested within larger social formations (the very loosely structured Holy Roman Empire, the interlaced bishoprics of the church), as it developed throughout the medieval period it forged its own political independence. It was autonomous in important ways. The city was both fortification and market, but to be a real city juridical independence was required.

Citizenship in the city was construed along familial lines or, perhaps better put, was dominated by fraternal metaphors. Members were bound to one another by oaths. In matters respecting land ownership, markets, and trade, citizens served as jurymen adjudicating cases affecting their own. Such legal establishments, writes Weber, originated or emerged either through settled practice or specific constitutive charters granted by medieval kings who thereby relinquished much of their right – or writ – to interfere in city affairs. For our purposes, the most salient feature of this city is the ideal of citizenship construed as a mode of genuine sharing in political rule.

A particular structure of belief is implicated in all of this. The narrative of city origins in the medieval period is that the city derives from human free will. Citizenship is a "complex relation of rights and duties to a body conceived as a public possession, and a relation to one's fellow citizens as one's own."[30] Let me add that women were more in than out of this picture. The great pioneer of social history, Eileen Power, apprises us of the fact that a medieval woman held a "full share...in private rights and duties" and lived a life that "gave her a great deal of scope."[31] Involved in trade guilds, women worked, marketed, hunted and tended animals, and went on pilgrimage. Sharp cleavages between civic and "private" persons did not exist. These categories in their modern form congealed only with the triumph of the nation-state. Cities established their own communal rules and their power to do so was part of a cluster of shared recognitions in the medieval period. Patriotism was local. All inhabitants shared in the peace of the city.

Over time, however, city-autonomy in Europe was eroded by the evolution of free-flowing capital in which exchange was not town-bound, and by the emergence of what I have called the "political theology of the Protestant nation-state." State sovereignty triumphs as a kind of secular mimesis of God as ultimate Law Giver whose commands must be obeyed and whose power to judge is absolute. Social divisions were sealed: between home life and public life; peace and war; family and state. In the formulation of Hegel, the greatest theorist of the state as triumphant *Kriegstaat*, the immediacy of desire is contrasted with the power of universal life achievable *only* in and through the state in war (for the male citizen, of course). The city is small potatoes in this abstract scheme of things.

If you have borne with me in this *grand jeté* across several millennia, perhaps you are ready to emigrate with me, conceptually and historically, to the shores of the New Land to explore what America, as a political space and as an idea, did to and with this complex heritage. The argument will take us down two tracks, one conceptual, the other legal, both historical. Carrying with them ideas about the city from Europe, the men and women of America intermingled with their commitment to "natural right" a bit of civic republicanism as well as a theology of the covenant. Hence they wavered between trust and skepticism in their attitudes toward self-governance and about what sort of governance was appropriate to the new democratic person. A town? A city? A small republic? A large, territorial nation-state?

Thomas Jefferson, you may recall, feared the propertyless, potentially anarchic mobs of the big cities of Europe as much as he detested highly centralized government. The communitarian moral-ity of the city-ideal inherited from the Middle Ages seems not to have touched Jefferson, in large part because he shared Enlightenment disdain for all things medieval, all things Catholic. For Jefferson, civic virtue, or the hope for such, reposed in the robust souls of independent, landed yeomen-farmers. Suspicion of the city was bred in the bones of our stalwart civic republicans. The city was often construed as a site of de-civilization rather than as a site for civility and citizenship.

Reenter Tocqueville. Acknowledging the "utility of an association with his fellow men," the Tocquevillian citizen "is free and responsible to God alone, for all that concerns himself. Hence arises the maxim, that everyone is the best and sole judge of his own private interest, and that society has no right to control a man's actions unless they are prejudicial to the common weal or unless the common weal demands his help. This doctrine is universally admitted in the United States... I am now speaking of the municipal bodies." Tocqueville extols the New England township as a "strong and free community."[32] Tocqueville's reading prevailed in part because it offered such a powerful contrast between the spirit of the free township and, alternatively, the dangers of undifferentiated mass opinion and an overly centralized, European-style government.

But the Jeffersonian cloud hovered, always looming, as the fear that cities – anything bigger than a manageable township – could easily become ulcers on the body politic, sites of squalor, vice, the city of darkness, the city as the dearth of the civic. For many American thinkers, the city becomes a problem rather than presaging a possibility. Views of the city as a site of disorder came to prevail in the minds of Progressive reformers in the early twentieth century. (A big dose of anti-immigrant, anti-Catholic prejudice shaped their analyses of problems and their prescriptions for change, which, almost invariably, involved stripping cities of genuine power.) A unified political system, so held the reformist-centralizers, was necessary to deal with the factions of the city. State control of cities came to be seen as a defense of, rather than a restriction of, freedom and became incoded as such in American constitutional law. The city as a real civic space was lost; the city as a site which needs to be administered by the state triumphed.

Lewis Mumford tags this development a form of "growth by civic depletion," as independent organs of communal and civic life other than the state are slowly extirpated or allowed to persist only in shadowy forms.[33] We wind up, at present, with a picture of the city as a place where the search for wealth predominates and civic possibilities stagnate, prompting Thomas Bender, in an essay, "The End of the City?," to write: "In current political discourse the city has no legitimate existence prior to or superior to the claims of the market. There is no political justification of the city."[34] The "city" has become a floating signifier, at once a real space but a destabilized site: it bodes good or ill; it breeds freedom or control, and so on. My point is that the faltering of our commitment to a flourishing civic life "beneath" the level of the state – and I name that civic life "city" given the theoretical and historical purchase of the term – is one constitutive feature of those enumerated discontents with which this essay began.

Now to the legal track, for that will lead us, finally, back to subsidiarity and to our central themes. Gerald Frug, in a provocative essay, "The City as a Legal Concept," traces the way the law has contributed to the "current powerlessness of American cities." He argues that "our highly urbanized country has chosen to have powerless cities, and that this choice has largely been made through legal doctrine."[35] Realization of subsidiarity as a way to break through various congealments that stifle citizenship by disempowering citizens requires restructuring American society: a tall order. Is it possible? Here is the story Frug tells.

American liberal thought and practice has no robust way to thematize entities intermediate between the state and the individual. The city as a "corporation" remains ambiguous, an anomaly within liberalism, because it cannot be construed as public or private in a simple sense. Liberalism, on the other hand, turns on strong demarcations, or the presumption of such, between public and private. In *Dartmouth* v. *Woodward* (1819), the court used the public–private distinction to insist that all public corporations were *founded* by government. Justice Story's concurring opinion was especially important in imbedding a particular understanding of the public–private distinction for corporations into American political, social, and economic life, leaving implications for the cities and their autonomy somewhat murky.

But all murkiness vanishes with Chancellor Kent's *Commentaries on American Law*, published seventeen years after the Dartmouth College case. Here we find the assertion, presented as a taken-for-granted that need not be argued, that cities are "created by the government," that they are brought into being rather than being independently incorporated, and that any power they have is derivative. Denying the entire history of the city in medieval and early modern Europe, Kent's assertions prevailed. The most important American treatise on municipal corporations, John Dillon's *Treatise on the Law of Municipal Corporations*, published in 1872, called for rational, objective governance of cities, staffed by a professional elite, as citizens of cities might be capricious and untrustworthy. State power over cities is "supreme and transcendent." Finally, in *Hunter* v. *City of Pittsburgh* (1907), the nails are pounded into the coffin and city autonomy is buried. The language in this holding is strong and unrelenting: "The State...at its pleasure may modify or withdraw all [city] powers, may take without compensation [city] property, hold it itself or contract the territorial area, unite the whole or a part of it with another municipality, repeal the charter and destroy the corporation. All this may be done, conditionally or unconditionally, with or without the consent of the citizens, or even against their protest. In all these respects the State is supreme, and its legislative body, conforming its action to the state constitution, may do as it will, unrestrained by any provision of the constitution of the United States."[36] This case corresponded with the attack on the cities by reformers and with the quest for efficient, businesslike management to curb the evils of the city. Political science joined the parade by assuming state control as a given. (See Polsby, Dahl, Banfield, and others.)

Frug goes on to offer an argument *for* recovery of city power, hence for the very possibility that the principle of subsidiarity might have some real civic "bite." This argument rests on the presumption that cities have served historically and might serve again as "vehicles to achieve purposes which have been frustrated in modern American life. They could respond to what Hannah Arendt has called the need for 'public freedom' – the ability to participate actively in the basic societal decisions that affect one's life."[37] Absolute self-determination is, of course, a fantasy, whether for individuals or the institutions of civil society in an epoch dominated by state formations. But Frug suggests that there remains some room to maneuver in recapturing a notion of public freedom that exists in tension with liberal constructions of "individual" and "the state." This requires softening or reconfiguring those constructions.

If the notion of subsidiarity, central to Catholic social thought, is to have any real purchase in dealing with our current discontents, it must be tied to notions of effective power. This becomes a very complicated proposition when one gets down to brass tacks. But that the law must be adapted is central. Writes Pierre Rosanvallon, a European theorist of civil society: "Our own particular individualist-cum-statist legal framework provides no scope for the existence of any other form of grouping that may come into being within civil society... The definition of positive alternatives to the welfare state requires, on the one hand, that segments of civil society (neighbourhood groups, mutual aid networks, structures for running a community service, and so forth) be recognized as legal subjects and enjoy the right to establish rules independent of state law." Such associations come into being all the time, Rosanvallon argues, but their situation is "extremely precarious" in light of state law and encroachment. Thus progress "towards a... less rigid society means that the law must become pluralist..."[38]

Similarly, Frug insists that, having lost structured guarantees of genuine power at municipal and state levels, we must work to restore such guarantees. He reminds us that, under the terms of an early New York City charter in 1730, New York had effective power over property. This autonomy enabled it to "shape its own identity independent of state control; its status as a property owner gave the city its power." That power, in turn, could be effectively deployed to require social responsibility of property owners. The city could, and did, impose conditions requiring those who purchased land to engage in *pro bono* construction of streets and docks, and so on.[39] Updated to the present, Frug proposes some half-dozen ways in which cities could increase their power, and citizens their effective democratic enfranchisement. I will not present the list here. Suffice it to say that Frug, along with many other contemporary legal scholars, is calling for both a new politics and a "new language" that "nurtures equality and mutual respect rather than deference to professional expertise."[40] I take the Catholic bishops, in their pastoral on the economy, to be up to something very similar. The call is *not* for some utopian vision of participatory democracy but for a more effective, more authentic form of democracy embodied in genuinely viable, overlapping social institutions. Here critical political theory, Tocquevillian "moments," and Catholic social thought come together to challenge hegemonic liberalism at its most rigid, in its overly abstract, overly legalistic conceptualizations of individual and state, private and public.

At the conclusion of *Public Man, Private Woman,* I articulated a vision of an "ethical polity." I wrote: "Rather than an ideal of citizenship and civic virtue that features a citizenry grimly going about their collective duty, or an elite band of citizens in their public space cut off from a world that includes most of us, within the ethical polity the active citizen would be one who had affirmed as part of what it meant to be human a devotion to public, moral responsibilities and ends."[41] I called my ideal one that preserves "a tension between spheres and competing ideals and purposes." At the conclusion of *Women and War,* I gave my citizen a name – the Chastened Patriot – drawing away from those nationalist conceptions of citizenship that have terrorized our century, to a civic character who is capable of modulating the rhetoric of high civic purpose in light of her recognition of multiple loyalties and responsibilities and her awareness of the way loyalty to the nation can shade into excess. This Chastened Patriotism constitutes men and women as citizens who share what Hannah Arendt calls "the faculty of action," action responsible to and for others as well as oneself. This citizen is skeptical about the forms and claims of the sovereign state. He or she understands that there are other possibilities within our reach, multiple ways to understand and to achieve power, to engage in civic activity.

This Chastened Patriot needs a civic home. The space that might sustain her is the city as a metaphor of encompassable civic space, not quite the shining city set on a hill, but certainly not the ugly, menacing, unruly city we have come so much to fear and call increasingly upon the "police powers of the state" to control. This city as an imagined civic place is a site in which diversity is recognized and commonality is a cherished achievement. Is this city a worthy ideal? I have argued yes, and have sketched the historical, legal, political, and religious ideals and concepts that can be called upon to help call her into being. I am reminded, in closing, of the words of "an old master of medieval history" cited at the conclusion of Peter Brown's "Preface" to his small masterwork, *The Cult of the Saints.* They read as follows: "Above all, by slow degrees the thoughts of our forefathers [and foremothers!], their common thoughts about common things, will have become thinkable once more. There are discoveries to be made; but also there are habits to be formed."[42]

NOTES

1 David Hollenbach, S. J., "Liberalism, Communitarianism, and the Bishops' Pastoral Letter on the Economy," *Annual of the Society of Christian Ethics*, ed. D. M. Yeager (1987): 30.
2 Stephen Knach, "Why We Don't Vote – or Say Thank You," *Wall Street Journal* (December 31, 1990).
3 I draw on my essay "Citizenship and Armed Civic Virtue: Some Critical Questions on the Commitment to Public Life," in Charles H. Reynolds and Ralph B. Norman, eds., *Community in America* (Berkeley: University of California Press, 1988), 47–55.
4 Whether our practices follow suit in some total sense is a question I take up below.
5 Charles Taylor, "Atomism," in Alkis Kontos, ed., *Power, Possessions and Freedom: Essays in Honor of C. B. Macpherson* (University of Toronto Press, 1969), 39.
6 Ibid., 41.
7 Ibid., 48.
8 I summarize points drawn from Christopher Lasch, *The True and Only Heaven: Progress and its Critics* (New York: W. W. Norton, 1991).
9 Pope John Paul II, "Sollicitudo Rei Socialis," *Origins* 17/38 (1988): 650.
10 Ibid., 654–655.
11 Alan Wolfe, *Whose Keeper? Social Science and Moral Obligation* (Berkeley: University of California Press, 1989), 2.
12 Ibid., 20.
13 Ibid., 30.
14 As well, all modern liberal welfare states increasingly transfer funds, not from rich to poor, but to the middle classes. Those who most need help get very little of it.
15 Ibid., 220.
16 David Hollenbach, "The Common Good Revisited," *Theological Studies* 50 (1989): 38.
17 Many of the most important theorists of civil society today are Central Europeans – Adam Michnik, Václav Havel, George Konrad – but there is no space to discuss their work in this paper.
18 Lisa Sowle Cahill, "Toward a Christian Theory of Human Rights," *Journal of Religious Ethics* 8 (Fall 1980): 278.
19 Ibid., 284.
20 Ibid.
21 Pope John XXIII, "Ad Petri Cathedram," in *The Encyclicals and Other Messages of John XXIII* (Washington: TPS Press, 1964), 24–26.
22 National Conference of Catholic Bishops, *Economic Justice for All: Pastoral Letter on Catholic Social Teaching and the U.S. Economy* (Washington: NCCB, 1986), nos. 28 and 24.

23 Ibid., no. 100.
24 Pius XI, *Quadragesimo Anno*, no. 79.
25 Hollenbach, "Liberalism, Communitarianism, and the Bishops' Pastoral Letter," 34.
26 Joseph A. Komonchak, "Subsidiarity in the Church: The State of the Question," *The Jurist* 48 (1988): 301–302. I have recast Komonchak's principles in my own language.
27 Ibid., 326–327.
28 The darker side of the story of civic virtue is one I tell in *Women and War* (New York: Basic Books, 1987) in my discussion of the tradition of "armed civic virtue." I have a rather different tale to tell here.
29 Max Weber, *The City*, trans. and ed. D. Martindale and G. Neuwirth (New York: Collier Books, 1958).
30 Nancy Schwartz, "Communitarian Citizenship: Marx and Weber on the City," *Polity* 17/3 (Winter 1985): 548.
31 Eileen Power, "The Position of Women," in C. G. Crump and E. F. Jacob, eds., *The Legacy of the Middle Ages* (Oxford: Clarendon Press, 1948), 432–433.
32 Alexis de Tocqueville, *Democracy in America*, ed. Phillips Bradley, 2 vols. (New York: Vintage Books, 1945), 1: 67.
33 Lewis Mumford, *The Culture of Cities* (New York: Harcourt, Brace & Co., 1938).
34 Thomas Bender, "The End of the City?" *Democracy* (Winter 1983): 8.
35 Gerald Frug, "The City as a Legal Concept," *Harvard Law Review* 93 (1980): 1058–1059.
36 Ibid., 1062–1063.
37 Ibid., 1068.
38 Pierre Rosanvallon, "The Decline of Social Visibility," in John Keane, ed., *Civil Society and the State* (London: Verso, 1988), 204–205.
39 Gerald E. Frug, "Property and Power: Hartog on the Legal History of New York City," *American Bar Foundation Research Journal* 3 (1984): 674.
40 Gerald E. Frug, "The Language of Power," *Columbia Law Review* 84 (1984): 1894.
41 Jean Bethke Elshtain, *Public Man, Private Woman: Women in Social and Political Thought* (Princeton University Press, 1981), 351.
42 Peter Brown, *The Cult of the Saints* (University of Chicago Press, 1982), xv.

CHAPTER 7

The common good and the open society

Louis Dupré

INTRODUCTION

The term common good has been used in so many ways that it would be difficult to find any political thinker, however individualistically oriented, who has not, in one form or another, embraced it. The classical definition, formulated in the Middle Ages on the basis of Aristotelian principles, referred to a good proper to, and attainable only by, the community, yet individually shared by its members. As such the common good is at once communal and individual. Still, it does not coincide with the sum total of particular goods and exceeds the goals of inter-individual transactions. In medieval Christian thought, conflicts between the communal and the individual were at least in principle avoided by the fact that both were subordinated to a common transcendent goal. Yet once the idea of community lost its ontological ultimacy (mainly under the impact of nominalist thought), a struggle originated between the traditional conception of the community as an end in itself and that of its function to protect the private interests of its members. Eventually the latter theory prevailed and, after it became reinforced by resistance movements against repressive national government policies, it led to a doctrine of individual rights as independent of society. The founders of the American republic, while fully accepting the theory of rights, reacted against the priority of private (primarily economic) interests by strongly reemphasizing the idea of community as endowed with a good of its own. The intellectual and moral pluralism of recent times has made theorists reluctant to attribute any specific content to the notion of a common good. Some have replaced it by a doctrine of "fairness" (Rawls). Such a change returns the idea of community once again to particular (though not necessarily individual) interests. At a time when national communities face an increasing integration with one another in a world of dwindling resources, such a privatization seems inappropriate. The present essay argues for a restoration of an idea of the common good which incorporates individual rights without separating them from their social context.

EARLY CONCEPTS AND THEIR TRANSFORMATION

The first treatise on the common good in Christian Europe appeared at the turn of the fourteenth century in Florence: Remigio de' Girolami's *De bono communi*. It deviated from the heretofore accepted principle that the commonwealth remained subordinate to the person's supernatural destiny, though in the natural order it was prior to the individual. Remigio defended the thesis that Christian virtue required first and foremost that one be a good citizen. In doing so he came closer to adopting Aristotle's position on public virtue than had any Christian thinker before him.[1]

Despite his idealization of the *civitas*, Remigio by no means wished to establish a secular state. Quite the contrary, only in a Christian *communitas* does civil society find the spiritual support it needs for survival. He conceived the common good as the well-being of a spiritual *corpus mysticum* rather than the realization of an immanently human potential in the manner of Aristotle. Remigio boldly declares: "Homo tenetur preamare commune sibi."[2] The *communitas* alone realizes the ideal of *caritas*. The commonweal displays a greater similitude to God than any private entity. It may even be said to be more essential to the individual than the individual is to himself, since a part as part is only a potential entity (*pars ut pars est ens in potentia tantum*).[3] The part exists with respect to the whole, and hence the good of the whole is the one most "natural" to the individual.[4]

The ideas developed in this *livre d'occasion* were a response to the crisis of a city at the brink of civil war. In this context even the Thomist synthesis of public communality and private spirituality no longer appeared sufficient in the political conditions that had come to prevail in the Northern Italian republics. The two major systems that, until then, provided Latin Christianity with its political principles were those of Augustine and Aquinas. For Augustine's doctrine it may suffice here to refer to Eugene TeSelle's and David Hollenbach's recent essays.[5] One cannot but be struck by the amazing complexity of Augustine's position. To refute the charges that held Christians responsible for the decay of the Empire, in *The City of God* he turns the tables on the accusers by attributing the decline to an absence of civic virtue and concern for the common good, qualities that Christians possessed as abundantly as their pagan contemporaries lacked them. Augustine does not equate the unholy *civitas terrena* with civil society as such. Rather, different states of mind – penetrating private as well as public life – divide the redeemed from the unredeemed city. The *civitas Dei* transcends any terrestrial commonwealth. Yet it alone is capable of grounding the true, that is, spiritual and moral, community needed to support a genuine commonwealth.

Aquinas's position differs substantially from Augustine's. For Aquinas, a concern for the common good of the political community is a constitutive element of Christian virtue as such. A doomed Empire had presented Augustine's contemporaries little opportunity for the practice of civic virtue. But in St. Thomas's time, the *res publica christiana* was as far on its way toward earthly realization as it would ever be. Fra Remigio found strong support in the ideas of the man who had probably been his former master in Paris. Yet their positions unmistakably differ.

The difference was the very issue that reemerged in a dispute between two factions of Thomists only a few decades ago in the 1940s. One party, led by Charles De Koninck, claimed that Aquinas granted the common good a "primacy" over individual goods. " [Le bien commun] s'étend davantage au singulier que le bien singulier : il est le meilleur bien du singulier."[6] On the other side I. T. Eschmann, OP, forcefully defended a position attributed to Jacques Maritain. According to this interpretation, the common good, though superior to any particular good pursued by the individual and though a *bonum honestum* in its own right, must nevertheless remain subordinate to the *summum bonum* of contemplation which, by its very nature, is individual.[7] As Maritain presents the relation in *The Person and the Common Good*, the dispute appears somewhat less substantial than the heated battle would have led one to suspect. Spiritual beings relate first and foremost to God rather than to the common good immanent in the universe (as other creatures do), but this transcendent Good is itself a common one.[8] "The highest good (*bonum summum*) which is God is a common good."[9] Nor must that *highest* common good be pursued individually rather than communally, since it is precisely through the *immanent* common good of civil society that individuals acquire the moral virtues which alone enable them to pursue the transcendent Good.[10]

St. Thomas describes the end of legislation in the "perfect community" as *felicitas communis*.[11] Though Aquinas shares Aristotle's communal goal of society, he interprets it in a sense that transcends the philosopher's moral idea altogether. For Aquinas, the *fruitio Dei* rather than either natural contemplation or the attainment of virtue is the end of human life. "Non est ergo ultimus finis multitudinis congregatae vivere secundum virtutem, sed per virtuosam vitam pervenire ad fruitionem divinam."[12] The *fruitio divina* surpasses any active practice of virtue. While Aristotle had never resolved the ambiguity of whether the practice of moral virtue is only a means toward the end of contemplation or whether it is constitutive of it, for Aquinas no such doubt exists. The ultimate end of human life consists in the eternal fruition of the divine Being.

But here a new problem emerges. Is such a fruition not, by its very nature, strictly individual? How then can he still call it a "common" good? Aquinas justifies his terminology – and his desire to remain within the Aristotelian tradition – by distinguishing a distributive from a collective sense of the common good. As a universal good, God is common to us all, even though God remains beyond any human community and fulfills each person's desire singularly. "In human affairs there is a common good, namely, the good of the city or of the nation... There is also a human good, not common to many, but belonging to an individual by himself, yet useful not to one only, but to many."[13] The common good here appears to be an end common to all, but lying beyond society. But it is not entirely extrinsic since it conveys to the human community a very real unity. St. Thomas relates the individual attainment of this supernatural "common good" to Aristotle's ideal of contemplation. Though this supernatural good is mediated through life in the community, it is personal in its actual realization. While the practical intellect leads toward a political end, the theoretical intellect leads to the personal beatitude of the contemplative life. This is, of course, true enough, but hardly applicable to eternal beatitude in the possession of God, which transcends theoretical as well as practical activity.

Maritain's interpretation of these texts goes further than Aquinas and attributes a communal quality to the ultimate (Christian) end, which derives from its participation in the divine (i.e., Trinitarian) life. This participation would give humans a share in common life beyond all separation created by material restrictions and social divisions.[14] At the same time this participation in a higher, mystical society relativizes the significance of the political society. "Man is not ordained to the body politic according to all that he is and has."[15] Though totally engaged in the political society of which he/she forms an integral part, the person is not part of it in his/her *entire* being.

What Aquinas proposes and Maritain explicates amounts to an ultimate identity of the goals of society with the conditions that allow its members to achieve full personhood. But we should not conclude from this *ultimate* convergence of personal fulfillment and common good that they must also coincide in the terrestrial stage of society, even if that society is Christian. The practical order may require a certain amount of legal compulsion to enforce the primacy of the common good and to assist individuals in overcoming their private interests in order to attain genuine personhood. A failure to take this discrepancy between theoretical ideal and practical achievement into account would reduce the Thomist solution, even in Maritain's version, to a medieval utopia. Nor should we consider these qualifications sufficient to transpose the Thomist conception of the common good to the modern situation. They merely suggest that the medieval priority of the common good rested on a solid basis of realism.

In describing Aquinas's social theory, I have distinguished it from the later developments of that theory. One such development has been caused by the introduction of the concept of human rights. John Finnis rightly argues that, despite its cloudy origins, the modern usage of claims of right "should be recognized...as a valuable addition to the received vocabulary of practical reasonableness (*i.e.*, to the tradition of 'natural law doctrine')."[16] Without questioning the link between the two concepts – a link assumed in Vatican II's *Gaudium et Spes* (no. 74) and repeated in the US bishops' pastoral letter *Economic Justice for All* (no. 79) – one may nevertheless wonder whether a common good defined as securing the conditions that favor the realization of each member's "personal development"[17] still corresponds to St. Thomas's idea of the common good. Even after Finnis's social reinterpretation, the human rights theory places an emphasis upon individual well-being *in this life* which I do not find in Aquinas's view.[18]

Comparing Aquinas's position with the one that came to prevail in the fifteenth century, we notice a dissolution of elements previously held in balance. In Fra Remigio, a one-sided emphasis on the common good, only partly justified by the historical circumstances of his time, tips the scale toward the good of society. Still Remigio retains the ultimate supremacy of the transcendent Good. That transcendent element weakened as the political crisis in Florence intensified. The great Florentine political writers, such as Bruni, Marsuppini, and Poggio, increasingly turned to the late Roman republic rather than to the Gospel for political enlightenment. Machiavelli, coming at the end of that line, extended the sacrifice which the common good may demand of the citizen as far as to include individual salvation. Rather than cynicism, this claim reveals a strong awareness of the insufficiency for public policy of an increasingly privatized morality.

One major factor contributing to this privatization of morality at the end of the Middle Ages was a nominalist philosophy that recognized no reality in the universal as such. It would be inaccurate to conclude that nominalism itself was an individualistic philosophy. The political involvements of Ockham and Marsiglio di Padua clearly contradict that. Yet its atomistic conception of the real was instrumental in shifting the purpose of society to the well-being of the individual.

The impact of nominalist philosophy upon political thought from the end of the Middle Ages until the eighteenth century is difficult to assess. But there can be no doubt that it included one influential principle: what may be distinguished logically can exist separately. Not only may any complex state of affairs be logically reduced to its simple components, but these components may actually have preceded their factual complex realization. Since human nature can be conceived independently of its social orientation, it must therefore, at least logically and possibly in reality, be detached from that orientation. Its social quality thereby appears as an accidental form to be added to the socially neutral *a priori* of human nature.[19] A human nature independent of any political structure was logically possible, and hence presumed to be at least hypothetically real. Attempts to give this hypothetical *a priori* an empirical content varied. Suarez assumed it to be already socially oriented, Locke potentially social, Hobbes not intrinsically social at all. Beyond these differences, all agreed in viewing the political structure as a historical addition to human nature in a manner that had been inconceivable to earlier social philosophies.

Despite the disintegrating impact of late medieval philosophy, a powerfully social conception of the common good survived at the beginning of the modern age, especially in Scholastic writers such as Suarez and Richard Hooker. Hooker, citizen of a country in which church and state had recently become united in one territory under one head, had synthesized Aristotelian philosophy with Christian theology even more intrinsically than Aquinas himself had done. The religious situation of England dispensed him from having to make the distinctions between the ecclesiastical and the political community. He could therefore argue that the state's care for the common good included a *full* concern for the religious well-being of its subjects. Of course, the very nature of Christian beatitude demanded a separation between two realms, a separation which he asserted as clearly as Aquinas. But the responsibility for preparing the way to the attainment of beatitude lay with a community that was both civil and religious.[20]

Suarez, writing for a religiously and politically divided Europe, adopted a very different position. For him, the entire human community is already united by the very fact of its being created by the same God and Father. Hence the effect of whatever "social" contract may take place is not to render people "social," but merely to enable them to pass from one social or political state to another. In *De legibus* Suarez describes the *natural unity* that, prior to the political unity, links all humans together in the act of divine creation and enables them to constitute "a mystical body" – part of the same divine scheme – through the political consensus.[21] This high potential for social coherence that humans possess even before achieving political unity rests on the religious foundation of their common divine origin and destiny. It derives its immediate motivation toward political union from a desire for a common good – *ut mutuo se juvent in ordine ad unum finem politicum*. Precisely from this anticipative concern for a common good yet to be attained, political institutions will emerge. By *pursuing* that common good, humans already achieve an organic unity even before constituting a political body. Nor does this "naturally constituted" democracy vanish when its members transfer sovereignty to the prince in an irrevocable *quasi alienatio*: the exercise of that sovereignty remains subordinate to the common good which led to its transfer. If the sovereign prince ever comes to obstruct the pursuit of the common good, he may be removed by force, even by regicide.[22]

If Suarez's political philosophy could result in an absolutist form of sovereignty, this would happen more easily in writers who described the pre-political state as socially neutral. For them, political unity alone provided social structure, and the holder of sovereign power functioned as the indispensable instrument of this unity. Once one accepted the premise that the social order is not natural to humans corrupted by the Fall, it took only a small step to consider the sovereign power as divinely imposed. Thus nominalist philosophy combined with reformed theology in preparing the way to the divine right theory.

THE GENESIS OF MODERN LIBERALISM AND THE DEMISE OF THE COMMON GOOD

In Hobbes we confront a more radical application of the nominalist principle than in Suarez or, indeed, than in any other sixteenth-century writer. In a modified form, his thorough elementarism will find its ways into most later British social philosophy. William of Ockham had patterned his theory of the human will after that of the divine *potentia absoluta* as totally indeterminate, directed neither to good nor to evil, nor to any common good. Hobbes applied Ockham's theory of the will to the social order. Only the imposition, from without, of a political rule can secure social unity and a common good for atomistic human individuals.

Locke and his followers explicitly rejected this anti-social conception. Yet they continued to regard the state of nature as merely potentially social and requiring an explicit social contract to become actually social. The assumption of natural rights inherent in the state of nature distinguishes their theory clearly from Hobbes's individualist *jus omnium in omnia*. Those natural rights however, especially the right of property, could not be safeguarded unless some social arrangement were made from the start. Political authority, then, emerges almost spontaneously from a potentially social body which retains the power to withdraw that authority if it does not fulfil its purpose.

Once the idea of society came to rest upon individualist premises, the common good was inevitably reduced to a collective well-being of its individual members. Since civil society had no other purpose than to protect the life, liberty, and security of its members, it provided scant support for any normative concept of the common good. Still governmental power was never more repressive of what we now call individual rights than in the strong, autocratic state of the sixteenth and seventeenth centuries. The national state, once firmly established, proceeded to justify its central authority in a variety of theoretical ways.[23] The divine right doctrine was only one of these. Philosophers provided whatever theoretical support the current political regime required. In Hobbes's England that was a defense of absolute monarchy, in Locke's of constitutional government. But regardless of the cause they embraced, British philosophers after Hooker argued on the basis of elementarist, nominalist principles. Their thought played a major role in preparing the liberal, individualist theories of the nineteenth century.

The political origins of the contract doctrines lie in the early resistance movements of religious minorities, in England Calvinists and Catholics, in France mainly Calvinists. These movements led to a doctrine of pre-social, individual rights. Once Locke had given that doctrine its definitive formulation, after the Glorious Revolution (1688), the state had a purpose firm enough to unify the previously anarchical variety of individual aspirations into a coherent matrix: the protection of basic individual rights, especially freedom, by a democratically organized society. The theory of absolute individual rights has remained controversial ever since its start. What would rights mean before being promulgated by a sovereign power? Hobbes had considered this problem and concluded that a pre-political right meant nothing since it included everything.

The equation of a doctrine of natural law with one of natural rights developed out of a more radically individualistic questioning of the social pretenses of the contractual theory. Though the theory of rights may be *reinterpreted* within the general context of natural law,[24] its original individualism was far removed from the natural law's fundamental assumption of the essentially social nature of the person. The theory of natural rights had started as a complement to the natural law doctrine. But, as Ernest Fortin has argued, "In contrast to the natural law theory, the natural rights theory proceeds on the assumption that these same human beings exist first of all as complete and independent wholes, endowed with prepolitical rights for the protection of which they 'enter' into a society that is entirely of their own making."[25] The individualist origin of the natural rights theory became blatantly manifest in the link it forged, almost from the start, with utilitarian ethics. *Right* thereby came to stand for what was expedient for satisfying individual needs.

How did such a pragmatic goal ever gain the deontological quality that a theory of natural rights requires? The argument seems to have run as follows. Some actions appear so useful to society that laws to enforce them *ought* to be instituted; hence such laws are demanded by a human *right* that precedes all laws.[26] Clearly, not all advocates of the natural rights theory were utilitarians, nor did all utilitarians support the theory. Bentham, Adam Smith, and Hume opposed a doctrine that they felt could not fail to provoke resistance to the established order. But in view of the theory's empirical origin, the temptation to link it to the prevailing concept of social utility was great. In Thomas Paine's *The Rights of Man* the two are juxtaposed before our very eyes. In the first part, he still upholds an abstract theory of natural right, while in the second part, written somewhat later, he places human rights on a basis of economic utility.

Government is nothing more than a national association; and the object of this association is the good of all, as well individually as collectively. Every man wishes to pursue his occupation, and enjoy the fruit of his labors, and the produce of his property, in peace and safety, and with the least possible expense. When these things are accomplished, all the objects for which government ought to be established are answered.[27]

"Public good" for Paine, then, is no more than "the collected good of those individuals."

It would be erroneous, however, to consider Paine's views as reflecting the position of the founders of the American republic. True, even James Madison had claimed in the tenth Federalist Paper: "The first object of government is the protection of different and unequal faculties of acquiring property." Yet this economic, functional governmental structure rests on the assumption that Americans already belong to a more fundamental society constituted through a tradition of common ideals and civil virtue. The same Madison who so strongly defended the role of commerce also exclaimed in the Virginia Assembly during the debate on the Constitution in 1788: "To suppose any form of government will secure liberty or happiness without any virtue in the people, is a chimerical idea."[28] Jefferson likewise saw no political alternative to a state that would provide a maximum of commercial opportunity. He wrote to Washington: "All the world is becoming commercial." But in his *Notes on the State of Virginia*, Jefferson expressed a concern that the members of the newly established commonwealth "will forget themselves but in the sole faculty of making money" (Query 17).[29] How could the Founders reconcile their insistent appeal to civic virtue with their dominant interest in creating the political conditions for maximum trade profit? The two could be combined only because of their particular conception of government's relation to an older, more comprehensive social order that had already shaped society in its more fundamental features. The American statesmen never envisioned a pre-social condition. The presence from the beginning of a real, articulated society that distributes its functions over a number of social bodies reduced the role of the political structures to the instrumental function of coordinating these existing social functions. Michael Novak has rightly emphasized this *social genius* of the founders: "One cannot properly think of the framers as preoccupied solely with the individualistic aspect of individual liberties. On the contrary, they were preoccupied with questions of social system, of social *ordo*, in all its institutional ramifications."[30] Those principles that guided the beginning of our republic have not lost their pertinence today, as the discussion of subsidiarity and of the indispensability of civic virtue will show.

What accounts for this distinctness of the American conception of the state? One factor was undoubtedly the pragmatic state of mind of political leaders confronted with urgent practical necessities. Whether a pre-social "state of nature" had ever existed was a subject of speculation for which the framers of the constitution had neither the leisure nor the interest. But their more modest view of the political enterprise allowed their mostly implicit theory to accommodate elements of an older, more intrinsically social tradition. Precisely because they did not consider civil government a social "first," they could speak of human rights without sharing the individualist premises by which modern Europeans had justified these rights. These rights were neither pre-social nor inherent in individuals independently of their social status. John Courtney Murray gave this point all due emphasis when comparing the Bill of Rights with the French *Declaration of the Rights of Man* of 1789, which he called "a parchment child of the Enlightenment, a top-of-the-brain concoction of a set of men who did not understand that a political community…has roots in history and in nature."[31] While the French document was based on an atomism that ignored any associations intermediate between the individual and the state, the framers of the

American Bill of Rights never forgot the social entrenchments of the pre-political rights they wanted to safeguard. The American founders started from a real, rather than a potential, community. Nor did their idea of *right* serve as a substitute for the *good*. As Alexis de Toqueville described it, the notion of rights consists in the first place in the moral demands the common good makes upon the members of society, rather than a set of individual privileges. "The idea of rights is nothing but the conception of virtue applied to the world of politics. No man can be great without virtue, nor any nation great without respects for rights; one might almost say that without it there can be no society, for what is a combination of rational and intelligent beings held together by force alone?"[32] In this perspective rights educate the citizens toward serving the common good.

In contrast, the liberal idea of rights, dispensing with any definition of the common good, provides the kind of unembarrassed freedom needed for individuals with divergent and often incompatible goals to pursue their sundry interests.[33] No agreement on the nature of the good-in-itself is necessary as long as the members agree on the priority of the individual's right to choice to the full extent compatible with a similar freedom for others. The idea of equality of choice later came to be complemented by that of equal opportunity. This addition caused substantial disagreements in the liberal camp during the nineteenth century. Old-style believers considered such a policy of public assistance an undue intrusion into the unlimited freedom that forms the basis of modern society. To favor some would violate the limits protecting one's freedom against the way others exercised theirs. Despite this split on strategies, both parties continued to agree on the fundamental goal of society – the preservation of the maximum possible individual choice according to one's private conception of the good.[34]

That such a total neutrality with respect to the nature of the common good could ever be considered the supreme social ideal, indeed one that became dominant in Western society, is in itself remarkable enough. That it continues to be so regarded today is almost unbelievable. Yet recently Francis Fukuyama asserted that the "unabashed victory of economic and political liberalism" spelled the end of all ideological differences on public policy.[35] Translated into traditional language that means: a definitive abandonment of any attempt to define the common good in terms other than those of private choice. For Fukuyama, the "end of history" consists in the absolute triumph of the theoretical truth of the liberal idea which has now absorbed all previous contradictions. Considering the fact that this idea has no content of its own, I find this an amazing conclusion. Amazing, but perhaps inevitable, given the model of personhood on which it rests. Contrary to all previous traditions it assumes that the individual, as sole source of meaning and value, bears the entire responsibility for defining the goals and destiny of human nature. For the exercise of individual freedom to reach agreement, even perhaps the unity of a general will (Rousseau), it only had to follow standards of rational choice.

In accepting no other standards than those of reason, the liberal project was by no means as free of presuppositions and ideologies as it claimed to be. The priority of individual choice over any commitment to a *given* ideal of the common good rests on particular assumptions of what *is good for* the person, even while its advocates decline to define the nature of that goodness. That model of humanity differed in a basic way from the traditional Christian as well as from the classical ideal, both of which had presented life in society as essentially *given* prior to any choice. Freedom itself had to be exercised within certain, well-defined parameters. The difference appears starkly in the present claim of a *right to choose*, which in this case refers to the option to accept or refuse life itself. In the US that choice is still mostly restricted to the life of the unborn foetus; but advocates of the right to choose have begun to include the right to die or even to kill as applied to older or disabled persons.

Obviously, a development has taken place in liberal doctrine since its beginnings. While the Enlightenment version of it still firmly held to a set of traditional beliefs concerning the nature of the person and the norms of right conduct, the newer version, more consistently, has shed all restrictions except those needed to protect the freedom of others to pursue their goals. Today's liberal society, in Bruce Douglass's words, "does not prejudge the question of what citizens ought to be, do, or believe."[36] But the modern version operates no more in an ideological vacuum than the older one had. The apparent indeterminacy of its content rests upon a particular equation of freedom with unrestricted choice. How little that equation can be taken to be self-evident has been shown by the resistance it encounters in traditional societies and by the attraction totalitarian ideologies (be they fascist or Communist) have exerted in liberal democratic countries even in our century.

The presence of a particular ideology has been pointed out (and later admitted by the author) in John Rawls's impressively consistent argument in support of an idea of justice based on the principles of liberal indeterminacy. The concept of fairness in Rawls's *A Theory of Justice* (1971) is superior to most in that it has none of the relativism that characterizes many utilitarian arguments. For Rawls, as for Kant, the dignity of the individual is an *absolute*, not to be sacrificed for any presumed social benefits. Civil society has an unconditional obligation to protect this dignity.[37] But soon that deontological imperative slips away in the more fundamental relativism of the liberal refusal to define what constitutes the good. What appeared to be a *good* in the firmness of the demand turns out to be no more than a *fairness* in the distribution of opportunities for each person to pursue whatever he or she may consider to be good. But once we relativize the good to being a matter of private choice, we *eo ipso* deprive both the choice and the obligation of that absolute quality that only the good itself can confer. To secure each individual's "right" to do what he or she pleases, as long as he or she does not hinder others in doing the same, may be expeditious, perhaps necessary from a practical point of view. But it can hardly pass for a common *good*. Without the ultimacy of what is good *in itself*, fairness can claim no more than being conducive to a hypothetical goal. In this case that goal consists in the ideological assumption that the realization of private objectives has a priority over social objectives. It implicitly rejects the idea that there may be a good that surpasses unlimited choice and that may occasionally restrict it. Unless we show that fairness in granting a free choice is the *necessary* road to the pursuit of what constitutes a good-in-itself (the Scholastic *bonum honestum*), Rawls's ideal can count for hardly more than a description of the civilized manner in which members of a modern society, especially one rooted in the Anglo-Saxon legal tradition, pursue their intensely private goals without becoming a nuisance to others.

It is difficult to disagree with the appropriateness of policies based on such a principle for furthering the economic objectives of a developed country. According to Rawls, what all rational parties would *have to* choose, in order to act fairly, is a particular mode of distribution that has proven successful within a capitalist economy. How little such a principle can serve as a universal norm for political *praxis* appears soon enough when we attempt to apply it to societies with an "undeveloped" economy or even, I suspect, to the rules of economic exchange with such societies. William L. McBride put it well: "Economics determines the very sort of answer that Rawls decides to seek; essentially the justice that he is looking for is a justice of distribution of goods."[38] One could, of course, argue that the common good consists precisely in the maximum economic well-being of the members of a society. But that goal differs substantially from the one Rawls and modern liberals set up at the start of their project. Besides, to consider economic progress the primary value of a politically organized society or at least the basis of all others is, except in the case of destitute societies living in conditions of extreme material hardship, no more than a modern ideology that did not come to be generally accepted until the nineteenth century. It is one that liberalism shares with its worst adversaries, totalitarian Communists. As such it presents a weak argument in favor of an ideal of freedom.[39] The primacy of the economic leads to a theory of society in which public interference is restricted in principle to the creation and regulation of opportunities for the fulfillment of material and educational needs.

Even if we accept the severe moral restrictions imposed by the liberal principle of choice as morally ideal or inevitable, the criterion of fairness itself quickly turns problematic. In a world of scarcity even a pragmatic success in satisfactorily defining entitlements and distributions becomes hard to achieve. The distributional priorities set by public authority are likely to run into conflict with the ideals of freedom and equality a liberal government professes. Once one declares maximum individual choice the highest common goal, it becomes difficult to define, for instance, the margin at which the supply of energy must be restricted by the protection of a natural environment endangered by increased burning of fossil fuel and the production of nuclear power. At what point does public restriction turn into improper interference with citizens' freedom? Any kind of society has to confront such questions, but one that refuses to accept any idea of a common good beyond that of maximizing the individual choices of its members will experience greater difficulty in justifying its decisions. Marx already perceived a related problem when he exposed a conflict between the nineteenth century's ideal of laissez-faire liberalism and the socialized mode of capitalist production and distribution. These problems can only increase when, in a period of instant communication, societies of different levels of economic development are in constant exchange with one another. At a time of global exchange and under the threat of social and ecological disasters, can we remain satisfied with a morally neutral concept of the common good? Can even a definition of the common good based upon a concept of society restricted to the nation-state still suffice? On the other hand, can a society whose members no longer share common ideals and norms afford to have any but a morally neutral concept of the common good without sacrificing its most precious value – the autonomy of its members? These are issues we must investigate in the final part of the chapter.

THE GLOBAL SOCIETY'S NEED OF A COMMON GOOD

The attitudes and objectives of traditional liberalism clearly no longer suffice for solving the problems that confront modern democracies. A social ideal of unlimited choice is hardly appropriate for a situation in which shrinking resources continuously reduce the effectiveness of that choice. We may eventually discover adequate substitutes for our dwindling fuel supplies. But how can we hope to discover acceptable space to house and feed an alarmingly growing population, or to dispose of our increasingly hazardous waste? Or how could a public policy that includes neither principles nor provisions for maintaining a balance in global distribution of goods avoid the threatening prospect of social warfare? To survive with dignity in a world so substantially different from the one in which the liberal theory was formulated, we can no longer afford to rely on programs of distribution depending entirely on the free choice of generous individuals.

Of course, many citizens of advanced democracies would concur in this criticism. But few, not including the writer of this essay, would be prepared to exchange democratic choice for some new form of enlightened despotism either on a national or an international scale. We feel, rightly I think, that respect for individual freedom ought to be a non-negotiable feature of any future polity. The demand of individual autonomy has so fully taken possession of our moral outlook that even to weaken it would inflict major injury to that very dignity that we are seeking to preserve. A person's "right" to exercise basic control over his/her destiny has, whatever the adequacy of its theoretical justification, become a moral cornerstone of our culture. This implies that any positive, trans-individual determinations of the common good must be freely accepted. No argument of *raison d'état* should be allowed to overrule democratic liberties. We need a conception of the *good* that itself includes individual autonomy. To what degree ought the relative well-being of some groups or nations with a legitimate claim to the fruits of their labor be lowered in order to secure a higher degree of well-being for others? To decide this by governmental (national or international) *decree*, except for cases of famine on a grand scale where the survival of many is at stake, may entail a sacrifice of the fundamental good of freedom to the lesser one of material equality. Both values must be respected and any agreement on the manner in which they may simultaneously be preserved requires some *consensus* on the nature of the common good itself. Clearly, then, choice remains an essential factor in our definition of the common good, but it must cease to function as a substitute for it.

What possible alternative, then, could replace the present public neutrality regarding the ways individuals realize their freedom? The argument proposed here attempts to show that autonomy and moral neutrality need not remain as united as a liberal ideology would have it. Democratic freedom is perfectly compatible with a positive conception of the common good. But here we immediately confront a formidable obstacle to such a positive conception. How would we be able to define the common good when we no longer share a common concept of society in our pluralistic culture? Before addressing the real problems created by this pluralism, we should realize that neither a "definition" of the common good nor an *a priori* agreement on what it demands is needed for solving it. It suffices that we agree on the principle that the good of the community takes precedence over the maximum fulfillment of the individual, and that we be prepared to accept this as a maxim for moral action. An axiom so general may appear trivial. Nevertheless it shows how our present assumptions concerning the nature and function of society differ from pre-modern ones. If Plato, Aristotle, and Aquinas, even Luther, Calvin, and Suarez, were still capable of taking the priority of the common good for granted, it was because they still shared the belief that the norms of fundamental social institutions do not depend on private choice but are *given* with the institutions themselves. The rule over human affairs was not presumed to rest entirely in human hands. Indeed, society itself rested on a *given a priori*. Once the source of meaning and value came to reside exclusively in the human subject, however, as it did in the modern age, any possibility of reaching a consensus on the common good beyond that of creating an environment conducive to individual self-realization became extremely difficult. Indeed, I see no chance of regaining even a minimal agreement on what constitutes the common good without some return to a religious-moral view of the human place in cosmos and society. Without the restoration of some sense of transcendence, there remains little hope for a consensus on what must count as good in itself. For such a good must present itself in an objective, *given* order.

Of course, it would be idle to expect members of a modern society to agree on dogmatically defined or homogeneously articulated concepts like those that grounded the medieval religious world view. Today one cannot even count on a general acceptance of those minimal Deist principles that still informed eighteenth-century European culture. Yet what I am advocating is not doctrinal orthodoxy, but an *attitude* that is once again ready to accept the human condition as, at least in its foundation, *given*. I once described this *practical* religiousness as follows:

What is needed is a conversion to an attitude in which existing is more than taking, acting more than making, meaning more than function – an attitude in which there is enough leisure for wonder and enough detachment for transcendence...What is needed most of all is an attitude in which transcendence *can be recognized again*.[40]

What I am defending, in plain terms, is a return to virtue on a religious basis as an indispensable condition for any possibility of a genuine conception of, and respect for, the common good. Such a thesis must appear utopian in light of today's mostly technocratic, morally relativist, and intensely secular political science. As an excuse for presenting it nonetheless, I would point to the bleak results achieved by a purely pragmatic *realpolitik*. Even as recently as the eighteenth century, the fathers of modern democracy, Montesquieu and Rousseau, still regarded civic virtue as indispensable for building a good society as Plato and Aristotle did. Moreover, to those who launched the American republic, both the religiously inspired Puritans and the more morally but still deistically motivated founders, nothing seemed more indispensable to the success of the republic than self-forgetting devotion to a common cause defined by a religious destiny. The republican founders resolutely revived a moral ideal that had never completely vanished yet that in the British tradition had more and more yielded to utilitarian considerations.

But they surpassed the older tradition by applying that ideal to a *democratic* form of government. In antiquity such a government was deemed nearly devoid of moral potential. Montesquieu, on the other hand, held that a democratic republic required a higher degree of virtue from its citizens than any other. The founders of the American republic not only assumed the need for virtue, but attempted to protect it by institutions, without "enforcing" it upon the citizens as Rousseau did. It would be naive to consider the pursuit of self-chosen, private fulfillment an adequate substitute for virtue in the vastly complex society of our own age. To be sure, the intelligent pursuit of private interests already constitutes in itself a certain social order. But the reason why socialism made such deep inroads during the nineteenth century is simply that the liberal model of society failed to meet the minimum requirements for social harmony in the community as a whole. Even less will it be adequate for the infinitely more complex global society of the near future, which starts from economic inequalities that can never be overcome by mere laissez-faire politics.

In stressing the need for virtue and emphasizing duty, I do not mean to question the existence of human rights, the only effective means by which modern political philosophy has defended itself against the dangerous subjectivism present in its own principles. That theory may be shorn from its individualist origins if we conceive of those rights as given *with and through* the concrete context of society, rather than rooted in a pre-social state of nature. John Finnis has made a notable attempt to link human rights to the notion of the common good. For him, rights define the requirements of those *objective* and absolute values that constitute the dignity of the person. He thus frees the theory from the shackles of modern subjectivism. But has he also rid them of an individualist conception of the common good? Undoubtedly, the political community must secure those conditions, including social relations, that tend "to favor the realization by each individual in the community, of his or her personal development."[41] Yet is the common good no more than the totality of conditions that assist each individual member to pursue his or her own objectives? If a theory of rights relates to the common good only "by providing a usefully detailed listing of the various aspects of human flourishing and fundamental components of the way of life in community that tends to favor such flourishing in all,"[42] then that common good itself hardly exceeds the goods of individuals protected by individual rights.

The doctrine of rights advanced in the encyclical *Pacem in Terris* impresses me as being more intrinsically social. John XXIII stresses that human beings are by nature social (*PT* 23). Yet he does not oppose the social to the individual as the totalitarian theory of the state does. Nor does he restrict the function of the common good to the preserving of individual rights. Rather, the social and the individual appear as two dialectical moments of a single reality that preserves individual interests without allowing them to take over the common good. The diverse groups of civil society mediate individual interests with the common good.

For the achievement of ends which individual human beings cannot attain except by association, it is necessary and indispensable to set up a great variety of intermediate groups and bodies in order to guarantee the dignity of the human person and safeguard a sufficient sphere of freedom and responsibility. (*PT* 24)

The principle of *subsidiarity*, here articulated by Pope John and asserted by all his predecessors since Leo XIII, prevents the common good from assuming an existence independent of private concerns, and thus turning into social ideology.[43] Only a social system based on subsidiarity can avoid turning the state into either a mere legal sanction of individual interests (as in nineteenth-century liberalism) or into a personification of a common good in which individual interests are not adequately represented (as in the dictatorial states of the twentieth century).

In such a system citizens build the common good up from the ground, so to speak, constantly revising and reconceiving it in accordance with the particular needs of the time. A major problem with the traditional presentation of the common good is that it appears as a fixed concept, immovable by the dynamic changes of human existence. It is, of course, true enough that the *basic* objective – to enable the person to attain the fullness of life which only life in political community can grant – remains a constant. But that objective is empty until we concretize it in historical, time-bound goals. The common good ought to reflect the ever-active choices of free individuals, which it grounds, guides, and restricts.[44]

A primary function of civil society remains that of encouraging and providing the proper circumstances for the development of *virtue* among its citizens. Virtue, however, should be taken not in today's narrowly moralistic sense of what a categorical imperative prescribes, but as possessing the full social and aesthetic scope that Plato and Aristotle granted the term. This includes what we *may* do in pursuing that perfection for which nature is the aesthetic as well as the ethical norm. The idea of the common good should play a significant part in guiding citizens toward the cultivation of such virtue. Without substituting for church or family, civil society has as a principal function to support those institutions that may be conducive to the good life. The question of *goodness* must not be bracketed. At the same time, the acceptance of the idea of a common good presupposes a minimum agreement on what is intrinsically good, and this itself rests on the presence of a certain amount of *virtue* among the citizens. One of the main predicaments of the modern liberal state is that virtue has been replaced by choice. In addition, the principle of subsidiarity prohibits the state from *enforcing* a particular ideal of goodness if it is not accepted by a major part of its citizenship. To do so would harm rather than benefit the common good. This implies that political society should adopt an educational rather than a coercive role. The common good may require the toleration of a good deal of vice rather than radical attempts to eradicate evil by measures for which the citizenship is not prepared.

Finally, the idea of a common good must not remain restricted to the political community as it exists in the nation-state. Modern states have become so interdependent that the concept of absolute sovereignty or political autonomy has become obsolete. The internationalization of economic relations (on which political societies depend) shows how inadequate the modern state has become as ultimate incorporation of the "common good." Already Aquinas had expanded the idea of *communitas perfecta* to the entire *res publica hominum sub Deo* for the constitution of which political societies played only an instrumental role. Yet in the modern theory of the state, the political community became an absolute – an unqualified *societas perfecta*.[45] When Hegel placed the state at the top of the ethical pyramid in which his social philosophy culminated, he formulated a concept that has been bypassed by historical reality. We now have reached a point in history where the principle of subsidiarity with respect to the common good must be applied to the states themselves in their relation to the global community. In the present intensified exchange among nations, the principle of subsidiarity may assist us in overcoming socially dangerous and ethically unjustifiable political divisions. It can also prevent the imposition of an international authority that ignores the particular economic and cultural interests of individual nations and contributes no more to the global common good than a universally resented international police corps.

Significantly, recent papal encyclicals have insisted upon the same principle of subsidiarity in discussions of the formation of a world community that they once emphasized solely *within* the political community of the nation-state. No one did so more explicitly than John XXIII in *Pacem in Terris*.

> A public authority, having world-wide power and endowed with the proper means for the efficacious pursuit of its objective, which is the universal common good in concrete form, must be set up by common accord and not imposed by force...Just as with each political community the relations between individuals, families, intermediate associations and public authority are governed by the principle of subsidiarity, so too the relations between the public authority of each political community and the public authority of the world community must be regulated by the same principle."
> (*PT* 138, 140)

NOTES

1 Maria Consiglia De Matteis, *La teologia politica communale di Remigio de' Girolami* (Bologna: Patron, 1977), cxxiii. All references are to this edition of the text of *De bono communi*.

2 Ibid., 42, also 15.

3 Ibid., 30.

4 Ibid., 39.

5 Eugene TeSelle, "The Civic Vision in Augustine's City of God," *Thought* 62 (1987): 268–280. David Hollenbach, "The Common Good Revisited," *Theological Studies* 20 (1989): 70–94.

6 Charles De Koninck: *De la primauté du bien commun, contre les personnalistes* (Quebec: Laval University Press, 1943), 8.

7 On the controversy and the necessary distinctions, see Gregory Froelich, "The Equivocal Status of *Bonum Commune*," *New Scholasticism* 63/1 (1989): 38–57.

8 Jacques Maritain, *The Person and the Common Good* (Notre Dame, IN: University of Notre Dame Press, 1966), 18–19.

9 *Summa contra Gentiles*, III: 17.

10 *In I Pol.* lect. 1.

11 *Summa Theologiae*, I–II, q. 90, 2.

12 *De regimine principum* 1: 14. I owe this reference as well as the next qualification to a set of lecture notes, "Stoic and Christian Sources of Mediaeval Social Doctrine" by I. T. Eschmann, OP, which, to the best of my knowledge, was never published.

13 *Summa contra Gentiles*, III: 80.

14 Maritain, *The Person and the Common Good*, 7.

15 *Summa Theologiae*, I–II, q. 21, 4, ad 3.

16 John Finnis, *Natural Law and Natural Rights* (Oxford: Clarendon Press, 1980), 220–221.

17 Finnis, *Natural Law and Natural Rights*, 154.

18 Ernest Fortin, "The New Rights Theory and the Natural Law," *Review of Politics* 44 (1982): 590–612. Similar objections might be leveled against Maritain's theory of natural rights conceived as *prior* to any social incorporation. See Frederick Crosson, "Maritain on Natural Rights," *Review of Metaphysics* 36/144 (1983): 895–912.

19 On all the complexities of this process one may consult André de Muralt, "La Structure de la philosophie politique moderne d'Occam à Rousseau," in *Souveraineté et pouvoir. Cahiers de la Revue de Théologie et de Philosophie* 2 (Geneva, Lausanne, Neuchâtel, 1978), 3–84. I have greatly profited from this penetrating essay.

20 See the introduction by A. S. McGrade to Richard Hooker, *Of the Laws of Ecclesiastical Polity* (London: Sidgwick and Jackson, 1975), 11–40.

21 "Alio modo consideranda est hominum multitudo, quatenus speciali voluntate seu communi consensu in unum corpus politicum congregantur uno societatis vinculo, et ut mutuo se juvent in ordine ad unum finem politicum, quomodo efficiunt unum corpus mysticum, quod moraliter dici potest per se unum." *De legibus* III, chap. 2, no. 4. See also Otto Gierke, *Natural Law and the Theory of Society. 1500 to 1800*, trans. Ernest Barker (1934) (Boston: Beacon Press, 1957), 243, especially Barker's footnote.

22 *Defensio fidei* VI, chap. 4, nos. 1ff. I follow André de Muralt's interpretation in *d'Occam à Rousseau*, 60–65.

23 See J. W. Allen, *History of Political Thought in the Sixteenth Century* (New York, Barnes & Noble, 1960; orig. London, 1928), 282.

24 As John Finnis does in *Natural Law and Natural Rights*. See also David Hollenbach's essay in this volume.

25 Ernest Fortin, "The New Rights Theory and the Natural Law," *Review of Politics* 44 (1982): 595.

26 See Elie Halevy, *The Growth of Philosophic Radicalism*, trans. Mary Morris (Clifton, NJ: Augustus Kelley Publ., 1972), 138.

27 Thomas Paine, *The Rights of Man* (New York: Doubleday Anchor Books, 1973), 434.

28 Jonathan Elliot, ed., *Debates in the Several State Conventions on the Adoption of the Federal Constitution* (Philadelphia: Lippincott, 1907). Quoted by Michael Novak, *Free Persons and the Common Good* (Lanham, MD: Madison Books, 1989), 50.

29 On the "commercialism" of the founders, see Thomas L. Pangle, "The Constitution's Human Vision," *Public Interest* 86 (Winter 1987): 85–88.

30 Novak, *Free Persons and the Common Good*, 46–47. One may, of course, question whether the modern use of the term "liberal" in America still corresponds to the insights of the Founders. The period beginning with

Jackson and culminating in the first World War places a dominant emphasis on economic values whereby, in my judgment, America *in practice* rejoins the British tradition. Novak himself stresses the economic aspect of the American revolution, calling it "a new type of economic system" (p. 46) to a degree that weakens his position on the political significance and the need for self-sacrificing civic virtue so prominent in the early documents.

31 John Courtney Murray, *We Hold These Truths* (New York: Sheed & Ward, 1960), 38.

32 Alexis de Toqueville, *Democracy in America*, trans. George Lawrence (New York: Doubleday, 1969), 237.

33 Alasdair MacIntyre, *Whose Justice? Which Rationality?* (Notre Dame, IN: University of Notre Dame Press, 1988), 336.

34 Is this agreement still present in those whom Nicholas Capaldi calls new-style liberals who ground their principles in a teleological theory of participation? Or has the term "liberal" ceased to function as a useful category, since it has come to embrace virtually opposite principles? Nicholas Capaldi, *Out of Order: Affirmative Action and the Crisis of Doctrinaire Liberalism* (Buffalo, NY: *Prometheus Books*, 1985), 5.

35 Francis Fukuyama, "The End of History?" *National Interest* 16 (Summer 1989): 3.

36 R. Bruce Douglass, "Liberalism as a Threat to Democracy," in Francis Canavan, ed., *The Ethical Dimension of Political Life* (Durham, NC: Duke University Press, 1983), 29.

37 John Rawls, *A Theory of Justice* (Cambridge, MA: Harvard University Press, 1971), 3–4.

38 William L. McBride, *Social Theory at the Crossroads* (Pittsburgh: Duquesne University Press, 1980), 99.

39 Louis Dupré, *Marx's Social Critique of Culture* (New Haven: Yale University Press, 1983), 210–215; 281–285.

40 Louis Dupré, *Transcendent Selfhood* (New York: Crossroad, 1976), 17.

41 Finnis, *Natural Law and Natural Rights*, 154.

42 Ibid., 211.

43 See Clifford Kossel, SJ, "Global Community and Individuality," *Communio* 8/1 (1981): 37–50.

44 Charles Sherover, "The Temporality of the Common Good," *Review of Metaphysics* 37/3, no. 147 (1984): 492.

45 Kossel, "Global Community," 44.

CHAPTER 8

Catholic classics in American liberal culture

David Tracy

AMERICAN CATHOLIC SOCIAL THEORY: A POSSIBLE CONSENSUS?

To a non-expert reader like myself, contemporary debate in political theory and ethics, including Catholic social ethics in the United States, is one of the more promising discussions of our period. Unlike many debates in epistemology or, I regret to say, in fundamental theology, the debate in Catholic social ethics and political theory seems to yield more of a consensus (although, by no means either a full or a non-controversial consensus) than other debates. It is always risky to formulate a possible consensus. However, I shall attempt to do so here. In Catholic social ethics (represented, in the US, not only by Catholic ethicists but by the pastoral letters on nuclear war and the economy of the American bishops), there seems to be something like a consensus on three points.

First, a responsible Catholic social ethics in a pluralist and democratic society will be obliged to make its case on grounds acceptable, in principle, both to the Catholic and wider Christian community on the one hand, and to the larger secular, pluralistic, democratic, and, in that basic sense, "liberal" society on the other.[1] Insofar as Catholic social ethics succeeds in that public enterprise it will also correlate[2] (as distinct from juxtapose) the arguments from inner-Christian resources and the distinct arguments from "reason," including some form of a general ethics and political theory. Second, appeals in Catholic social ethics to earlier versions of "reason," such as dehistoricized versions of natural law, have been replaced by more historically conscious but not relativistic defenses of "reason." This move is analogous, I believe, to the abandonment of dehistoricized Enlightenment notions of rationality in contemporary liberal social theory. At the least, liberal theory, for example in the recent work of

Rawls, has seriously modified earlier Kantian claims without abandoning either a defense of reason or a defense of the humane ideals of the liberal Enlightenment. Third, the appeals to inner-Christian resources have now rendered Catholic social ethics a fully theological enterprise. This is evident in appeals to biblical symbols in Catholic ethics.[3] For example, the creation of man and woman in the "image of God" discloses an understanding of the human person, the bond of "covenant" an understanding of community, and the eschatological promise of the "Kingdom of God" an understanding of the political realm. It is also evident in appeals to classical Catholic theological positions in social ethics. Thus Augustine's subtle contrast of the *civitas Dei* and *civitas terrena* yields an understanding of the *res publica*; the Trinitarian understanding of God suggests an understanding of the person as relational in contrast to the classic liberal "individual."

There are, of course, strong exceptions to these generalizations on a possible consensus in American Catholic social thought among both Neoscholastic and Straussian Catholic thinkers as well as among some "linguistic-cultural" (and, therefore, anti-correlational) Catholic theologians. However, insofar as it is correct to speak of a representative, American Catholic position at all (e.g., the pastoral letters of the American bishops), these three constants in the discussion do seem to form something like a consensus. In this chapter, therefore, I wish to assume that such consensus does exist in order to suggest how Catholic social thinkers might provide further "public" (i.e., liberal, democratic) grounds for their now frequent appeals to inner-Christian resources in public discussion. In order to make that case, I shall employ arguments I have developed elsewhere in various public forums and publications.[4] I repeat these arguments here in order to test their plausibility for illuminating the relation between Catholic social ethics and the canons of publicness for liberal, pluralistic society. I do so in the hope that my hermeneutical argument on the public character of all "classics," including the religious classics of biblical symbols and doctrines as well as theological metaphors and analogues, may prove helpful to those Catholic social theorists desiring to show, on public grounds, why an appeal to particular traditions need not be merely particularist or private.

This strategy may prove helpful given the irony of our present situation. One way to express that irony is Schillebeeckx's ob-

servation: after two centuries of resistance to liberal modernity, at
Vatican II Catholic Christianity embraced the humane ideal of
modernity just at the time when modernity began to distrust itself.

There are, in fact, several good reasons for liberal modernity to
distrust itself: the social reality of rampant individualism with the
attendant loss of earlier American republican and covenantal
resources for a working notion of the common good (Bellah, et al.);
the epistemological crisis of "foundationalism" now exposed in
classical liberal theory's quest for certainty in its ethics and its
political theory alike; the "dialectic of Enlightenment" where once
liberating notions of Enlightenment reason have often become a
merely technical (indeed technocratic) notion of rationality on
means and a "decisionism" on ends; a sometimes almost manic-
depressive cycle of over-confidence and despair as modern liberalism
faces the uncertainty of its own former epistemological foundations
and the resultant possibility that we may now live in a post-modern
era.

One of the most careful, persuasive, and revisionary defenders of
modernity, Jürgen Habermas, whatever the other problems with his
thinking may be, has three singular contributions to our present
discussion.[5] First, the theories of (liberal) rationality should be
related, in any full position, with a historically informed theory of
social system and social action. Second, "totalization" theories on
liberal modernity (e.g., Weber or Adorno) should be incorporated
piecemeal for their considerable insights into the dilemmas of liberal
modernity but not wholesale. Third, in a pluralistic, democratic
society, reason needs more than a cultural defense (Rorty) or a
historical critique (MacIntyre). Reason needs a philosophical defense
as intrinsically intersubjective and communicative. The latter can
occur as a historically and social-scientifically informed but not
determined defense of "communicative reason." Hence one may
focus on the role of argument, as well as (more than Habermas seems
to realize) on the wider role of dialogue as inquiry.[6] Moreover, this
historically conscious but not historically determined (i.e., relativist)
defense of reason in Habermas is analogous to the historically
conscious defense of reason in the Catholic thinker Bernard Lonergan, and, through Lonergan's epistemological and methodological
influence, the Catholic social and political theory of John Courtney
Murray.[7] In either case, the need to defend reason without either
"objectivism" or "relativism" (Bernstein) remains a crucial com-

ponent of such consensual Catholic social thought. The question that recurs, however, is whether the appeal to explicitly Christian resources such as *imago Dei*, "Kingdom of God," or "eschatological proviso" is an appeal only to the Christian participants in the public discussion on values in a pluralistic society. Or is that appeal also (not *only*) an appeal to any attentive, intelligent, reasonable, responsible person? To be sure, that is only one of the many questions that must be addressed to respond adequately to the question of the relation of Catholicism and liberalism. To that explicit question the rest of this chapter will now turn.

PUBLICNESS AND PARTICULARITY

For a theologian like myself who fully endorses the turn to inner-Christian resources without the loss of appeals to reason in contemporary Catholic social thought, the question of "publicness," and thus of "liberalism," is a pressing one. It is even more pressing for one, again including myself, who also endorses the humane ideals and achievements of the liberal tradition while bemoaning liberalism's present seeming inability to discuss the ends of the good life of a pluralistic society. This inability is partly the result of the mistaken belief that the marginalization of art and the privatization of religion are necessary in any liberal, pluralistic society.

My aim in this section is to explore a question: Do particular traditions bear public resources? The answer is not obvious. But the refusal to pose the question, I suggest, has hampered many discussions of the role of religion in the public life of liberal, pluralistic societies like our own.

Consider the contemporary discussion of the nature of that publicness intrinsic to any liberal society. In a pluralist culture, it is important to know what will and will not count as public, that is what resources are available to all intelligent, reasonable, and responsible members of that culture despite their otherwise crucial differences in belief and practice. In the liberal tradition, the existence of a public realm assumes that there is the possibility of discussion (argument, conversation) among various participants. The only hope for such discussion in a radically pluralist liberal culture is one based on reason. Yet to state that "reason" is needed is to restate the problem of publicness for contemporary liberal theory, not to resolve it.

For what can it mean to say that all parties in a pluralist culture (individuals, groups, traditions) can meet in the public realm, the realm of reason, if there does not seem to be a shared understanding of reason itself? For example, if reason can only function instrumentally, then the culture can reasonably agree on the appropriate instrumental (especially technological) means to achieve its ends, but the ends – the shared values – are, by definition, private, decisionistic, non-rational. They are a matter of choice, not reason. This problem – the so-called problem of instrumental reason and resultant technicization of the once-public realm of liberalism – is intensified by the contemporary insistence in philosophy, ethics, and theology alike that reason itself has a history. To affirm the latter is to pose yet another problem for liberal models of publicness: the problem that various models of reason are themselves *in some sense* dependent on particular social, cultural, historical forces. Has liberal publicness itself now been rendered private? Has liberalism become merely one more particular tradition?

The fact that the problem of the historicity of reason has surfaced most tellingly in reflections upon the truth-claims of the hard sciences themselves (or, more exactly, among philosophers of science such as Kuhn, Toulmin, and Putnam) has only made the problem of the public realm that much more difficult. For the rule of a purely instrumental reason – and thereby the technicization of a once public realm – can only be further enforced if the "checks and balances" on technical reason by the methods of verification and falsification in the hard sciences are to be interpreted as in some crucial sense historically bound. Indeed radical proposals to this effect can readily be found in Feyerabend and Rorty even before deconstructionist literary theorists have had their say on the social sciences and the humanities.

This much seems clear in the present debate over the character of reason (and, therefore, the nature of publicness itself) : earlier debates on strictly positivist understandings of natural science (and, by extension, of reason) and strictly instrumentalist understandings of the relationships of techniques and values (and, by extension, the technicization of the public realm) are now spent. The major and far more difficult discussion has shifted elsewhere. Now the question has become whether the collapse of earlier over-claims of positivism and instrumentalism means that what little remained in the liberal public realm (viz., positivist and instrumentalist notions of reason) has also gone. Must we resign ourselves to the absence of *any* public realm at all and to the destruction of any notion of "publicness"? But how can liberalism intellectually (as distinct from culturally or institutionally) survive without a notion of a shared reason for a shared public realm?[8]

I paint this picture, at once too bleak and too brief, recalling some contemporary discussions of reason and publicness, not to endorse the claims of Feyerabend or Rorty or Derrida. I paint it, rather, to suggest that the question of religion in the public realm is a question that can help to clarify both the character of the truth-claims of religion and the character of any claim to truth in the liberal public realm itself. For the fact is, there remain many thinkers who defend the public realm and rationality itself. These thinkers defend the possibilities of "publicness" without retreating into either historicist, positivist, or instrumentalist notions of reason. They also defend rationality and a pluralistic liberal society without endorsing positions so radically pluralistic that they are finally indistinguishable from classic forms of hard relativism or historicism, however bedecked in the more attractive apparel of the "radical indeterminacy of all meaning" and the always elusive, if not illusory, character of truth itself.

If the problems of publicness and rationality (and thereby of the public realm) are as difficult as I suggest above, then the introduction by Catholic social theorists of religion into this debate may seem singularly unpromising. What seems more obviously "private" than religion to most liberal thinkers? Religion seems private not just in the sociological sense of privatization, but private in the philosophical sense of "without reason": decisionistic, undemonstrated, and perhaps undemonstrable. There are, in fact, ethical and theological analogues to the positions represented in the philosophy of science by Feyerabend or Rorty. Through the discovery of the historical roots and narrative forms of reason itself, such ethicists as Alasdair MacIntyre, in his early work, can seem to leave us with but two choices: Nietzsche or a new St. Benedict.[9] The choices are, indeed, both apt and disheartening for the public realm: the deconstructionist recovery of the "new Nietzsche" has been, thus far, hardly conducive to revitalizing the public realm of ethics and politics. And many of the new Christian narrative theologies are self-consciously, even proudly, sectarian.

In this discussion, one crucial need, I suggest, is to shift the major focus of the debate away from "origins" to "effects." More exactly,

one can agree with and learn thankfully from the present redis-
coveries of the historical, communal, and narrative origins of all
models of publicness and reason. And yet we should remain
unpersuaded by the strict narrativists' conclusions on effects, viz.,
that all we have are particular traditions of both reason and religion
whose particularist effects are as non-public, non-shareable as their
origins. In Troeltschian terms this translates into the position that
there is no church, there are only sects. In ethical terms, it translates
into the insistence that no Kant-like enterprise ever has succeeded or
could succeed. Rather, only various aretaic positions grounded in
particular communities and narratives are possible. In more general
philosophical terms, this translates as: there are no persuasive
(linguistically informed and historically conscious) transcendental or
metaphysical arguments. Rather, there is only context-bound rhe-
torical persuasion within concrete communities of discourse. In
general theological terms, this translates as: there is no fundamental
theology. There are only various particular systematic theologies. In
terms of our present set of questions, this translates as: there is no
authentic public realm where a public, shared reason can rule. There
are only particular traditions which can either "witness" to their
truth and make temporary coalitions with other traditions, or
become, in a once public but now technicized realm, merely
particularist interest groups struggling with and against other equally
particularist groups. As we will see below, there is no good reason to
discourage either "witnessing" or "coalitions" in the public realm as
long as these are not considered exhaustive options. However, there
is good reason for all witnessing groups and all coalition partners to
be deeply troubled about the loss of a public realm in liberal,
pluralistic societies. The departure of shared norms for reason and
publicness may mean that reasonable argument may exit from the
public realm. But the exit of truth is not the exit of power – as the
quick contemporary slide from witness and coalitions to interest
groups in the presently impoverished "public" realm starkly
demonstrates.

The issue of publicness can be reformulated, therefore, in this way:
Is it or is it not the case that, however particular in origin and
expression any classic work may be, whether in art or religion or any
other realm in which the human spirit reveals itself, the effects of that
classic are nonetheless public?[10] To shift the questions of art, religion,
and even, as suggested above, reason itself away from origins to

effects is a first step to providing a more adequate list of candidates for public discourse in a pluralistic culture. My own work on the nature of "the classic" leads me to this conclusion. To summarize: every classic work of art or religion is highly particular in both origin and expression yet deeply public in effect. As reception-theory in modern hermeneutics attempts to show, even if we cannot agree on the origins of a classic work of art, we can still agree on its effects. Those effects can only be described as public, i.e., shareable, open to all human beings. The effects of a classic work of art or the classic symbols and narratives of particular religious traditions are public by hermeneutically providing disclosive and transformative possibilities for all reflective persons.[11] Their publicness, indeed their meaning and truth, is precisely their ability to disclose new transformative possibilities for the imagination of any inquirer. The spectrum of possible responses (as disclosive and transformative) to any classic varies widely. Across this spectrum, responses to genuine classics range from, minimally, a tentative sense of resonance to, maximally, an experience appropriately described as a "shock of recognition." In *every* case along the whole spectrum, however, *some* hermeneutical disclosure and transformation, and thereby some meaning and truth, is in fact present. And it is present as communicable, shareable, public.

If strictly positivist and instrumentalist notions of reason and publicness alone are allowed, then the possibility of the common concrete experience of the truths of art and religion as truth-as-disclosure and transformation is, of course, disallowed. Then, as the public realm itself falls more and more under the influence of scientific and technical thinking, art becomes marginalized and religion privatized. But if – to employ classic Aristotelian terms – poetics and rhetoric are also allowed to make claims to truth (poetics through disclosure-transformation; rhetoric through persuasive argument, not fanciful ornamentation), then the role of reason itself is properly expanded – and properly focused in its *de facto* effects, not its speculative origins. As Stephen Toulmin has observed, Aristotle's *Topics* is also a rediscovery of the claims to truth and to shareable, public meaning in rhetoric itself (and by a necessary expansion of Toulmin's position on rhetoric, in the poetics, ethics, politics, and even metaphysics of Aristotle).

I do not pretend to have defended this expanded list of candidates for truth-claims in this brief thought-experiment. Yet this much is warranted, I believe, even on this limited basis: the problem of the role of religion in the public realm needs, above all, to focus first on analyzing a more comprehensive notion of reason itself than contemporary liberal theory envisages and thereby of religion's own possible relationships to that more comprehensive role. One strategy for attempting that is to shift, as above, the major focus of the discussion away from origins to effects. In that shift, the role of any classic (and, by analogy, of reason itself) is the role of a phenomenon that is always particular in origin and expression yet public in effect.

It is not the case, therefore, that our only alternatives are a positivist and instrumentalist definition of the public realm or a sheer chaos, a multiplicity of positions on publicness, meaning, and truth sliding into the abyss of "power-politics" amidst competing interest-groups. It is the case that reason itself, however particular in origin and expression, is public in effect. Reason itself is comprehensive enough to include *both* argument on the conditions for the possibility of our common, shared, public discourse (including *de facto* transcendental arguments on "communicative reason") *and* conversation with all the classic expressions in the culture (including the religious classics of the culture). Such a scenario suggests the fuller meaning of an authentically public realm where argument and conversation are demanded of all participants. What this might mean more concretely for the present question of the possible role of religion in American culture I shall now try to address.

PUBLICNESS AS ARGUMENT AND CONVERSATION

In the classical liberal tradition, to produce public discourse is to provide reasons for one's assertions. To provide reasons is to render one's claims shareable, public. To provide reasons is to be willing to engage in argument. For argument is clearly the more obvious form of public discourse.[12] To engage in argument is to make claims and to give the warrants and backings for those claims. Argument is not exhausted by the purely deductive procedures of the traditional syllogism or by some contemporary narrow understandings of logic. To be reasonable is, however, to be logical. To be logical is to be coherent. To argue is to demand coherence. To argue is also to be satisfied, as Aristotle insists, with the kind of evidence appropriate to the subject-matter under discussion. To argue is to engage – to

defend and correct – one's assertions publicly by providing the
evidence, warrants, and backings appropriate to the concrete subject-
matter under discussion. Entailed in this liberal commitment to
public argument is also the willingness to render explicit the criteria
appropriate to the particular subject-matter under discussion. Those
criteria will prove to be, in any case where the question is other than
one of coherence, criteria of relative adequacy, that is, adequacy
relative to the appropriate subject-matter and relative to the evidence
presently available on this subject-matter. With this liberal understanding of argument one can argue publicly, as Dewey insisted, not
only over the appropriate means to achieve a particular end, but over
the particular end itself. Because of the nature of the subject-matter,
the structure of the argument on any question of ends must be
difficult, complex, and tentative. And yet, as argument, the discussion
of ends and values is public, not private or merely preferential.

The move to explicit argument is the most obvious way to assure
publicness. If there is a liberal public realm, this means that there is
a realm where argument is not merely allowed but demanded. It
means, as well, that truth in the public realm will yield some
consensus – a consensus of the community of inquiry cognizant of
and guided by the criteria and evidence of the particular subject-
matter under discussion. As Dewey insisted, a community of inquiry
must be democratic, even radically egalitarian, in the most fundamental sense. No one is accorded privileged status in an argument;
all are equal; all are bound to produce and yield to evidence,
warrants, backings. The emerging consensus must be a consensus
responsible to the best argument. That remains the epistemological-
ethical heart of liberalism.

The first responsibility of the pluralistic, liberal, democratic public
realm is, therefore, the responsibility to give reasons, to provide
arguments – to be public. Argument has traditionally been, and
must remain, the primary candidate for publicness. And yet there is
a second candidate for publicness usually unacknowledged by liberal
theorists. It is related to, yet distinct from, argument itself. That
candidate, as I suggested above, is the phenomenon of conversation
with classics. More exactly, conversation is a phenomenon that is
scarcely distinguishable from argument in a general epistemological
sense. This is so insofar as there is no genuine conversation unless the
general criteria for argument are also observed: criteria of intelligibility (coherence), truth (warrants-evidence), right (moral

integrity) and equality (mutual reciprocity). These general criteria (roughly identical to those of Habermas) can serve as *de facto* conditions of possibility for the presence or absence of both argument and conversation.

However, there are also forms of conversation that, although responsible to these general criteria, are nonetheless also so distinctive in the kind of truth they attain and so important for a pluralistic public realm that they demand explicit treatment: viz., a conversation with the classics of a culture.

A classic is a phenomenon whose excess and permanence of meaning resists definitive interpretation. The classics of art and religion are phenomena whose truth-value is dependent upon their disclosive and transformative possibilities for their interpreters. This does not mean, to repeat, that the conversation with the classics can abandon the general criteria for publicness cited above. It does mean, however, that the concrete classics of art and religion are likely to manifest disclosive and transformative meaning and truth in a manner that is not reducible to the structure of argument. Truth as disclosure-transformation is a primal understanding of truth (Heidegger, Gadamer, Ricoeur). It is available in principle to all who will risk entering into genuine conversation with the classics. Here, conversation becomes, first, the entry by the interpreter into the to-and-fro movement of the questions and responses of the classic itself.[13] The interpreter, of course, enters with a pre-understanding of those questions, for example, a pre-understanding of religion. Nonetheless the interpreter is willing to risk that pre-understanding by noting the claim to attention of the classic itself. That claim to attention may range across a whole spectrum from a tentative resonance to a shock of recognition. The experience is one, primarily, of a reality that is first recognized as important and as bearing a truth-claim, and which is acknowledged in the experience of conversation with the classic to be so.

It is important to note that this modern hermeneutical understanding of conversation does not involve either a purely autonomous text or a purely passive recipient-interpreter. The central key to a conversation with a classic is neither the text nor the interpreter but the to-and-fro movement between them. The central moment of truth for this conversation with the classics of art and religion is the moment of disclosure-transformation that *can* occur when the interpreter risks addressing the claim to attention of the classic by entering into genuine conversation with it. Precisely as conversation, this interaction is public. Precisely as the result of conversation, the disclosure-transformation is a public candidate for possible consensus in the public realm.

If we are really engaged with a classic and not a mere period-piece, this means that the interpretation-as-conversation will necessarily be a different interpretation than that of its original author or its original audience. It is the effect that remains public, not the origin. For, as Gadamer correctly observes, we understand at all insofar as we understand differently than did the original author. The classics of any culture have always functioned as phenomena in the public realm precisely through their shareable disclosive and transformative possibilities. Those possibilities come to us through the more elusive, but no less real, form of a conversation rather than through the more usual form of "argument." They appeal, first, to imagination of possibility, not to argument or to pure choice. But once those possibilities are acknowledged as imaginative possibilities, they become candidates for some new consensus for the entire pluralistic community. They then function with the public impact of a truth-as-possible-disclosure, not truth as the result of an explicit conclusion of argument.

Since the disclosures of the classics of art and religion come to *us*, they do not come to passive recipients interested only in reconstructing their origins. The classics appear with a claim to disclosure, a claim to our attention as *ours* – i.e., as those willing to enter into conversation with them. As conversation-*partners* we must remain open to the risk of a retrieval of their disclosures. As *conversation-partners*, we must remain equally open to any necessary suspicion or critique of the errors and systematic distortions also possibly present in them and in the history of their effects. Every great work of civilization, as Walter Benjamin justly observed, is also a work of barbarism. Every great classic, every classic tradition, needs both retrieval and critique-suspicion.[14] Every classic needs continuing conversation by the community constituted by its history of effects. The community of liberal inquiry, grounded in notions of public argument, thereby can be expanded, on grounds acceptable in principle to liberal theory, to become as well the community of interpretation of the classics. These interpretations are grounded in the general rules for conversation and argument alike cited above as well as in the particular demands and risks of a genuine conversation with the disclosive claim to attention of every classic. Both communities are in principle public.

The community of interpretation of the classics is also responsible for rendering explicit its criteria of relative adequacy for good, bad, better (more adequate) readings of the classics. Any personal response to the disclosive power of the classic is indeed highly personal in experience. But once that experience is expressed, it becomes a public concern – subject to the rules for publicness of the entire pluralistic community of inquiry and interpretation. It is unlikely, of course, that the same response to the classics of a particular religious tradition will be found among both participants in (believers in) that tradition and others interpreting that tradition from "outside." But if the religious classics of any particular tradition are genuine classics, then they will also provide public, disclosive possibilities, now as appeals to imagined possibilities (e.g. utopian possibilities) available for all.

AMERICAN LIBERAL CULTURE AND CATHOLIC SOCIAL THEORY REVISITED

In American culture, the phenomenon once named "atheists for Niebuhr" is worth puzzling about. The fact is that Reinhold Niebuhr's interpretation of the disclosive and transformative power of the Christian symbols of sin and grace provided public resources for understanding aspects of our common, shared life even for those who did not share Niebuhr's own Christian faith. This phenomenon of "atheists for Niebuhr" is not, therefore, as paradoxical as it at first seems. Insofar as there exists a full spectrum of possible responses to the disclosive power of any classic, shareability or publicness is achieved across the entire spectrum of responses despite all other differences in response. Anyone who both experiences and expresses an interpretation of any disclosure of any classic thereby shares that possibility in principle with *all* others – whether those others prove to be ones for whom a full "shock of recognition" has occurred (the religious analogue is "faith"), or those for whom only some resonance has happened. On this reading, both the classics of art and the classics of religion are candidates for the public realm. It is not the case that only "believers in" a particular classic (those who have experienced a full shock of recognition, and have "faith") can interpret these classics properly and publicly. All members of the pluralistic community of interpretation can and should risk interpreting all the classics, in order to see if these classics provide some new imagined disclosive and transformative possibility for the public realm itself. To marginalize art and to privatize religion is to encourage the drift toward a public realm dominated by scientific and technical thinking. To marginalize art and to privatize religion is to narrow the comprehensive notion of reason.

For the community of inquiry would contradict its own norms by refusing to admit that the criteria for reasonable argument (intelligibility, truth, rightness, mutual reciprocity) are also applicable in every genuine conversation – including conversation with the disclosive and transformative truths of the classics of art and religion. The liberal public realm, the community of consensus, is both a community of inquiry (argument) and a community of interpretation (conversation with the classics).

Both communities, moreover, have survived in the two classic traditions of the American experiment itself. The American Enlightenment tradition[15] is fundamentally a tradition of reason based on argument in the broad sense described above. And the second "founding" tradition, the Puritan "covenantal" tradition, is grounded in conversation with particular religious classics.

The Enlightenment tradition defines the classic American attempt at a public realm grounded in a rationality open to all, grounded therefore in a consensus appropriate to every community of inquiry. The Puritan covenantal tradition defines the classic American attempt to engage in a genuine conversation with the classics of both religion and art (recall Jonathan Edwards). In this way the American community of reason, inquiry, argument also becomes a covenanting community of interpretation of shared classic symbols. Insofar as the American experiment was guided by these two classic traditions, it developed a public realm that was both a community of inquiry (argument) and a community of interpretation (conversation with the classic religious and artistic symbols). The more comprehensive notion of reason implicit in the American Enlightenment notion of argument freed that Enlightenment tradition to engage in conversation with the principal religious and artistic classics as well, especially the biblical symbols. This conversation was classically exemplified in a later period by Lincoln. The hermeneutical model of truth as disclosure implicit in the Puritan tradition guided the trajectory of American tradition from Edwards though Emerson to

James, Dewey, and Royce. It includes a peculiarly American aesthetic understanding of ethics and an admission, in principle, of both art and religion as candidates for disclosive possibilities in the public realm.

The most original (and clearly the classic) American tradition of philosophy – the pragmatic tradition – is one that continued, in various ways, these two classic strands. The Enlightenment comprehensive notion of reason-as-argument in Jefferson, Madison, and Franklin became the explicitly liberal theory of truth for the community of inquiry and a necessarily democratic ethos in Pierce and Dewey. The Puritan tradition, with its implicitly hermeneutical notion of truth-as-disclosure-of-possibility in Edwards, Lincoln (on the ethos of society), and Emerson (on the ethos of nature) became the explicit community-of-interpretation position in Royce (recall his reading of Pauline texts on community).

The list of candidates for models of reason has expanded, to be sure, beyond Jefferson's or even Dewey's models. But the comprehensive notions of reason and argument which they defended in their day remain the classic American liberal resources for recovering a public realm grounded in the consensus of a community of inquiry become a democratic polity. The dialectic of the American Enlightenment may have proved more dialectical then either Jefferson or even Dewey foresaw. But the route from Enlightenment reason to sheer technique and ever narrower notions of reason cannot be laid to their account. They defended argument, reason, and publicness in a comprehensive sense. They never understood reason as pure technique or positivist verification.

The list of candidates for the status of religious and artistic classics has also expanded beyond the earlier Puritan beginnings. Yet the implicit appeal to the model of disclosure in the Puritan notion of covenant can, in principle, break that earlier hegemony without abandoning that heritage. For pluralism can mean that the list of American artistic and religious classics has expanded to the point where the Puritan classics are now joined by others as well (African-American, native American, Catholic, Jewish, Southern, feminist, etc.). All are candidates for the public realm. All need to be included in conversation, implying retrieval, suspicion, and critique.

Insofar as one defends argument and conversation, one defends a public realm. Insofar as one allows argument to be narrowed to scientistic and technological models, one abandons the classic

American Enlightenment tradition of "civic discourse" and its comprehensive notion of reason. Insofar as one exiles conversation with the classics to the margins of the society, to the privacy of an individual's heart, or even to the wider privacy of a witnessing community become one more "reservation of the spirit," one abandons the classic American covenantal tradition grounded in a model of conversation with the classics. Consensus is the hope of the public realm. But consensus prevails as a claim to truth and not merely a survey of interests when consensus lives in an arguing community of inquiry and a conversing community of interpretation. The two classic traditions of the American experiment with a public realm suggest as much. More importantly, both demand no less of all their later descendants.

Among those later descendants are American Catholic social theorists.[16] They, too, have learned to abandon earlier notions of an ahistorical reason without abandoning reason itself. They have learned, like the Puritans, to employ their own central inner-Christian symbols and doctrines (*imago dei*, "Kingdom of God," *civitas Dei*, the Trinitarian understanding of God) in a public manner. Indeed, on this latter issue, contemporary Catholic social theorists have come to resemble Reinhold Niebuhr rather than their otherwise dominant mentor, John Courtney Murray. Niebuhr's own defense of his use of biblical and Reformed symbols for the public realm – a defense he sometimes called "empirical" and, more confusingly, the "mythical method" of inquiry – needs retrieval and revision as much as John Courtney Murray's account of reason needs both. Is it too much to hope that seemingly obscure and "foreign" herme-neutical reflections on conversation and on truth as manifestation may provide some useful resources for this aspect of Catholic social theory's present task? As both the classic liberal tradition and the classic Catholic social tradition rethink their epistemological-ethical grounds, it can be hoped that they may do so in conversation with each other. In that conversation, neither side need retreat to objectivism or relativism. Both may affirm a pluralistic, democratic realm without assuming that inner-Christian resources must be relegated to privacy – even the wider privacy of the "witnessing community." Such at least is my hope. And such are some of the reasons for the hope that lies in me for the contemporary fruitfulness of the American Catholic social tradition in a pluralistic, democratic public realm.

NOTES

1 The debates over the meaning of the term "liberal" will probably never cease. "Liberalism," like all such concepts (e.g., "Romanticism" or "conservatism"), is and will remain an essentially contested concept. For present purposes, the concept refers politically to democratic realms, sociologically to pluralistic societies, and epistemologically (the principal emphasis of the present analysis) to an appeal to public, shareable reasons rather than "private" beliefs for any common, shareable ideals in a pluralistic and democratic society. In that latter sense I share the emphases of John Dewey in *The Public and Its Problems* even if I find wholly inadequate his reading of religion as purely ideal in *A Common Faith*. A fine study of the dilemmas of "liberalism" is Thomas A. Spragens, Jr., *The Irony of Liberal Reason* (University of Chicago Press, 1981). For a good recent defense of the "liberal tradition" broadly construed, see Charles Taylor, *Sources of the Self: The Making of the Modern Identity* (Cambridge, MA: Harvard University Press, 1989).

2 On this concept for theological method, see David Tracy, *The Analogical Imagination: Christian Theology and the Culture of Pluralism* (New York: Crossroad, 1981), and Leonard Swidler, ed., *Consensus in Theology? A Dialogue with Hans Küng and Edward Schillebeeckx* (Philadelphia: Westminster, 1980).

3 The category "symbol" moreover is usually interpreted in both hermeneutical and theological ways (Rahner, von Balthasar, Tillich).

4 Most recently, on conversation and the dilemmas of "publicness" in a post-modern situation in *Plurality and Ambiguity* (San Francisco: Harper & Row, 1987); for the debate on human rights, the special issue on *Human Rights* of *Daedalus* 112 (1983): 237–254, where I first tried to develop these categories for a "public" use of religious symbolic resources – there "imago dei" and "eschatological symbols" for the human rights debate. Forms of this argument on classics are employed elsewhere as well in my published work.

5 See especially Jürgen Habermas, *Theory of Communicative Action*, trans. Thomas McCarthy, 2 vols. (Boston: Beacon Press, 1984).

6 I have tried to defend the thesis that "conversation" rather than "argument" is the more inclusive category in *Plurality and Ambiguity*, chap. 1.

7 It seems clear that Lonergan's *Insight* as well as his reflections on the shift from classical to historical consciousness were deep and explicit influences on Murray.

8 The latter, purely cultural, defense is the position of Richard Rorty and, possibly and far more surprisingly, of the later Rawls.

9 Alasdair MacIntyre, *After Virtue: A Study in Moral Theory* (Notre Dame, IN: University of Notre Dame Press, 1981). See also Stanley Hauerwas

and L. Gregory Jones, eds., *Why Narrative? Readings in Narrative Theology* (Grand Rapids, MI: Eerdmans, 1989).

10 I have tried to defend this notion of the "public" character of the classic in *The Analogical Imagination*, chap. 3, "The Classic."

11 The development of the categories of "disclosure" (or "disclosure-concealment" and transformation) are largely those of the hermeneutical tradition. For two representative studies, see John Macomber, *Poetic Interactions: Language, Freedom, Reason* (University of Chicago Press, 1989); Diana Culbertson, *The Poetics of Revelation: Recognition and the Narrative Tradition* (Macon, GA: Mercer University Press, 1989).

12 The "obviousness" of argument should not tempt us to make it foundational for all exercises of reason. For one analysis of the limits of argumentation, see Wittgenstein on "following a rule" in Ludwig Wittgenstein, *Remarks on the Foundations of Mathematics*, ed. G. H. von Wright, R. Rhees, G. E. M. Anscomb, trans. G. E. M. Anscomb, rev. edn. (Cambridge, MA: MIT Press, 1978); *Wittgenstein's Lectures on the Formulations of Mathematics: Cambridge, 1939*, ed. Cora Diamond (Ithaca, NY: Cornell University Press, 1976). Neither work is a finished work. Indeed, the latter are the reconstructed notes of his students, R. G. Bosanquet, Norman Malcolm, Rush Rhees and Yorick Smythies.

13 See Hans-Georg Gadamer, *Truth and Method* (New York: Seabury, 1975), 325–345.

14 On hermeneutics of suspicion, see Paul Ricoeur, *Freud and Philosophy* (New Haven: Yale University Press, 1981).

15 On the didactic and pragmatic character of the American Enlightenment as distinct from the Continental, see Henry F. May, *The Enlightenment in America* (New York: Oxford University Press, 1976).

16 See here the representative work of David Hollenbach, *Claims in Conflict: Retrieving and Renewing the Catholic Human Rights Tradition* (New York: Paulist Press, 1979); and *Justice, Peace and Human Rights: American Catholic Social Ethics in a Pluralistic World* (New York: Crossroad, 1988). See, also, the writings on these issues of J. Bryan Hehir and John Coleman.

PART III

Practices and institutions

CHAPTER 9

Catholicism and liberal democracy

Paul E. Sigmund

It is only a little over five decades since Sidney Hook stated, "Catholicism is the oldest and greatest totalitarian movement in history." Some years after Hook's remark, Paul Blanshard declared, "You cannot find in the entire literature of Catholicism a single unequivocal endorsement by any Pope of democracy as a superior form of government."[1] Much has happened – both in theory and in practice – to mitigate the suspicion of the inherent authoritarianism of Roman Catholicism on the part of Americans of Protestant, Jewish, and secular backgrounds. Yet there is still a lingering suspicion that there remains what Weber called an "elective affinity" between a hierarchical church organized around a leader not popularly elected and authoritarianism in politics, a basic opposition between Catholicism and liberal democracy. While the stereotyped thinking of a Hook or a Blanshard receives little credence today, it may still be useful to examine the historical and contemporary record on the relation of Catholicism and democracy in order to arrive at a more nuanced view.

This chapter will begin by reviewing that relationship historically, sketching patterns of ecclesial theory and practice in the early church and the medieval period, followed by discussions of the defensive centralization of church governance that took place during and after the Reformation, of the church's reaction to the Enlightenment and to continental liberalism, and of the new tendencies of the last hundred years in the social teachings of the church. Second, the emergence of the Christian Democratic movement will be outlined. Third, we will review the practical impact of the shift that took place in official Catholic thought in the mid 1960s from a relative indifference to forms of government to endorsement of democracy as a morally superior form of government. Fourth, this will be followed by a discussion of the belief that there is an inherent tension or conflict between liberal democracy and contemporary Catholic political and social thought, as well as the alternative claim that the two traditions supplement and reinforce one another.

When we examine the record of the early church, it appears to be neither a democracy nor a centralized hierarchical structure, but something in between. Peter and his successors were understood to have received a special commission from Christ, "Thou art Peter and upon this rock I will build my church" (Mt. 16:18), but the apostles and their successors, the bishops, were also given a universal charge by Christ ("Going therefore teach ye all nations," Mt. 28:19) and the early Christian communities were seen as direct recipients of divine grace and inspiration ("Where two or three are gathered in my name, there am I in the midst of them," Mt. 18:20). The Christian communities often acted as quasi-independent self-governing entities to make decisions, especially in times of persecution. The apostles elected a replacement for Judas and in the Council of Jerusalem that was to decide on whether circumcision was required for Gentiles, Peter was corrected by Paul, and decisions were made by consensus. The government of the early church partook of elements of all three of the classic forms, monarchy, aristocracy, and democracy, and when later Christians looked back to it as a model they could find evidence of all three forms of government.[2]

Also relevant to later ideas of limited government that were important in the development of liberal democracy was the dualism both of loyalties and of institutional structure implied by Christian belief in an independent source of legitimation of government. Not only did this give special religious character to political power, but it also limited its area of authority ("There is no power but of God. The powers that be are ordained of God," Rom. 13:1–2. "We must obey God rather than men," Acts 5:29).

When the church emerged from the catacombs in the fourth century and was first tolerated and then formally established as the religion of the Roman empire, there was a danger that it would be swallowed up in the imperial bureaucracy, and indeed something close to that process took place in the Eastern church. Yet even there collegial decision-making structures existed, notably the ecumenical councils, seen principally as assemblies of bishops and patriarchs, although usually called by the emperor and with a special place for the representative of the pope. In Western Europe and North Africa, councils of bishops enacted legislation with or without participation of temporal authorities, and Rome demanded – but did not always receive – a special role in resolving disputes. Bishops were selected in various ways, most commonly by a vote or consensus of the diocese, and while the episcopal dioceses were in communion with Rome, the pope was not seen as exerting a strong governing role in the diocese. Often the strongest influence was the local ruler – but in theory, as argued explicitly by Pope Gelasius (c. 590 AD), "there are two" structures of rule, a dualism of spiritual and temporal authority.

The centralization that is associated with the modern Roman Catholic Church dates from the twelfth century. A revitalized papacy developed a system of law, courts, records, and bureaucracy that made Rome increasingly important in the government of the church. Neoplatonic hierarchical models ("The Great Chain of Being"), particularly as mediated through the writings of Pseudo-Dionysius, who was mistakenly believed to be the convert of St. Paul mentioned in Acts 17:34, were seen as an earthly reflection of the order of angels, a view which was reinforced by feudal theory and practice that conceived of medieval political and social life in terms of ranks and orders. John of Salisbury (1120–80) and others employed classical organic images to describe the organization of society along lines analogous to the structure of the human body, and medieval canon and civil lawyers used analogies of the relation between head and members in the human body to describe the organization and legal status of emerging "corporate" groups such as guilds, cathedral chapters, religious orders, etc.

Yet there were also more democratic elements in the practice and the theory of medieval Catholicism. Gratian's *Decretum*, a twelfth-century compilation of earlier church documents that was used by all medieval canon lawyers, insisted that "Bishops are to be elected by the clergy and requested by the people" (*D.* 62 c. 1) and "No bishop should be assigned to the people against their will" (*D.* 62 c. 1). It cited as a condition for the validity of laws that they must be "approved by the practice of those under them" (D. 4 c. 2). A Roman law phrase that originally applied to water rights, "What touches all, should be approved by all," was incorporated in the official canon law collection, the *Liber Sextus*, in 1298, and new religious orders such as the Dominicans developed elaborate systems of election and representation for their internal governance. In the church–state conflicts between the spiritual and temporal powers, each side appealed to the legitimizing role of the consent of the people to weaken the claims of the other side. In the fourteenth and fifteenth centuries, the writers of the conciliar movement appealed to the democratic elements in the church tradition (elections, consent to law, and even original equality in natural law) to argue that the council as representative of all the members of the church was superior to the pope.[3]

Yet in standard university courses on "Western Civilization" or "The History of Political Thought," the classic expression of medieval Catholic political thought is taken to be *Unam Sanctam* (1302), the papal bull of Boniface VIII which, appealing to "Blessed Dionysius," concludes that "every human creature must be subject to the Roman pontiff." A more accurate version of the medieval Catholic political tradition is contained in the writings of St. Thomas Aquinas, who combines both hierarchical and democratic elements. On the one hand, law is made by "the whole community or the person who represents it" (*Summa Theologiae*, i–ii, q. 90, art. 3) and the best form of government is one in which "all participate in the selection (*electio*) of those who rule" (*ST* i–ii, q. 105), but, on the other, government by a monarch is best because it promotes unity and follows the pattern of God's monarchical government of the universe (*De Regimine Principum*, chap. 3). The pope leads the church to a higher spiritual goal, but (at least in one interpretation – there are conflicting texts) he can only intervene in temporal affairs "with respect to those things in which the temporal power is subject to him" (*ST*, ii–ii, q. 60, art. 6). Law obliges morally and reflects the divine purposes in the world, but an unjust law that violates natural or divine law is no law at all but an act of violence (*ST*, i–ii, q. 96, art. 2). All men are equal in the sight of God and even slaves have rights, but "there is an order to be found among men" according to which even before the Fall the more intelligent were to lead the less intelligent (*Summa contra Gentiles*, 4, 81 and *ST* i, q. 92, arts. 3–4). Thus authoritarian, constitutionalist (Aquinas as "the first Whig"), and democratic conclusions can all be drawn from Aquinas's writings – and from the tradition of medieval Catholicism.[4]

The process of papal centralization that had been initiated in the twelfth century was carried much further in the period of the

Counter-Reformation with the imposition of a common liturgy ("the Roman rite"), discipline, and control over appointments of bishops. That control was shared with Catholic monarchs through the *jus patronatus*, the right to name candidates for episcopal sees to the Vatican, and through concordats (i.e., treaties) that guaranteed the rights of the church, especially state support for Catholicism and enforcement of religious uniformity, as well as special rights in the areas of education and marriage. Yet this apparent endorsement of absolute monarchy was qualified by the Jesuit and Dominican opponents of the theory of "the divine right of kings" including Robert Bellarmine and Francisco Suarez, who argued that political authority came from God through the people. Some of their arguments for a conditional transfer of authority contributed to the constitutional tradition that led ultimately to Locke's *Second Treatise of Civil Government*, but none of the Catholic writers argued as Locke did for religious toleration. The Catholic writers still endorsed religious uniformity and the rule of the monarch while arguing for moral and constitutional limits on his exercise of rule. In a comfortable but corrupting arrangement the Catholic Church in Western Europe was the state church in the principalities and kingdoms of Southern and Central Europe, while Protestantism held a similar position in Northern Europe ("the union of throne and altar"). In Italy the pope was also temporal ruler of the papal states.

In the eighteenth century, the emergence of the Enlightenment was seen as another threat to Catholicism. Voltaire exclaimed, "Ecrasez l'infame" and Rousseau proposed an obligatory civil religion, viewing the Vatican's religious authority as a threat to civic loyalty (as had Locke, by implication, in his *Letter on Toleration*).

The republican movement associated with the French Revolution was opposed to the privileges of the church, and Italian republican-nationalists saw the papal states as the major obstacle to Italian unification. Pope Gregory XVI's encyclical *Mirari Vos* (1832) reacted to an uprising in the papal states that he had suppressed with the aid of Austrian troops by recommending "trust and submission to princes." It denounced those who "consumed with the unbridled lust for freedom are entirely devoted to impairing and destroying all rights of dominion while bringing servitude to the people under the slogan of liberty" and who attempted "to separate the Church from the state and to break the mutual concord between temporal authority and the priesthood."

In the next pontificate, Pius IX (1846–78) reacted to the seizure of the papal states in 1860 by denouncing liberal ideas (quoting Gregory XVI) as "insanity" and "injurious babbling" in his encyclical *Quanta Cura* (1864), which was accompanied by a compilation of past papal statements on related topics, the Syllabus of Errors. Among the errors condemned were the proposition that "it is no longer necessary that the Catholic religion be held as the only religion of the state" and (the most famous error) "that the Roman pontiff can and ought to, reconcile himself to, and agree with, progress, liberalism, and modern civilization."[5]

When Rome was seized by the Italian nationalists, Pius IX imposed a ban on Catholic participation in Italian politics. His successor, Leo XIII, did not lift that ban but he encouraged French Catholics who had opposed the Third Republic because of its anti-clericalism to involve themselves in French political life through the so-called *ralliement* policy. In Bismarckian Germany too, Catholics organized the Catholic Center Party in resistance to the Iron Chancellor's anti-Catholic *Kulturkampf*. The Vatican's opposition to democracy was modified somewhat with the publication of Leo's encyclical *Immortale Dei* (On the Christian Constitution of States) in 1885. Leo wrote that "no one of several forms of government is to be condemned... Neither is it blameworthy in itself in any manner, for the people to have a share, greater or less, in the government; for at certain times and under certain laws, such participation may not only be of benefit to the citizens, but may even be of obligation" (*ID* 36). Yet this does not mean that Leo had suddenly become a liberal democrat. In both this encyclical and in *Libertas Humana* (Human Liberty) issued in 1888, he reaffirmed his predecessors' denunciations of freedom of worship, of expression, and of teaching, accusing the liberals of making "the state absolute and omnipotent" and of proclaiming "that man should live altogether independently of God." Indeed, the pope denounced liberalism as "the sullied product of a revolutionary age of man's unbounded urge for innovation." Yet having opposed religious freedom in principle, he then added that the church "does not forbid public authority to tolerate what is at variance with truth and justice, for the sake of avoiding some greater evil or preserving some greater good."[6] (This is the passage that gave rise to the distinction later made by Catholic theologians between the "thesis" or ideal situation of Catholicism as the established true religion, and the "hypothesis" or pragmatic compromise of religious toleration in a situation of religious pluralism.)

Liberal democracy was identified by the nineteenth-century papacy with the separation of church and state, the removal of public support for Catholicism, the secularization of education and marriage, and efforts to replace the Catholic religion with an all-encompassing rationalism and anti-clericalism. The Vatican was only vaguely aware that in the Anglo-American world liberalism did not take the anti-Catholic stance of the liberals on the continent – if only because Catholics were a small, although increasing, percentage of the population with no pretensions to public recognition or financial support. Nevertheless, the Vatican was suspicious of ecumenical developments in the United States, and in 1895 the Apostolic Delegate saw to it that the rector of the Catholic University of America was removed and that the "naturalism" of the American church and its tendency to minimize its differences with Protestantism were condemned.

The establishment of the Center Party in Germany was followed by the creation of Catholic parties in Holland, Belgium, and Austria, which like it were also primarily concerned with the protection of the rights of the church. Those parties, however, began to take a more active social role with the publication of Leo's encyclical *Rerum Novarum* in 1891. While *Rerum Novarum* rejected Marxist notions of the class struggle and argued for the natural law status of private property, it focused mainly on the plight of the working classes in a rapidly industrializing Europe. Its call for a living wage to enable the worker to support himself and his family, its assertion of the right of the laboring man to form (preferably Catholic) trade unions to defend his rights, and its argument for the promotion of intermediate groups between the individual and the state formed the basis of the development of the social teaching of the church with important effects in Europe and Latin America.

Yet this Social Catholicism should be distinguished from Christian Democracy, the political movement to form parties that endorsed pluralistic democracy as the form of government most in keeping with Christian teaching. When France was racked by the Dreyfus affair that had divided the country along religious lines and by the controversies that accompanied the separation of church and state, a French Catholic leader, Marc Sangnier, established Le Sillon, a movement to encourage Catholic participation in French political life. Pius X, Leo XIII's successor, suppressed Le Sillon, because "in order to justify their social dreams, they appeal to the gospel, interpreted in their own manner, and what is still more grave to a disfigured and diminished Christ." Le Sillon had fallen afoul of the general suspicion of the heresy condemned by Pius as "Modernism," which the pope accused of "proposing a reform of church government to bring it into harmony with men's conscience which is turning toward democracy."[7]

Thus while in those European countries with parliamentary governments such as Belgium, Holland, Germany, and Austria, Catholic parties participated in political life (in the German case, the Center became one of the bulwarks of the Weimar Republic after World War I), in France and Italy parties of Catholic inspiration were not active because of Vatican opposition. After the *Non Expedit* ban on Catholic participation in Italian politics was lifted in 1919, a socially oriented priest, Don Luigi Sturzo, organized the Popular Party, which had spectacular success; but it was in effect dissolved in 1924 by the Vatican after Mussolini came to power, and Sturzo went into exile. In France, many Catholics (including the young army officer Charles de Gaulle) were monarchists and opposed to the parliamentarism of the Third Republic. But a small party of Christian Democratic inspiration, the Popular Democratic Party, was organized in the 1930s and involved young leaders who were later to be active in the Resistance to Nazism and in the creation of a Christian Democratic party, the Mouvement Republicain Populaire (MRP), after World War II.[8]

Under Pius XI (1922–39) the church entered into ill-fated agreements with Mussolini and Hitler. The Lateran Treaty of 1929 established Vatican City and guaranteed religious instruction in the Italian schools, and a concordat was reached with Hitler's Germany in 1933, both soon violated by the dictators. Pius XI's social encyclical, *Quadragesimo Anno* (1931), further developed Leo's endorsement in *Rerum Novarum* of intermediate groups between the individual and the state, which the pope called the principle of subsidiarity. His support for vertical vocational groups ("orders") in industry and the professions involving cooperation of labor and management seemed to resemble the corporatism adopted by authoritarian regimes in Portugal, Italy, and Austria in the twenties and thirties. But as the totalitarian character of the German and Italian regimes became evident, the pope issued two denunciatory encyclicals, *Non Abbiamo Bisogno* (1931) and *Mit Brennender Sorge* (1937).

One indication of the state of Catholic political thought in Latin Europe in the 1930s was its relation to the Falange in Spain. Jose Antonio Primo de Rivera, organizer of the Falange and the son of the former dictator, could appeal to Catholicism in support of a third position between Marxist collectivism and liberal parliamentarism in politics, and between socialism and capitalism in economics. There seemed to be an affinity, not between Catholicism and totalitarianism, but between the Vatican and authoritarian regimes that were willing to grant the church certain rights in the areas of education and marriage. The ease with which Francisco Franco could take over the Falange as his official party, and the support that he received from Spanish ecclesiastical authorities seemed to prove this.

CHRISTIAN DEMOCRACY

The single person who did most to relate democracy and human rights to the Catholic tradition and to argue against a link between Catholicism and authoritarianism was the French philosopher Jacques Maritain. Converted to Catholicism in 1906 and to Thomism in 1912, Maritain only began to write about politics in the late 1920s following the condemnation by Pius XI of Action Française, a right-wing movement with which Maritain had been sympathetic.[9] Maritain argued that an "integral" democracy that is both "personalist" and "communitarian" is the best application of Christian and Thomist political principles, and that the modern democratic state is the result of the "leavening influence of the Gospel principles in human history."[10]

Maritain distinguished his religiously based personalism both from what he considered to be the egoistic individualism of "bourgeois liberalism" and from the collectivism of Marxism – thus maintaining a continuity with early papal "third positionism." However he drew from the Thomist tradition to argue for a religiously pluralistic and socially concerned democratic state that was almost indistinguishable from the contemporary democratic welfare states of Europe. Along with other Catholic political thinkers of European background, such as Yves Simon and Heinrich Rommen, he was responsible for a new development in Catholic thought that had been anticipated but not articulated by earlier European writers.[11] He argued that democracy was not simply one of several forms of government, all of which were acceptable to the degree that they promoted "the common good," but was the one political structure that was most in keeping with human nature and with Christian values.

Maritain's writings on democracy were read, quoted, and used by the leaders of the incipient or revived Christian Democratic parties in Europe after World War II and in Latin America in the 1950s and 1960s. For the Mouvement Republicain Populaire in France, the CDU–CSU in the German Federal Republic, and the Democrazia Cristiana (DCI) in Italy, Christianity implies democracy. Maritain's personalism and communitarianism provided the theoretical justification for these developments. It drew on Catholic and Thomistic conceptions of human nature to argue for free institutions, the welfare state, religious pluralism, and political democracy.

During World War II the Catholic integralists and authoritarians were discredited by their support for fascism, and the Vatican began to take a more positive attitude toward democracy. Pope Pius XII in his Christmas messages drew direct links between political freedom, democracy, and the Christian tradition. His well-known 1944 *Christmas Message* stated that "a democratic form of government appears to many people as a natural postulate imposed by reason itself." However, he maintained some continuity with earlier papal criticisms by distinguishing between "the people" and "the mass." The latter he described as "the main enemy of true democracy and of its ideal of liberty and equality," since "a democratic state left to the arbitrary will of the mass" acts as if "the authority of the state is unlimited ... and there is not left any appeal whatsoever to a superior and morally binding law." "A sound democracy," the pope insisted, must be "founded upon the unchanging principles of natural law and revealed truths."[12]

It was ironic that just as the Vatican and Catholic Europe were finally opting for democracy, a bitter debate broke out in the United States over the relation of Catholicism and democracy. The immediate policy issue was whether Catholic schools could receive financial support from the government. The Supreme Court had argued in the New Jersey Bus Case (*Twining* vs. *Ewing Township Board of Education*, 1947) and in the *Everson* case (1948) that the First Amendment forbade even non-discriminatory aid to church-related schools, although it allowed "aid to the child" in the form of bus transportation. The appearance of Paul Blanshard's *American Freedom and Catholic Power* in 1949 just at the time that the American bishops were making a drive for aid to their schools provided evidence to American liberals that the growing influence of Catholicism constituted a fundamental threat to American democracy. For a time the editorial and letters pages of the *Washington Post* were full of references to nineteenth-century papal encyclicals and quotes from such otherwise little known works as John Ryan and Francis Boland's *Catholic Principles of Politics* to demonstrate that Catholics believed only in religious toleration when they were in a minority and that once they reached power they would establish Roman Catholicism as a state religion. It did not help that Ryan and Boland printed extracts from *Immortale Dei* in their text, following them with an argument that although "error has not the same rights as truth," "the foregoing propositions have application only in a completely Catholic state" (pp. 318–319), or that there were still restrictions on the rights of Protestants to proselytize in Colombia and Spain.[13]

Beginning in 1948, John Courtney Murray, SJ wrote several articles criticizing the theory that the establishment of a state church was the Catholic ideal, and arguing that indeed the American arrangement was closer to that ideal than Franco's Spain. Cardinal Alfredo Ottaviani, the head of the Holy Office in Rome, publicly attacked Murray's view and it was extensively debated in the *American Ecclesiastical Review*.[14] In 1955 Murray was advised by his superiors in Rome to discontinue his writing on the subject and he cleared his study of all books related to the topic. Yet ten years later he was one of the principal influences upon the preparation of the Second Vatican Council's (1962–65) Declaration on Religious Freedom (*Dignitatis Humanae Personae*).

As the Latin title indicates, the Vatican II statement bases its argument for religious freedom on the dignity of the human person as a free moral being. During the intervening ten years European historians and theologians, such as Joseph Lecler, had prepared the way for the Declaration. But the most important breakthrough in the official Vatican position was the publication of Pope John XXIII's encyclical *Pacem in Terris* in 1963. After what appears to be a classically conservative beginning, a discussion of "order between men," the pope states that every human being is a "person" by virtue of which "he has rights and duties of his own, flowing directly and simultaneously from his very nature." Among those rights is "the right to honor God according to the dictates of an upright conscience, and the right to profess his religion privately and publicly" (*PT* 8–9, 14).[15] The reference to public worship seemed to indicate a change in the official position that had endorsed the policy of Franco's Spain that tolerated non-Catholic worship only in private.

The encyclical makes a similar argument on democracy stating that "the dignity of the human person involves, moreover, the right to take an active part in public affairs and to contribute one's part to the common good of the citizens" and that "the human person is also entitled to a juridical protection of his rights" (*PT* 26–27). In the next section the pope says that "It is impossible to determine, once and for all, what is the most suitable form of government," but he refers again to the advantages of participation and of ministers holding office only for a limited time, in effect arguing for periodic elections (*PT* 67, 74).

The encyclical swept away the single most important obstacle to the acceptance of democracy by the Vatican – its belief in the theoretical superiority of the union of church and state. The liberal democratic state necessarily entails religious freedom, and it took until the 1960s for the Vatican to accept its desirability on philosophical and theological grounds. (Indeed Father Murray had been "disinvited" as an expert advisor at the first session of the Council and only came in that status to the second session at the insistence of Cardinal Spellman.)

A similar link between religious freedom and endorsement of democracy is evident at the Second Vatican Council. The same session that adopted the Declaration on Religious Freedom also voted the Pastoral Constitution on the Church in the Modern World (*Gaudium et Spes*) that included the following formal commitment of Catholicism to democracy:

It is in full accord with human nature that juridical-political structures should, with ever better success and without discrimination, afford all their citizens the chance to participate freely and actively in establishing the constitutional bases of a political community, governing the state, determining the scope and purpose of various institutions, and choosing leaders.[16] (*GS* 75)

The Declaration on Religious Freedom restated in more forceful terms what Pope John had said in *Pacem in Terris*. Arguing that "the human person has a right to religious freedom," the Council declared that "the right to religious freedom has its foundation in the very dignity of the human person." The Council defined that right as freedom "from coercion on the part of individuals or of social groups and of any human power in such wise that in matters religious no one is to be forced to act in a manner contrary to his own beliefs. Nor is anyone to be restrained from acting in accordance with his beliefs, whether publicly or privately, whether alone or in association with others, within due limits" (*GS* 2).

Religious freedoms were not the only liberties endorsed by the Council. Again drawing its arguments from the development of "a keener awareness of human dignity," and repeating what had been argued in *Pacem in Terris*, *Gaudium et Spes* endorsed the contemporary aspirations for

a political-juridical order in which personal rights can gain better protection. These include rights of free assembly, of common action, of expressing personal opinions, and of professing a religion privately and publicly. For the protection of personal rights is a necessary condition for the active participation of citizens, whether as individuals or collectively, in the life and government of the state. (*GS* 73)

CONTEMPORARY APPLICATIONS

The formal commitment of the official church to democracy and human rights as well as to religious freedom meant, in effect, the abandonment of the long-standing opposition between the Vatican and liberal democracy. The Council's statement on democracy contained footnotes to Pius XII's wartime Christmas messages, but it marked a much clearer and unambiguous commitment to democracy and political participation than ever before. There remained a suspicion and indeed a moral critique of economic liberalism. But the opposition to liberalism's political program, much of which had been fueled by now-obsolete struggles over education and financial support, had disappeared. While in many ways this was simply a recognition of political changes that had taken place at the grassroots and in the national communities in Europe and Latin America, the fact that democracy was now formally endorsed at the highest level had an important impact on the conduct of church leaders and the clergy in subsequent decades. The bishops themselves had received a kind of political and moral education as a result of their attendance at the Council from September until December for four years (1962–65), and it affected their attitudes toward their own role as moral leaders. Catholic seminaries and educational institutions used the Council's decrees as an educational reference point, and old-line conservatives and integralists could no longer cite the Vatican to legitimate their political views.

In countries like France, Germany, Italy, and the Low Countries the battle had already been won. The election of Charles de Gaulle in 1958 marked the beginning of the end of the division between Catholic monarchists and anti-clerical republicans that had begun with the French Revolution. Before that the collaboration of conservative Catholics with the Vichy regime during World War II had discredited the anti-republican cause, and the MRP had become the largest party in France until the creation of the Gaullist party split its ranks. The Gaullist regime and later the Socialists were finally able to work out compromises on the vexing question of state financial aid to church schools. In Germany the Christian Democratic Union included both Catholics and Protestants among its leaders and no longer saw its primary function as the defense of the rights of the Catholic Church. Similarly the Christian trade unions and their international confederation signified by changing their names that there was no longer a direct link to the church. While for geographic and historical reasons Italian Christian Democrats were more concerned with the role of the church, they too began to lose their confessional character and to make compromises and alliances with Republicans, Liberals, and Socialists who had earlier been sworn enemies.

All this had begun to take place well before the Council. A more measurable impact of the Council's commitment to democracy can be discerned in Spain, Portugal, and Latin America. In Spain the tight link between the hierarchy and the Franco regime began to loosen – especially among Catholic student and labor groups and the younger clergy and bishops. By the time of the transition that followed Franco's death, Catholics, Socialists, and Communists could work out constitutional solutions to problems that had caused a civil war forty years earlier. In Portugal the church was less prepared for the downfall of the authoritarian regime, but once the mid-seventies radicalism of the military and the peasantry wore off, it too developed a system that involved compromise and cooperation among liberals, Catholics, and Socialists.

The most striking impact of the change was in Latin America. In the Alliance for Progress period of the early 1960s the Christian

Democratic parties were seen as "the last best hope" (the title of a book by Leonard Gross, published in 1967) for Latin America. In Chile and Venezuela large and well-organized Christian Democratic parties emerged to challenge the old link between conservatism and Catholicism with programs of agrarian reform, and improved housing, education, and welfare that appealed to Maritain and the social encyclicals. Christian Democratic parties were also founded in Central America that were to play a significant role in the coming decades.

By the time of the Conference of Latin American Bishops (CELAM) in Medellín in 1968, however, many of the elected civilian governments of Latin America had been overthrown – often in the name of Western and Christian values. The church's public endorsement of democracy prevented the military regimes from using Catholicism as a source of legitimacy as earlier authoritarian rulers had been able to do. More importantly the church became an umbrella under which human rights groups and opponents of the regime could find protection and support. In post-1973-coup Chile, for example, the church set up the ecumenical Committee for Peace and later the Vicariate of Solidarity to aid victims of the repression, and a Human Rights Commission was established headed by Jaime Castillo, a Thomist theorist and former Minister of Justice of the Christian Democratic government of Eduardo Frei (1964–70). In Brazil, the National Conference of Brazilian Bishops became an outspoken critic of government repression in the 1970s, and in El Salvador and Nicaragua the hierarchy repeatedly denounced instances of torture and murder by authoritarian regimes. The single exception was Argentina where, except for the activities of a Catholic layman, Adolfo Perez Esquivel, the Catholic church was strangely silent in the face of the disappearances of 9,000 Argentines between 1976 and 1979.[17]

The pattern continued in the 1980s. The Guatemalan church, which had previously been supportive of the military, encouraged and assisted the transition to an elected government in 1983. The Haitian church was one of the few institutional structures that could operate to assist that troubled country's search for a stable democratic government after the departure of the Duvaliers. In Chile a church-inspired group promoted a massive registration campaign that was a major factor in the defeat of Augusto Pinochet's 1988 bid for an extension of his mandate until 1997. In the Philippines, Cardinal

Jaime Sin played a central role in the defeat of the Marcos government at the polls and Marcos's subsequent departure from power. In Panama, the Catholic hierarchy wrote a pastoral letter calling for democracy in June 1987 that began the process of popular mobilization against General Manuel Noriega. In Brazil the church promoted the transition from military rule, and a leftist candidate from the trade unions with strong connections to the Ecclesial Base Communities (CEBs) came close to winning the presidency in December 1989.

Catholic conservatives now found it more difficult to justify their position by appealing to order, hierarchy, and property as intended by God. Latin American conservatism in general began more and more to resemble its North American counterpart arguing for efficiency, law and order, economic freedom, and the importance of the private sector and private property. In Chile there was a curious amalgam of two previously antithetical traditions in the argument of Chilean Catholic conservatives (e.g., Jaime Guzman) that the encouragement of the market economy was an example of Pius XI's principle of subsidiarity. The Latin American neoconservatives' ideological shift is important because besides endorsing market capitalism they now accept the necessity and even the desirability of a democratic political system. Since many of them have been educated in Catholic schools, the shift in Catholic theory and practice has been an important influence in their change of attitude.

Returning to Europe in the eighties, one is struck again by the salience of the church in the political openings in Eastern Europe. The link between the Catholic church and the Solidarity movement in Poland is an evident one, and it should not be surprising that a democratized Poland is in the process of reintroducing (optional) religious instruction in the government schools. A somewhat less obvious but nevertheless important role was played by the Catholic church in Czechoslovakia, while in East Germany the Evangelical (Lutheran) church ministers emerged as important leaders in 1989.

In the United States, while there was never any doubt about the commitment of American Catholics to democracy, there were important changes in the relationship of Catholics to the American political process. Since the election of John Kennedy in 1960, Catholics no longer felt discriminated against in American life. The close historical link to the Democratic Party has been broken, and the ideological spectrum in American Catholicism runs from the *National*

Catholic Reporter on the left, through the *National Catholic Register* in the center, to *The Wanderer* on the right. The two Catholic senators from New York, Daniel Patrick Moynihan and Alfonse D'Amato, symbolize in their differences the range of contemporary Catholic political views. While there are lingering problems, mostly centered around the abortion issue (especially some bishops' efforts to impose ecclesiastical sanctions on those who favor legalized abortion), considerable public attention has been given to the Catholic bishops' pastoral letters on nuclear weapons and on the American economy. While this may not be what Richard Neuhaus has called the "Catholic moment" in the United States,[18] the church and its spokesmen are regarded as respected contributors to national political debate, especially when its leadership takes account of differing opinions and makes appeals to rational norms as it did in the two pastoral letters. Both those letters evoked strongly critical responses by Catholic conservatives, notably Michael Novak, confirming for the case of American Catholicism Robert Wuthnow's thesis that the divisions in American religion are now more along ideological than sectarian lines.[19]

CATHOLICISM AND LIBERAL DEMOCRACY TODAY

The endorsement of liberal democracy by the institutional church has not been a wholly uncritical one, and there has been an attempt to maintain continuity with earlier statements. This is particularly true in the case of economic liberalism or free market capitalism. In 1967, for example, Pope Paul VI wrote an influential encyclical, *Populorum Progressio* (On the Development of Peoples) that attacked capitalism as a system "which considers profit as the key motive for economic progress, competition as the supreme law of economics, and private ownership of the means of production as an absolute right that has no limits and carries no corresponding obligation." Paul VI quoted Pius XI on "the international imperialism of money" and argued that "unchecked liberalism" is itself a form of dictatorship (*PP* 26). The encyclical focused on the economic relations of rich and poor countries and called for action to favor the Third World, since "development is another name for peace" (*PP* 30). In the following year, the Medellín Conference of Latin American Bishops denounced both liberal capitalism and Marxism as "against the dignity of the human person" with Latin America "caught between the two options" (*On Justice*, no. 10).[20] It is not surprising, therefore, that the liberation theology movement was able to use the Conference's description of the "institutionalized violence" in Latin America to extend the traditional just war criteria to include revolutionary counter-violence against capitalism.[21]

Pope John Paul II is often described as a conservative in theology and ecclesiology, but he has exhibited a critical attitude toward liberal individualism and free enterprise economics, which was expressed in *Laborem Exercens*, his 1981 encyclical that endorsed the priority of labor in economics. *Libertas Conscientiae*, the second (1985) Vatican Instruction on Liberation Theology, sums up the state of contemporary Catholic social thought in its commitment to *solidarity* – the obligation of all persons to contribute to the common good – against individualism, and to *subsidiarity* – the promotion of the initiative of individuals and intermediate communities – against collectivism (*LC* 73). The Instruction reiterates the church's commitment to democracy, arguing that there can only be "authentic development in a social and political system which respects freedoms and fosters them through the participation of everyone," while guaranteeing a "proper pluralism in institutions and social initiatives" (*LC* 95).[22]

Papal criticism of capitalism was modified in John Paul II's encyclical *Sollicitudo Rei Socialis* (On Social Concern), issued in 1988 in observance of the twentieth anniversary of *Populorum Progressio*. Perhaps for the first time in papal documents, it listed among the human rights that everyone should be guaranteed, "the right of economic initiative... which is important not only for the individual but for the common good," but it balanced this with a denunciation of the international economic, financial, and social mechanisms "that accentuate the situation of wealth for some and poverty for the rest" (*SRS* 15). It added that there is a "social mortgage" on property and that "the goods of this world are originally meant for all" (*SRS* 22 and 42). The pope emphasized once again the importance of democratic and participatory institutions, since the "free and responsible participation of all citizens in public affairs" and "respect for the promotion of human rights" are necessary conditions of authentic development (*SRS* 44).[23]

Are we to conclude from this review that after a long history of opposition, Catholic social thought has now not only reconciled itself to liberal democracy, but has embraced it? Not exactly. A number of tensions and conflicts remain between the views of most liberal democrats and contemporary Catholic thinking on politics.

Some would hold that a central difference is that contemporary liberalism is relativistic and skeptical, while Catholicism is committed to a transcendent source of absolute religious and moral values. This understanding of liberalism seems to me to be an excessively reductionist one, since it lumps all liberals into the camp of what I would call "procedural" or "value-neutral" liberals such as Bruce Ackerman, Robert Nozick, or Ronald Dworkin (and, much earlier, Thomas Hobbes), as distinct from what I might call "substantive" liberals like John Locke, Immanuel Kant, or among contemporary writers, Joseph Raz.[24] For these latter, liberal democracy is grounded in absolute values intrinsic to the human person, whether they are derived from a conception of the free individual in "the state of nature which has a law of nature to govern it" (Locke, *Second Treatise*, no. 6) or from the nature of a free self-legislating moral person (Kant), or from the freely-choosing, morally committed, and socially-oriented individual (Raz). In the case of natural law liberal democrats such as John Hallowell, democracy is based on a view of the nature of the human person that closely resembles the views of Catholic theorists.[25] For them, to use the terminology of John Rawls, liberal democracy is not just about the right, but also "a thick theory of the good."[26]

Thus there is a convergence of contemporary Christian Democrats and those liberals who argue that something more than a commitment to individual freedom is necessary to undergird social cooperation in a democracy, namely a moral and social view of the human person. In the case of the Christian, this view of the person sees the human being as endowed with an immortal soul and a special right and duty to make moral and social choices for which he or she is responsible to God. In the case of "substantive liberals" it is a conception of the human person as moral, free, and aware of his/her responsibility to respect the equal moral rights of other human beings. The differences are not that great between the two. Both believe that the state should respect human rights and resolve differences democratically – and both do so for moral reasons – as distinct from the "procedural liberal" who supports democracy because of skepticism about the possibility of knowing the good.

There still remain areas of tension, however, between liberalism and Catholicism. Several come to mind. In the area of sexuality and the family, liberalism tends to tolerate – and even in some cases, endorse – greater diversity of "lifestyles" than does Catholicism. The church continues to oppose abortion, contraception, divorce, homosexuality, and pornography while for most liberals these are matters of individual "choice." Historically and even today the church has extended its opposition to such practices to support for the enactment of coercive legislation against them. Whatever liberals may think of those practices, and some liberals, certainly most Catholic liberals, believe that they are wrong, they are opposed to the legislation of morality. There is a long tradition in Catholic social thought that permits the toleration of evil to avoid a greater evil (e.g., St. Augustine was prepared to tolerate houses of prostitution on such grounds). Some contemporary Catholic politicians appeal to this tradition when they distinguish between their personal moral views on abortion or homosexuality and the advisability of enacting coercive legislation against these practices.

However, the Catholic church has been reluctant to leave what it considers to be serious moral ills to the area of individual choice. It has long since ceased to press for legislation outlawing contraception, and only in a few countries is it still fighting a losing battle to prevent the enactment of legislation permitting divorce. In the areas of pornography, homosexuality, and abortion, however, it is still hostile to liberal permissiveness. It views these practices as fundamental violations of natural law – the murder of the fetus and the corruption of family values that are important to a stable democracy. In a democracy any group is entitled to make an argument on philosophical grounds about the areas of morality that are essential to a stable society. Provided that the results are arrived at after open debate and by majority rule, it seems to many Catholics that there is nothing wrong with legislation in these areas.

Liberals however – including Catholic liberals – would argue that the area of sexual conduct is a matter of private choice, and not for public legislation. Their opposition as liberals is reinforced by their opposition as democrats to the pressure tactics used by some members of the hierarchy – and more generally to what they see as an undemocratic structure of authority and decision-making in the church itself.

It is true that Vatican II's Dogmatic Constitution on the Church (*Lumen Gentium*) defined the church as "the people of God" and stated that "the order of the bishops is successor to the college of the apostles in teaching authority... together with its head, the Roman pontiff and never without this head" (chaps. 2 and 3). In line with this teaching, there has been a partial decentralization of the internal structure of the church. Since Vatican II national councils and international synods of bishops have taken a more active role, and the laity has been more deeply involved. However, the church has not become a democracy and those, like the Brazilian liberation theologian Leonardo Boff, who have argued for an increase in internal democratization have had difficulties with the Vatican. There is still a tension and there always will be between a hierarchical church that sees itself as a guardian and interpreter of divine revelation and a sociopolitical structure that decides public questions on the basis of free discussion, majority rule, and individual rights.

A second area of tension between Catholicism and liberal democracy is that of education. Arguing that common schooling is essential to promote the cultural preconditions of democratic coexistence, most liberal democrats in America have opposed direct support to church schools, although compulsory education laws recognize that they are performing a valuable social service. The tortured state of contemporary constitutional law in the area of church and state as it applies to aid to religious schools demonstrates that a rigid application of the "wall of separation" doctrine is not historically, philosophically, or practically valid. More generally the recent church–state cases seem to demonstrate, as William Galston and others have argued, a doctrinaire commitment by many judges to the privatization of religion as well as a refusal to recognize that religious beliefs are an important source of moral and social insights in a pluralistic society.[27]

A third area of tension in the past, which has been mentioned earlier, is the historic hostility of Catholicism to capitalism, the economic system of all Western democracies. It is true that there is now much less resistance in Catholic circles to free markets than in the past. Christian Democratic parties worldwide from the CDU in Germany to the PDC in Chile have moved from an initially anti-capitalist position to one that accepts and even endorses market freedom, provided that it is supplemented by a substantial program of social legislation ("the social market economy"). Michael Novak and others have tried to make a stronger religious argument for the virtues of capitalism. But there remains in the Catholic tradition a belief that capitalism is based on greed and exploitation, and is therefore suspect from a moral point of view. Thus state action is required to limit its excesses.

The social orientation of Catholic political thought is derived from a belief in the common creation of all human beings by God and in an objective common good. Historically this has meant that Catholicism has been more favorable than has liberalism to welfare programs, unionization, and government action to respond to basic needs. Here again, however, there has been a convergence in this century as contemporary liberals, at least in the English-speaking world, have accepted and endorsed welfare legislation. In theory, however, even where its model of the human person is not quite as starkly individualist as what Michael Sandel has called its concept of "the unencumbered self,"[28] liberalism seems to arrive at social obligations from premises that are initially more individualist in concept than does Catholicism.[29]

Since Vatican II, as I have argued earlier, official Catholic commitment to political democracy and human rights has been added to the church's earlier support for social legislation. Recent statements both by the Vatican and by national episcopates in Latin America and the Philippines have stressed the moral duty of political participation that goes beyond the more permissive attitude of liberalism. Public service is lauded as a morally praiseworthy and religiously legitimated calling. From being a critic and even opponent of democracy, the church has become its strong supporter, and while there may be differences concerning the morality of some democratic outcomes there is no dissent on the moral superiority of democratic political structures and the religious grounding of human rights. As developments in Latin America and Eastern Europe have demonstrated, the church now provides an important reinforcement for democracy and an institutional refuge for human rights activists in times of oppression. In addition, at least some critics of contemporary liberal culture would endorse the efforts of the church to warn of the corrosive social and moral effects for democracy of materialism, unrestrained sexuality, and declining family values.

Thus the relation between Catholicism and liberal democracy has now become a positive and, one would hope, a mutually reinforcing one, even if there are a number of continuing tensions between them. The public square is not yet bereft of religious people committed both to democracy and to fundamental moral values. If, as Robert Bellah and others have argued, an inherent problem for democracy is the lack of moral commitment to community and to participation that seems to result from the individualism and pluralism of the liberal society, the changes that we have traced in this article will provide significant support for the future of democracy in the contemporary world.

NOTES

1 Sidney Hook, *Reason, Social Myths and Democracy* (New York: John Day, 1940), 76; Paul Blanshard, *American Freedom and Catholic Power*, 2nd edn. (Boston: Beacon Press, 1958), 64 (orig. edn.: Boston: Beacon Press, 1949).

2 On the documentary evidence for and against papal claims, see James T. Shotwell, ed., *The See of Peter* (New York: Columbia University Press, 1940). On the emergence of the monarchical episcopate, see Elaine Pagels, *The Gnostic Gospels* (New York: Harper & Row, 1979), chap. 2. For more general accounts see Maurice Goguel, *The Primitive Church* (London: Allen & Unwin, 1984), and Wayne Meeks, *The Moral World of the First Christians* (Philadelphia: Fortress Press, 1986).

3 See the documents in Brian Tierney, *The Crisis of Church and State (1150–1300)* (Engelwood Cliffs, NJ: Prentice-Hall, 1964), and Tierney, *Religion, Law, and the Growth of Constitutional Thought, 1150–1650* (New York: Cambridge University Press, 1982), as well as Paul E. Sigmund, *Nicholas of Cusa and Medieval Political Thought* (Cambridge, MA: Harvard University Press, 1963), chap. 4, and Antony Black, *Council and Commune: The Conciliar Movement and the Fifteenth Century Heritage* (London: Burns and Oates, 1979), chaps. 16–17.

4 See the selections in Paul E. Sigmund, ed. and trans., *St. Thomas Aquinas on Politics and Ethics* (New York: W. W. Norton, 1988).

5 For the English texts, see Claudia Carlen, ed., *The Papal Encyclicals: 1740–1878* (Raleigh, NC: McGrath, 1981), 235–240 and 381–385. For the *Syllabus of Errors*, see Henry Bettenson, ed., *Documents of the Christian Church* (New York: Oxford University Press, 1960), 382.

6 All quotations are taken from the translations of Leo XIII's encyclicals in Joseph Husslein, SJ, *Social Wellsprings*, vol. 1 (Milwaukee: Bruce Publishers, 1940).

7 Quotations are from Alec R. Vidler, *A Century of Social Catholicism* (London: SPCK, 1964), 138.

8 See Michael Fogarty, *Christian Democracy in Europe, 1820–1953* (London: Routledge, 1957).

9 The best-known of Maritain's books applying Thomist principles to democracy are *Integral Humanism*, Eng. trans. (New York: Scribner, 1938); *Scholasticism and Politics* (New York: Macmillan, 1940); *The Rights of Man and the Natural Law* (New York: Scribner, 1943); and *Man and the*

State (lectures delivered at the University of Chicago in 1949 and published by its press in 1951).

10 On the development of Maritain's political theory, see my article "Maritain on Politics" in Deal Hudson and Matthew Mancini, eds., *Understanding Maritain* (Atlanta, GA: Mercer University Press, 1987). Maritain's early writings were critical of liberalism and capitalism, but after a lengthy stay in the United States, he wrote a book that praised the most bourgeois liberal of all modern states as the best application of Christian principles; see his *Reflections on America* (New York: Scribner, 1958).

11 See Yves Simon, *The Philosophy of Democratic Government* (University of Chicago Press, 1951); Heinrich Rommen, *The State in Catholic Thought* (St. Louis: Herder, 1945).

12 See the 1944 Christmas Message in Michael Chinigo, ed., *The Pope Speaks: The Teachings of Pope Pius XII* (New York: Pantheon, 1957), 292–299.

13 John A. Ryan and Francis Boland, *Catholic Principles of Politics* (New York: Macmillan, 1940), 318–319.

14 For Ottaviani's statement, see *New York Times*, July 23, 1953.

15 Citations are from the collection of recent papal documents edited by Joseph Gremillion, *The Gospel of Peace and Justice: Catholic Social Teaching since Pope John* (Maryknoll, NY: Orbis, 1976).

16 References to Vatican II are from Walter M. Abbott and Joseph Gallagher, eds., *The Documents of Vatican II* (New York: America Press, 1966).

17 See Eric O. Hanson, *The Catholic Church in World Politics* (Princeton University Press, 1981), chap. 7; Brian Smith, *The Church and Politics in Chile* (Princeton University Press, 1982); Thomas C. Bruneau, *The Church in Brazil: The Politics of Religion* (Austin: University of Texas Press, 1982); Philip Berryman, *The Religious Roots of Rebellion: Christians in the Central American Revolutions* (Maryknoll, NY: Orbis Books, 1984); Emilio Mignone, *Witness to Truth: The Complicity of Church and Dictatorship in Argentina* (Maryknoll, NY: Orbis Books, 1988); and Paul E. Sigmund, *Liberation Theology at the Crossroads: Democracy or Revolution?* (New York: Oxford University Press, 1990).

18 See Richard John Neuhaus, *The Catholic Moment* (New York: Harper & Row, 1987).

19 Robert Wuthnow, *The Restructuring of American Religion* (Princeton University Press, 1988).

20 The citations of Paul VI and the CELAM Medellín Documents are from Gremillion, *Gospel of Peace and Justice*.

21 See my *Liberation Theology at the Crossroads* for a discussion of the relation of revolution and democracy in liberationist thinking. In the 1980s the liberation theologians moved away from the socialist revolutionism of the 1960s to an endorsement of grass-roots democracy, because, in the

words of Hugo Assmann, long regarded as one of the most radical of the liberation theologians, "Democratic values are revolutionary values" (quoted on p. 175).

22 Citations from the English translation of *Libertas Conscientiae, Origins* 15 (April 17, 1985).

23 The text of "On Social Concern" appears in Gregory Baum and Robert Ellsberg, eds., *The Logic of Solidarity* (Maryknoll, NY: Orbis Books, 1989), 1–62.

24 See Joseph Raz, *The Morality of Freedom* (Oxford: Clarendon Press, 1986).

25 See John Hallowell, *The Moral Foundations of Democracy* (New York: Cambridge University Press, 1954).

26 See the discussions in R. Bruce Douglass, Gerald M. Mara, and Henry S. Richardson, eds., *Liberalism and the Good* (New York: Routledge, 1990), esp. chap. 11.

27 William Galston, "Public Morality and Religion in the Liberal State," *PS* [newsletter of the American Political Science Association] 19 (1986): 807–824.

28 Michael Sandel, *Liberalism and the Limits of Justice* (New York: Cambridge University Press, 1982).

29 For an example of the difference in reasoning patterns compare John Rawls's use of a quasi-contractual theory in *A Theory of Justice* (Cambridge, MA: Harvard University Press, 1971) to argue for a constitutional system that only tolerates inequalities that benefit the least advantaged, with the more communitarian, scriptural and philosophical arguments given by the bishops of Latin America for the "preferential option for the poor."

CHAPTER 10

Feminism, liberalism, and Catholicism

Mary C. Segers

The global women's movement and the varieties of feminist theory informing this movement require imaginative thinking about how issues of gender justice and equality affect attempts to address tensions between liberalism and Catholicism in the American milieu. This essay will consider liberal and Catholic traditions from a feminist perspective and argue that feminist theory presents an alternative vision of social justice which criticizes yet incorporates elements from liberalism. It also maintains that while Catholic thought and practice has not adequately addressed the challenge of contemporary feminism, Catholic tradition is rich in resources which feminists can use to press the case for theoretical and practical change in church and society.

There are three reasons for such a study. The first is apologetic (in the sense of an apologia or defense). Many deficiencies of contemporary liberal capitalist society – abstract individualism, subjective and relativist conceptions of the good, the cultural excesses of an untrammeled exercise of individual choice, the decline of the family, and a decrease of volunteerism in community life – are attributed at least in part to the contemporary feminist movement. Some worry that as women become more concerned with asserting their worth as individuals, they will lose what Carol Gilligan has identified as a special moral emphasis on care and responsibility for others and, as a result, society will be diminished. I think this characterization of the effects of the women's movement is inaccurate and seek to defend feminism against such criticisms.

Second, liberal feminism, that strand of feminist theory upon which I focus here,[1] derives from the liberal tradition historically and builds upon its central notions of human dignity and individual rights. Yet liberal feminism is critical of liberal social thought and has moved beyond it in important respects. Not coincidentally, feminism generally – even liberal feminism – provides a critical perspective on American liberalism that should be of interest to Catholics and others with communitarian concerns.

A third factor is the use in Catholic circles of a distinction between "Christian feminism" and "radical feminism."[2] The latter phrase is a catch-all term for all varieties of feminist theory outside "true Christian feminism." Since most secular and religious feminists regard Catholic tradition as deeply patriarchal, they view the church hierarchy's attempts to define "true Christian feminism" with irony and skepticism. Nevertheless, the church's efforts to respond to the challenges of the women's movement by coopting the feminist label indicates the need to discuss the relation between Catholicism and feminism. It is necessary to review some major feminist criticisms of Catholic thought as well as positive elements in the Catholic tradition that might promote justice for women in modern society.

The discussion has four parts. The first briefly defines feminism and the varieties of feminist theory. The second examines what feminism has appropriated from liberal theory as well as ways feminism has criticized and progressed beyond liberalism. The third analyzes Catholic conceptions of womanhood articulated in recent papal teaching and summarizes the major feminist criticisms of Catholic Christianity. It also indicates positive elements in Catholic tradition and practice that some women have appropriated in their quest for social justice. The final section summarizes points of contact between liberal feminism and Catholicism that offer alternatives to the dominant cultural ethos of American liberalism.

THE FEMINIST CHALLENGE

Feminism can be defined in terms of what feminists oppose as well as what they support. Thus Nancy Holmstrom defines a feminist as "anyone, male or female, who opposes the exploitation and oppression of women," while Gloria Steinem states that "Feminism is the belief that women are full human beings. It is simple justice."[3] Nevertheless, despite its many varieties, feminism insists that women be taken seriously as moral agents. An instrumentalist conception of women is rejected by all feminists, no matter what their ideology. As Dame Rebecca West wrote in 1913, "I myself have never been able to find out precisely what feminism is: I simply know that people call me a feminist whenever I express sentiments that differentiate me from a doormat or a prostitute."[4]

Feminist theory is a more systematic articulation of feminist goals and commitments. Feminist thought is astonishingly diverse; it is not one but many theories or perspectives. The varieties include liberal, Marxist, radical, socialist, psychoanalytical, existentialist, and post-modern feminism as well as eco-feminism, pro-life feminism, and libertarian feminism.[5] In general, each feminist theory attempts to describe women's oppression, to explain its causes and consequences, and to prescribe strategies for women's liberation. Many different theoretical currents flow into feminist thought; the "woman question" has been around for at least two centuries and socialist, liberal, and Marxist theoreticians have felt compelled to address it. There is much disagreement about the causes and nature of the oppression of women, and the remedies for it. Nevertheless, diverse feminist theories do not so much compete with as complement one another. Each feminist theoretical perspective is a partial, provisional answer to "the woman question."[6] The different varieties of feminist thought overlap and enrich one another. One of these varieties is liberal feminism.

LIBERALISM AND LIBERAL FEMINISM

The relation of feminism to liberalism is complex. Feminism has emerged from liberalism, yet clearly transcends it. As Susan Okin notes, "Though by no means all contemporary feminists are liberals, virtually all acknowledge the vast debts of feminism to liberalism. They know that without the liberal tradition, feminism would have had a much more difficult time emerging."[7]

Historically, the development of liberal feminism from liberalism is evident in the work of such feminists as Mary Wollstonecraft and John Stuart Mill. In *Feminism, Marriage, and the Law in Victorian England*, Mary Lyndon Shanley describes how traditional liberal concepts of individual rights, natural freedom, and consent or contract were powerful tools in the hands of feminist reformers in the nineteenth and early twentieth centuries.

Individualistic and contractual ideas, particularly the notion that consent is at the root of all human obligations, were crucial to early divorce law reform. Ideas about contract were also at the heart of the battle against the common law doctrine of coverture, which took away a woman's independent legal status when she married… The argument made by opponents of women's suffrage that women were adequately represented by their fathers, husbands, or brothers (who voted, in effect, for the "household") was for a while successful, but was ultimately doomed in a polity based on the notion that government was created by the free consent of individuals endowed with "inalienable rights."[8]

In the 1960s and 1970s, feminists used similar liberal principles to secure legislative statutes and court decisions undermining the sexual division of labor and enabling more women to participate in the public world of marketplace and politics. Indeed, it is liberal feminism that has been most influential in American society, providing the justification for many of the political, legal, and social reforms of the 1970s and 1980s.[9]

Liberal feminists maintain that women's subordination "is rooted in a set of legal and customary constraints that block women's entrance or success in public life. Because society has the false belief that women are, by nature, less intellectually and physically capable than men, it excludes women from the academy, the forum, and the marketplace."[10] As a result of such exclusionary policies, the true potential of many women goes unfulfilled and society is deprived of the contributions they could make. As remedies, liberal feminists appropriate from the parent tradition principles of individual rights, equality of opportunity, natural freedom, consent or contract, an emphasis on education as a means of social reform, and a focus on law as a key to political and social change. They place special emphasis upon women's dignity and individual rights.[11] Moreover, liberal feminists are usually committed to major economic reorganization and considerable redistribution of wealth, since one of the political goals most closely associated with liberal feminism is genuine equality of opportunity in education and employment.

While feminists utilize major elements of the liberal tradition, they also strongly criticize important aspects of it. According to these critics, liberalism is flawed by a false gender neutrality, a failure to recognize that the liberal state historically has not been and is not now neutral in its policies toward women, children and families. It is faulted for its failure to recognize that the family, a basic unit of private life, is very much a political institution to which principles of justice should apply. Liberalism's formalistic ethic of rights is said to deny difference by bringing all separate individuals under a common measure of rights, an impartial standard of equal treatment which in reality is partial – i.e., is derived from men's experiences of the world of work and public life.[12] Finally, a major difference between liberalism and contemporary feminist thought centers on the public–private dichotomy. Feminists contend that liberal polities have been slow to extend to women crucial political and legal rights largely because of traditional distinctions between public and domestic realms. Traditionally, this public–private dichotomy has assumed that men inhabit both realms, easily moving from one to the other, while women inhabit only the realm of family life, where they are properly subordinate to their husbands. The "autonomous individuals" dear to most classical liberal thinkers were traditionally male heads of households.[13]

Indeed, liberal feminism has outgrown its parent tradition in significant respects. Feminist theorists have criticized the abstract individualism associated with the liberal view of the self, liberalism's conception of social relations as largely contractual or voluntary, and the liberal view of political community. Sometimes liberal feminists sound like communitarians in their critique of some fundamental premises underlying liberal thought; however, as we shall see, there are major reasons why feminists find communitarian perspectives inadequate as an alternative to liberalism.

Let us first consider the abstract individualism associated with the liberal view of the self. According to this atomistic individualism, society is composed of individual human beings who are unsituated, unencumbered, and unrelated. This "disregards the role of social relationships and human community in constituting the very identity and nature of individual human beings."[14] Thus it is an essentially false depiction of human beings because it ignores factors of interdependence including, among other things, the fact that men's autonomy rests on women's subordination. As Susan Okin states, "Claims that the subjects of classical liberal theory are autonomous, basically equal, unattached rational individuals rest on the often unstated assumption of women's unpaid reproductive and domestic work, their dependence and subordination within the family, and their exclusion from most spheres of life."[15] Or, in Naomi Schmeman's words, "Men have been free to imagine themselves as self-defining only because women have held the intimate social world together, in part by seeing ourselves as inseparable from it."[16]

From a feminist perspective, therefore, a major task for women is to extricate themselves from webs of social interdependence. Men may need to sensitize themselves to the social construction of their identities, but women need to do exactly the opposite – to realize some degree of autonomy and assert some independence from social definition. Seyla Benhabib and Drucilla Cornell express this idea eloquently:

the vision of the atomic, "unencumbered self," criticized by communitarians, is a male one, since the degree of separateness and independence it postulates among individuals has never been the case for women ... Precisely because to be a biological female has always been interpreted in gendered terms as dictating a certain psychosexual and cultural identity, the individual woman has always been "situated" in a world of roles, expectations and social fantasies. Indeed, her individuality has been sacrificed to the "constitutive definitions" of her identity as a member of a family, as someone's daughter, someone's wife and someone's mother ... If unencumbered males have difficulties in recognizing those social relations constitutive of their ego identity, situated females often find it impossible to recognize their true selves amidst the constitutive roles that attach to their persons.[17]

Like communitarians, feminists reject liberalism's vision of atomistic individualism because it draws a picture of the self that is incomplete and because it encourages people to think of themselves first, fostering egoism and rewarding selfishness. Unlike communitarians, however, feminists see validity in liberal notions of individuality and individual rights, especially for women. Feminists "begin with the situated self but view the renegotiation of our psychosexual identities, and their autonomous reconstitution by individuals as essential to women's and human liberation."[18]

In addition, some feminists have argued that justifications for liberal principles of political equality and individual liberty need not logically imply a commitment to abstract individualism.[19] Alternative justifications – advanced historically, for example, by liberals such as John Stuart Mill – employ arguments based on utility, the protection of people's interests, and representative government. Susan Wendell contends that one might maintain that political equality is "the best system for helping people to protect their own interests ... [and] that it has proven dangerous to the interests, happiness or self-development of human beings to allow others to make major decisions affecting their lives without their representation or consent ... [Moreover] while human beings are often bad at ensuring our own wellbeing or development, history seems to indicate that we are even worse at ensuring other people's wellbeing, and therefore the best arrangement is individual liberty and political equality."[20] These practical considerations yield arguments supporting liberal principles without assuming a state-of-nature condition of free unsituated individuals. Thus liberal feminism need not imply a commitment to abstract individualism. Indeed, as indicated above, there are good reasons why liberal feminists do not assume such a view.

A second liberal feminist critique of the parent liberal tradition concerns its conception of social relations as largely contractual or voluntary. "The boundaries of human relations are drawn by the nature of the self, understood in liberalism as competitive, privatistic, isolated, and self-interested."[21] These assumptions limit the potential bonds that can be created between people to ones that are instrumental and self-imposed. The individual is not seen as related to other individuals in intrinsic ways.

Again, the feminist critique on this point stresses how partial, limited, and therefore inaccurate the liberal account of human relations is. Feminists argue that the liberal analysis not only leaves out a broad range of human experience, but that it systematically ignores the experiences of women and children. As Virginia Held writes, "If the epitome of what it is to be human is thought to be a disposition to be a rational contractor, human persons creating other human persons through the processes of human mothering are overlooked."[22] Elizabeth Wolgast adds that "Atomism cannot...represent non-peer relationships like those of parent and child, teacher and student, or any where one person takes care of the interest of another."[23]

The model of interpersonal relations preferred by liberal feminists to that of traditional liberalism is one that allows for organic connections among people, relations of dependency and interdependency of many kinds. A model such as this captures the diversity of human relationships and does not ignore women and children. Liberal feminism therefore resists the tendency to "contractualize" relationships and opts for something different. In Held's words:

Instead of importing into the household principles derived from the marketplace, perhaps we should export to the wider society the relations suitable for mothering persons and children...relations...characterized by more care and concern and openness and trust and human feeling than are the contractual bargains that have developed so far in political and economic life, or even that are aspired to in contractarian prescriptions.[24]

Finally, the liberal feminist critique of traditional liberal theory is directed at its view of political community. While liberalism claims to provide a neutral state which protects the rights of individuals to pursue their private interests and goods as they define them, a feminist critique of liberal politics challenges this pretense to gender neutrality. The standard view is that by its non-intervention, the state maintains its neutrality concerning what goes on within the private sphere. However, gender scholars point out that the liberal state has regulated and controlled the family in innumerable ways that have tended to reinforce patriarchy. In nineteenth-century England, the common law doctrine of coverture deprived women of legal personhood upon marriage, including rights to own property, to veto a husband's decisions, to sue for separation or divorce, or to retain custody of one's children. By exempting the family from principles of justice applicable to the public sphere, nineteenth-century liberal thought, supposedly neutral, rationalized and justified women's domestic and political subjection.

Similarly, twentieth-century feminists question the neutrality of a state that has condoned sex discrimination in employment, continues in public policy to privilege the nuclear family over all other familial arrangements, and refuses to intervene in cases of domestic violence on "privacy" grounds. They also worry that extending formal rights to individuals may not amount to much if people do not have the financial resources necessary to exercise those rights. In a formal sense the state may be a neutral arbiter between competing interests, but in reality the state simply recognizes and legitimates an existing balance of forces, a balance in which one of the strongest forces is that of male dominance. Perhaps this is why Catherine MacKinnon argues that "liberal neutrality" in fact amounts to "substantive misogyny." In the context of sexual inequality, a government which refuses to take sides in the name of "neutrality" is in reality taking sides with the more powerful, men, allowing them to maintain their dominance through a state policy of non-interference.[25]

To summarize, liberal feminism is not classical liberalism. Historically, it has emerged from the liberal tradition and it is indebted to liberal theory for fundamental concepts of liberty, individual dignity and equality of opportunity. But it distances itself from other, more negative aspects of liberalism: abstract individualism, a contractarian view of social relations, and the concept of the neutral state. Moreover, liberal feminists reject an understanding of equal rights and equal opportunity that assumes that what is most worth having and doing is what men think worth having and doing. The equal opportunity doctrine does not necessarily commit liberal feminists to either a meritocratic model of society or a competitive form of individualism. In fact, equal opportunity turns out to be a surprisingly radical political goal for liberal feminists because it means, for example, educating men and women equally, and ending the "double work-day" for women by requiring men to share parenting and homemaking. Liberal feminists do not promote self-fulfillment to the exclusion of concern for others nor are they committed to the denigration of women's traditional role as homemaker. The equal opportunity formula does not propose that women should become just like men; rather it suggests a fluidity of social roles for women and men according to individual ability and aspiration.

Finally, while liberal feminism has outgrown traditional liberalism, it has not embraced, in uncritical fashion, communitarianism. Feminists and communitarians both find fault with liberalism, but they do not agree on remedies for the deficiencies of liberal capitalist society. While communitarians are concerned with the loss of "traditional boundaries," feminists are concerned with the costs of those boundaries, especially for women. Communitarians tend to gloss over or ignore the oppression of women in traditional communities; this is especially true of the family. Whereas feminists are wary of an ahistorical idealization of the traditional family, communitarians tend to speak uncritically of "the family" as a universal and undifferentiated unit. Furthermore, communitarian thinkers have generally had little commitment, and sometimes great hostility, to gender equality. In fact, as Penny Weiss notes, some feminists wonder why there is so much interest in community among feminists, and so little interest in feminism among communitarians.[26]

CATHOLICISM AND FEMINISM

Liberal feminists and traditional liberals may have their differences, but they are united in criticizing the views of the institutional Catholic church on women's role in church and society. Indeed, in analyzing the interaction of liberalism and Catholicism in American public life, feminists will invariably find much to applaud in liberalism and much to criticize in Catholic conceptions of womanhood. While secular feminists are likely to dismiss Catholic Christianity as hopelessly patriarchal and anti-feminist, religious feminists struggle valiantly within the church to increase awareness of sexism and to prod the church into action on issues of gender justice. Their trenchant critique of Catholic views on women is especially noteworthy precisely because they do not dismiss Catholic tradition as irremediably flawed, but try instead to salvage positive elements from Catholic social teaching which feminists can use to promote gender justice.

Feminists and scholars in women's studies in religion have criticized Catholic Christianity for its traditional conception of women as primarily wives and mothers, for the denial of voice to women in church life, for its long history of fear and distrust of women.[27] As a cultural force in Western history, the church has, for the most part, either excluded women from education or selectively educated them primarily for social roles in domestic life. Institutionally, the Catholic church in the United States actively opposed women's suffrage and has been slow to support women's greater political participation. Most gender scholars are not surprised by the church's failure to champion women's rights in the public (political) sphere. To them, this failure of the institutional church is merely the public reflection of an exclusion of women from priestly ordination and a refusal to include women in high administrative posts within the official church. There seems to be a parallelism between public and private, between the treatment of women in church polity and in the liberal state.

The issues raised by Catholic feminists – new ecclesiological models, questions of authority, revisionist understandings of "women's place" – have challenged the papal, curial, and episcopal authorities and created tensions within the church in the United States. These tensions have carried over to the church's external relations with the larger society and government. Traditional views on women's role as wife-and-mother are reflected, for example, in the primacy accorded by the church to the abortion issue in American politics. Indeed, because of their heightened concern with abortion, the American bishops have been single-issue-oriented in their approach to issues of women's rights and public participation.

Compared with the bishops' extensive pro-life lobbying, the record of the American church on other questions of women's rights has been modest indeed. On issues such as equal credit opportunity, comparable worth, equal educational opportunity, childcare, child support, and social security for spouses, the bishops' support has been lukewarm and qualified. Moreover, the American hierarchy has used the abortion issue to justify its refusal to support other public policy initiatives – the Equal Rights Amendment, the Pregnancy Discrimination Act of 1978, and the Civil Rights Restoration Act of 1988 – designed to end discrimination against women and improve the quality of their lives.[28]

Judging by the record, then, the Catholic hierarchy does not really support women's full participation in the public life of the church or the public sphere of civil society. Moreover, it is difficult to think this is unrelated to the traditional conception of women in official church teaching. As Mary Jo Weaver notes, "Official Catholic teaching about women is a religious form of sex-role stereotyping which Catholic feminists oppose."[29]

A useful way both to analyze Catholic conceptions of womanhood and to delineate feminist criticisms is to examine Pope John Paul II's 1988 apostolic letter *Mulieris Dignitatem*. This letter was written in response to a request by the 1987 World Synod of Bishops on the Laity for a deeper consideration of church teaching on women. *Mulieris Dignitatem* includes the pope's reflections on several topics: Catholic conceptions of womanhood; papal reflections on marriage; the defense of Catholic traditional teaching against feminist criticism; papal Mariology; the policy implications of the pontiff's traditional view of women's special role as mothers; and his emphasis upon nurturing and caring as special feminine qualities.

The pope's apostolic letter is important, first, because of the influential role of papal statements in Catholic teaching. Such statements generally set the tone for subsequent pronouncements of episcopal conferences, individual bishops, clerical preachers and diocesan educators at lower levels of the church hierarchy. Concretely, this means that if the American bishops decide to issue a pastoral letter on women's concerns, as they did in 1988, they will make sure their pastoral letter reflects the views stated in the pope's apostolic letter. Second, the pope's letter is significant because it is a strikingly clear and complete expression of the ideology or worldview which feminists strongly challenge. Since it is a contemporary statement of authoritative church teaching on the status of women, it will shape official discussion of these topics for years to come. After examining the pope's letter, I shall recount briefly the views of several Catholic feminists in evaluating the pope's conception of the role of women. Finally, I shall suggest some positive elements in Catholic tradition which would enable the church to better affirm and support women.

Mulieris Dignitatem (On the Dignity and Vocation of Women) is written in the form of a philosophical reflection on the theology of women; it is also the first pontifical statement which attempts to answer feminist objections to the use of exclusive language in liturgy and worship and feminist claims to priestly ordination.[30] The letter begins with an extended meditation on biblical texts from Genesis (1:27–28; 2:18–25) and Ephesians (5:25–32) as establishing the equality of the sexes before God and the sanctity of marriage. Human beings are made in the image and likeness of God, and as free, rational creatures they are to imitate the loving communion of a Trinitarian Creator. However, men and women are created to complement one another. "Whatever violates the complementarity of women and men, whatever impedes the true communion of persons according to the complementarity of the sexes offends the dignity of both women and men."[31]

John Paul II emphasizes the significance of marriage in Genesis and the Christ-Bridegroom/Church-Bride analogy in Ephesians as definitive of the dignity and vocation of women. Woman is to be open to love in order to love in return. She is equal with man, but has "feminine" qualities – not defined by the pope – which specially qualify her to care for human persons in family and society. This theological construction of Genesis and Ephesians explains why marriage and family are important, as central religious symbols, for the church. A whole ecclesiology is made to turn on the nuptial analogy in Ephesians. Women as loving wives and mothers are to image the church as the loving, faithful Bride of Christ, the Bridegroom. In this interpretation, as women go, so goes the church; that is, if the conduct of women is disorderly, then church order and the social order are threatened.

Women, then, are seen primarily in relation to marriage and family. The pope refers to "the naturally spousal predisposition of the feminine personality" (*MD* 20). The role of women is to witness prophetically to the order of love. They do this through motherhood and virginity; these are "two particular dimensions of the fulfillment of the female personality" (*MD* 17). Mary, mother of Jesus, is the model for women since she was both virgin and mother.

A good part of the pope's exhortation is given over to defending Christian tradition against some aspects of the feminist critique while accommodating other parts of the feminist challenge. For example, the pope minimizes the role of Eve in the story of the Fall and original sin, so as to counter the identification of women with sinfulness. He reinterprets the celebrated passages in Ephesians 5:25–32 to imply mutuality and an egalitarian relationship between marriage partners rather than relations of subjection and authority (*MD* 24).[32] With respect to language and terms such as "the fatherhood of God," he contends that anthropomorphism is characteristic of biblical language, that maternal imagery was sometimes used to depict God, and that, in any case, God as pure spirit is beyond the language of gender (*MD* 8).

The pope seeks to counter arguments for the admission of women to the ordained priesthood. He maintains that the Jesus of the Gospels was a promoter of woman's true dignity, whose words and works always expressed the respect and honor due to women. The pontiff therefore insists that Christ's calling only men as his apostles was an intentional and deliberate action, not an unthinking acquiescence in the prevalent customs of his age and culture.

Mulieris Dignitatem is also informed by the strong Mariology characteristic of John Paul II. The pope offers Mary as "a model of discipleship and a sign of hope to all, and at the same time as a special symbol and model for women" (*MD* 24). Christ reveals to us how men should live while Mary is the model for women of true dignity and feminine humanity. The pope focuses especially on the Annunciation and Mary's willing consent to be united with God as the mother of his son. John Paul II suggests that Mary's fiat is the exemplary attitude for women; he repeatedly emphasizes the analogy between Mary's gracious acceptance of motherhood and that of ordinary women (*MD* 19).

The conclusion seems inescapable that women find their dignity and vocation primarily through marriage and motherhood and that women should, like Mary, be good mothers thereby cooperating in God's salvific plan.[33] The pope's language suggests a mystification of motherhood and an exaggerated expectation of maternal sensitivity. In his words, a pregnant woman's unique contact with the new human being developing within her gives rise to an attitude toward human beings – not only toward her own child, but every human being – which profoundly marks the woman's personality. It is commonly thought that women are more capable than men of paying attention to another person and that motherhood develops this predisposition even more. (*MD* 18)

According to the pope, both parents should share in child-rearing, but "the mother's contribution is decisive in laying the foundation for a new human personality" (*MD* 18). Thus complementarity for this pope means that, though men and women are essentially equal (both are created in God's image), women bear primary responsibility for parenting and for the welfare of the family.

The pope is willing to draw out the policy implications of this traditional view of women's special role as mother. Since parenthood "is realized much more fully in the woman, especially in the prenatal period," he contends that "No program of 'equal rights' between women and men is valid unless it takes this fact fully into account" (*MD* 18). In *Laborem Exercens*, John Paul II's 1981 encyclical On Human Work, he urged that since motherhood and care of children and family are primary tasks of women, a "family wage" is mandatory in a well-ordered society. That is, wages must be sufficient to enable women to stay at home caring for their children. He also called for the restructuring of the labor process so that working women might carry out their primary maternal responsibilities while being gainfully employed (note that the pope said little about changing society to enable fathers to combine career and fatherhood).

Mulieris Dignitatem concludes by emphasizing caring love as the fundamental special calling of women universally. Not only must women care for children and family; they must exemplify love and caring for all human beings. In the post-modern age, they must take care of the marginalized persons left behind by advancing science and technology; they must clean up after men, so to speak (*MD* 30). The pope indicates no awareness that women themselves might be in science and technology, but instead continues and reinforces age-old sex-stereotyping of human abilities and predispositions.

To summarize: the church's response to the feminist challenge – at the level of the papacy – has been, first, to reassert the traditional view of woman as wife and mother with some modification to accommodate changing social conditions. It is clear that women are to be at the service of the family in the papal worldview. John Paul

II continues the emphasis in Catholic social thought upon the importance of the family as the basic unit of society (*MD* 31). The pope generally ignores the responsibilities of fathers and sees care of the family as especially entrusted to women. Thus while women should have access to public life, the private role of wife and mother is primary. There is little awareness of diversity of family types in different societies and little recognition of the feminist insistence upon equitable division of labor within families.

Second, the papal response to the feminist critique is characterized by considerable ambiguity. In his writings, John Paul II indicates an awareness of women's oppression and condemns the objectification and exploitation of women.[34] He holds the church up as a defender of woman's dignity, yet reaffirms the ban on women's ordination. He does not seem to recognize that unequal treatment of women and men within the church might be related to discrimination against women in society.

Third, the pope reiterates the traditional view that while men and women are equal before God, women are not identical with men but have complementary qualities which fit them to be companions and helpmates. In this typically functionalist, biologically deterministic approach, being determines function, and the physiological and psychological differences between the sexes indicate a divine intention about their respective roles. However, it is difficult to know exactly what to make of sex differences. As one Catholic feminist has remarked, it is uncertain whether there is a measurable connection between sex and gender differences and the conclusions we should draw about them in our public life.

If men and women are different, does that mean only men should be priests – or only women? Or does it mean that priests should come in equal proportions of both sexes? If women are likely to have tender hearts, as one curial official recently warned, does that mean they should not serve on marriage tribunals, or does it mean that no marriage tribunal should be without them? If men are less likely to have tender hearts, should that restrict them to football fields and basketball courts while women deal with questions like third-world debt?[35]

Proponents of complementarity are usually quick to assert that differences do not mean diminishment, that although women are different, they are not inferior. But Mary Jo Weaver insists that "We must ask what inferiority means in the church. How would it be demonstrated? Is the usual complementary choice for Catholic women – motherhood or a convent – a way to keep women in powerless positions? And is powerlessness linked with inferiority?"[36] Other feminists note that in the traditional Catholic view, women serve as complements to men, but men are not complementary companions and helpmates to women. They criticize the language of complementarity as designed "not to name a relevant reality but to evade real equality in the church." Margaret Steinfels contends that if advocates of complementarity are to be taken seriously, then let them install women in positions of power within the institutional church, so that the link between difference and inferiority-power-lessness can be broken. Arguing that the ban on ordination does not mean a ban on women in organizational leadership, she advocates that women be appointed to positions as chancellors, heads of tribunals, heads of curial congregations, members of the college of cardinals, and Vatican diplomats. Such appointments would signify a commitment to genuine equality within the church.

Fourth, *Mulieris Dignitatem* contains considerable ambiguity about feminine symbolization in Christian theology. For example, men and women are both called to consecrated virginity as well as to marriage and parenthood; yet virgin and mother (parent) symbols are feminine, and the pope wishes to draw special implications from these symbols as to how women should behave (he speaks of "feminine" characteristics and conduct). On ordination, only men can be priests (imaging the person of Christ, the Bridegroom), although the church as Christ's bride includes all Christian women and men. The pope is ambiguous on such symbolization, using it in two ways. But this is precisely where the feminist theological critique is relevant. It insists that contemporary theologians and churchmen (churchwomen also) cannot discount the gendered character of many Christian symbols. Anne Carr puts it this way:

Jesus was a male; the dominant biblical images of God are male. And inherently male symbols are no help to alienated women *because* they have functioned so effectively in history to legitimate the subordination of women. This point may not be trivialized. Feminist reflection on the doctrines of God and of Christ, that shows that God is not male and that Jesus' maleness is a purely contingent fact, must further attend to the effective history of these doctrines, their practical and political uses. Only if the effects of these symbols and doctrines are transformed now and in the future can it be claimed that the symbols and doctrines are not intrinsically patriarchal, that they can be made available to women. A pragmatic criterion of the future emerges that holds that the truth of theological formulation lies in its effects. Given the effects of the past, any adequate contemporary formulation of the doctrine of God or of Christology must unmask past ideological uses of the symbols and attend to their transformative, ethical, and futural [sic] horizons of interpretation.[37]

What resources in the Catholic tradition would enable it to better acknowledge, recognize, affirm and support women? Obviously, the contemporary church's human rights tradition and its concern for social justice is a starting place. Another resource is the work of feminist theologians and ethicists which has, for the most part, been underutilized by the church hierarchy. It might help if church authorities tried to discern the complexity of contemporary feminist thought, instead of speaking only of "Christian feminism" and dismissing all the other varieties of feminist thought as "radical feminism." Still another positive step is exemplified by Archbishop Rembert Weakland of Milwaukee's "listening sessions" in which he set about trying to hear women speaking frankly on the basis of their own experiences. Finally, admitting women to positions of high church authority would certainly give some credibility to papal and episcopal claims that the church really supports equality of the sexes.

CONCLUSION

Just as liberalism challenged the Catholic worldview in the nineteenth and early twentieth centuries, feminism is surely a major challenge to Catholic Christianity in the last quarter of the twentieth century. However, as I have indicated, feminism also criticizes and qualifies liberalism to a significant extent. Indeed, because of the pervasive, deep, and lasting effects of patriarchy, feminists apply a healthy skepticism to *all* claims made by established authorities, institutions, and traditions. Adopting a critical, feminist perspective means standing on the margins of society and asking *who* defined the reigning conventions and practices, and *who* benefits primarily from these existing social arrangements? Neither Catholicism nor liberalism can withstand scrutiny from a feminist perspective; both must adapt to meet this new challenge which, when all is said and done, concerns the well-being of half of humanity.

Nevertheless, if the criterion of this scrutiny is the degree to which an institutional tradition opposes the oppression of women and works diligently to promote equity and equality, then liberalism looks somewhat better than Catholicism in terms of ideology and practice. Liberals at least recognize the problem of sex-stereotyping and sex-based discrimination, and they espouse principles of equality of opportunity, human dignity, and individual rights which naturally can contribute to the struggle for gender justice.

Catholicism also emphasizes human dignity and global human rights, but the church seems light years behind liberalism and liberal feminism in efforts to support the advancement of women. Limitations on the church's ability actively to support the women's movement include the following. First, its official teaching endorses a biological determinism or anatomy-is-destiny approach that conceives women's natural, primary role to be that of wife and mother. Acceptance of this traditional way of conceptualizing women's role in society seems to render many churchmen insensitive to the realities of injustice against women in private and public life. Second, a narrow, rigid teaching on sexuality, evident in the prohibition of artificial contraception as a means of limiting the size of the family is far from persuasive to many Catholics and many feminists. Third, the refusal to ordain women or to give them high administrative positions within the church undermines church support for the advancement of women in secular society. In addition, feminist theologians and Scripture scholars have shown how the church is also limited by linguistic sexism in liturgy, spirituality, and in theological conceptions of God. And they have emphasized the fact that much Catholic moral theology on the position of women in society was written by men, from the perspective of men. This continues in efforts by contemporary American churchmen to write pastoral statements defining women's role in church and society. Needless to say, such a practice is contrary to the thrust of the feminist movement which stresses decision-making and role definition by women themselves.

Cumulatively, these limitations of the institutional church amount to a refusal to accord women full status within the ecclesia of Catholic Christianity, and an attempt to circumscribe women's moral decision-making. Compared to this legacy, the liberal tradition is obviously more progressive and seems, to women at least, to offer more hope and greater relevance. If there is a spectrum or scale of progress towards women's empowerment, Catholicism would have to be seen as lagging behind liberalism because it has not yet granted women the signs and symbols of basic respect, individual dignity, and equal opportunity necessary to the full inclusion of women in social life. Liberal feminism by contrast would occupy a point on the scale in advance of liberalism; that is, liberal feminism has improved upon liberalism by rejecting some negative aspects of the liberal tradition while reaffirming greater individualism, freedom, and equality for women.

The liberal tradition is of course very complex. It should be emphasized that liberal feminists are more committed to political liberalism with its emphasis on individual rights and equal opportunity while they are distinctly less comfortable with laissez-faire economic liberalism and with cultural liberalism (defined as a kind of libertarianism in matters of culture, morals and style). In distancing itself from the parent tradition, liberal feminism has been more influenced by the critique of liberalism made by radical feminists and socialist feminists rather than the critique emanating from communitarians or Catholic cultural conservatives.

How can Catholic tradition affirm and support women? What is or could be a Catholic contribution to the feminist project? Catholicism is a rich heritage which contains many resources of potential use to the feminist cause. Through the centuries, Catholic tradition and practice has furnished us with many examples of heroic, pioneering women who made significant contributions to the public good: Joan of Arc, Teresa of Avila, Elizabeth Seton, Katharine Drexel, Dorothy Day. In the United States, religious sisterhoods nursed wounded soldiers during the Civil War, built and operated schools, hospitals, colleges, and social service agencies, and worked in other ways to build a decent, humane society. There must be some powerful, attractive sources of commitment within Catholic tradition to have inspired these kinds of activities.

In liturgy and spirituality, Catholic tradition also contains sources of nurturance and sustenance for religious feminists. In contrast to a first generation of feminist theologians whose pioneering work was critical of the tradition, a second generation has emerged whose work is more synthetic. Sandra Schneiders, Anne Carr, and Elizabeth Johnson belong to this second generation of feminist theologians whose work joins the insights of feminist theory with the riches of Catholic thought.[38] The Scripture scholar Schneiders, for example, wonders why among the hundreds of images of God in the Bible – God as mother, father, friend, sower, baker, lamb, gate, water, wind, fire, light – Christians have chosen the image of Christ the king as their predominant image. She maintains that the overwhelming message in Scripture is that humans cannot define God: "God is beyond anything we can box into one image or category." She argues that Catholics, particularly Catholic women, have been offered a very limited and sometimes unhealthy spirituality, and insists that "We need some theological therapy of the religious imagination." To do this Catholics should avoid all sexist language and come to understand that just as men in Scripture "are role models for all Christians, so too are the women in Scripture role models for all Christians, male and female."[39] It is this kind of deconstruction and reconstruction of the tradition which religious feminists propose.

Finally, Catholic social thought is potentially an important resource for feminists in the struggle for gender justice. Catholic social teaching tries to chart a middle way between the negative aspects of capitalism and the liabilities of socialism. Its concepts of human dignity, rights correlative with duties, the common good, subsidiarity, and participation in economic life comprise a rich tradition which could be tapped. Without revision, however, there is some question as to how much assistance this tradition could provide. Catholic social teaching itself badly needs a solid infusion of feminist theory in order to offset its general neglect of "the woman question."

Thus while liberal feminism has outgrown liberalism, Catholic thought has yet to appropriate fully those positive elements of the liberal tradition that would help to promote women's greater recognition and self-value as individuals. This means that there is some distance – some would say a great divide – between Catholic tradition and liberal feminism. But there is also some room for dialogue between these traditions. On three issues – pornography, contract pregnancy, and abortion – there are some surprising and interesting common themes which liberal feminists and Catholics can explore.

Radical feminists such as Catherine MacKinnon and Andrea Dworkin have characterized pornography as debasing and exploitative of women, and have sought civil statutes to protect women's rights. The Catholic church has also opposed pornography – though for different reasons. What is surprising is that liberal feminists, who might be expected to defend First Amendment rights of individuals to determine what they see and read, have agreed with their radical feminist sisters in questioning whether pornographers should be allowed to sell their wares. I think especially here of two liberal feminists, Susan Wendell and Elizabeth Wolgast, who have argued against pornography in ways that suggest some commonalities with Catholic thought. Both authors argue that a good case can be made, on the basis of Mill's principle of liberty alone, for restricting pornography that portrays violence and coercion of women and children. Mill's principle, they contend, permits interference with expression when it causes serious harm to others, provided that the harm cannot be prevented by acceptable means other than restricting the expression. Insofar as pornography is exploitative of women and children or is felt by women to be demeaning and insulting, its protection by the government under the First Amendment cannot be easily argued in a society committed to equal respect for individual persons.[40]

Catholic moral teaching condemns pornography as corrupting of people's minds and imaginations and as depicting sexuality in a manner that is debasing and demeaning as well as exploitative of women and children. It would appear that Catholic sexual ethics and liberal feminist views agree at least in their opposition to violent pornography.

A second point of contact between Catholic perspectives and those of some liberal feminists concerns contract pregnancy (also known as surrogacy or surrogate motherhood). The Catholic church officially opposes contract pregnancy on grounds that it interrupts the essential, necessary relationship between human sexuality, marriage, and parenthood. The church maintains that surrogacy violates human dignity because it exploits women and treats children as commodities. The church also views surrogacy as a threat to the integrity of the family and an attack on the institution of marriage that will weaken further its place and role in society. Finally, the hierarchy recognizes that the practice of surrogacy may put pressure on poor women to participate in such arrangements to help support themselves and their families.[41]

Again, among feminists surrogate motherhood is controversial. The feminist debate on surrogacy pits supporters of contract pregnancy as a legitimate expression of women's autonomy against critics who deplore surrogacy as destructive of families and who worry that poverty will force women to resort to contract pregnancies for income. Under such circumstances, it makes little sense to these feminists to speak of women's "freedom" to bear children for others in return for payment. Indeed, some liberal feminists criticize surrogacy as the quintessential expression of contractarian liberalism with all its shortcomings. Contractarian liberal arguments for enforcing pregnancy contracts are said to conflate contract and freedom, and to present contract as the paradigmatic bond linking people to one another in human society. As Mary Lyndon Shanley argues, "The model upon which contract pregnancy rests – of the self-possessing individual linked to others only by contractual agreements – fails to do justice to the complex interdependencies involved in human procreative activity, family relations, and human social life in general."[42] This criticism sounds markedly similar to the official church criticism stated above.

Of course, a critical difference between feminist opposition to surrogacy and the Catholic hierarchy's opposition is the church's insistence upon the absolute inseparability of the unitive and procreative dimensions of sexual intercourse. This position leads the church to reject all forms of artificial conception (just as it rejects all forms of artificial contraception). However, feminists approach reproductive technologies with more flexibility and evaluate them with respect to their safety and efficacy in terms of the goal of childbearing, not the physical integrity of a single act of intercourse. Feminists also give much greater emphasis to a class and gender analysis of artificial reproduction. Nevertheless, despite their differences, a curious but complementary blending of concerns and principles links Catholics and feminists on the matter of contract pregnancy. As Shannon notes, "The methodology of the bishops and feminists is not similar. Yet each group, beginning from different starting points, identifies similar concerns and comes to similar conclusions."[43] Perhaps there is room here for dialogue – to develop further the shared critique of atomistic individualism and contractarian liberalism which underlies arguments for the enforcement of pregnancy contracts.

A third point of contact between Catholic perspectives and those of liberal feminists concerns public policy on abortion. Liberal jurisprudence resists coercive laws restricting abortion as a violation of women's autonomy and as poor public policy. While liberal feminists support the legality of abortion, many have moral reservations about the high incidence of abortion in the United States. Nevertheless, for these feminists, the way to reduce the incidence of abortion is not to burden or coerce involuntarily pregnant women but to press for reform policies to create alternatives for such women. This sounds remarkably similar to what some Catholic pro-lifers are currently doing regarding abortion policy in the United States – educating public opinion and sponsoring programs which offer alternatives to abortion for involuntarily pregnant women. This is not to minimize basic differences between Catholics and feminists concerning the moral status of fetal life and the primacy of women's autonomy. Rather, it is simply to point out possible areas of agreement and cooperation between these two groups at least with respect to public policies to assist women.

It would be naive to suggest that these points of contact are anything more than openings for dialogue. One must be realistic about the grounds for rapprochement between feminism and Catholicism. Nevertheless, it would seem that these two traditions have nothing to lose by exploring their common critique of classical contractarian liberalism.

In this essay, I have tried to show that liberal feminism is not "ultraliberalism," and that liberal feminists have thoughtfully appropriated positive elements from the liberal tradition while distancing themselves from excessively individualistic strains of contractarian thought. Feminism offers a conception of the person as a social self, whose identity is shaped from the start by social interdependence. Catholic social thought also emphasizes the social situatedness of the person. But before Catholics and feminists can find common ground, the church must make a major effort to address the feminist critique. One possibility is a feminist project of recovery of the riches of the Catholic tradition – done within the church by religious feminists. In such a project, Catholics have much to learn from the nuanced views of liberal feminists.

NOTES

1 The fact that I discuss liberal feminism does not mean that I am a liberal feminist or that I prefer this variety of feminism to other feminist perspectives. I focus on liberal feminism because of the issues studied in this volume, the relation between liberalism, Catholicism, and American public philosophy. I myself think that liberal feminism is properly balanced and enriched by other feminist theories, e.g., socialist feminism and radical feminism.

2 This distinction was made during a March 1989 meeting in Rome between American archbishops and the heads of Vatican curial congregations to discuss the state of the American Catholic church; see

Origins, February 23, March 23, and March 30, 1989; also *The New York Times*, March 12, 1989; *National Catholic Reporter*, March 10, 1989; and *Origins* 18 (September 22, 1988): 242.

3 Gloria Steinem, "Reflections," in Lynn Gilbert and Gaylen Moore, eds., *Particular Passions* (New York: Clarkson Potter, 1981), 167. The source for Nancy Holmstrom's definition was her lecture at the Newark campus of Rutgers University in March, 1986.

4 Dame Rebecca West, quoted in *The New York Times Book Review* by John Leonard, May 28, 1982, 25. I acknowledge that this quotation from West is troubling. I do not subscribe to the elitism implicit in this statement which ignores the fact that prostitution is often undertaken as an alternative to poverty. However, while the reasons for engaging in prostitution may be mitigating circumstances, they do not diminish or alter the instrumental use of women which underlies prostitution.

5 See, for example, Rosemarie Tong, *Feminist Thought* (Boulder, CO: Westview Press, 1989); Alison Jaggar, *Feminist Politics and Human Nature* (Totowa, NJ: Rowman & Allanheld, 1983); Zillah Eisenstein, *The Radical Future of Liberal Feminism* (New York: Longman, 1981); and Jean Bethke Elshtain, *Public Man, Private Woman: Women in Social and Political Thought* (Princeton University Press, 1981) for more on types of feminist theory.

6 Tong, *Feminist Thought*, 1.

7 Susan Moller Okin, *Justice, Gender, and the Family* (New York: Basic Books, 1989), 61.

8 Mary Lyndon Shanley, "Afterword: Feminism and Families in a Liberal Polity," in Irene Diamond, ed., *Families, Politics, and Public Policy* (New York: Longman, 1983), 357–358. See also Shanley, *Feminism, Marriage, and Law in Victorian England: 1850–1895* (Princeton University Press, 1989).

9 Prominent liberal feminists include Pat Schroeder, Eleanor Smeal, Elizabeth Holtzman, Bella Abzug, and Geraldine Ferraro, as well as leaders and members of the National Organization for Women. Liberal feminists (loosely defined) include philosophers and political theorists such as Susan Okin, Elizabeth Wolgast, and Mary Lyndon Shanley.

10 Tong, *Feminist Thought*, 2.

11 Susan Wendell, "A (Qualified) Defense of Liberal Feminism," *Hypatia: A Journal of Feminist Philosophy* 2/2 (Summer 1987): 66.

12 See Zillah Eisenstein, *The Female Body and the Law* (Berkeley: University of California Press, 1988) for analysis of the problem of equal treatment in liberal theory; see also Iris Marion Young, *Justice and the Politics of Difference* (Princeton University Press, 1990), chap. 8.

13 Susan Moller Okin, "Humanist Liberalism," in Nancy L. Rosenblum, ed., *Liberalism and the Moral Life* (Cambridge, MA: Harvard University Press, 1989), 39–40.

14 Marilyn Friedman, "Feminism and Modern Friendship: Dislocating

the Community," in Cass R. Sunstein, ed., *Feminism and Political Theory* (University of Chicago Press, 1990), 143.

15 Okin, "Humanist Liberalism," 41.

16 Naomi Schmeman, "Individualism and the Objects of Psychology," in Sandra Harding and Merrill B. Hintikka, eds., *Discovering Reality* (Boston: D. Reidel, 1983), 240.

17 Seyla Benhabib and Drucilla Cornell, eds., *Feminism as Critique* (Minneapolis: University of Minnesota Press, 1987), 12.

18 Ibid., 12–13.

19 Michael Walzer also contends that "Contemporary liberals are not committed to a presocial self, but only to a self capable of reflecting critically on the values that have governed its socialization." See his "The Communitarian Critique of Liberalism," *Political Theory* 18/1 (February 1990): 21.

20 Benhabib and Cornell, *Feminism as Critique*, 70–71.

21 Penny A. Weiss, "Feminism and Communitarianism: Exploring the Relationship" (unpublished paper presented at the 1990 Annual Meeting of the American Political Science Association, San Francisco, August 31, 1990), 14.

22 Virginia Held, "Non-Contractual Society: A Feminist View," in Marsha Hanen and Kai Nielson, eds., *Science, Morality and Feminist Theory* (University of Calgary Press, 1987), 120.

23 Elizabeth H. Wolgast, *Equality and the Rights of Women* (Ithaca, NY: Cornell University Press, 1980), 154.

24 Held, "Non-Contractual Society," 122.

25 Catherine MacKinnon, *Feminism Unmodified: Discourses on Life and Law* (Cambridge, MA: Harvard University Press, 1987), 15. See also Weiss, "Feminism and Communitarianism," 24.

26 Weiss, "Feminism and Communitarianism," 1.

27 For a sampling of feminist theology and scholarship in women's studies in religion, see the writings of Elisabeth Schüssler-Fiorenza, Rosemary Radford Ruether, Mary Daly, Anne Carr, Margaret Farley, Mary Hunt, and Bernadette Brooten. See also the following volumes in the Harvard Women's Studies in Religion Series: C. W. Atkinson, C. H. Buchanan, and M. R. Miles, *Immaculate and Powerful: The Female in Sacred Image and Social Reality* (Boston: Beacon Press, 1985), and C. W. Atkinson, C. H. Buchanan, and M. R. Miles, *Shaping New Vision: Gender and Values in American Culture* (Ann Arbor: UMI Research Press, 1987).

28 The bishops' opposition to the ERA developed initially in the mid 1970s because the Equal Rights Amendment appeared to be a blank check for possibly radical social change which the bishops feared. Later in the decade and in the early 1980s, the possible linkage of abortion rights with the ERA deterred the NCCB from supporting the ERA. For the story of the failure of the US Catholic Church to support the 1920s ERA, see Antoinette Iadarola, "The American Catholic Bishops and Woman:

From the Nineteenth Amendment to the ERA," in Yvonne Y. Haddad and Ellison Banks Findly, eds., *Women, Religion, and Social Change* (Albany: State University of New York Press, 1985), 457–476.

29 Mary Jo Weaver, *New Catholic Women: A Contemporary Challenge to Traditional Religious Authority* (San Francisco: Harper & Row, 1985), xiv.

30 In 1976, the Vatican Doctrinal Congregation issued, with the permission of Pope Paul VI, its "Declaration on the Admission of Women to the Ministerial Priesthood" (*Inter Insigniores*), reiterating the church's ban on female priests. This Declaration is contained in Leonard Swidler and Arlene Swidler, eds., *Women Priests: A Catholic Commentary on the Vatican Declaration* (New York: Paulist Press, 1977), 37–52.

31 "Human Rights and the Rights of Women," an *ad limina* address by Pope John Paul II to American bishops from the western United States, September 2, 1988, in *Origins* 18/15 (September 22, 1988): 243. See also *Mulieris Dignitatem*, no. 6.

32 The Pope reinterprets the celebrated passages in Paul's Letter to the Ephesians – "Wives, be subject to your husbands, as to the Lord. For the husband is the head of the wife... Husbands, love your wives, as Christ loved the church and gave himself up for her" – to imply mutuality and an egalitarian relationship between married partners: "Whereas in the relationship between Christ and the church the subjection is only on the part of the church, in the relationship between husband and wife the 'subjection' is not one-sided but mutual" (*MD* 24).

33 An earlier pope was more straightforward and explicit about the Christian duty of women as mothers. Leo XIII wrote that the purpose of marriage was not only the propagation of the human race but "the bringing forth of children for the church, 'fellow citizens with the saints, and the domestics of God.'" Pope Leo XIII, *Arcanum (On Christian Marriage)*, no. 10, in Claudia Carlen, ed., *The Papal Encyclicals: 1878–1903* (Raleigh, NC: McGrath, 1981), 31.

34 *Familiaris Consortio (The Role of the Christian Family in the Modern World)* (Boston: St. Paul Editions, 1981), 41–42.

35 Margaret O'Brien Steinfels, "The Church and Its Public Life," *America* (June 10, 1989): 554. This was the 1989 John Courtney Murray Forum Lecture delivered at Fordham University on May 18, 1989. The reference to women and tender hearts is to a remark made by Cardinal Edouard Gagnon, former President of the Pontifical Council for the Family, at the March 1989 meeting between American archbishops and the Pope and curial officials in Rome. Referring to the presence on diocesan marriage tribunals of women trained in canon law, Cardinal Gagnon stated: "Women religious can be very helpful in dealing with marriage cases, but we have to be careful that their tender hearts do not play tricks on them." *The New York Times*, March 12, 1989; also *The Washington Post*, March 10, 11, and 12, 1989; also "Catholics for a Free Choice," *Conscience* 10/2 (March–April 1989): 7–8.

36 Weaver, *New Catholic Women*, 52.

37 Anne E. Carr, *Transforming Grace: Christian Tradition and Women's Experience* (San Francisco: Harper & Row, 1988), 109.

38 Among the first generation of religious feminists drawn from the Catholic community, one might include Mary Daly, Rosemary Ruether, and Elisabeth Schüssler Fiorenza. Admittedly, the work of some feminist theologians and ethicists is both critical and synthetic: I am thinking especially of Schüssler Fiorenza, Bernadette Brooten, Margaret Farley, Mary Hunt, and Rosemary Ruether.

39 "God Is More than Two Men and a Bird," Editors' Interview with Sandra M. Schneiders, *U.S. Catholic* (May 1990): 20–27.

40 See Elizabeth H. Wolgast, *The Grammar of Justice* (Ithaca, NY: Cornell University Press, 1987), 112–120.

41 Thomas A. Shannon, "Bishops, Feminists, and Surrogate Motherhood," in Mary Segers, ed., *Church Polity and American Politics: Issues in Contemporary American Catholicism* (New York: Garland Publishing, 1990), 251–271.

42 See Mary Lyndon Shanley, "A Critique of Contractarianism in Feminist Theory: 'Surrogate Mothering' and Women's Freedom" (unpublished paper presented at the 1990 Annual Meeting of the American Political Science Association, San Francisco, California, August 31, 1990).

43 Shannon, "The Bishops, Feminists, and Surrogate Motherhood," 251.

CHAPTER 11

The family, liberalism, and Catholic social teaching

Laura Gellott

Few issues, few institutions, have the capacity to rouse such contradictory images, emotions, and passions as does "the family." On the most personal level, family is the source of one's identity. Family is the basis for stability; for some, however, it is a lived experience of oppression, even abuse. The family is "a meeting place for different generations,"[1] but that meeting can be an occasion for the transmission of values and wisdom, or a battleground upon which the generations meet in an atmosphere of rejection, intolerance, violence, and pain.

On the level of politics and policy, electoral campaigns of the last decade have demonstrated the efficacy of "family" as a slogan. Equally evident is the fact that the word stands as a symbol for a host of differing values and assumptions.[2] Those differences can be seen most sharply at the point where discussions of family touch on the question of women's rights, roles, and responsibilities. Two decades after the rebirth of feminism and the women's movement, the family is a critical arena, perhaps *the* arena, where the tensions and contradictions surrounding women's roles in contemporary society are played out.

It is clear that the family in America is in a state of transition, in both the public as well as the private realm. In the area of public policy, courts, legislatures, school boards and human service agencies wrestle with issues such as parental consent for abortion or for issuing contraceptives to minors, parental choice in schooling and the public funding concerns that accompany it, welfare policies that seemingly discourage the presence of the male parent in the family. On the personal level, there are the problems presented by the incidence of divorce, of households headed by single parents, and households where both parents work full-time outside the home. Another change involves the increase in the number of persons who have never married or who have married but do not have children. By far the most disturbing statistics point to the degree of violence within families, directed both at spouses and at children.

Even in the best of circumstances, where individuals surmount the odds and remain committed to a marriage and to the raising of a family, there are the challenges of economic uncertainty and the risks involved in rearing children in the context of a materialistic and secular society beset by temptations of peer pressure, drugs, and premature sexual activity. In the dilemmas posed by these challenges the crisis of the identity and authority of families in contemporary society is perhaps most apparent.

At this point in history the liberal tradition, which has informed so many of our institutions, stands mute before these dilemmas. Daily we are confronted with the evidence of social breakdown in our cities, in our schools, in homes and workplaces. Commenting on the 1988 US presidential campaign, an event which can have left few sanguine about the state of political discourse in America, one observer wrote:

Liberalism has a proud history of defending individual rights. The breadth of religious and personal freedom we now enjoy is an expression of its successful struggles...But liberalism, wrapped as it is in the defense of personal autonomy, is unable to speak to the social breakdown which increasingly plagues us.[3]

This essay will explore the origins of the modern family as the product of industrialization and the accompanying development of liberal ideology. It will examine in particular the implications of the dichotomy at the heart of the liberal tradition: the division of the public from the private sphere. It will argue that liberalism's difficulty in conceptualizing a realm between the public and private domains, reinforced by its defense of individual autonomy, has led it into a state of paralysis when confronted with questions surrounding the place of the family in contemporary society. It will then examine what the tradition of Catholic social thought, developed over the last century, has to say about the family, focusing on several critical notions from that body of teaching – notions which, I will argue, have the potential to engage liberalism, especially the program of reform liberalism as it has developed in recent decades, in a fruitful dialogue.

In examining both traditions, insights provided by gender scholarship will be considered. Classical liberalism and Catholic teaching, it will be apparent, rest upon certain assumptions about women which may no longer be valid, and, in some cases, may even be offensive. At the least they are no longer credible to growing numbers of women and men. It is my belief that this lack of credibility is particularly tragic in the case of Catholic social teaching. It is one of the contentions of this essay that Catholic teaching, especially as it turns to pastoral concerns, introduces a vocabulary or way of thinking about the family which has the potential to speak to the vacuum found in much of contemporary discussion; and has the possibility, I would assert, to strike a responsive chord with many individuals. But until Catholic teaching is able to come to grips with issues of sexuality and the equality of women the wisdom that it speaks on issues of family will, I fear, go unheeded.

LIBERAL SILENCE ON THE FAMILY

Classical liberalism took as its metaphors the parliamentary state and the marketplace. Access to both was through individual talent, labor, and capital.[4] Moreover, classical liberalism emphasized the primacy of the individual, and the need for the "fullest possible freedom for individual belief, expression, and production... Intellectual freedom is justified as competition in the 'marketplace' of ideas."[5]

But that marketplace and state in which liberalism's free, autonomous – and male – individual functioned was only half of existence, namely, the public realm. The public world of political participation and production was distinguished from the realm of home and family: the realm of reproduction, the private sphere toward which women were to devote their efforts. In Western thought the notion of the public versus the private sphere, defined along gender lines, is as least as old as Aristotle.[6] But the division was given new weight in modern, industrial society where – concurrent with the expanded economy and the diffusion of liberal democracy – women were denied access to both by virtue of a lack of financial independence and the vote.[7]

At the same time, exclusion from the public realm became the basis for the "cult of domesticity," a hallmark of nineteenth-century middle-class existence. Woman's role was that of "angel in the home"; the guardian of values unsullied by contact with the sordid practices of the public, capitalist world. The historian Jeffrey Weeks has characterized the dichotomy, evident by the mid nineteenth century, which resulted from liberalism's construction of public and private spheres:

> Victorian morality was premised on a series of ideological separations: between family and society, between the restraint of the domestic circle and the temptations of promiscuity; between the privacy, leisure and comforts of the home and the tensions and competitiveness of work. And these divisions in social organisation and ideology were reflected in sexual attitudes. The decency and morality of the home confronted the danger and the pollution of the public sphere; the joys and the "naturalness" of the home countered the "corruption"... of the streets... This was the basis of the dichotomy of "the private" and "the public" upon which much sexual regulation rested.[8]

While "morality" was assigned to the private realm, it would be wrong to infer that liberals *sought* to create a public realm devoid of moral or religious influence.[9] In fact, the separation between public and private sphere ironically formed the basis for the family's role as guarantor of the presence of virtue in the public sphere. The family was, however implicitly, essential to the functioning of the public sphere. It served not only as a counterweight to the vicissitudes and the amorality of public society, it was the source of moral formation, emotional satisfaction and renewal for individuals. Separate from the public sphere and sheltered within the walls of the home, the family would shape individuals equipped to venture forth daily to do battle in the marketplace and the political assembly.

Just as the private realm played an important public function, so too the realm of family was not immune from encroachments by the public sphere. The literature on the cult of domesticity argues convincingly that marital and paternal relationships were frequently described in market terminology. Women, after all, were legally the "property" of their husbands. Peter Stearns states that "modernization includes... the extension of a profit-making, market mentality to shops, farms, and even individual families."[10] The historian Edward Shorter makes the point even more forcefully, anticipating the social changes which have helped to bring the family to the present situation:

> [An] important dimension of capitalism lay in the mentality of the market place. In the eighteenth and early nineteenth centuries the market economy encroached steadily at the cost of the moral economy, and the values of individual self-interest and competitiveness that people learned in the

market were soon transferred to other areas of life... [C]apitalism's mental habits of maximizing one's self-interest and sacrificing community goals to individual profit transfer easily to other thought processes. It seems a plausible proposition that people assimilate in the market place an integrated, coherent set of values about social behavior and personal independence and that these values quickly inform the noneconomic realms of individual mentalities.[11]

Thus, for all the inclination to exempt the family from the ethos cultivated by liberalism in the public realm, the family was drawn into that very ethos, becoming in time one more institution that served, rather than countered, the interests of atomistic individuals. We could argue that this tendency has today reached its logical conclusion in a society that embraces a version of liberalism stressing rights but not responsibilities, defending personal autonomy above all. This kind of society emphasizes the values of the marketplace – "competition, independence, self-reliance and aggression, making of them the organizing principles around which we construct our politics, our ethics, and even many of our personal relationships."[12]

Nevertheless, the thrust of liberal *policy* remained that of separating the realm of the public from that of the private. Hence the "benign neglect" of the private sphere, with all its consequences:

[Liberals] appreciated the need for a sphere of personal belief that was to be protected and set apart from the power of the state. However, to set matters of conscience outside the power of the state is to consign them to irrelevance when it comes to the main business of the community... It is this arrangement that gives to liberal communities their amoral aspect.[13]

The course of classical liberalism in the United States was altered by the evolution of reform liberalism. More a movement than an ideology, "there is a thread that ties reform liberalism together and distinguishes it from other ideologies. That limited vision is simply the notion that government should act to assist disadvantaged individuals so that they can compete effectively in the market-place."[14] The sources of reform liberalism include Populism, Progressivism, the New Deal, and more recently the Great Society. Reform liberalism advocates governmental assistance to those whose access to the marketplace or parliamentary assembly (i.e., political power and influence) is limited by deficiencies occasioned by illness, racism, poverty, or family background.[15] Stated most simply, reform liberalism does not seek to abolish, or even to alter fundamentally the key institutions of market and state. Instead, it assigns to one institution – the state – the task of coming to the aid of individuals so as to allow them to compete on an equitable basis in the market. "The fundamental assumption of reform liberalism is that governmental action can overcome inequalities in background, wealth, and most especially power."[16]

In times when reform liberalism flourished, the gulf between the public and private spheres was seemingly bridged. Such was the case during the Progressive Era at the end of the nineteenth century and beginning of the twentieth. Ironically, it was the centrality accorded to individualism in the liberal tradition, coupled with the notion of separate spheres and the moral superiority of true womanhood, that provided the opening for women – as individuals – to move out of the home and into the public realm, albeit in defense of "family values." History labels these women – Jane Addams being a prime example – social feminists. Working from the setting of the settlement house, characterizing their work as "social housekeeping," these reformers sought to transfer the values of the home to society at large. Settlement workers and social feminists were particularly concerned with women, children, and families. Programs at the settlements included sessions devoted to childcare and homemaking skills. Settlements provided day care for children of working mothers. In all of this, reformers were guided by a vision of American society *as* family. In other words, a new metaphor took its place alongside those of the market and the parliamentary assembly.[17]

It is safe to assert that in the United States both the Democratic and Republican parties have long shared a consensus on the validity of the liberal institutions of market and parliamentary assembly. However, through the legacy of reform liberalism's project of using the state to assist individuals in competing in the market, the retreat from a "pure" market economy increasingly became a hallmark of Democratic Party policy. Conversely, conservative Republicans in our day have laid claim, at least in theory, to the functioning of a market unhindered by government intervention or assistance to all but the "truly needy," again, at least in theory. The Democrats, the "liberal" party, meanwhile retained the notion of the market in the intellectual realm. More precisely, in the realm of cultural values, Democrats expanded their commitment to freedom of expression and sought to give the individual the fullest possible scope for personal expression over the widest range of beliefs and choices. This marketplace of beliefs, values, and cultural norms is an expression, again, of the historian Edward Shorter's "marketplace mentality," wherein "capitalism's mental habits of maximizing one's self-interest and sacrificing community goals to individual profit transfer easily to other thought processes."[18]

The commitment to a marketplace of values and beliefs was the corollary of the Democratic Party's embrace of the constituencies created by various liberation ideologies and movements of the 1960s and 1970s, movements aimed at securing new rights and recognition for minorities, for women, for gays and lesbians. The influence of the women's movement on notions of family was and remains enormous. At the outset of this essay I stated that political and philosophical differences over the family emerge most sharply and clearly at that point where discussions of family begin to touch the question of women's rights, roles, and responsibilities. Much of the impact of feminist thinking upon the family has been healthy. Jean Bethke Elshtain has noted that feminist criticism has helped in "stripping away the old ideological guises that celebrated motherhood yet denigrated women, extolled an ideal of private life yet disallowed parents the means with which to live in decency and with dignity."[19] Underlying the feminist movement is the recognition not only that women have been denied access to the market and the political assembly by their lack of capital and political power, but also that any corporate or collective institution, including the family, runs the risk of limiting, stifling, even oppressing its members.

Yet there is another side to this. In embracing at least one set of lessons from the feminist movement, women tacitly accepted the goals and definitions of the marketplace. As long as women played the role assigned them by classical liberal theory and the ideology of domesticity, the family could function, to some degree at least, as both the "haven in the heartless world," as one recent writer has put it, and as a moral teacher and source of emotional sustenance to participants in the public realm. But the more "modern" life has become, i.e., the more women as well as men have embraced individualism and autonomy, the less the family has been able to perform that traditional function. And with the values supporting individualism in the ascendancy, liberals are channeled into thinking of the family as one more instrument for the pursuit of self-interest. Such a utilitarian conception of the family (as opposed to a Kantian or ontological one) serves to diminish other significant functions of the family: rearing of children, for example, or maintaining traditions and caring for one another across the generations. And this has become all the more evident now that women are refusing in principle to carry the caring burden alone.

And right it is that they should refuse to carry that burden alone. It would be an error to construe the above as a simple-minded proposition that, were women to return to their "proper sphere," all would be right with the family and society. I noted above that women (and men) have embraced one set of lessons from the feminist movement – namely the maximizing of self-interest. That there were and remain other lessons to be learned from feminism is stated eloquently by Suzanne Gordon:

The promise of women's liberation, after all, was more than just the attainment of abstract equality with men, important as that goal was and remains. It also contained the hope that qualities and activities long despised or condescended to as "feminine" would be valued as vital social necessities to be shared by women and men alike. Women would not just change men... they would change the world... But transformative feminism... ran squarely up against the market... Thus women entering the workplace were forced to make the same choice between work and care that men have long had to make. That is what it meant to be equal to men in a man's world. This is equality of deprivation and it is not enough.[20]

And of what does this deprivation consist? For one thing, the triumph of the values of the marketplace has meant a devaluing of care. Gordon cites shortages of nurses and teachers, the comparative lack of monetary reward in the caring professions, and the Congressional failure in 1990 to override President George Bush's veto of the Family and Medical Leave Act as evidence that "as a society we cannot seem to muster the political will to care for the most precious things we produce – other human beings."[21] Behind the devaluing of care, and contributing to it, is a lack of *time*. This often stems from real economic necessity, but just as often results from a disordered set of priorities: working longer and harder in pursuit of individual ambition or material gain, "a society dominated by what Hegel rightly saw as an endless dialectic of 'needs creation.'"[22]

The consequences both for individual welfare and for family as a source of nurture and care are debilitating:

We have children other people care for, friends we have no time to socialize with, spouses about whom we complain but with whom we have no time to struggle to create more fulfilling relationships... As we become a nation of work addicts and moonlighters we are depriving ourselves of the time necessary for child-rearing and other family or leisure activities – in other words, the time required to enjoy a rich and varied life.[23]

The atomistic tendencies of liberalism, evident in the marketplace of cultural values and mores, coupled with the asserted inability of liberals to conceptualize a realm between the public and the private, leave us in a state of confusion on how to address the role, the responsibility, the identity of family. Furthermore, as the result of efforts – laudable in intent – to include all comers we are as a society unable even to define what we mean by "family."[24] There is a deep irony about the situation in which we now find ourselves. Reform liberalism's achievement has been the softening of the asocial or anti-social tendencies of classical liberalism through the introduction of the notion that government has a responsibility to care for the victims of the marketplace. But welfare state liberalism offers the possibility of a caring society at the very moment when we are least confident about the one institution that historically has made it possible for people truly to support and nurture one another – namely the family.[25]

CONTRIBUTIONS FROM CATHOLICISM

The question at this juncture is, then: What might the tradition of Catholic social thought bring to a dialogue with liberalism, enabling us to sort our way through the marketplace of values, giving direction to the actions and impulses of the parliamentary assembly? What does Catholic social teaching offer to an understanding of the role and function of the family that liberalism cannot?

I will argue that the Catholic tradition makes a contribution in four significant areas. They are: (1) the principle of solidarity over against liberal individualism; (2) a claim for the realm of mediating institutions, bridging the liberal dichotomy of private and public, individual and state; (3) the principle of subsidiarity, which points a direction for the proper role of the [welfare] state in assisting the mediating institution of family; and (4) an appreciation for the historical dimension of the lives of individual families.

These principles are both philosophical and pastoral. The philosophical teachings that address the issues of the relationship of the individual and the family to the larger community received their first modern formulation in the encyclicals *Rerum Novarum, Quadragesimo Anno*, and *Casti Connubii*. The teaching on the family in *Rerum Novarum* is consistent with the wider intent of that encyclical – the attempt on the part of the church, after a century on the defensive, to address and come to terms with the challenges posed by the modern state. The more pastoral principles are the product of Vatican II, best exemplified by the treatment of family in *Gaudium et Spes*, and in recent encyclicals and pastoral letters, up to and including *Centesimus Annus* and the American bishops' pastoral letter on women. The pastoral statements, however, continue to address the family within the philosophical framework informed by the principles of solidarity and subsidiarity established in *Rerum Novarum* and the other landmark social encyclicals.

Consider first the principle of solidarity. Whereas the point of departure – and destination – of liberalism is the autonomous individual, Catholic social theory sets forth the belief that human beings "by their very nature stand completely in need of life in society."[26] True, more contemporary formulations of Catholic teaching advance a personalist philosophy which values the *individual* in the uniqueness of his or her spiritual nature (seeing, incidentally, in human beings something more than citizens of a state or producers and consumers in the market). Moreover, rights inhere in the individual. But in *Rerum Novarum* those rights "are seen in much stronger light when considered in relation to man's *social* and domestic *obligations*."[27] The rights of the individual assume their full meaning in the context of society, and rights directly imply responsibility. This assertion speaks to the sense that something in modern America has gone awry, that in cherishing our freedom we have failed to recognize the social obligations that make freedom possible in the first place.[28]

Closely tied to the challenge to individualism is Catholic teaching's critique of materialism. In our day materialism is perhaps the most pronounced expression of individualism. It is materialism and consumerism that drive the vicious cycle of needs and wants, in turn contributing to the deprivation of time available for the caring and nurturing of families. The "increasingly driven and harsh cultural surround" of contemporary American society has made it almost impossible for families to flourish. At the "emotional core of family concerns in grassroots America" there is a pervasive fear that "children are adopting the values of an aggressive materialistic individualistic and consumerist culture." Parents recognize that they need more time to teach "sound values," but time "more and more evaporates. Here the classic fissure in American society between individualism and community really hits home, and individualism, cast in a distinctly materialistic mode, seems to be winning."[29]

Catholic social teaching, from *Rerum Novarum* to *Centesimus Annus*, has addressed the corrosive effects of materialism upon society.[30] Most recently John Paul II stated:

It is not wrong to want to live better; what is wrong is a style of life which is directed toward "having" rather than "being"... It is therefore necessary to create lifestyles in which the quest for truth, beauty, goodness and communion with others for the sake of common growth are the factors which determine... choices.[31]

Likewise, the second draft of the American bishops' ill-fated pastoral letter on women warned that

A home has to be more than a stopping place where family members come and go, meeting functional needs but not engaging in quality times of togetherness that foster intimacy and respect... If individual fulfillment becomes an end in itself, if monetary gain becomes the prime value, family life suffers.[32]

A second key notion from Catholic teaching is the claim for the existence of a realm of mediating institutions between the public world of the assembly and marketplace, and the private. I have argued above that liberalism's difficulty in conceptualizing a realm between the public domain and the private, reinforced by its defense of individual autonomy, has resulted in a state of paralysis in the face of questions surrounding the place of the family in contemporary society. For "private" liberals read only "individual." This becomes highly problematic when dealing, for example, with questions relating to sex education or "values clarification" within the public schools. The proper functioning and role of the family is lost, dismissed, or viewed as an obstacle to the enlightenment of the child who, treated as an autonomous – and adult – individual, is invited to browse the marketplace of cultural values and norms. In Catholic teaching's enunciation of the realm of mediating institutions lies the possibility for an escape from the public–private, state–individual dichotomy.

In response to the claims of the liberal state, Leo XIII staked out the relationship of the individual and the individual's most fundamental social unit, the family, to the state. In *Rerum Novarum* and in subsequent encyclicals, the force of Catholic teaching argues that there is no rigid divide between the private and public realms. Instead, we as individuals, possessing rights, live and act and assume our fullest meaning within the context of social obligations. Hence we have *civil society*. Its terrain is the space between the individual and the state. Its forms are those natural, local, professional, and voluntary associations in which we live our daily lives in relationship with others. In this space created by the mediating institutions of civil society – families, friendships, communities, workplace – we have the potential to realize the fullest dimension of the term "human integrity." By uniting the public with the private in this way, Catholic teaching locates its claim to address public, policy issues in a pastoral voice.

John Paul II reasserts this vision of the human person and society in *Centesimus Annus*:

According to *Rerum Novarum* and the whole social doctrine of the church, the social nature of man is not completely fulfilled in the state, but is realized in various intermediary groups, beginning with the family and including economic, social, political and cultural groups which stem from human nature itself and have their own autonomy, always with a view to the common good. This is what I have called the "subjectivity" of society which, together with the subjectivity of the individual, was canceled out by "real socialism."[33]

Rerum Novarum was written at that moment in history when the church confronted the dual ideologies of the nineteenth century: liberal capitalism and Marxist socialism. In light of the fact that *Centesimus Annus* makes its appearance at the moment of the "defeat of so-called 'real socialism,'"[34] it is interesting to note that perhaps the most creative analysis of the meaning of civil society is occurring today in the countries of Central Europe, among people liberated from the oppression of the one ideology, while remaining skeptical of the other. The foremost English-speaking observer of that scene, Timothy Garton Ash, has developed the notion of Central Europe as a "kingdom of the spirit," a community emerging from the post-Yalta dichotomy of East and West. He asks: "If not in state or Party power structures then where, if at all, are these individual men and women 'living in truth' to combine? In *civil society* [Ash's emphasis]."[35] For our purposes in this essay it is instructive to note that among the "uses of adversity" witnessed by Ash under the recently vanished era he cites those spaces between the individual and the state, those things which could yet, if we pay heed, instruct the West in the ways of a more human life:

comradeship, deep friendship, family life; time and space for serious conversation, music, literature, not disturbed by the perpetual noise of our media-driven and obsessively telecommunicative world; Christian witness in its original and purest form; more broadly, qualities of relations between men and women of very different backgrounds, and once bitterly opposed faiths – an ethos of solidarity.[36]

Contrast this with the lament that we in contemporary American society find ourselves with families others care for, friends we have no time to socialize with, no time, in short, to enjoy a rich and varied life.

It is, of course, one thing to assert the existence and claim the worth of the family as a mediating institution but another to legitimate and empower it. I shall return to that challenge at the end of this essay. Moreover, in reasserting the importance of family, care must be taken that it not become a vehicle for stifling the legitimate aspirations of its female members. Here especially is an area where Catholic teaching to this day contains some serious flaws, and where the Catholic tradition could be served by some of liberalism's more generous and expansive character. That notion too I will develop in greater detail in what follows.

A third key notion in Catholic teaching is that of subsidiarity. The 1981 encyclical *Familiaris Consortio* provides a classic formulation of subsidiarity, while addressing both policy implications and the need for legitimation.

The family and society have complementary functions in defending and fostering the good of each and every human being. But society – more specifically the state – must recognize that "the family is a society in its own right" and so society is under a grave obligation in its relations with the family to adhere to the principle of subsidiarity.[37]

The encyclical continues:

By virtue of this principle, the State cannot and must not take away from families the functions that they can just as well perform on their own or in free associations; instead it must positively favor and encourage as far as possible responsible initiatives by families.[38]

John Paul II goes on to reassert the connection between the well-being of the family and that of society:

In the conviction that the good of the family is an indispensable and essential value of the civil community, the public authorities must do everything possible to ensure that families have all those aids – economic, social, educational, political and cultural assistance – that they need in order to face all their responsibilities in a human way.[39]

Here perhaps lies a key to the way out of the "by now familiar ritual dance between 'more welfare state' as the panacea or 'more free market and individual responsibility' as the solution to our ills."[40] Taken together, these passages stake out the appropriate arena for action on the part of the state on the one hand, and the mediating institution of the family on the other. It is the responsibility of families to do that for which they are best suited: provide love, nurturance, and the transmission of identity and values. The state cannot do this. Jean Bethke Elshtain states emphatically that it is only

through powerful, eroticized relations with specific others, parents or their permanent not temporary surrogates, that children will be nurtured and protected in a way that allows their creation of self and other to be structured and mediated.[41]

On the other hand, it is the responsibility of the state to do what states, at their best, are suited to do. The state must *provide the context* in which family life can flourish. At its simplest this means providing for the peace and economic prosperity of its citizens. It means economic policies that provide jobs at a level of remuneration which allows for a decent and human standard of living.[42] The phenomenon known as the "working poor" is a scandal. In *Centesimus Annus* John Paul II reminds us that Leo XIII attributed to public authority the strict duty of providing properly for the welfare of the workers, including fair pay, because failure to do so violates justice.[43] "Providing the context" means addressing the need for a system of national health care. Medical costs are such that assuring care in times of catastrophic illness or even in situations short of that definition is something families cannot do unassisted.

The state must do more, however, than provide social services. Families need affirmation, and legitimation of their function. There needs to be a climate of opinion, a culture that takes seriously such things as the commitment involved in marriage and family, and the obligation that one generation owes to the next. Liberalism has failed to offer a coherent affirmation of either the stability of the family as a social good, or the value of preserving ties and obligations across the generations. In their silence on these matters, liberals have aided and abetted in the trivialization of such concerns in our public life. Conservatives *have* addressed these issues, at least on the level of rhetoric, tapping into an evident longing among Americans for stability and organic wholeness in their lives. The danger there, of course, is that what one writer has called "the shabby 'return to family values' that haunts American politics"[44] is often a thinly veiled disguise for the stifling of the legitimate aspirations of women for dignity and equality. But in dialogue with Catholic teaching, particularly its pastoral dimensions, liberalism could develop ways of thinking about the family that have the potential to strike a responsive chord and shape the necessary context. And Catholic teaching could likewise profit from the exchange with liberalism.

Since Vatican II Catholic teaching has emphasized pastoral concerns over philosophical questions regarding the relationship of family to state and society. However, those pastoral directives are grounded in both the spirit and the principles set forth by the earlier landmark social encyclicals. In other words, there exists an essential continuity between the classical teachings and those of Vatican II.

We thus turn to what the Catholic tradition, speaking in a pastoral voice, has to say to individuals and families in the concreteness of their daily lives. And this brings us to the fourth key notion in Catholic teaching: its sense of the historical dimension of family life. Catholic teaching appreciates the fact that marriage (and by extension family life), although intended to be permanent, "is lived differently at the different stages of the life of the married couple."[45] Indeed each family can be said to have a history of its own, a history given shape and texture by the religious and cultural traditions of the family, by its own lived experience as individuals and as a community.[46] In *Familiaris Consortio* John Paul II acknowledges this historical character, noting that "marriage and the family touch men and women in the concreteness of their daily existence in specific social and cultural situations."[47] Among "those situations within which marriage and the family are lived today"[48] are "a more lively awareness of personal freedom and greater attention to the quality of interpersonal relationships in marriage, in promoting the dignity of women, to responsible procreation, to the education of children."[49]

I believe that this addresses what Barbara Dafoe Whitehead calls the grassroots concerns among families about what they are and what they do. She distinguishes this "family language," concerned with how parents can raise their children in a culture that is unfriendly to children and parents, from the "official language" spoken by opinion leaders in politics, the media, and the academy.[50] Within that mediating realm from which so much of our existence springs and to which we constantly return, families know the energy and commitment that must be invested to make family life work in the concreteness of daily life. It seems to me that an understanding that family life will and *should* change in its particulars over time is one that speaks reassuringly to families in transition, as children grow and form attachments of their own, or as spouses mature in their own identities and talents, with consequences for the nature of the relationship between them. To conceive of the family as having a history of its own acknowledges the inevitability of change, but offers the reassurance that, as in all history, there abide elements of "duration and continuance."[51]

By identifying the realm of mediating institutions, thus uniting the public with the private, Catholic teaching locates its claim to address political issues in a pastoral voice. Perhaps nowhere do the political-philosophical teachings and the pastoral dimensions of this teaching better come together, giving direction to both policy and personal priorities, than in the question of *time*. The lack of time that so many experience makes it difficult to cultivate family and friendships, difficult for parents to counter the environment of materialistic values. We know, "in the concreteness of daily existence," the pressures that often seem to implode upon us in the face of the lack of time. The answer, the commitment, must come both on the level of the political and the personal. The state must "provide the context" for family life by paying attention to what might be called "the politics of time." We need policies allowing for parental and family leave to care for newborn, sick, and aging family members. Longer vacations (the norm in Western Europe) would be desirable, as would efforts at reduction of the work-day and week. And the state must insure that wages and salaries are just, thereby obviating the need experienced by many individuals – sometimes by both parents – to work more than one job to support their families.[52]

But this is more than an issue of public policy. The lack of time experienced by individuals can stem from real economic necessity, true; but it can just as easily result from a disordered set of personal priorities: the pursuit of individual ambition or material gain. Here is an area where Catholic teaching serves to remind us that it is "necessary to create lifestyles in which the quest for... goodness and communion with others for the sake of common growth are the factors which determine... choices," and that if "individual fulfillment becomes an end in itself, if monetary gain becomes the prime value, family life suffers."[53] But there is more to reordering our priorities than just having more time. It is a question of "time for what?" Here too Catholic teaching points a direction, by virtue of its sense of something little acknowledged today: namely "hierarchy." Every society, whether it enunciates it in those terms or not, values some things more than others. Catholic teaching ascribes to the family – as the cell and school of society – a higher place in the order of institutions than others.[54] In dialogue with liberalism, Catholic insights on the corrosive effect of materialism and individualism, coupled with a sense of the reordering of priorities to a hierarchy of ends, can provide an alternative to liberalism's present inclination to view "choice" as good *per se*, regardless of the choices people make in fact.

Another area where I believe Catholic teaching, especially in its pastoral dimensions, can engage in a fruitful dialogue with liberalism is the definition of family. This touches upon priorities and choices; it has to do with channeling, for policy purposes, some of liberalism's expansive, all-inclusive tendencies. A staple of Catholic teaching has long been the idea that the purpose of marriage is the procreation and education of children.[55] This emphasis on the presence of children as an essential constitutive element of family is worth pondering. There are implications for policy in a child-focused definition of family. Assisted by the notion of distributive justice, governments are called upon to aid those families – with children – who are most in need of health care, day care, and additional schooling.

In raising the issue of definition one must be cautious lest we, by our definition, demean or exclude from consideration the lived experience of individuals and families for the sake of some abstract ideal. It is the spirit of inclusion that liberalism, in large measure from noble motives, has sought to accommodate. Neither is there an intent here to discount the experience of individuals who, through choice or circumstance, have not as adults formed a nuclear family of their own. The lived experience of many single people testifies to the fact that they feel themselves very much a part of a family. But in what sense? *Familiaris Consortio* addressed "filiation and fraternity" (and, one would hope, "sorority") in the same breath as "fatherhood and motherhood."[56] I would suggest that for those individuals – married or single – who do not have children the full meaning of family is to be experienced in the ties of "filiation and fraternity," as aunts and uncles, as partners in the work of transmitting identity and shared values across the generations. The second draft of the American bishops' pastoral letter on women spoke to the fact that "single aunts and uncles can... seek in appropriate ways to become a vital part of an extended family."[57] I see in this the possibility of recovering a sense of the genuine importance of the extended family. *Gaudium et Spes* eloquently states the vision of the family as "the place where different generations come together and help each other to grow wiser."[58] This is a task in which all members of a family – a historical community bound by the necessity of ties of blood and animated by love – can participate.

Likewise, we should guard against definitions of family that are so broad they become meaningless and useless for both policy and personal application. It strikes me that, for some time now, on both the policy and personal level, we have allowed "family" to be a vessel into which any and every human arrangement is poured, thus making it bear the weight of every human tie and relationship.[59] I would suggest that we spend some time developing enhanced definitions of and appreciation for other categories of human relationship. Among others, we need to give more attention and weight to the category of friendship. Here again the Catholic bishops' pastoral on women offered some insight:

Friendship between men and women as well as relationships between persons of the same sex can nourish a person's sense of discipleship and enhance the capacity for committed service. Friendship involves the risks associated with honest, open expression... but this effort is amply rewarded by wholesome intimacy and the graced capacity to resolve grievances and anger... The relationships found in... friendships are precious gifts to be nourished and expanded.[60]

All of this – the appreciation of the historical dimensions of family life, issues of priorities and definition – is essential to creating the cultural and political climate which legitimates family. In questioning why reform liberalism has so far failed to articulate this legitimation, one can point beyond the aspect of the marketplace of values and look to the tendency, inherent in liberalism, to have the state assume those obligations which properly belong to the family. If capital is the currency of the market, and power the currency of parliamentary institutions, the "currency" of the mediating institutions is obligation, responsibility, and authority. All are closely bound together. Without the latter, the former two are meaningless, without the first two the justification for the latter is non-existent. Alan Wolfe argues that where the welfare state has come to predominate, as in Scandinavia, the sense of obligation on the part of individuals and intermediary institutions, including the family, has been weakened, followed by a weakening of the authority of those mediating institutions.[61] We need to ask whether the usurping of the family function – either overtly or through attitudes which simply ignore the family's proper role – has not helped to create the present situation rather than ameliorating it. Thus the irony that welfare state liberalism seeks to provide a caring society at the very moment when we are least confident about the institution which has historically been the model and metaphor for care and nurturance, namely the family. The condition of families does matter to the health of our society; indeed, it matters to the whole vitality and possibility of the liberal project. Liberals need to assert that value in language and in actions loud and clear.

UNAVOIDABLE CHALLENGES TO CATHOLICISM

I have stated above that Catholic teaching likewise could profit from dialogue with the reform liberal tradition, particularly its expansive vision and sense of inclusivity. Catholic teaching is in some respects deeply flawed, especially in those areas which relate to questions of sexuality and to the equality and dignity of women.

Inasmuch as Catholic teaching acknowledges the historical character of the family, it is appropriate to remind ourselves that Catholic teachings on the family evolved in response to the historical situation posed by the rise of industrial society and the liberal state. Moreover, it is essential to grasp the fact that in formulating its modern teachings on the family the church accepted as a starting point a separation of spheres and division of labor along gender lines. Thus in decrying the implications of classical liberalism and modern industrial society for the family, church teaching allowed those very conditions to set the terms of the debate. The implications for the role and status of women, found in the classical liberal tradition, are therefore present in Catholic teaching as well. In both, the responsibility for a harmonious family life falls disproportionately to the woman. The acceptance of the division of spheres (not only male and female, but implicitly public and private), opened a breach in the tradition of Catholic thought, and introduced a flaw into the integralist nature of that teaching. This distorts a body of teaching that professes to see the good of family and society as intimately linked and that seeks to disallow dualism of the public and private spheres fundamental to classical liberalism. Pushed to its logical conclusion, this breach places the family outside of society rather than anterior to it, and threatens the connecting links that the Catholic tradition sought to forge when it identified the family as "the first and vital cell of society."[62] This is a breach, I would argue, that will only be mended when the Catholic tradition is able to come to grips with questions concerning the role of women in the church and in society.

One example of the problem is the fact that Catholic teaching retains a tendency to address women in their "proper roles" as wives and mothers, regarding employment outside the home as at best a necessary evil. In this regard, as in others, *Familiaris Consortio* represents a step backward from the tone of *Gaudium et Spes*.[63] Here is an area where Catholic social teaching could profit from some of liberalism's openness to change and its moral imagination. Just as liberalism needs to legitimate the family as a social good, Catholic teaching needs to acknowledge the fact that for many women a career or employment outside the home may be in the best interest of the family financially; but more importantly it may be the way in which the woman realizes her potential and her legitimate aspirations for individual human dignity. This can have a positive effect on the children in that family, particularly daughters. It may even be that some female spouses today are the ones with the potential to earn the "family wage."

Another area where the issue of equality for women is troublesome is in the church's refusal to ordain women to the priesthood. The claim that, in the hierarchy of states of life, celibacy is superior to marriage[64] is one that is troubling in its own right, but doubly so if women, by virtue of their gender, are automatically excluded. The adherence to a male celibate priesthood is indicative of the church's difficulties in the whole realm of sexuality as well. The recent pronouncement whereby married men in Brazil may be ordained priests on the condition that conjugal relations with spouses be terminated is an insult to women and to married people everywhere, and makes a mockery of the Catholic claims for the nobility of the married state and the permanence of the marriage bond.

The church's teachings regarding sexuality go to the heart of its credibility when speaking on issues concerning family. Particularly disturbing for many has been the steadfast adherence to *Humanae Vitae* and the ban on artificial birth control. In this, the church might be guided by more careful attention to the totality of its own teachings, particularly its appreciation for the historical character of individual family life. Lisa Sowle Cahill points out that "one of the hallmarks of contemporary thought is the repudiation of dualism." This is at one, I hasten to point out, with Catholic social thought's project of "reconstructing the public and private." In that spirit, Cahill asks that the church acknowledge that "a non-dualistic view of sex requires that we premise a sexual morality on the goodness of the sexual acts and sexual pleasure. It also requires that we look at these acts and their reproductive potential as an integrated whole or process" over the *history* of the relationship. "Spousehood and parenthood are linked in the long-term commitment of the couple, sexually expressed." Sexuality "as mutual physical pleasure, as intimacy, and as parenthood (or at least receptivity to it)...come together in the ongoing relationship," in the *lived historical experience* of the couple.[65]

In this whole question of the credibility of Catholic social teaching the fate of the American bishops' pastoral letter on women is instructive. I have already cited the contributions made by this letter to an appreciation of the intergenerational nature of family life. Likewise valuable are the letter's statements on the equality of states of life – countering the superiority-of-celibacy claim[66] – and the recognition of the realm of friendship. Beyond this, the pastoral makes a genuine effort to address the changed circumstances and situations according to which family life is lived today. While reaffirming earlier statements about the family as a "school of deeper humanity," and "a domestic church," the bishops display pastoral sensitivity to the heartbreaking helplessness of minority women trapped in a cycle of crushing poverty; the exhaustion of mothers trying to maintain a family, a home and outside employment; the frustration of intelligent women being stereotyped as emotional and incapable; the injustice of women receiving unequal pay or having unequal opportunities for advancement.[67]

However, the credibility as well as the viability of the letter were compromised by its reaffirmation of both *Humanae Vitae*[68] and an all-male, celibate priesthood.[69] Reeling under criticism from liberals within the church, the letter failed to gain enough votes to be issued by the bishops and the questions it addressed have been set aside for the time being. The fate of the pastoral is an example of what may well befall any attempt to introduce the Catholic perspective on family into the public dialogue.

This would be a tragedy. The Catholic tradition contains much that speaks to the lack of direction and clarity found in discussions of the family today. The principles of solidarity and subsidiarity, the critique of materialism, the transcendence of the public–private dichotomy through the claim for the importance of the realm of mediating institutions, and the pastoral appreciation of the realities of family life as a lived experience: all these hold the possibility for assisting liberalism in finding a direction and a voice with which to address questions of family policy. The stakes in this undertaking are high. A nation deprived of a legitimate and viable role for families is one in which the possibilities for a nurturing, caring – indeed a civil – society are remote indeed.

NOTES

1 *Study Guide* for the Synod of Bishops, "The Role of the Christian Family in the Modern World" (Washington: US Catholic Conference, 1979), 35.
2 Kristin Luker has set forth a useful framework for examining attitudes towards motherhood and family within the context of wider social and ideological world views. See *Abortion and the Politics of Motherhood* (Berkeley: University of California Press, 1984), 158ff.
3 Fred Siegel, "What Liberals Haven't Learned, and Why," *Commonweal* (January 13, 1989): 17.
4 Kenneth R. Hoover provides a graceful interpretation of liberalism and the institutions of representative government and marketplace in *Ideology and Political Life* (Monterey, CA: Brooks/Cole, 1987), 10–28. "The liberal community is organized by two basic institutions: the marketplace and representative government... Access to goods and services

is determined by the resources, whether in the form of labor or capital, of each individual" (pp. 10–11). Alan Wolfe has likewise developed the primacy of the market and the state in modern society: "Modern societies come to rely ever more thoroughly on either the market or the state to organize their codes of moral obligation..." See Wolfe, *Whose Keeper? Social Science and Moral Obligation* (Berkeley: University of California Press, 1989), 20.

5 Hoover, *Ideology and Political Life*, 12.

6 See Jean Bethke Elshtain, "Aristotle, The Public–Private Split, and the Case of the Suffragists," in Jean Bethke Elshtain, ed., *The Family in Political Thought* (Amherst, MA: University of Massachusetts Press, 1982), 51–65.

7 "The woman's wage communicated to women their inevitable inferiority in nondomestic spheres... and taught women that mobility and independence were cultural goals not appropriate to their sex. And the woman's wage underscored the individual woman's need for male economic protection, thus directing women, quite literally every payday, to devote their best energies to social life and eventual marriage." Leslie Woodcock Tentler, *Wage Earning Women: Industrial Work and Family Life in the United States, 1900–1930* (New York: Oxford University Press, 1979), 25.

8 Jeffrey Weeks, *Sex, Politics and Society: the Regulation of Sexuality Since 1800*, 2nd edn. (London and New York: Longman, 1989), 81. The historical literature on "separate spheres" and the burden placed on women as the guardians of the private sphere is voluminous. Much of it is a product of the flourishing, over the last two decades, of the fields of social history and women's history. See, for example, Michael Anderson, *Approaches to the History of the Western Family, 1500–1914* (London: Macmillan, 1980), in particular chap. 3; J. A. Banks, *Prosperity and Parenthood* (London: Routledge & Kegan Paul, 1954); J. A. and Olive Banks, *Feminism and Family Planning in Victorian England* (New York: Schocken Books, 1964); Patricia Branca, *Silent Sisterhood: Middle Class Women in the Victorian Home* (London: Croom Helm, 1975); J. F. C. Harrison, *The Early Victorians 1832–1851* (New York: Praeger, 1971); and Martha Vicinus, ed., *Suffer and Be Still: Women in the Victorian Age* (Bloomington: University of Indiana, 1972). On the cult of domesticity in the United States, see Nancy Cott, *The Bonds of Womanhood: "Women's Sphere" in New England, 1780–1835* (New Haven: Yale University Press, 1977). An especially stimulating treatment of the public–private, male–female worlds in nineteenth-century France, and one that addresses the role of Catholicism in creating the rich texture of the female world of domesticity, is found in Bonnie G. Smith, *Ladies of the Leisure Class: The Bourgeoises of Northern France in the Nineteenth Century* (Princeton University Press, 1981).

9 Indeed, the historian Peter Stearns has argued that "the principal

cultural interest of the middle class in the early nineteenth century was religion." Peter N. Stearns, *European Society in Upheaval*, 2nd edn. (New York: Macmillan, 1975), 134.

10 Ibid., 2.

11 Edward Shorter, "Female Emancipation, Birth Control, and Fertility in European History," *American Historical Review* 78 (1973): 621–622; see also Shorter, "Illegitimacy, Sexual Revolution and Social Change in Europe, 1750–1900," *Journal of Interdisciplinary History* 2 (1971): 237–272.

12 Suzanne Gordon, "A National Care Agenda," *The Atlantic Monthly* (January 1991): 65.

13 Hoover, *Ideology and Political Life*, 20.

14 Ibid., 62.

15 Ibid., 63–64.

16 Ibid., 65.

17 Laura Gellott, "Staking Claim to the Family: Will Liberals Rediscover a Heritage?" *Commonweal* (September 20, 1985): 488–492.

18 Shorter, "Female Emancipation," 621–622.

19 Jean Bethke Elshtain, *Public Man, Private Woman* (Princeton University Press, 1981), 322.

20 Gordon, "National Care Agenda," 68.

21 Ibid., 64.

22 Jean Bethke Elshtain and John Buell, "Families in Trouble," *Dissent* 38 (Spring 1991): 265.

23 Gordon, "National Care Agenda," 65.

24 See, for example, the discussions surrounding the 1981 White House Conference on Families. After identifying as among the "growing problems" confronting American families divorce and children born out of wedlock, the White House statement promised that the conference would "recognize the pluralism of family life in America. There are families in which several generations live together, families with two parents or one and families with or without children. The Conference will respect this diversity." But one-parent families were numbered among the "problems" identified in the original statement. Were they a problem, or an expression of diversity to be respected? An editorial in *Social Work* states: "The discrepancy in these statements reflects a considerable problem in designing family policy." See *Social Work* 24 (November 1979): 447–448.

25 Wolfe, *Whose Keeper?*, 60, 129, 164.

26 *Gaudium et Spes* [*GS*] no. 25, which cites in turn St. Thomas Aquinas.

27 *Rerum Novarum* [*RN*], in Claudia Carlen, ed., *The Papal Encyclicals: 1878–1903* (Raleigh, NC: McGrath, 1981), 243.

28 Wolfe, *Whose Keeper?*, 2.

29 Elshtain and Buell, "Families in Trouble," 264.

30 "Therefore, those whom fortune favors are warned that riches do not

bring freedom from sorrow and are of no avail for external happiness...
It is one thing to have a right to the possession of money and another to
have the right to use money as one wills." *RN*, in Carlen, *Papal Encyclicals
1878–1903*, 245–246.

31 *Centesimus Annus [CA]*, no. 36, in *Origins* 21/1 (May 16, 1991).

32 "One in Christ Jesus: A Pastoral Response to the Concerns of Women
for Church and Society," no. 49, in *Origins* 19/44 (April 5, 1990).
Because this document satisfied almost no one, the bishops failed to issue
a final version of the draft.

33 *CA* 13.

34 *CA* 35.

35 Timothy Garton Ash, *The Uses of Adversity: Essays on the Fate of Central
Europe* (New York: Vintage, 1990), 179ff.

36 Timothy Garton Ash, *The Magic Lantern: The Revolutions of '89* (New
York: Random House, 1990), 154.

37 *Familiaris Consortio* (The Christian Family in the Modern World) [*FC*],
no. 45 (Washington: United States Catholic Conference, 1981); citation
to *Dignitatis Humanae*, no. 5.

38 *FC* 45.

39 *FC* 45.

40 Elshtain and Buell, "Families in Trouble," 263.

41 Elshtain, *Public Man, Private Woman*, 32.

42 The "Charter of the Rights of the Family," the 1983 document that
grew out of the same 1980 Synod on the Family that also produced
Familiaris Consortio, reasserts this right, calling for a "family wage" or
"other social measures such as family allowances or the remuneration of
the work in the home of one of the parents" so that the family may
exercise its "right to a social and economic order... which permits the
members to live together and does not hinder the unity, well-being and
the stability of the family..." See *Charter of the Rights of the Family*
(Washington: United States Catholic Conference, 1983), art. 10, a.
Likewise, the American Catholic bishops, in the second draft of their
pastoral letter on women, stated that "the church... teach[es] that
society should foster family life by making sure a family wage is available." See "One in Christ Jesus," no. 60.

43 *CA* 8.

44 Erazim Kohák, "Can There be a Central Europe?," *Dissent* (Spring
1990): 197. Kohák treats many of the themes of civil society, in the
context of newly liberated Central Europe that Timothy Garton Ash
discusses in his books.

45 *Study Guide* to Synod of Bishops, "The Role of the Christian Family in the
Modern World," 25.

46 *Familiaris Consortio*, no. 46, cites as among the rights belonging to families
"the right to bring up children in accordance with the family's own
traditions and religious and cultural values."

47 *FC* 4.

48 Ibid.

49 *FC* 6.

50 Cited in Elshtain and Buell, "Families in Trouble," 264.

51 *FC* 46.

52 Gordon, "National Care Agenda," 65–66; Elshtain and Buell, "Families in Trouble," 264–266.

53 *CA* 36; "One in Christ Jesus," no. 49.

54 Vatican Council II, *Apostolicam Actuositatem* (The Decree on the Apostolate of the Laity) [*AA*], no. 11, cited in *FC* 42; Vatican Council II, *Gravissimum Educationis* (Declaration on Christian Education) [*GE*], no. 3.

55 *Casti Connubii*, as one example, states that "amongst the blessings of marriage the child holds the first place"; and "first consideration is due to the offspring." See Claudia Carlen, ed., *The Papal Encyclicals: 1903–1939*, 393 and 399.

56 *FC* 15.

57 "One in Christ Jesus," no. 81.

58 *GS* 52.

59 Elshtain criticizes "modes that call themselves familial but replicate family ties through hollow, sentimentalized repetition of terms for family relations...rather than a serious attempt to recreate and resituate genuine intergenerational, not simply peer or generation-specific bonds." See *Public Man, Private Woman*, 330.

60 "One in Christ Jesus," no. 90.

61 Wolfe, *Whose Keeper?*; see especially chaps. 5 and 6.

62 *FC* 42, *AA* 11.

63 See Jan Grootaers and Joseph Snelling, *The 1980 Synod of Bishops: "On the Role of the Family,"* An Exposition of the Event and An Analysis of Its Texts (Leuven University Press, Bibliotheca Ephemeridum Theologicarum Lovaniensium LVIV, 1983), 166–175. Grootaers and Snelling describe the frustration and disappointment of the bishops with the Synod. Factors which they cite include the personality of John Paul II; the pressures and limitations on expression, including self-censorship exercised by a number of bishops; the clear message that *Humanae Vitae* was not to be contradicted, despite the expectations of some of the bishops; a "greater closedness surrounding [the Synod's] procedure than any of the earlier," exemplified by the strict secrecy which surrounded the final formulation of the Propositions. All in all, the two argue, "the 1980 Synod exhibited the narrowest sense of 'collegiality' and the poorest connection with the local churches." This was compounded, especially in view of the topic, by the "actual exclusion of laypersons." "Behind the facade of deliberation and dialogue, all the conditions were filled to limit this Synod to a monologue."

64 *FC* 16.

65 Lisa Sowle Cahill, "Can We Get Real About Sex," *Commonweal* (September 14, 1990): 502.
66 "One in Christ Jesus," no. 43. "The church's focus on marriage and the family must not be placed in opposition to the authentic realization of other life-giving roles and vocations... that the church's recognition of distinct offices must never justify clericalism or the exclusion of women from participation in the full life of the Christian community."
67 Ibid., no. 5.
68 Ibid., nos. 72–78.
69 Ibid., nos. 113–119.

CHAPTER 12

Rights of persons in the church

James H. Provost

The Catholic church has recently adopted codes of law which for the first time include lists of rights and duties common to all Catholics.[1] This is a significant development within the last decade, for it introduces within the church's law an echo of the Catholic social teaching on rights in society at large. For some time there have been appeals to the rights of Christians within the church occasioned by a variety of concerns, ranging from the concern of church officials to promote evangelization and the action of Catholics in the world, to the interests of individuals or groups who assert claims to the celebration of the Eucharist in a time of a shortage of celibate priests, or in regard to the role of women, or on behalf of academic freedom.[2] Now even official codes of church law use rights language to describe the common status of church members.

This paper examines the adoption of this rights language in church law, and explores the extent to which it has been taken seriously in the system of canon law. Some preliminary cautions, however, are in order. First, in canon law the rights language itself tends to be somewhat ambiguous. It reflects an understanding that some rights are based in human nature (human rights), whether they are recognized by a given legal system or not. A specific legal system may recognize a variety of rights, some of which are human rights and others of which are the result of how the legal system itself is organized. Canon law includes both types of rights, and at times it is not easy to determine whether a given right should be considered a natural human right, or rather the creation of the canonical system.

Second, this obviously cannot be an exhaustive review of the topic, either in its contemporary expression or in its historical precedents. The effort here is only to sketch the main lines of the contribution which can be made from the perspective of canonical studies.

Third, attention will be limited to the rights of individual persons, rather than the rights of the church as such, or the rights of juridic persons (e.g., religious orders, dioceses, chapters of canons, etc.), or even the rights which pertain to a specific status in the church (e.g., the rights of clergy, rights of bishops, rights of religious, etc.). The specifically contemporary issue focuses on the rights of the individual Christian faithful – sometimes called "personal" rights – even while continuing to affirm these other traditional classes of rights.

Finally, the study is limited to the Catholic church; the issue of whether "rights" are even admitted within other Christian traditions would lead us too far afield.[3] For the Catholic church the law applicable to both Latin and Eastern Catholics will be reviewed as it stands today, but for the history of this topic attention will be directed only to the Western or Latin canonical tradition, even though an exploration of personal rights in the Eastern tradition could be quite interesting.

THE ADOPTION OF A LIST OF COMMON RIGHTS

The adoption of a list of rights and duties common to all the faithful may be new in the church's law, but attention to rights has a long history in canon law. This section of the paper has four parts: an overview of the canonical tradition up to and including the 1917 code; the debate among canonists in the twentieth century about "subjective rights" in the church; the development of the list of rights in the new codes; and some commentary on the meaning of these rights in the context of the studies in this volume.

At the start it is important to acknowledge the ambiguity in the use of a key concept which runs throughout this history, that of "subjective rights." In some usages the term seems to mean basic human rights, arising from the fact of being a human being ("subject"). In other usages the term seems to connote the legal claims of a person within a society (whether the church or secular society), either because of the duties the person has in that society or because of the legal system of the society itself.[4]

Canonical tradition

There is a venerable tradition among canonists affirming the rights of persons in the church. Historians of canon law and of the medieval period in general have explored the development of "subjective" or personal rights in canon law from various angles.[5] Whether it was the law affecting the poor,[6] or children,[7] or the right to active and passive voice in elections,[8] or the right to conjugal acts,[9] medieval canonists were deeply embroiled in practical questions relating to personal rights. They did not develop an abstract treatment of rights, but they did use concepts such as rights, duties, liberties, immunities, interests, actions, and so on, which clearly reflect an underlying framework based on an acceptance of personal rights.

Their discussions did not distinguish rights within the church and rights within society at large; for them, Christendom formed a whole, church and state were the two swords or powers on which Christendom was based, and distinctions framed on a separation of the two were not part of their horizon. This does not mean that all claims were treated equally; but it took for granted that claims could be made within the church as well as within secular life. Indeed, many concerns which we identify today with the state were the proper domain of the church at that time: marriage, care for the poor, etc.

This medieval tradition provided the foundation on which bishops, missionaries, and canonists built their interventions on behalf of the Indians in Spanish America shortly after the initial conquests of Mexico, Central America, and Peru. While the lawfulness of the conquests was defended by Juan Ginés de Sepúlveda, they were rejected altogether by Fray Bartolomé de las Casas who argued the Spanish had no right to take over the newly discovered lands. Francisco de Vitoria and the School of Salamanca took a middle ground, denouncing the injustices perpetrated by the conquistadors and arguing for the rights of the Indians.[10] The Salamanca canonists constructed their arguments based on the natural rights of the Indians as human persons. But given the heritage of Christendom with which they were working, they applied this not only to the need for reform of the political regime imposed in New Spain but also to the work of the church itself, insisting on the freedom of the act of faith in opposition to any forced conversions.[11] While the project for renewal and redress of the colonial regime ultimately failed because the Spanish authorities in Latin America would not implement the royal decrees developed in consultation with the Salamanca canonists, the insistence on rights within the church had at least some effect through the legislation of the various particular councils, particularly the Third Council of Lima in 1583.[12]

This rich Salamanca tradition is frequently cited as one of the sources for the Enlightenment's development of human rights in a secular setting as the distinction between religious and secular life continued to grow. However, it did not bear fruit within the church, nor did it result in a listing of rights and duties of the Christian faithful when the church's law was given its first modern codification in 1917. Why? The reasons are various. Canon law did not recognize a fundamental equality of all the faithful; on the contrary, at least since Gratian's Decree (1140) a basic inequality was presumed by the law.[13] The anti-religious polemic of the Enlightenment, the anti-Catholic character of European liberalism, and particularly the devastating effects of the French Revolution on the Catholic church, contributed to an attitude which was hardly favorable to emphasizing rights in the church.[14] The primarily hierarchical concerns of the 1917 codification left little room for a listing of rights which might be considered claims against church authorities.[15]

Concern for the rights of persons, however, was not absent from the 1917 Code of Canon Law. It contains the traditional affirmation that with baptism come the rights and duties proper to Christians (c. 87). While generally it made no attempt to list those rights directly, canon 682 did state explicitly that "The laity have the right to receive spiritual goods from the clergy according to the norm of ecclesiastical discipline, especially the aids necessary for salvation." From one perspective the remainder of the church's law could be understood as structuring the implementation of this right.[16]

Canon 1524 also introduced a new requirement into church law that laborers be paid a just wage and that they be assured appropriate working conditions. The canon is an initial attempt to incorporate into church law the social teaching developed in *Rerum Novarum*, a tentative exploration of how applicable the church's teaching about rights in secular life might be to life within the church. But it is restricted to the church as employer, in which it is difficult to differentiate a specifically ecclesial reality in contrast to secular employers.

Twentieth-century debate

Since the early 1940s there has been considerable discussion among canon lawyers about the rights of persons within the Catholic church. The debate was often phrased in terms of whether "subjective rights" exist within the church. It was an almost entirely European discussion, framed in the context of European political theory and systems.[17] Prior to Vatican II canonists dealt with the church in terms of a theory they considered to be based on principles which also applied to secular political theory, which explains why debate about "subjective rights" in European secular circles found such an echo in canonical discussions about inner church life.[18]

"Subjective rights" are rights which inhere in the person, respecting the autonomy as well as the social nature of human persons. They are often presented as claims of the individual over against an all-encompassing public authority. It was in this sense that Pio Fedele argued that canon law has no room for subjective rights.[19] He claimed that church law considers only the utility of the church (*utilitas Ecclesiae*); it is a law of the public order only, an order which is directed toward the salvation of souls (*salus animarum*). How can an individual stake out a claim over against the public order which by definition is for the individual's good?

Such an extreme position stimulated an animated debate among canonists, and even an entire congress of canon lawyers dedicated to the topic.[20] Some argued that subjective rights are the same as those basic rights (also called "fundamental rights") which arise from human nature; with the church proclaiming its support for these rights in its social magisterium, it must be consistent and recognize these same rights in its own legal order.[21] Others argued that fundamental rights and subjective rights are different; these canonists based subjective rights in the legal system rather than in the nature of the human person. The European legal system makes a major distinction between public law and private law, a distinction the canonists carried over into their discussion of the church. In light of this some canonists claimed that in addition to private subjective rights which are exercised in the sphere of private law such as contracts or managing one's own finances, there are also public subjective rights which incorporate the individual into society and are essential to understanding the role of the faithful in the church itself.[22]

The debate remained somewhat academic until John XXIII announced Vatican II and called for the revision of the Code of Canon Law. The council resolved the question of the rights of persons within the church not by engaging in the theoretical debate of canonists, but by stating quite forcefully the basic equality of Christians and by listing various rights within the church.

"Right" (*ius*) in the sense of personal rights was applied internally to the life of the church in a number of conciliar documents.[23] For example, there is the basic right and duty of all the faithful to full, conscious, and active participation in liturgical celebrations (*Sacrosanctum Concilium*, no. 14). The "rights" of Christians within the church constituted one of the frameworks for the discussion about lay persons. They have the right to receive help from the spiritual goods of the church, to express their needs and desires to church authorities, to express their opinion about what is for the good of the church (*Lumen Gentium*, no. 37). They have a basic duty and right to the apostolate, and to exercise in the church as well as in the world the charisms they receive from the Holy Spirit (*Apostolicam Actuositatem*, no. 3). Christian parents have the right and duty to provide a Christian education for their children (*AA* 11). The laity have the right to found associations, to run them, and to give them a name of their choice (*AA* 19). Bishops, pastors, and other clergy are reminded that all the faithful, lay as well as clergy, have the right and duty to carry out the apostolate (*AA* 25).

The bishops also spoke of the "freedom of the children of God." In addition to the generic meaning of redemption, Christian "liberties" were addressed in specific contexts. Church pastors are to recognize the proper liberty of lay people in secular matters (*LG* 37). Scientific liberty, or academic freedom, is proclaimed for those who work in the church's colleges and universities (*Gravissimum Educationis*, no. 10, *Gaudium et Spes*, no. 62). The freedom of the act of faith is one of the bases for religious liberty, so much so that the constant teaching of the church is that no one is to be coerced to believe (*Dignitatis Humanae*, no. 12).

More fundamentally, the bishops affirmed the basic equality of all in the church insofar as they are called to the same sanctity and share the common lot in God's justice as believers. "There is among all a true equality with regard to the dignity and action which is common to all the faithful for building up the Body of Christ" (*LG* 32).

Rights in the new codes

The work of revising church law began in earnest once the council concluded. Those responsible for this effort were charged by Paul VI to incorporate in the law the "new way of thinking" characteristic of the council. The commission appreciated from the beginning the significance of the conciliar statements on rights and proposed as two of its guiding principles that the rights of persons be "defined and safeguarded," and that procedures be assured for "safeguarding subjective rights."[24]

Proposals for a listing of Christian rights were developed by a number of canonists in the late 1960s and early 1970s.[25] Two approaches developed. Some modeled their approaches on those of basic human rights, even attempting to transpose the 1948 Universal Declaration of Human Rights into canon law.[26] Even the principles for the code's revision alluded to a natural law basis for the rights of Christians, similar to the basis adopted in church teaching for fundamental human rights.[27]

The 1971 Synod of Bishops addressed the practice of justice and cautioned that "anyone who ventures to speak to people about justice must first be just in their eyes." Therefore, "within the Church rights must be preserved. No one should be deprived of his ordinary rights because he is associated with the Church in one way or another."[28] The synod went on to address specific rights including those to a just wage, participation and responsibility, freedom of expression and thought. This seems clearly to be taking the church's teaching on rights in secular life, and applying them internal to the life and operations of the church itself.

Others approached rights from a theological, ecclesiological perspective, affirming the uniqueness of the church and therefore the unique character of rights within the church. Rather than drawing on secular parallels they sought to root their listing of rights in the magisterium, especially in Vatican II.[29]

The actual drafting of a list of "fundamental rights" common to all Christians was undertaken by two different sub-committees of the code revision commission.[30] The first list became public when the draft *Lex Ecclesiae Fundamentalis* was circulated for comment in 1971. It occasioned some criticism and underwent various revisions. Eventually the second list was dropped, and the listing of rights developed for the *Lex* was incorporated into the church's codes.[31] The 1983 Code of Canon Law for the Latin Church has a special section at the beginning of its first substantive book, "On the People of God," which deals with the "Obligations and Rights of All the Christian Faithful" (cc. 208–223). The 1990 Code of Canons for the Eastern Churches follows a different organization of the material, but among the very first canons is the same list taken from the *Lex* with some editorial modifications, entitled "On the Christian Faithful and the Rights and Obligations of All of Them" (cc. 10–26).[32]

The first canon on the Christian faithful in both codes gives a basic context for understanding the rights which follow. Through baptism the faithful are incorporated into Christ and constituted as people of God, they share in Christ's priestly, prophetic and royal functions, and they are called to exercise the mission God entrusted to the church to accomplish in the world. The rights and duties of Christians come from baptism and of their nature can be exercised only within the context of the community of the church. This already establishes a communitarian setting for understanding rights.

The listing contains both rights and duties, sometimes relating to the same reality. There does not seem to be an especially systematic organization to the list, so no special importance need be attributed to where a particular right (or duty) appears in relation to the others.

Here is a brief summary of the rights and obligations. Fundamental is the statement of "true equality with regard to dignity and the activity whereby all cooperate in the building up of the Body of Christ."[33] This equality is based on baptism and looks toward the mission of the church. It does not claim that everyone has an equal role in the church, but that all equally share in carrying out the work of the church in whatever role they may serve. The canon serves to affirm a common juridic status in the church for all the faithful, whatever other divisions may exist according to legal status (age, place, clergy–laity, etc.).

Christians are then said to have obligations to maintain communion with the church and to fulfill their duties toward the whole church and their own particular church, to live a holy life, and to promote the church's growth and continual sanctification. They have the duty and right to work so that the Gospel is preached to everyone, everywhere. They are to obey the official teachings and discipline laid down by the bishops, but are also free to petition, making known their needs, and to express their opinion privately and publicly, both to church officials and to others in the church.

The faithful have the right to worship God according to the prescriptions of their own rite, and to pursue their own spirituality. For charitable and religious purposes and to promote the Christian vocation in the world they are free to found and to run associations in the church, and to hold meetings. They have the right to promote or sustain apostolic actions on their own initiative.

Christians have a right to a Christian education leading to the maturity of a human person, and to greater knowledge and living of the mystery of salvation. Those engaged in theology and related fields enjoy a lawful freedom of inquiry and expression of opinion on matters in which they have some expertise.

The faithful have the right to be free from coercion in selecting a state in life, and no one is permitted to damage unlawfully another's good reputation or to violate another's right to privacy.

Christians can vindicate and defend their rights before a competent ecclesiastical court. When called before competent authority for judgment they have the right to be judged in keeping with the law, and to have it applied with equity. They also have the right not to be punished with canonical penalties except as provided by law.

All Christians are obliged to help meet the material needs of the church, to promote justice in society, and to assist the poor. In exercising their rights they must observe personal and social responsibility, and church authorities can restrict the exercise of these rights for the sake of the common good.

Commentary

A detailed commentary on these canons is beyond the scope of the present study.[34] Three topics, however, are significant for the present study: the communitarian base and understanding of rights in the codes; the relationship of obligations and rights; and the relationship of the canons to human rights.

Communitarian base

Because the rights and obligations arise with baptism, of their nature they relate to being in the church and participating in its mission. They are not presented as some autonomous base for making a claim over against the church, but rather as the expression of the common juridic status of all within the church community.

There is some equivocation in many of the authors who have analyzed the relationship of these personal rights and the church. The equivocation is in the understanding of "church" in this context. In canon 204 "church" clearly means the people of God, the community of the faithful – laity, religious, clergy, hierarchy. The focus is on the mystery of the church as it is lived out in this world. In this sense there can be no standing over against the community in the name of personal rights, for this is the community of salvation which exists for the *salus animarum*, the salvation of the individual.

But in addressing the question of whether the obligations and rights of the faithful can be a claim over against church authorities, many of the commentators shift to an understanding of "church" as hierarchy. They assert that rights cannot constitute a claim against the hierarchy but rather must take into account the "exigencies of charity and of a delicate respect for the hierarchical authority of the church."[35] Yet even in the very statement of some of the rights, it is the hierarchy which is charged to provide certain services for the rest of the faithful. The nature of at least these particular rights presupposes a claim for services from the hierarchy. Other rights are an affirmation of a sphere of liberty; although this liberty must be exercised responsibly within the church community, it also implies some restriction on the discretion of others, including church authorities.

It is in this light that the canon on the limitation of rights bears greater scrutiny.[36] The canon is taken from *Dignitatis Humanae*, no. 7, dealing with limitations on the exercise of the right to religious liberty in the context of personal and social responsibility, which imposes limits on the use of any liberty. The council teaches that individuals and social groups "are bound by the moral law to have regard to the rights of others, to their own duties toward others and to the common good of all."[37] The codes take this general principle of the moral law and apply it to the exercise of rights within the church. It is the exercise of the rights, not the rights themselves, which is limited.

The conciliar text immediately takes up the limitation on the exercise of rights which can be imposed by governments in order to defend society against possible abuses committed on the pretext of the exercise of rights. Government is not to act in an arbitrary manner, but in conformity with the objective moral order. The council then describes the elements of public order, which constitute a fundamental part of the common good. The code applies the same principles to the role of church authorities.[38]

In effect, the code incorporates the magisterium's teaching about the limitation of the exercise of one of the most fundamental human rights – religious liberty[39] – to church authority's role in the limitation of rights within the church. While not stating explicitly the limitation on church authority this imposes, it provides a basis for interpreting when the abuse of ecclesiastical power can be punished.[40]

It is in this context that the concept of "common good" is applied to limitations on rights. The canons speak of the "good" in a variety of ways. For example, "good" is used in an objective sense – the good of a portion of the people of God or diocese, of a religious institute, of the missions; the good of religion; the good of the whole church, of the churches, of dioceses; the greater good which is produced when several bishops or bishops' conferences cooperate.[41] Here "good" seems to mean benefit, advantage, etc.

Another objective sense of the term is the "public good" – for which public juridic persons are established, which is safeguarded by warnings when church officials judge it to be endangered, and on whose behalf a promoter of justice (a sort of public prosecutor in the church courts) is to be named in each diocese. In cases involving the public good the judge has greater discretionary authority but also must administer an oath to the parties, weigh confessions more carefully, follow special procedures, and cannot resolve the matter by settlement or compromise.[42] Here "good" seems to refer to the good order of society, the public welfare.

Sometimes public good is joined with mention of the salvation of souls: Eastern authorities must keep both of these in mind when issuing decrees; an oath has no effect on an act which would be harmful to either the public good or eternal salvation; judges can proceed ex officio in cases involving the public good of the church or the salvation of souls.[43] Here the public good has equal importance with the salvation of souls, but it is not the same thing.

There is also a more personal use of "good" – the good of the faithful, their spiritual good or well-being.[44]

Then there is the "common good." Sometimes the canons qualify it as the common good of society.[45] At other times it clearly means common good in the same sense as the social teaching of the church: clergy can be permitted to be active in political parties or labor unions if it will protect the rights of the church or promote the common good.[46] The "common good of the church" is invoked in two instances. The first is to exempt some juridic persons from the seminary tax.[47] The other concerns self-regulation in the exercise of rights. That is, in exercising one's own rights in the church a person must consider the common good of the church along with the rights of others and one's own duties toward others.[48] Finally, common good is the basis for authorities to regulate the exercise of personal rights and to supervise private associations.[49]

The purpose for this detailed analysis of how the canons use these concepts is to highlight the fact that there is no well-developed technical meaning of "good" or "common good" applied with consistency throughout the church's law. As with other key concepts in the codes, there is an ambiguity in the meaning and use of "common good." An interpreter must attempt to determine the correct meaning in canon law not on the basis of some general principle of common good, but according to the usual canonical principle of understanding the meaning of terms in their text and context (c. 17). But underlying all this is the understanding of the church as a communion of persons which is fundamentally a communion of each of them with Christ, and at the same time a bonding among all of them as God's people, Christ's body, a holy communion of those who share this same divine life. In light of this the law expects a communitarian concern to inform the exercise of any rights in the church.[50]

Who are the "community" about which one is to be concerned? The canon on self-limitations of rights identifies three considerations: others who have rights in the same situation, others toward whom one has duties in this situation, and the welfare of the rest of the people of God. At least, this latter would seem to be the meaning of "church" in the phrase "common good of the church," rather than the institutional benefit associated with other uses of "good" in the law. Indeed, one might argue that the "common good of the church" is to be understood in terms of those conditions under which the people of God can seek their perfection, in keeping with the technical meaning *Dignitatis Humanae*, no. 6 gives to the common good.[51]

The rights specific to Christians in church law, then, are not independent bases for making claims over against the institution; they are communitarian in their very nature, arising out of baptism and rooted in the dignity of being a member of God's people. But by the same token, they are not merely privileges extended by a benign sovereign. They are truly bases for personal action and responsibility which must be respected by church officials. It is not merely the benefit of the institution that is at stake in limiting a Christian's rights, but rather the conditions under which Christians themselves can pursue their perfection in the church. These two are not necessarily the same: what institutional authorities may prefer, or even consider necessary, may or may not have a bearing on the conditions under which Catholics can seek perfection in the context of the church community.

Since the canon is dealing with the limitation on the free exercise of rights, it must be interpreted strictly (c. 18); that is, only so much restriction is permitted as the technical meaning of the words of the law warrant. *Dignitatis Humanae* provides a similar reading of the role of authorities with reference to the exercise of personal rights: "That principle of full freedom is to be preserved in society according to which people are given the maximum of liberty, and only restrained when and in so far as is necessary."[52] The communitarian nature of rights in the church reinforces the sphere of liberty of the Christian, even while pointing to the sense of responsibility which is implied in a legitimate exercise of those rights.

Obligations and rights

Rights and duties are closely interwoven in the codes. Some even seek to derive rights from duties: identify persons' duties, and you will know their rights.[53] In such a view rights are limited, first, to the fulfillment of duties that a person has; and second, by society's organization of who has what role, that is, of who has what duties. The wording of the title in the Latin code ("obligations and rights") has been taken by some as confirming this view in the law.

But the Eastern code retains the more traditional formula, "rights and obligations," and authoritative reports indicate there was no intention to adopt a particular theory of the source of rights in drafting even the Latin code.[54] What the law does attempt, however, is to emphasize the correlation between duties and rights. While some rights arise from human dignity or baptismal status, other rights are related to one's responsibilities for the mission of the church. Moreover, if someone has a duty to provide me with something, that gives me a right to their services. Similarly, if I have a duty to carry out some responsibility, I have the right to do it. Indeed, if my failure to exercise a right would endanger the community, then I even have an obligation to exercise my right.

As mentioned above, these rights must all be seen within the framework of the church community. The close relating of rights and duties is one way of trying to spell out this tie to the community, while at the same time respecting the freedom and personal responsibility of each Christian.

Human rights and the canons

Some of the rights recognized in the church's law are fundamental human rights (e.g., freedom from coercion in choosing a state in life, the rights to a good name and to privacy, and the right to vindicate rights). Other rights arise from the condition of being a Christian and are fundamental in the sense of being rights which come from baptism. Still other rights arise from the way in which the church is organized; they are practical determinations which can and may change as the church's organizational life changes.

The final draft of the *Lex Ecclesiae Fundamentalis* proposed to acknowledge all the rights and duties which come from the dignity of the human person; in other words, to give legal recognition to all fundamental human rights within the church.[55] The canon, however, was not incorporated into the codes. Its implications were so broad that it would be difficult to give legal precision to the canon.[56]

Several commentators remark that the church has officially recognized human rights in many settings; there was no need to do so internal to the church's law where the focus should be on life within the Catholic community itself, presuming the human rights which Catholics have in common with all people. Indeed, it is not the role of the church, but rather that of the state, to guarantee basic human rights.[57]

In some ways the list of rights in the codes resembles other catalogues of human rights.[58] The codes' rights and duties could also be categorized according to the classifications in use for human rights: liberties, entitlements, and participation. The list reflects its historical conditioning and is not an attempt at an abstract theory of rights.[59]

But in other ways, they differ from the usual lists of human rights. Secular lists have often been drafted to address specific problems in the body politic: denials of rights leads to their reaffirmation; grievances which affect the basic liberties of people lead to a claim for those same liberties.[60] The codes' list, however, does not seem to have been drafted in light of specific grievances or burning issues felt throughout the church. Instead, it is selected primarily from the teachings of the hierarchy, some concerning human rights and some concerning the role of lay persons in the church.

Bills of rights in civil constitutions are frequently presented as "fundamental," which means they must be taken into consideration by the authorities in carrying out their activities, and they can be claimed against other parties in society. It is disputed whether the rights listed in canon law can be considered fundamental in the canonical system.[61]

Finally, the statements of rights are so hedged about with cautions and qualifiers that some have questioned the seriousness of the codes in stating them.[62] This may be designed to provide within the law itself the principles for its interpretation. Canon law belongs to the system of "legislative supremacy" in the interpretation of law. That is, the law itself contains the principles for its own interpretation (cf. for example cc. 14, 16–22 in the Latin code), or else the legislator (not the courts) issues binding interpretations which are themselves laws rather than precedents (c. 16). At times the means for interpreting a law are spelled out in detailed qualifications inserted into the text of the law itself.[63] But this style of law-making does lead observers who are not conversant with the technicalities of the canonical legal system to raise this question.

SERIOUSNESS OF THE RIGHTS

These cautions in the way rights are stated are not the only reason some question the seriousness of the listing of rights in present church law. For a right to be considered realistic, it must be defensible. That is, there must be some way to vindicate the right when it is threatened or violated. Does the canonical system provide such a system, does it work, or is it even workable?

Maintaining a long standing principle in canon law, the new codes affirm that "every right whatsoever is safeguarded not only by an action but also by an exception unless something to the contrary is expressly stated."[64] An action is a petition for a judicial decision on some matter; an exception is a request by a respondent in a case to change some procedure or to quash the case.[65] So in addition to affirming the right to vindicate and defend rights before a competent church court,[66] the law expressly provides for a procedure (action or exception) by which this can be done.

Actions and exceptions are usually made as part of a canonical trial in a church court.[67] The codes recognize this by including as the first purpose for a trial "to prosecute or to vindicate the rights of physical or juridic persons."[68] So it would seem that a system is in place for the vindication and protection of personal rights in the church. But this is only partially true.

As church courts gradually developed during the Middle Ages the decision of a lower court could be appealed to a higher court. The courts developed the practice of hearing appeals not only from the decision of a lower court, but also appeals from a decision made by a church official outside of a tribunal setting. These were called "extra-judicial" appeals, or the presentation of a case against a church official in a higher tribunal. They were an alternative to going to the official's hierarchical superior for redress.[69] The ability of the courts to hear cases vindicating rights against bishops' actions was gradually limited by the growing competencies of the Roman congregations. With Pius X's reorganization of the Roman Curia in 1908, the courts were eliminated entirely as an avenue for vindicating personal rights against a church official's actions.[70] Proposals drafted as part of the development of the 1917 code to reintroduce the courts as an alternative to recourse to a superior were not adopted.[71] An authentic (authoritative) interpretation of the 1917 code excluded from the Roman Rota even cases for damages resulting from improper administrative acts.[72]

In effect, after 1909 when the reforms of *Sapienti Consilio* took effect, courts have been a place to vindicate rights, but not when the conflict arises from the act of a bishop or similar superior. The only exception had to do with financial administration.[73]

In drafting the current codes, an effort was made to develop a systematic law governing administration in the church.[74] It included basic principles for good administration as well as procedures for vindicating rights which may have been harmed by administrative actions of bishops or other officials. While this draft law was not adopted, elements of it were incorporated in the final draft of the code sent to the pope in 1982, including the optional development of administrative tribunals by bishops' conferences. These would have been an alternative to having recourse to the bishop's superior to vindicate rights.

The final version of the codes, however, does not contain the option for administrative tribunals, and restricts to "hierarchical recourse" the vindication of rights in these situations.[75] Catholics who claim their rights have been violated or illegally limited by a pastor or other official subject to a diocesan bishop must take the case to the bishop. If the complaint concerns an action by the bishop, they must take the case to an appropriate office of the Roman Curia. If they have a complaint against an action by an office of the curia, they can ask the

Supreme Tribunal of the Apostolic Signatura to review whether the curial office erred in procedure, or in understanding and applying the law; if the Signatura agrees, the case goes back to be reconsidered by the curial office.[76]

On the face of it, this is at least a basic system for vindicating rights. However, there are a number of technicalities which must be observed and failure to do so could lead to the case being thrown out. For example, there are strict time limits which must be met. If the complaint is against a bishop's action, within ten working days he must be asked to reconsider. If he refuses, or if he does not answer for a month (which is taken to be equivalent to refusing), the recourse to the Roman Curia must be made within fifteen working days. These time limits are "peremptory"; that is, if they are not observed, the right to have recourse in this case is lost.

Restricting recourse from a bishop's decision to Rome makes access to relief more difficult by reason of distance, difference in language, and the complexity of dealing with curial offices. The time and money involved can be beyond the resources of the individuals concerned, discouraging legitimate cases while at the same time favoring those who have the finances and time, even if theirs is only a nuisance case.

There is no regular reporting of cases handled on hierarchical recourse, so it is difficult to learn the practice of the Roman Curia in these cases. This increases the difficulty in advising people with a grievance on whether there is even any hope in approaching the Apostolic See with their petition.[77]

In short, the system is inadequate and has been recognized as such by various authors.[78] Despite the emphasis on rights in the early pages of the codes, the section dealing with the vindication and protection of rights leans heavily in favor of administrators and institutional concerns rather than the rights of the Christian faithful.

An element of the system which mitigates somewhat this bleak evaluation is the provision for mediation of disputes.[79] This can be a means to vindicate rights, provided all parties agree to the mediation. Such a system has been attempted in various dioceses of the United States since the early 1970s, and a formal system was adopted for Bavaria around the same time.[80]

The American system was adopted as a pattern which dioceses could adopt or modify. It proposed a system of conciliation and arbitration which conceivably could address most of the grievances in the church outside of truly doctrinal or sacramental issues. A survey of experience in United States dioceses from 1970 through 1975 learned that over half the dioceses had some experience with diocesan "due process," over 40 percent had some experience in processing a case, and that for a number of people it has been a means to vindicate their rights, especially when dealing with a lay person, religious, or cleric below the bishop.[81] But the survey also learned that people generally are not aware of the services which are available, that the process does not work effectively when the bishop is a party to the case, and that only about a quarter of the dioceses in the country could be considered "actively" involved in "due process" efforts. The survey also found that more than voluntary compliance is needed in many cases for solutions developed through mediation to have any effect.

Possible ways to close this gap are under study by a special committee of the Canon Law Society of America. Among the options under consideration is the possibility of establishing administrative tribunals within the United States. While officials of the Apostolic Signatura have indicated an openness to such a possibility,[82] it remains to be seen whether the technical details can be worked out in practice.

CONCLUDING REFLECTIONS

The language of rights has found a new emphasis in the law of the Catholic church. While it resonates with canonical tradition, the present formulation of a list of rights and duties common to all the Christian faithful is something new in canon law. It is not at all clear, however, whether the Catholic church has taken over the liberal ideas usually connected with statements of human rights. Key expressions relating to rights (including the term "rights" itself) appear to be used ambiguously in the new church codes. Although some human rights are contained in the list, there is no explicit affirmation of the acceptance of all human rights within the canonical system. Moreover, the expression of the rights is so cautionary that it has led some to question whether these are truly rights in the generally accepted sense.

Although the rights and duties are set forth in a communitarian context and can be limited for the sake of the common good, it is not clear that they exercise any significant role within the community. It is debated whether they are to be understood as fundamental rights which can be used as criteria for judging the actions of church officials. The legal provisions for vindicating the rights appear to be inadequate. Without effective means to vindicate rights, and without a consensus to support their significance in the social life of the church, can they even be considered "rights" in the modern sense?

It would seem that the church has yet to come to grips with the issue of how to incorporate into its own legal order the language of freedom and rights which Vatican II applied within the church. Whether it is possible to make this incorporation cannot be judged from the canonical data, for the revision of the codes appears to have avoided the hard questions.

Two closing comments, however, may help to place this situation in perspective. The first has to do with how long it takes for a community to come to grips with the practical implications of rights. For example, within the church it has taken many centuries to come to a clearer understanding of the rights of the pope and bishops, despite centuries of attention to the issue. The concept of a common juridic status for all the faithful is so new in canon law as to be practically revolutionary. It is to be expected that its full implications will take time to work out.

The second comment has to do with the reception of law.[83] While the codes may have come into existence with their promulgation, whether they will have lasting effect on the life of the church will depend on the extent to which they are put to work – the extent to which they are received by the communities for which they were promulgated. The major factor in what the rights of Christians will eventually mean in the Catholic community is the community itself. How it understands these rights, the way in which people act in light of their rights, the commitments they make and the actions which follow from these, will eventually determine whether personal rights do indeed exist within the Catholic church.

NOTES

1 See *Codex Iuris Canonici*, January 25, 1983; *AAS* [*Acta Apostolicae Sedis*] 75/2 (1983): cc. 208–223 (for the Latin Church), and *Codex Canonum Ecclesiarum Orientalium*, October 18, 1990: *AAS* 82 (1990): 1033–1363, cc. 7–26 (for the Eastern Churches). In this article citations from the Latin code are taken from *Code of Canon Law, Latin–English Edition* (Washington: CLSA, 1983); see also *Code of Canons of the Eastern Churches, Latin–English Edition* (Washington: CLSA, 1992).

2 See, for example, *The Right of the Community to a Priest*, ed. Edward Schillebeeckx and Johann-Baptist Metz, *Concilium* 133 (Edinburgh: T. & T. Clark, 1980); *A Catholic Bill of Rights*, ed. Leonard Swidler and Herbert O'Brien (Kansas City, MO: Sheed & Ward, 1988).

3 See, for example, J. H. Lochman, "Les Eglises réformées et la théologie des 'droits de l'homme,'" *Revue théologique de Louvain* 10 (1979): 348–352.

4 For a further discussion, particularly of nineteenth- and twentieth-century debates, see Hans Coing, "Signification de la notion de droit subjectif," *Archives de philosophie de droit* 9 (1964): 1–15.

5 See Antonio García y García, "Los derechos de la persona humana en el ordenamiento canónico medieval," in *I diritti fondamentali della persona umana e la libertà religiosa. Atti del V Colloquio Giuridico (8–10 marzo 1984)*, ed. Franco Biffi (Vatican City: Libreria Editrice Vaticana, 1985), 85–100; Heinz-Meinholf Stamm, "Die Grundrechte der menschlichen Person im Dekret Gratians," in ibid., 497–503; Brian Tierney, "Origins of Natural Rights Language: Texts and Contexts, 1150–1250," *History of Political Thought* 10 (1989), cited by Charles J. Reid, Jr., of Cornell Law School in an unpublished manuscript, "The Canonistic Contribution to the Western Rights Tradition: An Historical Inquiry."

A contrary view has been developed over many years by Michel Villey. See, for example, "L'Idée du droit subjectif et les systèmes juridiques," *Revue historique de droit français et étranger* 24 (1946): 201. For a critique, see Brian Tierney, "Villey, Ockham and the Origin of Individual Rights," in *The Weightier Matters of the Law: Essays on Law and Religion. A Tribute to Harold J. Berman*, ed. John Witte, Jr., and Frank Alexander (Atlanta, GA: Scholars Press, 1988).

6 Brian Tierney, *Medieval Poor Law: A Sketch of Canonical Theory and Its Application in England* (Berkeley: University of California Press, 1959).

7 See García y García, "Los derechos," 88–90.

8 That is, to vote (active voice) or to be a candidate (passive voice). See Anscar Parsons, *Canonical Elections: An Historical Synopsis and Commentary*, Canon Law Studies 118 (Washington: Catholic University of America, 1939); Jean Gaudemet, *Les Elections dans l'église latine des origines au XVIᵉ siècle* (Paris: ed. Lanore, 1979).

9 See, for example, James Brundage, *Law, Sex, and Christian Society in Medieval Europe* (University of Chicago Press, 1987); Reid, "The Canonistic Contribution," 49–71.

10 See García y García, "Los derechos" 97–100. See also Luciano Pereña, ed., *Derechos y deberes entre Indios y Españoles en el nuevo mundo según Francisco de Vitoria* (Salamanca: Universidad Pontificia Cátedra V Centenario, 1991).

11 See Luciano Pereña, *Carta magna de los Indios* (Madrid: Universidad Pontificia de Salamanca, 1987).

12 See Antonio García y García et al., *La proteccion del Indio* (Salamanca: Universidad Pontificia de Salamanca, 1989).

13 "Duo sunt genera christianorum," c. 12 q. 1 c. 7. The inequality between clergy and laity received special attention in the nineteenth- and early twentieth-century canonists. See Jean Gaudemet, "La condition des Chrétiens dans la doctrine canonique des XVIIIe et XIXe siècles," in Eugenio Corecco et al., eds., *Les Droits fondamentaux du chrétien dans l'église et dans la société. Actes du IVe Congrès International de Droit Canonique Fribourg (Suisse) 6–11 Octobre 1980* (Fribourg: Editions Universitaires, 1981), 645–667.

14 See discussion in Eugenio Corecco, "Il Catalogo dei doveri-diritti del fedele nel CIC," in *I diritti fondamentali della persona umana e la libertà religiosa*, 101–102; Jean Imbert, "Droit canonique et droits de l'homme," *Année Canonique* 15 (1971): 383–395.

15 See Juan Ignacio Arrieta, "I diritti dei soggetti nell'ordinamento canonico," *Persona y derecho, suplemento lex nova de derechos fundamentales del fiel* 1 (1991): 10–11.

16 See Robert T. Kennedy, "Canonical Tradition and Christian Rights," in James A. Coriden, ed., *The Case for Freedom: Human Rights in The Church* (Washington: Corpus, 1969), 91–106, esp. 96.

17 For an overview of the discussion see José M. G. Del Valle and Cienfuegos Jovellanos, *Derechos fundamentales y derechos publicos subjetivos en la Iglesia* (Pamplona: EUNSA, 1972). For a contrast of "subjective rights" and English law, see Geoffrey Samuel, "'Le Droit Subjectif' and English Law," *Cambridge Law Journal* 46 (1987): 264–286.

18 Generally, the canonists' theory was framed in terms of the church as a "perfect society," a claim to sovereignty in the spiritual realm on a par with national sovereignty in the secular realm. The theory continues in the diplomatic practice of the Holy See, where diplomatic relations are always between a secular government and the "Holy See" as an international spiritual entity, not the Vatican City State.

19 Fedele first presented this view in his *Discorso generale sull'ordinamento canonico* (Padua: CEDAM, 1941), and continued to defend it in subsequent publications.

20 See *De iure subiectivo deque eius tuitione in iure canonico. Acta congressus internationalis iuris canonici 1950 [1950 Congress]* (Rome: Catholic Book Agency, 1953).

21 See, for example, Luigi De Luca, "I diritti fondamentali dell'uomo nell'ordinamento canonico," in *1950 Congress*, 88–103.

22 See Alfonso Prieto Prieto, "Los derechos subjectivos publicos en la Iglesia," in *Iglesia y Derecho*, Semana de Derecho Canonico x (Salamanca: CSIC, 1965), 325–361.

23 See the analysis in Paul Hinder, *Grundrechte in der Kirche. Eine Untersuchung zur Begründung der Grundrechte in der Kirche* (Fribourg: Editions Universitaires, 1980), 91–98.

24 Pontifical Commission for the Revision of the Code of Canon Law,

"Principia quae Codicis Iuris Canonici recognitionem dirigant," *Communicationes* 1 (1969): 82–83, principles 6 and 7.

25 See, for example, Jean Beyer, "De statu iuridico Christifidelium iuxta vota Synodi Episcoporum in novo Codice iuris condendo," *Periodica* 57 (1968): 550–581; "Toward a Declaration of Christian Rights: A Position Paper," in Coriden, ed., *The Case for Freedom*, 5–14; José Maria Gonzales, *Derechos fundamentales y derechos publicos subjetivos en la Iglesia* (Pamplona: EUNSA, 1971); John F. Kinney, *The Juridic Condition of the People of God: Their Fundamental Rights and Obligations in the Church*, excerpt from JDC dissertation (Rome: Catholic Book Agency, 1972).

26 See especially the very interesting but still unfinished study by Jean Beyer, "De iuribus humanis fundamentalibus in statu iuridico christifidelium assumendis," *Periodica* 58 (1969): 29–58.

27 *Communicationes* 1 (1969): 82. "The rights of each of the Christian faithful are to be recognized and safeguarded, both those contained in natural law and divine positive law, and those which are fittingly derived from them due to the social condition which they acquire and possess in the Church."

28 1971 Synod of Bishops, *The Ministerial Priesthood and Justice in the World* (Washington: USCC, 1972, 1982), 40.

29 Hinder is one of the leading theorists along this line. See the analysis of these two positions by Jean Bernard, "Les droit fondamentaux dans la perspective de la 'Lex fundamentalis' et de la revision du Code de Droit Canonique," in Corecco, ed., *Les Droits fondamentaux du chrétien*, 367–395.

30 One group worked on a proposed *Lex Ecclesiae Fundamentalis* (a sort of common foundational law for the whole Church, Eastern as well as Latin), and the other group drafted canons on the laity. This second group became involved in developing a list of "fundamental rights" because they had to sort these out from the rights which are specific to the laity. Both lists drew heavily on the statements from the Second Vatican Council. For a detailed history see Rosalio Castillo Lara, "Some General Reflections on the Rights and Duties of the Christian Faithful," *Studia Canonica* 20 (1986): 7–32.

31 The *Lex* itself was never promulgated, nor were any reasons given for the decision not to proceed after the work of drafting was completed and approved by a special commission in 1981.

32 The first canon in this list is new with the Eastern code. It states the obligation to safeguard and transmit the faith, to profess it openly, and to bear fruit in works of charity (c. 10).

33 Primary reference is made here to the listing in the Latin code, c. 208; practically the same wording appears in the Eastern code, c. 11.

34 More detailed commentaries can be found in Matthäus Kaiser in Joseph Listl et al., eds., *Handbuch des katholischen Kirchenrechts* (Regensburg: Pustet, 1983), 173–179; James H. Provost in James A. Coriden et al., eds., *The Code of Canon Law: A Text and Commentary* (New York/Mahwah,

NJ: Paulist Press, 1985), 134–159; Heinrich J. F. Reinhardt in Klaus Lüdicke, ed., *Münsterischer Kommentar zum Codex Iuris Canonici* (Essen: Ludgerus Verlag, 1987).

35 Arrieta, "I diritti dei soggetti nell'ordinamento canonico," 36. See also Corecco in *I diritti fondamentali della persona umana e la libertà religiosa*, 118–120.

36 The full text of the canon deserves quoting here:

"§1. In exercising their rights the Christian faithful, both as individuals and when gathered in associations, must take account of the common good of the Church and of the rights of others as well as their own duties toward others.

"§2. In the interest of the common good, ecclesiastical authority has competence to regulate the exercise of the rights which belong to the Christian faithful."

Canon 223 of the Latin code; c. 26 of the Eastern code makes some slight changes in word order and in connecting words, but retains the substance of the Latin code's canon.

37 Translation from *Decrees of the Ecumenical Councils*, ed. Norman P. Tanner (Washington: Georgetown University Press, 1990), II: 1005.

38 After affirming the existing power of the pope and diocesan bishops, principle 6 for the revision of the code stated that the use of this power cannot be arbitrary in the church – natural law, divine positive law, and church law forbid this. Whether the code has been successful in appropriately delimiting the exercise of such power is a matter of some discussion. See, for example, John P. Beal, "Confining and Structuring Administrative Discretion," *The Jurist* 46 (1986): 70–106, where he contrasts American administrative law with the provisions of the 1983 code.

39 John Paul II even considers this to be "the basis of all other freedoms." See "Message for the Thirtieth Anniversary of the Declaration of Human Rights," December 2, 1978: *AAS* 71 (1979): 121–125.

40 Abuse of ecclesiastical power is listed in both codes as a crime which can receive an "appropriate punishment"; cf. Latin code, c. 1389, §1; Eastern code, c. 1464, §1.

41 See Latin code, cc. 447; 459, §1; 460; 473, §1; 495, §1; 498, §1, 2°; 501, §3; 591; 626; 633, §1; 790, §1, 2°. See Eastern code, cc. 84, §1; 148, §3; 202; 267, §1, 2°; 270, §3; 322, §1; 412, §2.

42 See Latin code, cc. 116, §1; 1348; 1430; 1431, §1; 1481, §3; 1532; 1536, §§1–2; 1598, §1; 1691; 1696; 1715, §1; 1728, §1. See Eastern code, cc. 1094; 1095, §1; 1139, §3; 1213; 1217, §§1–2; 1281, §1; 1376; 1165, §1; 1471, §1.

43 See Eastern code, cc. 1110, §1; 1519, §1; Latin code, cc. 1201, §2; 1452, §1.

44 See Latin code, cc. 87, §1; 88; 1233. Eastern code, cc. 82, §1, 2°; 148, §3; 1536, §2; 1538, §1.

45 Latin code, c. 795; Eastern code, c. 405.
46 Latin code, c. 287, §2; Eastern code, c. 384, §2.
47 Latin code, c. 264, §2. The exemption applies to juridic persons which include a college of students or teachers to "promote the common good of the Church." Examples are schools or even institutes of higher learning run by a religious institute.
48 Latin code, c. 223, §1; Eastern code, c. 26, §1.
49 Latin code, c. 223, §2; 323, §2; Eastern code, c. 26, §2.
50 See Rinaldo Bertolino, *Il nuovo diritto ecclesiale tra coscienza dell'uomo e istituzione. Saggi di diritto costituzionale canonico* (Turin: G. Giappichelli, 1987).
51 The text in *Dignitatis Humanae* speaks of the "common good of all," but canon 223 has changed this to "common good of the Church." See Provost in *The Code of Canon Law: A Text and Commentary*, 158–159. Reinhardt interprets both sections of the canon on the limitation of rights to deal with the "common good of the Church" and equates this with the public welfare of the Christian community. Julio Manzanares in *Código de derecho canónico: Edición bilingüe comentada*, ed. Lamberto de Echeverría (Madrid: BAC, 5th edn., 1985) 142, argues the canon protects against those who would use a claim of rights against proper solidarity; he also argues the presumption must still be for liberty, in light of *DH* 7's principle that limitations must be only when necessary and to the degree that they are needed. Javier Hervada in *Codigo de derecho canónica: Edicion anotada*, ed. Pedro Lombardía and Juan Ignacio Arrieta (Pamplona: EUNSA, 1983), 180, argues for "public order" as the basis for limitations, not the common good.
52 *DH* 7; Tanner, 1006.
53 Hinder, *Grundrechte in der Kirche*, provides the clearest articulation of this view. It was not the theory followed by the code commission, however; see Castillo Lara, "Some General Reflections," 25, 32. See also the critique by Remigiusz Sobanski, "'Iura Propter Officia'? Remarques lieés aux en-têtes des Ier et IIe titres du livre II du nouveau CIC," in *Vitam impendere vero. Studi in onore di Pio Ciprotti*, ed. Winfried Schulz and Giorgio Feliciani (Vatican City: Libreria Editrice Vaticana, 1986), 221–233.
54 See response from the secretariat of the code revision commission to comments raising this point, *Communicationes* 14 (1982): 168, at cc. 244–264, no. 2. See also Castillo Lara, "Some General Reflections," 25, 31–32; see also Provost in *The Code of Canon Law: A Text and Commentary*, 137–138.
55 *Communicationes* 12 (1980): 32, c. 3. "The Church recognizes and professes the dignity proper to the human person of each and every human being, as created in God's image, and it also acknowledges the duties and rights which flow from it, and even safeguards these because of the call of all persons to salvation."

56 The many listings of rights in civil constitutions, or in the UN Universal
Declaration of Human Rights, attempt to identify specific rights rather
than to give an overly broad statement whose meaning could remain so
indeterminate as to be unenforceable.

57 See Peter Krämer, "Menschenrechte – Christenrechte. Das neue Kir-
chenrecht auf dem Prüfstand," in André Gabriels and Heinrich J. F.
Reinhardt, eds., *Ministerium Iustitiae. Festschrift für Heribert Heinemann zur
Vollendung des 60. Lebensjahres* (Essen: Ludgerus Verlag, 1985), 169–177;
Gerhard Luf, "Grundrechte im CIC/1983," *Österreichisches Archiv für
Kirchenrecht* 35 (1985): 107–131.

58 See the comparison of the list when it was still part of the *Lex*, with
catalogues in modern state constitutions, by Heinz-Meinholf Stamm,
"Os direitos fundamentais do homem e do christão e os poderes das
autoridades eclesiásticas segundo a nova lei fundamental da Igreja, á luz
das constituições civis modernas," *Revista Eclesiástica Brasileira* 42
(1982): 289–306.

59 This is also fairly characteristic of secular lists of rights. See Castillo Lara,
"Some General Reflections," 21; Provost, *The Code of Canon Law: A Text
and Commentary*, 135.

60 The Bill of Rights, the Declaration of the Rights of Man and of the
Citizen, and even the Universal Declaration of Human Rights reflect
this fact.

61 James A. Coriden, "A Challenge: Making the Rights Real," *The Jurist*
45 (1985): 1–23, argues they are fundamental. He points to several bases
for the continued foundational role of these rights in the church, ranging
from the principles for the revision of the code and the origin of the list
in the draft for the *Lex*, to John Paul II's statements affirming their
importance in the revised code both when he promulgated the new
Latin code and in subsequent statements. Castillo Lara, "Some General
Reflections," 15–19, argues on the other hand that the title of
"fundamental rights" used in the *Lex* was not transferred with the list
and that a doctrinal consensus does not exist to support the meaning of
"fundamental" when applied to rights in the Church. They express,
however, the common juridic status of the faithful.

62 See the criticism of this and other aspects of the codes' lists in Hans F.
Zacher, "Grundrechte und Kirche," *Stimmen der Zeit* 111 (1986):
454–462.

63 For example, Latin code, c. 212, § 3 on expressing opinion in the Church,
which contains rules relative to libel, slander, and "national security"
style concerns for the faith and the Church. See Provost in *The Code of
Canon Law: A Text and Commentary*, 138–139.

64 Latin code, c. 1491. Eastern code, c. 1149, has a somewhat different
formulation, exactly the same as 1917 code, c. 1667.

65 See Lawrence G. Wrenn in *The Code of Canon Law: A Text and Commentary*,
p. 969.

66 Latin code, c. 221, §1; Eastern code, c. 24, §1.

67 Latin code, c. 1400, §1, 1°; Eastern code, c. 1055, §1, 1°.
Church courts are to be set up in each diocese (Latin code, c. 1420) or eparchy (Eastern code, c. 1086). Decisions of a diocesan court can be appealed to the metropolitan court, or if the diocese is an archdiocese, to some other diocesan court which serves as the regular appeals court for it. Anyone can appeal a judicial decision to the Apostolic See (Latin code, c. 1417; Eastern code, c. 1059); in Patriarchal churches, there is also an appeal court set up at the level of the patriarchate (Eastern code, c. 1063).

68 Latin code, c. 1400, §1, 1°; Eastern code, c. 1055, §1, 1°.

69 See Jaime Traserra, *La tutela de los derechos subjetivos frente a la administracion eclesiastica* (Barcelona: Herder, 1972); Ulrich Tammler, *Tutela Iurium Personarum. Grundfragen des Verwaltungsrechtsschutzes in der katholischen Kirche in Vergangenheit und Gegenwart* (Amsterdam: B. R. Grüner, 1981). See also Justin D. McClunn, *Administrative Recourse*, Canon Law Studies 240 (Washington: Catholic University, 1946), 1–10; Rinaldo Bertolino, *La Tutela dei Diritti nella Chiesa. Dal vecchio al nuovo Codice di Diritto Canonico* (Turin: G. Giappichelli, 1983), 53–54.

70 Pius X, apostolic constitution *Sapienti consilio*, June 29, 1908: *AAS* 1 (1909): 7–19.

71 Tammler, *Tutela Iurium Personarum*, 36–50.

72 *AAS* 16 (1924): 251.

73 Under the 1917 code, c. 1572, §2, if a bishop agreed to it, he could be sued in his own diocesan tribunal in cases involving his own rights or temporal goods, or those of entities he represented in law. If he did not agree to his diocesan court taking the case, the appellate court could hear it.

74 The *Schema De Procedura Administrativa* has never been published. A first draft was prepared in 1970, then revised and enlarged by 1972 when it was sent to the bishops and various church agencies for consultation. It was generally well received at the time. See discussion in Bertolino, *La tutela dei diritti*, 55–62.

75 Latin code, cc. 1732–1739; Eastern code, cc. 996–1006. The Eastern code's organization of the material is somewhat clearer than the Latin code.
No official reason has been given for the sudden disappearance of the canons on administrative tribunals between the final draft and the 1983 code, although see Corecco in *I diritti fondamentali della persona umana e la libertà religiosa*, 123, for the views of one of the special group of advisors who worked with the pope as he prepared the final version of the Latin code. Similarly, no explanation has been given for the disappearance of the canons on administrative tribunals from the final draft of the Eastern code and its promulgated version.

76 For further explanation of these steps, see John P. Beal, "Protecting the Rights of Lay Catholics," *The Jurist* 47 (1987): 129–164.

77 For a review of the limited experience reported in a survey of US dioceses, see James H. Provost, "Recent Experiences of Administrative Recourse to the Apostolic See," *The Jurist* 46 (1986): 142–163.

78 See Bertolino, *La tutela dei diritti*, 150–156; Castillo Lara, "Some General Reflections," 23–25; Zacher, "Grundrechte und Kirche," 460–462.

79 Latin code, c. 1733; Eastern code, c. 998. The Latin code contains details about setting up an office or council of mediation; the Eastern code has not included these structural details, leaving them to the law of the various churches *sui iuris*.

80 NCCB, *On Due Process* (Washington: USCC, rev. edn. 1972); *Kirchliche Verwaltungsprozessordnung der Kirchenprovinzen in Bayern*, as reported in Bertolino, *La tutela dei diritti*, 71, note 11.

81 *Due Process in Dioceses in the United States 1970–1985. Report on a Task Force Survey*, ed. James H. Provost (Washington: CLSA, 1987).

82 See Zenon Grocholewski, "Atti e ricorsi amministrativi," in *Il nuovo codice di diritto canonico: novità, motivazione e significato* (Rome: Libreria Editrice della Pontificia Università Lateranense), 516–519.

83 See James A. Coriden, "The Canonical Doctrine of Reception," *The Jurist* 50 (1990): 58–82; Geoffrey King, *The Acceptance of Law by the Community as an Integral Element in the Formation of Canon Law: An Historical and Analytical Study*, Canon Law Studies 498 (Washington: Catholic University of America, 1979).

Afterword: a community of freedom

David Hollenbach

The Catholic church crossed a watershed in its relationship to modern democratic government in the late 1950s and early 1960s. During this period, the transnational church fully committed itself to the constitutional democracy and human rights that had long been taken for granted in American Catholicism. The subsequent public activity of the church in regions such as Eastern Europe, Latin America, Southern Africa, Korea, and the Philippines suggests that this commitment is being pursued even at great cost and can be expected to be irrevocable. The Second Vatican Council marked the cessation of the battle of attrition fought between Catholics and liberals in the nineteenth and first half of the twentieth centuries.

On one reading of this recent history, the terms for the end of hostilities were Catholic surrender and liberal victory. The essays in this volume, however, tell a considerably more complex tale. The church has not simply taken over liberal ideas uncritically, but is putting its own interpretation on them and has begun to develop its own distinctive understanding of the meaning and purpose of democracy. Most importantly, the Catholic rapprochement with democratic freedoms has been accompanied by repeated insistence on the importance of commitment to the common good for the well-being of the societies in question. The documents of Vatican II and the writings of popes from John XXIII to John Paul II are filled with affirmations that communal solidarity is a prerequisite for a social existence worthy of human beings.

What makes this pertinent to the United States today is that our own experience of community is increasingly wanting. A central theme in this book is that there are ominous signs today of a thinning of the sense of community and solidarity that holds the people of the United States together, and that the result is an impoverishment of our capacity for self-government. Just as the experience of totalitarian

323

tyranny led to the church's affirmation of democratic freedoms a generation ago, the experience of many today is raising deep questions about how much genuine freedom and real power citizens in liberal democracies actually enjoy in living out their daily lives. One can fairly conclude that current democratic practice is facing a genuine crisis and is in need of the sort of fresh thinking that recent Catholic teaching emphasizes. The importance of the common good and the possibility of a spirit of solidarity has reemerged with a new salience in the Catholic–liberal dialogue. The essays in this volume suggest that today Catholicism has an important contribution to make to American public life precisely because it is the bearer of a tradition that emphasizes community and the common good. The Catholic–liberal encounter in the United States thus promises to be one of ongoing mutual enrichment, not victory for one side and surrender for the other. Or so, at least, it might be hoped.

The discussions in this book point to three ways the Catholic tradition can contribute to such an enrichment of American public life and the liberal public philosophy that has figured so prominently in its development.

The first is institutional. Growing out of its historic understanding of subsidiarity, Catholic thinking about the social order points in the direction of a politics that can move beyond the current polarization of statist versus market-dominated thinking. It does this by giving particular attention to the fate of "civil society" as the seedbed of the sort of freedom that is realized in community. It promotes social empowerment through participation.

The second contribution from Catholicism comes from its belief that civil conversation and argument can yield shared under-standings of the social good, even shared religious understandings. The recovery of openness to the possibility that visions of the good life may not be simply personal preferences but can be subjected to intelligent assessment in a community of genuine discourse is urgently needed to counteract the breakdown of serious political debate and cultural self-criticism in American life today.

The third potential Catholic contribution to American public life is its challenge to the primacy assigned to self-interest (however enlightened) in much liberal theory and, increasingly, in the practices of Western liberal democracies. Catholicism, like other Christian traditions, Judaism, and indeed all the great historical world religions, affirms that self-transcendence is essential to the achievement of both freedom and genuine community among persons. It also affirms that such self-transcendence is a real though precarious possibility. The need to recover a sense of this possibility is increasingly evident in the United States today.

STATE, MARKET, AND CIVIL SOCIETY

Liberalism as a vision of the social order today commonly focuses primarily on individuals and their fate. It then proposes institutional means, either the state or the market, as instruments for securing the interests of these individuals. Though the Catholic concern for the fate of the individual is deep, the emphasis in Catholic thought is different. The sociological realism that is woven into past and present Catholic teaching asks us to focus on the fate of social institutions, as the places where individuals are formed and nurtured, as well as on individuals themselves. This is evident in the Catholic emphasis on the importance of securing the well-being of "intermediary" institutions such as families and voluntary associations, and it is a key to understanding how the Catholic tradition can envision a form of political life that is communal without being statist.

The outlines of this vision were evident in the arguments that led the church to embrace democratic politics during the middle decades of this century. A key element in the argument that led to this commitment to democracy in the 1950s was the distinction drawn between state and society by Jacques Maritain and John Courtney Murray among others. Society is composed of a rich and overlapping set of human associations and communities such as families, neighborhoods, clubs, churches, labor unions, businesses, corporations, professional associations, credit unions, cooperatives, universities, and a host of other associations. They are the soil for the growth of human sociality. Especially when they are small or of intermediate size, they enable persons to come together in ways that can be vividly experienced. The bonds of communal solidarity formed in them enable persons to act together, empowering them to shape some of the contours of public life and social institutions. The government of a democratic society is a servant of the social "body" that develops out of the activity of these intermediate communities. As Pius XI formulated the matter in what came to be known as the principle of subsidiarity, government "should, by its very nature, provide help (*subsidium*) to members of the body social, it should never destroy or absorb them."[1] Or in Maritain's words, "the state is inferior to the body politic as a whole and is at the service of the body politic as a whole."[2] This body politic or civil society is the primary locus in which human solidarity is realized.

In the writings of Maritain and Murray, this principle leads immediately to the affirmation of religious liberty and constitutional democracy and, *eo ipso*, to opposition to all forms of totalitarianism and state absolutism. Churches, just like all the other associations that make up the rich fabric of civil society, must be free from domination by the state. As Murray concluded,

The personal or corporate free exercise of religion, as a human and civil right, is evidently cognate with other more general human and civil rights – with the freedom of corporate bodies and institutions within society, based on the principle of subsidiary function; with the general freedom of association for peaceful purposes, based on the social nature of man; with the general freedom of speech and of the press based on the nature of political society.[3]

This argument reveals one way that a Catholic understanding of the institutions of democracy and the human rights that undergird them presents a challenge to those forms of liberalism concerned primarily with the defense of the freedom of individuals to act as they please in a zone of privacy. The Catholic presupposition about the basis of democracy is not the sovereignty of individual autonomy. Participation in public life and the exercise of freedom in society depend on the strength of the communal institutions that give persons a measure of real power to shape their environment, including their political environment. As John Coleman has argued, the Catholic commitment to democracy rests on "a presumptive rule about where real vitality exists in society."[4] The public and the social are not to be identified with the political. Therefore a practice or institution can be truly public even though not under governmental control.

The importance of a public sphere that is not dominated by the state has become luminously clear in the way the collapse of Communism was so rapidly brought about in Eastern Europe. The power of the dissident workers and intellectuals of the "velvet revolutions" of 1989 grew out of their success in creating the solidarity of a genuine civil society, not out of direct seizure of state power or out of the barrel of a gun. What were initially extra-political bonds of community at Gdansk's shipyard and Prague's Magic Lantern Theater empowered men and women to effect a stunning transformation of supposedly untransformable totalitarian regimes. Though the Catholic church was surely not the sole agent of this transformation, there is no question that its commitment was crucial in sustaining the many overlapping communities that make up civil society – communities that refused to submit to state domination. As the Jewish intellectual and Solidarity activist Adam Michnik stated before the revolution, "The problem faced by Polish society is that civil society doesn't exist. Society is not recognized as capable of organizing itself to defend its particular interests and points of view ... [T]he present totalitarian system insists that every person is State property. The Church's view is that every person is a child of God, to whom God has granted natural liberty ... It follows from this that in Poland and other communist countries religion is the natural antidote to the totalitarian claims of the State authorities."[5]

This vision of the importance of the institutional fabric of civil society faces a very different threat in the United States today than the one that existed in Central and Eastern Europe until very recently. The presupposition of those who advocate a fuller and more unequivocal Catholic embrace of liberal practice and theory is that the social and political institutions of the United States are organized in a way that is just about right. The interpretation of both Catholicism and liberalism offered here questions this presupposition. To be sure, if the alternatives to American institutions are Communist totalitarianism, the authoritarian oligopolies that have been dominant in much of Latin American history, or the one-party states common in Africa, there can be no doubt of the superiority of the democratic institutions of the North Atlantic. But this is not the choice either liberals or Catholics face in the United States today. There is more than one way to sap the strength of civil society and undermine the freedom and capacity of persons to exercise genuine power in shaping their lives together. State absolutism is surely one way to do so, and it must be guarded against with vigilance. But there is a more immediate threat to the life of a community capable of nurturing freedom in the United States today: the dominance of the market over increasingly large domains of social and cultural life.

This is one of the central themes of John Paul II's recent encyclical, *Centesimus Annus*. This document endorses the important role markets must play in overcoming the stifling suppression of economic initiative in Eastern Europe. In a way long familiar to American Catholics, the pope also highlights the efficiency of free markets as means for the generation of wealth. He does so in a manner that embodies a new emphasis in the tradition of papal teaching on social matters, and that is clearly the result of the harsh experience of Eastern Europe. But the pope also has much to say about the limits of markets and the threat posed by the expansion of the values of the marketplace into domains where other human values should prevail. He is clearly convinced that this is exactly what has happened and continues to happen in the West.

The pope's words are markedly similar to those written some years ago by the American economist Arthur Okun. Okun argued strongly for the freedom and efficiency of market economies and against the repression and inefficiency of centralized command economies. At the same time he stressed that the commitment of American public philosophy to the fundamental equality of all citizens sets limits on what can be bought and sold. This should put us on guard against "the imperialism of the market's valuation," whose unchecked expansion would turn society into a "giant vending machine that delivers anything and everything in return for the proper number of coins." Other values – such as political rights of citizens, the basic conditions of survival, the bonds of affection in friendship and family, and the honor and recognition due to genuine human excellence – should not be up for sale. These other values, Okun says, "are the glue that holds society together."[6]

The protection of these values and the human communities in which they can be realized is a precondition for what the pope calls solidarity. To the extent that values of the market override them, human beings face "increased isolation in a maze of relationships marked by destructive combativeness and estrangement." If the market becomes the dominant organizing principle in society we experience "a reversal of means and ends" in which persons serve the laws of supply and demand rather than the other way around.[7]

There is considerable evidence that the pope's warning is no false alarm in the United States today. During the past several decades a number of sectors of social life formerly subject to direction by non-market values have been increasingly commercialized. In the provision of health care, for example, the growth of hospitals run for profit by investor-owned companies operating multiple facilities, and the heightened competition among an increased number of physicians for a limited number of patients and health-care dollars, has led to a basic transformation of the medical profession. Health care is treated more and more like a commodity. In the words of one study, "Although charitable institutions and selfless professionals have not disappeared, health care has become an increasingly commercialized and competitive set of activities that make up the fastest-growing element in the service sector of the nation's economy. The behavior of both providers of health care and third-party purchasers is driven more and more by the dollar. The question can be raised whether a role remains for idealism, for altruism, for looking for the needs of the patient and the community before attending to the bottom line."[8]

A similar transformation has been underway in the legal profession, where litigation is increasingly seen as desirable service rather than a regrettable necessity provided to clients. It has also led an increasing number of lawyers to view their work less as a profession and more as participation in a profit-making industry. The result has been heightened adversarialism and increased suspicion not only in the courtroom but also in many of the daily social interactions that are needed to hold society together.[9]

In the world of business itself, non-market values such as respect for employees and responsibility to communities affected by corporate decisions both in the present and in future generations are also threatened by the narrow focus of short-term market outcomes. Corporations have been destroyed and communities deeply wounded by the failure to recognize that successful enterprises depend on the recognition of relations, values, and goods that cannot be treated as commodities. Business and business people themselves will surely be the victims if these values are subject to growing commercialization. The recent rash of corporate take-overs and the crisis in the savings-and-loan industry suggest that this is just what has been happening in some sectors of the United States economy.

The art of politics also appears to be increasingly driven by an informal market in government services and campaign contributions. Though the line between a legitimate political contribution and a flat-out bribe is exceedingly difficult to draw, the cynical view that the political process is controlled by "special interests" and "big business" has grown. The heavy reliance on media consultants drawn from Madison Avenue advertising agencies heightens the suspicion that electoral politics is a matter of marketing even if it is not literally up for sale. The United States Catholic bishops themselves have retained one of the same media consultants who helped design recent presidential campaigns to help them communicate their position on abortion to the public more effectively. Has even pastoral leadership become a form of marketing?

None of this proves that the United States has become Okun's "vending machine society," nor does it mean to imply this. But it does suggest that the fabric of civil society being rediscovered in Eastern Europe is at least seriously threatened in the United States by the dominance of the market. The Catholic tradition can contribute much to American public life today by strengthening those forms of community that empower people to act on the basis of values that resist commodification. These include communities of family and friendship, associations concerned with the quality of neighborhood and local community life, and all the other small and intermediate-sized groups traditionally referred to in discussions of the principle of subsidiarity and of "mediating institutions." These groups are not in danger of being absorbed or suppressed by the state. Rather the prime threat comes from a market cut loose from the institutional and moral constraints needed to keep it in its proper place – in service to the common good of society whose vitality depends on the existence of a network of many different kinds of human interrelationship. As Norman Birnbaum points out, if this network is understood to be a dynamic, developing reality rather than a set of institutions that is already in place, commitment to this kind of solidarity has the potential to be deeply transformative of society, not reactionary. Both the theoretical vision this entails and the fact that the church itself is a living example of such community provide an important resource for enriching the public life of the United States today. Just as the idea of civil society was a force for change in Eastern Europe, it can and should play such a role in the United States, though in a very different direction. Though the pope's reflections do not provide a blueprint for what these changes might be, they do offer an approach – a set of leads, if you will – that point toward a recovery of community that steers clear of state dominance. Development of specific policies and practices that can follow up on these leads is a matter to be worked out in the continuing dialogue between Catholicism and liberalism in the United States.

In such dialogue, it will be important to remember that the Catholic tradition continues to maintain that democratic government has an important role to play in supporting and strengthening the thick weave of communal relationships constituting civil society. The principle of subsidiarity demands that government be limited, but it is neither a libertarian principle nor an endorsement of the sort of neo-liberalism represented by thinkers like von Hayek and von Mises that is being newly discussed today. Nor, despite efforts to maintain the opposite, is it a principle compatible with those forms of American neoconservatism that supported Reaganite views of political economy. The government has an important role to play both in protecting the place of the market in society and in simultaneously keeping the market in its place. Government intervention "encourages, stimulates, regulates, supplements, and complements" the operation of the market, "as the occasion requires and necessity demands."[10] Or in John Paul II's formulation, democratic government should establish a "juridical framework" that directs both the economy and civil society in ways that serve the common good. This framework "presupposes a certain equality among the parties, such that one party would not be so powerful as practically to reduce the other to subservience." Government and the private sector working together should assume responsibility "for protecting the worker from the nightmare of unemployment" – both through "policies aimed at balanced growth and full employment" and "through unemployment insurance and retraining programs." Government and the private sector together are responsible to insure wage levels adequate for living in dignity, "including a certain amount for savings," as well as improved training for "more skilled and productive work." Legislation is needed "to block shameful forms of exploitation, especially to the disadvantage of the most vulnerable workers, of immigrants and of those on the margins of society." Trade unions play a "decisive" role in insuring this latter protection. International markets must be opened up, breaking down "the barriers and monopolies which leave so many countries on the margins of development."[11]

This vision of public life, therefore, is pluralistic in that it assumes no single form of human community is capable of embodying the full human good. It encourages, instead, active participation in multiple forms of human association. Such participation is threatened when any single social institution gains the power to control the whole of human life, whether this institution be the state, the market, or, for that matter, the church. This, practically, is what the principle of subsidiarity means. And it carries the warning that the danger of encroachment by the state or the market into ever larger domains can be averted only when persons are empowered for common action by strong communities in civil society.[12]

PUBLIC DISCOURSE AND THE PUBLIC GOOD

Of course, talk about common action by strong communities always raises the spectre of coerced cohesion. This raises the question of whether anything like the vision of solidarity held out by Catholic thought can be achieved without sacrificing intellectual freedom and social pluralism. Liberals today tend to be very skeptical that any such thing is possible. For that reason they fear allowing any talk about "the good" to enter into public discourse in a society where persons hold many different conceptions of what this good is. The prevailing liberal view is that any attempt to bridge the gaps that separate those who hold diverse conceptions of the full human good is bound to fail. Because the effort to achieve some consensus about the public good is judged to be futile, we have to get along with a politics that is neutral on competing conceptions of the good life. The fact is, however, that people's conceptions of how life ought to be lived are being introduced into public discourse all the time. In a Catholic view of the matter, even those who profess to support public neutrality on the meaning of the good life have a hard time achieving it in practice. Our lives are too intertwined and we rely too much on common institutions for it to be otherwise. Catholic thought suggests that we need to question the liberal premise on this crucial matter. Is neutrality on the meaning of the good life the best we can do? Are the values implicit in it the ones on which we want to base our common life as a society?

We need to ask, for example, whether it really makes sense to act as though the various visions of the good life available to us are simply preferences determined by tradition and/or taste. Can we really maintain that such preferences are private rather than public affairs in a society where persons are so deeply interdependent on each other and linked to the biosphere? In the prevailing liberal ethos, we can debate publicly which means will satisfy the maximum number of these preferences. But this public debate can rely only on what John Rawls calls "public reason." By this he means "the shared methods of, and the public knowledge available to, common sense, and the conclusions of science when these are not controversial."[13] This is a very thin reed on which to rest the civic unity of the nation.

In addition, there is a practical danger in such a strategy. For there is considerable evidence that the "common sense" that is in fact shaping American public life today is increasingly governed by a cynical "I'll get mine" attitude precisely because actual political discourse fails to address the real needs of communities. And this failure is itself partly the result of the fact that interest group politics is frequently incapable of even naming the social bonds that increasingly destine us to sharing either a common good or a "common bad."[14] Politics threatens increasingly to become a quasi-market in preferences and power. A principled commitment to avoiding sustained discourse about the human good can easily produce a downward spiral in which shared meaning, understanding, and therefore community become even harder to achieve.

Admittedly, it will be difficult to find an alternative to the liberal commitment to neutrality on the good in a nation and a world whose awareness of diversity is increasing, not decreasing. But this is not the first time that people have run up against the problem of conflicting beliefs. And Catholic historical memory provides notable encouragement that the sort of discourse across the boundaries of diverse communities that is needed is both possible and potentially fruitful. The Catholic tradition, in its better moments, has in fact experienced considerable success in efforts to bridge the divisions that have separated it from other communities with other understandings of the good life. For example, in the first and second centuries, the early Christian community moved from being a small Palestinian sect to active encounter with the Hellenistic and Roman worlds. In the fourth century, Augustine synthesized biblical faith with Stoic and Neoplatonic thought in a way that profoundly transformed both Christian and Graeco-Roman thought and practice. In the thirteenth century Thomas Aquinas once again transformed Western Christianity through his appropriation of an Aristotelianism he learned from Arab Muslims and from Jews, and he transformed Aristotle in the process. And though the church resisted the liberal discovery of modern freedoms through much of the modern period, this book has demonstrated how liberalism has been transforming Catholicism once again through the last half of our own century and how Catholicism might in turn contribute to a transformed liberal theory and practice. The memory of these events in social and intellectual history as well as the experience since Vatican II leads many Catholics to the hope that communities holding different visions of the good life can get somewhere if they are willing to risk conversation and argument about these visions. Injecting such hope back into the public philosophy of the United States would be a signal achievement. Again, it appears to be not only a desideratum but a necessity today.

The spirit that is required for such discourse about the public good might be called intellectual solidarity – a willingness to take other persons seriously enough to engage them in conversation and debate about what they think makes life worth living. This differs in important ways from the standard liberal appeal to tolerance as the appropriate response to pluralism. Tolerance is a strategy of non-interference with the beliefs and lifestyles of those who are different or "other." Intellectual solidarity entails engagement with the other through both listening and speaking, in the hope that understanding might replace incomprehension and that perhaps even agreement could result. Since it is *mutual* listening and speaking, it can only develop in an atmosphere of genuine freedom. But also because it is mutual, this freedom will not be that of an atomistic self. Where such conversation about the good life begins and develops, a *community* of freedom begins to exist. And this is itself a major part of the common good.

What might such public discourse look like? First, it would address the question of how to secure both the vitality and the justice of civil society. The Catholic contribution to this discourse will stress that the twin principles of solidarity and subsidiarity provide insight into the roles of a limited state and a limited market in the institutional framework of society. These principles will be advanced for the positive contribution they can make to understanding the shape of a good society. They will also be proposed to argue critically against theories or practices that adopt single-minded institutional commitments, whether these be to government (in the form of either a minimal state or a highly centralized one) or to the market (in either laissez-faire or centrally planned forms). Within this broad framework, the discussion can move to argument about more specific social practices and public policies. In fact, public discourse about these matters will move back and forth between general principles and more concrete applications, with the general and the specific mutually illuminating and criticizing each other. In this way, a public conversation about the good of society might be generated. Only when this occurs does a free society or a community of freedom really exist.

Second, this public discourse must also concern visions of those human goods that are neither strictly political nor strictly economic. Broadly speaking, this is conversation and argument about the shape of American culture. It seeks understanding of the authentically human through the full array of the arts and sciences. It will undertake the tasks of retrieving, criticizing, and reconstructing understandings of the human good from the historical past and transmitting them to the future through education. As Murray once noted, "the great 'affair' of the commonwealth is, of course, education."[15] He was referring to education in the broadest sense: the organization of schools and their curricula, but even more to the level of critical cultural self-understanding among both the populace at large and among its elites. In much liberal theory and practice today, this entire cultural and educational project of understanding, criticizing, and reconstructing visions of what it is to be authentically human (Rawls's "comprehensive understanding of the good") is treated as a private affair. Murray's insistence that this project is not only *an* affair but *the* great affair of the commonwealth challenges this liberal presupposition frontally. David Tracy's essay in this book shows that the privatization of these cultural concerns threatens so to instrumentalize and technicize public life as to destroy it altogether. In much liberal thought, tolerance of diversity becomes the premier cultural lesson to be learned. But if a community of freedom is to be realized, engagement with the other, and not just tolerance, is required. In such engagement, a person's own deeper convictions are set forward as potential contributions to public understanding and simultaneously placed at risk of revision.

Seen in this light, it is no accident that the arts, especially the theater, played a central role in breaking the grip of totalitarianism in Czechoslovakia.[16] Though the task of sustaining and strengthening public life in the United States today is doubtless very different than in Central Europe, the importance of genuinely public conversation and argument about what forms of human living are truly good is equally important here. And as Norman Birnbaum has argued, such discussion occurs partly in our discourse both about the institutions of political and economic life and also in discussion of more particular policies in both spheres. The quality of these political and economic debates, however, will be dependent on the depth of the larger cultural exchange. The achievement of solidarity in the political and economic domains is therefore dependent on the strengthening of free discourse in the cultural sphere – intellectual solidarity in a cultural community of freedom.

Third, and doubtless most provocative, the growth of such solidarity also suggests a reconsideration of the notion that religious convictions about the good must be kept out of public view in a religiously pluralistic society. It suggests the possibility of conversation about the visions of the human good held by diverse religious communities and of intellectual engagement with them. Such a suggestion is anathema to most contemporary liberal theorists, for religion is often viewed by them as a rigid set of beliefs held on non-rational grounds. In this view, religion is very likely to be a source of division, conflict, and even violence when it appears in public. It is inherently uncivil. There is, of course, no lack of historical evidence to back up this fear, nor are all contemporary American religious communities immune from the rigidity and fissiparous qualities that lead many liberals to object to their presence in public life.

The Catholic tradition, however, rejects the notion that religious faith must be irrational and, therefore, uncivil. Faith and understanding go hand in hand in the Catholic view of the matter; they are not adversarial but mutually and reciprocally illuminating. As Tracy puts it, Catholic social thought seeks to correlate arguments drawn from the distinctive religious symbols of Christianity with arguments based on shared public experience. This effort at correlation moves back and forth on a two-way street. It rests on a conviction that the classical symbols and doctrines of Christianity can uncover meaning in personal and social existence that common sense and uncontroversial science fail to see. So it invites those outside the church to place their self-understanding at risk by what Tracy calls conversation with such "classics." At the same time, the believer's self-understanding is also placed at risk because it can be challenged to development or even fundamental change by dialogue with the other – whether this be a secular agnostic, or a Christian from another tradition, or a Jew, Muslim, or Buddhist. Intellectual solidarity has religious implications. It means that in a community of freedom, religion should be represented in the discourse about the goods of public life. It equally means that religious believers must enter this discourse prepared to listen as well as to speak, to learn from what they hear, and, if necessary, to change as a result of what they have learned. The experience of the Catholic church over the last half century has been a vivid example of such listening, learning, and changing through its encounter with liberalism. This process must and will continue as Catholics develop their self-understanding into the future. Is it too much to expect that the experience of transformation through engagement rather than tolerance could strengthen America's public philosophy in an analogous way?[17]

The achievement of a community of freedom in a religiously pluralistic society thus challenges both religious and non-religious persons alike. For Christian believers, it is a challenge to recognize that their faith in God and the way of life it entails is a historical reality – it is rooted in historically particular scriptures and symbols and it is lived and sustained in historically particular communities. This historicity means that the task of interpreting the meaning of their faith will never be done as long as history lasts. The God in whom they place their faith can never be identified with any personal relationship, social arrangement, or cultural achievement. God transcends all of these. Though Christians believe that in Jesus Christ they have been given a definite revelation of who this God is, they cannot claim to possess or encompass God in any of their theologies or understandings of the ultimate good of human life. Thus, in the words of Avery Dulles, "The Christian is defined as a person on the way to discovery, on the way to a revelation not yet given, or at least not yet given in final form."[18] Because the Christian community is always on the way to the fullness of its own deepest faith, hope, and love, it must be continually open to fresh discoveries. Encounter with the other, the different, and the strange must therefore characterize the life of the church. Active participation in a community of freedom is a prerequisite to such discovery.

In particular, the church still has much to learn from its liberal interlocutors, particularly with regard to the way it conducts its internal affairs. The liberal insistence that any just community must be based on a commitment to the equal dignity of every person can teach Catholicism important lessons about its own institutional life, as Mary Segers and James Provost pointedly show in their contributions to this volume. This is especially the case in the way it responds to the demands of women for equal respect and participation in family, society, and the life of the church itself. It is also evident in the need to develop much more serious protections for the freedom of intellectual inquiry within the church regarding the meaning of Christianity and its relation to other currents in our culture. The conditions necessary for the realization of a community of freedom apply to the church, not just to civil society. In both, the continuing dialogue between liberalism and Catholicism must be ongoing. If the church is to contribute to the building of a stronger community of freedom in the United States, it must itself be a community of freedom.

Non-believers and agnostics are challenged by this dialogue and engagement as well. We need considerably more imagination about how to be authentically human than instrumental rationality can provide if we are to deal creatively with the problems that face American society today. We need a broader and deeper vision of the good. In Martha Nussbaum's words, such a vision arises from "myths and stories from many times and places, stories explaining to both friends and strangers what it is to be human rather than something else. The account is the outcome of a process of self-interpretation and self-clarification that makes use of the story-telling imagination far more than the scientific intellect."[19] Religious traditions and communities are among the principal bearers of these imaginative sources for our understanding of the human. They can evoke not only private self-understanding but public vision as well. Unbelievers therefore have reason to risk considering what contribution religious traditions might make to our understanding of the good life. For society to try to exclude religious narratives and symbols from public simply because they are identified with religion would be to impoverish itself intellectually and culturally. It would *a priori* cut itself off from one of the most important forms of intellectual exchange necessary in a community of freedom.

SELF-INTEREST AND SELF-TRANSCENDENCE

Finally, one other opportunity for dialogue between Catholicism and liberalism as they seek to contribute to American public life today has to do with self-interest and the possibility of self-transcendence. The issue is both moral and spiritual. It concerns the very meaning of freedom itself.

Central to the entire liberal tradition is a tendency to think of freedom as the liberty to pursue the good life as one sees fit. Or as liberal theorists usually construe it, freedom is the liberty to seek one's enlightened self-interest. And, as noted above, the presumption is that we can be neutral about how this liberty will be used. Many of these theorists argue that the pursuit of self-interest is not necessarily identified with the selfishness of philosophical egoism. A liberal citizen may have a conception of the good life that includes a significant commitment to altruistic values. Such a person's self-interest will include acting on the basis of these values. But it is up to that citizen to determine for herself whether to make such a commitment to other-regarding behavior and what it means in practice.

In this view, the freedom of the individual is a natural given; the goal of liberal institutions is to protect it. This does not mean, of course, that human beings are entirely self-sufficient. No realistic understanding of persons can deny that children are profoundly dependent on their parents, or that adults continue throughout their lives to depend on the integrity of the environment and on communities ranging from the family to the interdependent global economic network. The impossibility of total self-sufficiency is the reason why a social contract is necessary for human survival and flourishing. But the pattern of social cooperation this contract makes possible is a means, not a value to be sought for its own sake. Its aim is to maximize the natural liberty of the individual to the degree consistent with the necessity of social interaction. Freedom, therefore, is essentially a private matter; it exists in the public sphere only to protect this zone of privacy. This view of freedom is hardly neutral about how freedom should be used. For it assumes that other-regarding behavior is not necessary to sustain a successful democratic society. It also invites people to concern themselves with others only as useful means to private ends.

Yves R. Simon has drawn a distinction between a societal partnership based on contract and a richer notion of community based on what Aristotle called civic friendship.[20] This distinction helps clarify how the Catholic tradition's understanding of freedom in community is notably different from the liberal one. A partnership is entered into to enhance the private well-being of each of the contracting parties. The partnership benefits both and serves the good of both. Therefore the partnership is itself a social good. But, in Aristotle's terms, it is a useful good rather than a good in itself. It serves the private purposes of those who enter into it in an instrumental way. In much liberal thought, the institutions of democratic government are such instrumental goods.

Recent Catholic discussions of the values of democracy have a broader base. Freedom is not only a naturally given attribute of human personality, it is also a human achievement.[21] This fuller reality of freedom is attained through self-transcendence and the formation of bonds of relationship with realities other than the self – primarily other persons. Freedom is achieved in relationality, solidarity and community. Such achievement is at once a moral and a spiritual attainment.

Consider a child's growth from a state of utter dependence to the maturity marked by self-possession and self-determination. Psychological theories of human development trace this process in well-known ways. An aspect of this growth is a process of becoming more independent and self-determining. But equally important is growth in the ability to form relationships with others, relationships that are freely entered into because they are recognized as good in themselves. In fact, mature self-possession and self-determination grow in and through the self-transcendence that makes such relationships possible and actualizes them. The Christian tradition calls this self-transcendence love – the valuation of the other for its own sake and the formation of mutual relationship with the other as a good in itself.[22]

The Catholic tradition is fully aware of the tendency of persons to be, in Augustine's words, "curved in on themselves." This tendency is manifest in the "lust for domination" and the conflict and violence that mar human history. The human capacity for relationality and community is subject to profoundly destructive perversions. In theological language, these are what is meant by sin. It is a condition that can only be counteracted by a recognition that human beings are not their own creators, not the sole sources of the meaningfulness of their own lives. Being free does not mean that a human being is *causa sui*.[23] Rather, human freedom is always responsive; it begins with a recognition of a world beyond the self, given to the self. The beginning of freedom, therefore, is self-transcendence. And it bears fruit in a further self-transcendence as well – the self-transcendence of a fuller harmony and union with other persons, with social communities of various kinds, with the world of nature, and ultimately – believers affirm – with God.

An expansion of these possibilities for self-transcendence and for the creation of new bonds of relationship and solidarity is both a moral and spiritual task. It will not be brought about simply by arguments that employ instrumental rationality to reflect on the means that can most effectively secure private self-interests. It is on this point that Catholicism differs fundamentally from liberal contract theories. The self is inherently relational and achieves depth and solidity only by going beyond itself in solidarity and community. Christians call the move from private interests to other-relatedness conversion – a turning to the neighbor in love, based on a recognition that the neighbor is a gift rather than a threat.

There are important ethical and social preconditions for such recognition, preconditions that show the continuing importance of the values of freedom and equality so highly prized by liberalism. The neighbor and fellow citizen can sometimes truly be a threat to both self-possession and self-transcendence. The danger of this stress on relationality and solidarity is that it can trap persons in patterns of domination and even encourage them to connive in their own exploitation. To prevent this latter outcome, the equal dignity of all citizens must be central in both the theory and practice of American public life. Such equality is a precondition for any community that is truly a community of freedom, where relationships are built on mutuality rather than superordination and subordination. Both liberals and Catholics can and must affirm this, as Catholics have learned during the past half century. But in the continuing conversation, Catholicism will continue to point out that liberal notions of freedom and of the self encourage the separation of people into private and isolated worlds. And it offers an alternative vision of solidarity and community that can renew the promise of American democracy as a community of freedom that is both urgently needed and possibly even inspiring.

This book has aimed to stimulate and enlarge the dialogue between the Catholic and liberal traditions. It has not provided detailed prescriptions for the outcome of such a dialogue. But even partial realization of the hope that the conversation can move to a deeper level would contribute much to the public life and public philosophy of the United States today.

NOTES

1 *Quadragesimo Anno*, no. 79.
2 Jacques Maritain, *Man and the State* (University of Chicago Press, 1951), 13.

3 John Courtney Murray, *The Problem of Religious Freedom* (Westminster, MD: Newman Press, 1965), 26–27.

4 John A. Coleman, "Religious Liberty in America and Mediating Structures," in his *An American Strategic Theology* (New York: Paulist Press, 1982), 226.

5 "Towards a Civil Society: Hopes for Polish Democracy," interview with Adam Michnik by Erica Blair, *Times Literary Supplement* (February 19–25, 1988): 199.

6 Arthur M. Okun, *Equality and Efficiency: The Big Tradeoff* (Washington: Brookings Institution, 1975), 12–14. Okun's discussion has been elegantly elaborated and deepened in Michael Walzer, *Spheres of Justice: A Defense of Pluralism and Equality* (New York: Basic Books, 1983).

7 John Paul II, *Centesimus Annus*, no. 41.

8 Bradford H. Gray, *The Profit Motive and Patient Care: The Changing Accountability of Doctors and Hospitals*, A Twentieth Century Fund Report (Cambridge, MA: Harvard University Press, 1991), 5.

9 See Walter K. Olson, *The Litigation Explosion: What Happened When America Unleashed the Lawsuit* (New York: Dutton, 1991).

10 John XXIII, *Mater et Magistra*, no. 53; Pius XI, *Quadragesimo Anno*, no. 79.

11 *Centesimus Annus*, nos. 15 and 35.

12 This interpretation of the Catholic tradition's understanding of pluralism resembles that of Michael Walzer. In addition to Walzer's *Spheres of Justice*, cited above, see his "The Idea of Civil Society: A Path to Social Reconstruction," *Dissent* (Spring 1991): 293–304. The following discussion will indicate, however, that the Catholic tradition is more hopeful than Walzer that the particularisms of differing communities can be transcended, at least sometimes, in a more universal solidarity.

13 John Rawls, "The Idea of an Overlapping Consensus," *Oxford Journal of Legal Studies* 7 (1987): 8.

14 See, for example, E. J. Dionne, Jr., *Why Americans Hate Politics* (New York: Simon & Schuster, 1991).

15 John Courtney Murray, *We Hold these Truths: Catholic Reflections on the American Proposition* (New York: Sheed & Ward, 1960), 9.

16 See Václav Havel, *Disturbing the Peace: A Conversation with Karel Hvizdala*, trans. Paul Wilson (New York: Vintage Books, 1991).

17 For a most illuminating and original discussion of these themes, see Michael J. Perry, *Love and Power: The Role of Religion and Morality in American Politics* (New York: Oxford University Press, 1991). See also Robin Lovin, "Perry, Naturalism, and Religion in Public," *Tulane Law Review* 63 (1989): 1517–1539. Both Perry's earlier work and Lovin's theological reflection on it are discussed in David Hollenbach, "Religion and Political Life," *Theological Studies* 52 (1991): 87–106. Perry, Lovin, and Hollenbach are all indebted to the work of David Tracy, exemplified in his contribution to this volume.

18 Avery Dulles, "Revelation as Discovery," in William J. Kelly, ed., *Theology and Discovery: Essays in Honor of Karl Rahner* (Milwaukee: Marquette University Press, 1980), 27.

19 Martha Nussbaum, "Aristotelian Social Democracy," in R. Bruce Douglass, Gerald R. Mara, and Henry S. Richardson, eds., *Liberalism and the Good* (New York: Routledge, 1990), 217.

20 Yves R. Simon, *Philosophy of Democratic Government* (University of Chicago Press, 1951), 48–50, 64–68.

21 The ideas of freedom to be found in the two-thousand-year history of Catholicism are, of course, multiple. The discussion here makes no claim to deal with all of these. Rather the goal is to highlight an emphasis found in Catholicism that needs particular emphasis in the contemporary American context.

22 For a much deeper discussion of the understanding of love only sketched here, see Margaret A. Farley, *Personal Commitments* (San Francisco: Harper & Row, 1986).

23 For a probing exploration of this theme, see Ernest Becker, *The Denial of Death* (New York: Free Press, 1973).

Index

344